LINUX®

ESSENTIALS

LINUX®

ESSENTIALS

Roderick W. Smith

WILEY

John Wiley & Sons, Inc.

Acquisitions Editor: Agatha Kim
Development Editor: David Clark
Technical Editor: Ross Brunson
Production Editor: Rebecca Anderson
Copy Editor: Elizabeth Welch
Editorial Manager: Pete Gaughan
Production Manager: Tim Tate
Vice President and Executive Group Publisher: Richard Swadley
Vice President and Publisher: Neil Edde
Book Designer: Happenstance Type-O-Rama
Compositor: James D. Kramer, Happenstance Type-O-Rama
Proofreader: Scott Klemp, Word One New York
Indexer: Ted Laux
Project Coordinator, Cover: Katherine Crocker
Cover Designer: Ryan Sneed

For general information on our other products and services or to obtain technical support, please contact our Customer Care Department within the U.S. at (877) 762-2974, outside the U.S. at (317) 572-3993 or fax (317) 572-4002.

Wiley publishes in a variety of print and electronic formats and by print-on-demand. Some material included with standard print versions of this book may not be included in e-books or in print-on-demand. If this book refers to media such as a CD or DVD that is not included in the version you purchased, you may download this material at http://booksupport.wiley.com. For more information about Wiley products, visit www.wiley.com.

Library of Congress Control Number: 2011939652

Dear Reader,

Thank you for choosing *Linux Essentials*. This book is part of a family of premium-quality Sybex books, all of which are written by outstanding authors who combine practical experience with a gift for teaching.

Sybex was founded in 1976. More than 30 years later, we're still committed to producing consistently exceptional books. With each of our titles, we're working hard to set a new standard for the industry. From the paper we print on, to the authors we work with, our goal is to bring you the best books available.

I hope you see all that reflected in these pages. I'd be very interested to hear your comments and get your feedback on how we're doing. Feel free to let me know what you think about this or any other Sybex book by sending me an email at nedde@wiley.com. If you think you've found a technical error in this book, please visit http://sybex.custhelp.com. Customer feedback is critical to our efforts at Sybex.

Best regards,

NEIL EDDE
Vice President and Publisher
Sybex, an Imprint of Wiley

ACKNOWLEDGMENTS

Although this book bears my name as its author, many other people contributed to its creation. Without their help, this book wouldn't exist, or at best would exist in a lesser form. Agatha Kim was the acquisitions editor, and so helped get the book started. Denise Lincoln and David J. Clark, the development editors, and Rebecca Anderson, the production editor, oversaw the book as it progressed through all its stages. Ross Brunson was the technical editor, who checked the text for technical errors and omissions—but any mistakes that remain are my own. Liz Welch, the copy editor, helped keep the text grammatical and understandable. The proofreader, Scott Klemp, checked the text for typos. I'd also like to thank Neil Salkind and others at Studio B, who helped connect me with Wiley to write this book.

ABOUT THE AUTHOR

Roderick W. Smith, LPIC-2, LPIC-1, CompTIA Linux+, is a Linux consultant, author, and open source programmer. He is the author of over 20 books on Linux and other open source technologies, including *Linux+ Complete Study Guide*; *LPIC-1 Study Guide, 2nd Edition*; *LPIC-2 Study Guide*, and *Linux Administrator Street Smarts*, all from Sybex.

Contents at a Glance

Introduction   *xvii*

CHAPTER 1   Selecting an Operating System   1

CHAPTER 2   Investigating Linux's Principles and Philosophy   21

CHAPTER 3   Understanding Software Licensing   33

CHAPTER 4   Using Common Linux Programs   49

CHAPTER 5   Managing Hardware   75

CHAPTER 6   Getting to Know the Command Line   99

CHAPTER 7   Managing Files   117

CHAPTER 8   Getting Help   131

CHAPTER 9   Using Programs and Processes   149

CHAPTER 10   Searching, Extracting, and Archiving Data   165

CHAPTER 11   Editing Files   185

CHAPTER 12   Creating Scripts   203

CHAPTER 13   Understanding Users and Groups   217

CHAPTER 14   Creating Users and Groups   235

CHAPTER 15   Setting Ownership and Permissions   257

CHAPTER 16   Navigating the Linux Filesystem   271

CHAPTER 17   Managing Network Connections   285

APPENDIX A   Answers to Review Questions   307

APPENDIX B   LPI's Certification Program   325

Index   *329*

CONTENTS

Introduction   *xvii*

CHAPTER 1   **Selecting an Operating System**   **1**

What Is an OS? 1

     What Is a Kernel? 1

     What Else Identifies an OS? 2

Investigating User Interfaces 4

     Using a Text-Mode User Interface 4

     Using a Graphical User Interface 6

Where Does Linux Fit in the OS World? 8

     Comparing Linux to Unix 8

     Comparing Linux to Mac OS X 10

     Comparing Linux to Windows 11

What Is a Distribution? 13

     Creating a Complete Linux-Based OS 13

     A Summary of Common Linux Distributions 14

     Understanding Release Cycles 17

The Essentials and Beyond 18

CHAPTER 2   **Investigating Linux's Principles and Philosophy**   **21**

Linux through the Ages 21

     Understanding Linux's Origins 22

     Seeing Today's Linux World 24

Using Open Source Software 24

     Understanding Basic Open Source Principles 24

     Linux as a Software Integrator 27

Understanding OS Roles 27

     Understanding Embedded Computers 27

     Understanding Desktop and Laptop Computers 28

     Understanding Server Computers 29

The Essentials and Beyond 30

CHAPTER 3   **Understanding Software Licensing**   **33**

Investigating Software Licenses. 33
    Copyright and Software. 34
    Using Licenses to Modify Copyright Terms 36
The Free Software Foundation. 36
    Understanding the FSF Philosophy. 37
    Free Software and the GPL 38
The Open Source Initiative. 39
    Understanding the Open Source Philosophy 39
    Defining Open Source Software 40
The Creative Commons 41
Using Open Source Licenses 42
    Understanding Open Source Licenses. 42
    Understanding Open Source Business Models 44
The Essentials and Beyond. 45

CHAPTER 4   **Using Common Linux Programs**   **49**

Using a Linux Desktop Environment. 49
    Choosing a Desktop Environment. 50
    Launching Programs. 52
    Using a File Manager 54
Working with Productivity Software 56
    Finding the Right Tool for the Job 57
    Using a Web Browser 58
    Using Email Clients 59
    Using Office Tools. 60
    Using Multimedia Applications 61
    Using Linux for Cloud Computing 62
    Using Mobile Applications 62
Using Server Programs. 63
    Identifying Common Server Protocols and Programs. 63
    Installing and Launching Servers. 67
    Securing Servers 68
Managing Programming Languages 69
    Choosing a Compiled vs. an Interpreted Language 69
    Identifying Common Programming Languages 70
The Essentials and Beyond. 72

CHAPTER 5   **Managing Hardware**   **75**

Learning About Your CPU 75
    Understanding CPU Families. 76
    Identifying Your CPU 78
Identifying Motherboard Capabilities 78
Sizing Your Power Supply. 80
Understanding Disk Issues 81
    Disk Interfaces 81
    Partitioning a Disk. 81
    Understanding Filesystem Issues 85
    Using Removable and Optical Disks 88
Managing Displays 89
    Understanding the Role of X 89
    Using Common Display Hardware. 90
Handling USB Devices 92
Managing Drivers 93
    Understanding Types of Drivers. 93
    Locating and Installing Drivers 94
The Essentials and Beyond. 95

CHAPTER 6   **Getting to Know the Command Line**   **99**

Starting a Command Line 99
    Launching a Terminal 100
    Logging Into a Text-Mode Console 102
    Logging In Remotely 103
Running Programs 103
    Running Text-Mode Programs 104
    Running GUI Programs. 105
    Running Programs in the Background. 105
Manipulating Files 106
    Obtaining File Listings 106
    Changing Directories. 108
    Using Absolute and Relative File References. 108
    Using Common File Manipulation Commands 110
Using Shell Features 111
    Using Command Completion 111
    Using Command History. 112
The Essentials and Beyond. 114

CHAPTER 7   **Managing Files**   **117**

Manipulating Files 117
    Creating Files 118
    Copying Files 118
    Moving and Renaming Files 120
    Using Links 121
    Deleting Files 122
    Using Wildcards 123
    Understanding Case Sensitivity 123
Manipulating Directories 124
    Creating Directories 125
    Deleting Directories 125
    Managing Directories 127
The Essentials and Beyond 127

CHAPTER 8   **Getting Help**   **131**

Using *man* Pages 131
    Understanding the Purpose of *man* Pages 131
    Locating *man* Pages by Section Number 132
    Searching for a *man* Page 133
    Reading *man* Pages 134
    Using *less* 135
Using *info* Pages 138
    Understanding the Purpose of *info* Pages 138
    Reading *info* Pages 139
Finding Additional Documentation 140
    Locating Program Documentation on Your Computer 141
    Locating Program Documentation Online 144
    Consulting Experts 145
The Essentials and Beyond 146

CHAPTER 9   **Using Programs and Processes**   **149**

Understanding Package Management 149
    Linux Package Management Principles 149
    Understanding Package Systems 150
    Managing RPM Systems 152
    Managing Debian Systems 153

Understanding the Process Hierarchy 154

Identifying Running Processes 155

Using *ps* to Identify Processes 155

Using *top* to Identify Processes 157

Measuring Memory Use 159

Using Log Files 160

Locating Log Files 160

Producing More Verbose Log File Entries 162

Examining the Kernel Ring Buffer 162

The Essentials and Beyond. 163

CHAPTER 10   Searching, Extracting, and Archiving Data   165

Using Regular Expressions 165

Searching for and Extracting Data 167

Using *grep*. 168

Using *find* 170

Using *wc* 171

Redirecting Input and Output 172

Using Basic Redirection Operators 173

Using Pipes 175

Generating Command Lines 175

Archiving Data 176

Using *tar* 176

Using Compression. 179

Using *zip* 180

The Essentials and Beyond. 183

CHAPTER 11   Editing Files   185

Understanding the Role of Text Files 185

Choosing an Editor 187

Launching an Editor. 189

Editing Files with *pico* or *nano* 189

Using Text Editor Conventions 190

Exploring Basic *nano* Text-Editing Procedures 190

Saving Your Changes from *nano*. 193

Editing Files with Vi. 193

Understanding Vi Modes 193

Exploring Basic Vi Text-Editing Procedures. 194

Saving Your Changes from Vi 197

Using Configuration File Conventions. 197
Editing Formatted Text Files 199
The Essentials and Beyond. 200

CHAPTER 12   Creating Scripts   203

Beginning a Shell Script. 204
Using Commands 204
Using Arguments 207
Using Variables 208
Using Conditional Expressions. 210
Using Loops. 212
Using Functions 213
Setting the Script's Exit Value 214
The Essentials and Beyond. 215

CHAPTER 13   Understanding Users and Groups   217

Understanding Accounts 217
   Understanding Account Features 218
   Identifying Accounts 220
   Understanding Groups. 222
Using Account Tools 223
   Discovering Your Own Identity 224
   Learning Who's Online 225
Working as *root*. 226
   Why Work as *root*? 227
   Acquiring *root* Privileges. 227
   Using *root* Privileges Safely 230
The Essentials and Beyond. 232

CHAPTER 14   Creating Users and Groups   235

Creating New Accounts 235
   Deciding on a Group Strategy 235
   Selecting a Good Password 236
   Creating Accounts Using GUI Tools 239
   Creating Accounts from the Shell. 241
Modifying Accounts 244
   Deciding When to Modify Accounts 244
   Checking for Logged-in Users 245

Modifying Accounts Using GUI Tools 245
Modifying Accounts from the Shell 247
Deleting Accounts 250
Avoiding Account-Deletion Pitfalls 250
Deleting Accounts Using GUI Tools 251
Deleting Accounts from the Shell 251
Managing Groups 252
Managing Groups Using GUI Tools 252
Managing Groups from the Shell 253
The Essentials and Beyond 255

CHAPTER 15　　**Setting Ownership and Permissions**　　　**257**

Setting Ownership 257
Understanding Ownership 258
Setting Ownership in a File Manager 259
Setting Ownership in a Shell 260
Setting Permissions 261
Understanding Permissions 261
Setting Permissions in a File Manager 266
Setting Permissions in a Shell 266
Setting the umask 267
The Essentials and Beyond 268

CHAPTER 16　　**Navigating the Linux Filesystem**　　　**271**

Understanding Where Things Go 271
User Files vs. System Files 271
The Filesystem Hierarchy Standard 273
Important Directories and Their Contents 274
Using Special Permission Bits and File Features 277
Using Sticky Bits 277
Using Special Execute Permissions 279
Hiding Files from View 280
Viewing Directories 281
The Essentials and Beyond 282

CHAPTER 17　　**Managing Network Connections**　　　**285**

Understanding Network Features 285

Configuring a Network Connection. 287
    Deciding Whether to Use DHCP 288
    Creating a Wi-Fi Connection. 289
    Using a Network Configuration GUI 293
    Using Text-Based Tools 295
Testing Your Network Connection. 299
    Checking Your Routing Table 299
    Testing Basic Connectivity 299
    Finding Breaks in Connectivity. 300
    Testing DNS 302
    Checking Your Network Status 302
Protecting Your System from the Bad Guys 303
The Essentials and Beyond. 304

APPENDIX A   **Answers to Review Questions**   **307**

Chapter 1. 307
Chapter 2. 308
Chapter 3. 309
Chapter 4. 310
Chapter 5. 311
Chapter 6. 312
Chapter 7. 313
Chapter 8. 314
Chapter 9. 315
Chapter 10. 316
Chapter 11. 317
Chapter 12. 318
Chapter 13. 319
Chapter 14. 320
Chapter 15. 321
Chapter 16. 322
Chapter 17. 323

APPENDIX B   **LPI's Certification Program**   **325**

The Linux Essentials Certification. 325
Certification Objectives Map 326

Index   *329*

Introduction

The book you hold in your hands is an introductory textbook on the Linux operating system. As the title suggests, it provides you with the essential knowledge to begin using and managing this powerful operating system (OS), which is an important one in today's computing world. The following pages describe why you should care about Linux, describe the purpose of the Linux Professional Institute's Linux Essentials certification, offer advice on who should buy this book, describe how the book is organized, and explain some of the typographical and organizational elements within the book's chapters.

What Is Linux?

Linux is a clone of the Unix OS that has been popular in academic and business environments for years. Linux consists of a kernel, which is the core control software, and many libraries and utilities that rely on the kernel to provide features with which users interact. The OS is available in many different *distributions*, which are collections of a specific kernel with specific support programs. Popular Linux distributions include Arch, CentOS, Debian, Fedora, Gentoo, Mandriva, openSUSE, Red Hat, Slackware, SUSE Enterprise, and Ubuntu, but there are hundreds, if not thousands, of other Linux distributions. This book focuses on tools and techniques that are used in most or all distributions, although from time to time it demonstrates more distribution-specific tools.

Linux has several characteristics that make it worth learning and using:

- ► Linux is open source software, meaning that the files used to create the working programs that make up Linux are freely available and may be modified and redistributed. Thus, if you dislike something about the way Linux works, you can change it yourself! (You may need modest to considerable programming skill to do so, however.)

- ► Linux is available free of charge. Although some distributions require payment, most can be downloaded from the Internet and used without paying a cent. This is a great boon for students, businesses on a shoestring budget, or anybody wanting to save money. Those who want to pay for greater support can do so by hiring consultants or purchasing service contracts.

▶ As a clone of the older Unix OS, Linux has inherited a great deal of Unix software, including many very important Internet server programs, databases, programming languages, and more.

▶ Linux is highly scalable—it runs on everything from cell phones to supercomputers. The Linux versions described in most detail in this book run on a more limited range of hardware, but they can run on PCs that are several years old or on the very latest hardware. Linux can make good use of PCs that are too old for the latest version of Windows.

▶ Many businesses and non-profit organizations rely on Linux. Although desktop systems still usually run Windows, Linux is often used to run the organizations' Web sites, route their Internet traffic, and do other critical behind-the-scenes tasks. In some cases, Linux is used as the desktop OS, too. Thus, learning Linux will help your employment prospects.

You can install Linux on almost any PC on which you normally run Windows or Mac OS X. You can install Linux by itself or side by side with another OS, so you can learn Linux without losing your ability to get work done in your regular OS.

What Is the Linux Essentials Certification?

The Linux Professional Institute (LPI; http://www.lpi.org) offers a series of Linux certifications. These certifications aim to provide proof of skill levels for employers; if you've passed a particular certification, you should be competent to perform certain tasks on Linux computers. The LPI exams include Linux Essentials, LPIC-1, LPIC-2, and several LPIC-3 exams. As the name implies, the Linux Essentials exam is the lowest-level of the exams, covering the most basic tasks of using and administering a Linux computer. Its specific objectives can be found at http://wiki.lpi.org/wiki/LinuxEssentials. This book covers all of these topics, although not in the exact order in which they appear on the LPI Web site.

Who Should Read This Book?

You may have been assigned this book for a class you're taking, but if not, it can still have value for self-study or as a supplement to other resources. If you're new to Linux, this book covers the material you will need to learn the OS from the beginning. You can pick up this book and learn from it even if you've never used

Linux before. If you're already familiar with Linux, you'll have a leg up on many of the topics described in these pages.

This book is written with the assumption that you know at least a little about computers generally, such as how to use a keyboard, how to insert a disc into an optical drive, and so on. Chances are you have used computers in a substantial way in the past—perhaps even Linux, as an ordinary user, or maybe you have used Windows or Mac OS X. I do *not* assume that you have knowledge of Linux system administration.

System Requirements

As a practical matter, you'll need a Linux system with which to practice and learn in a hands-on way. You can install Linux in several ways:

- ► Alone as the only OS on the computer

- ► Side by side with another OS

- ► In an emulated computer environment provided by a virtualization program such as VMware (http://www.vmware.com) or VirtualBox (http://www.virtualbox.org)

If you're taking a course on Linux, you may be able to use Linux in a lab environment, but if you're using this book in a self-study manner, you should plan to install Linux yourself. Although you can learn something just by reading this book, no amount of reading can substitute for hands-on experience with Linux!

You can use any popular Linux distribution with this book, although if you're new to Linux, you'll probably be happiest with one of the more user-friendly distributions, such as CentOS, Fedora, openSUSE, or Ubuntu. This book does not include instructions for how to install Linux; you should consult distribution-specific documentation to help with this task.

To install Linux and use all its GUI tools, your computer should meet the following requirements:

CPU   400 MHz Pentium Pro or better

Minimum RAM   640 MiB

Recommended RAM   At least 1,152 MiB

Hard disk space   At least 9 GiB in unpartitioned space

Some distributions can work on less powerful computers than this, and others may require better hardware to take full advantage of all features. Consult your distribution's documentation to fine-tune these requirements.

How This Book Is Organized

This book consists of 17 chapters plus this introduction. The chapters are organized as follows:

Chapter 1, "Selecting an Operating System,"   provides a birds-eye view of the
world of operating systems. This chapter will help you understand what Linux is
and the situations in which you might want to use it.

Chapter 2, "Investigating Linux's Principles and Philosophy,"   covers Linux's
history and the ways in which Linux—and other OSs—are commonly used.

Chapter 3, "Understanding Software Licensing,"   describes copyright law
and the licenses that both Linux and non-Linux OSs use to expand or restrict
users' right to use and copy software.

Chapter 4, "Using Common Linux Programs,"   covers the major categories of
Linux software and provides pointers to some of the most popular Linux programs.

Chapter 5, "Managing Hardware,"   provides advice on how to select and use
hardware in Linux. Specific topics range from the central processing unit (CPU)
to device drivers.

Chapter 6, "Getting to Know the Command Line,"   tackles using typed commands to control Linux. Although many new users find this topic intimidating,
command-line control of Linux is very important.

Chapter 7, "Managing Files,"   describes how to move, rename, delete, and edit
files. Directories are just a special type of file and so are covered as well.

Chapter 8, "Getting Help,"   covers Linux's help resources. These include the
built-in man and info packages and using off-computer resources such as Web sites.

Chapter 9, "Using Programs and Processes,"   describes how you can install
programs in Linux and how you can adjust the priority of running programs or
terminate selected programs.

Chapter 10, "Searching, Extracting, and Archiving Data,"   summarizes tools
you can use to find data on your computer, as well as how you can manipulate
data archive files for data transport and backup purposes.

Chapter 11, "Editing Files,"   introduces the topic of editing text files. This
includes basic features of the pico, nano, and Vi text-mode text editors as well
as some common configuration file and formatted text file conventions.

Chapter 12, "Creating Scripts,"   describes how to create simple scripts, which are programs that can run other programs. You can use scripts to help automate otherwise tedious manual tasks, thus improving your productivity.

Chapter 13, "Understanding Users and Groups,"   introduces the concepts that are critical to understanding Linux's multi-user nature. It also covers the root account, which Linux uses for most administrative tasks.

Chapter 14, "Creating Users and Groups,"   covers the software and procedures you use to create, modify, and delete accounts and groups, which define who may use the computer.

Chapter 15, "Setting Ownership and Permissions,"   describes how to control which users may access files and in what ways they may do so. In conjunction with users and groups, ownership and permissions control your computer's security.

Chapter 16, "Navigating the Linux Filesystem,"   describes where files go in Linux—where you can look for program files, configuration files, user files, and so on.

Chapter 17, "Managing Network Connections,"   covers the critical topic of telling Linux how to use a network, including testing the connection and some basic network security measures.

Broadly speaking, the chapters are arranged in order of increasing complexity of the tasks and systems described. The book begins with background information on Linux and the philosophies that drive its development. Subsequent chapters describe basic user tasks, such as moving files around. The book concludes with tasks that are of most interest to system administrators, such as account management and network configuration.

Each chapter begins with a list of the topics that are covered in that chapter. At the end of each chapter, you'll find a few elements that summarize the material and encourage you to go further:

The Essentials and Beyond   This is a one-paragraph summary of the material covered in the chapter. If when you read it something sounds unfamiliar, go back and review the relevant section of the chapter!

Suggested exercises   Each chapter includes two to four exercises you should perform to give yourself more hands-on experience with Linux. These exercises do not necessarily have "correct" answers; instead, they're intended to promote exploration and discovery of your own computer and of Linux.

Review questions   Each chapter concludes with a series of nine review questions, in multiple-choice, true/false, or fill-in-the-blank format. (Answers to review questions appear in Appendix A.) These questions can help you test your knowledge and prepare for the Linux Essentials exam. Note, however, that these questions are *not* taken from LPI's exam. You should *not* memorize the answers to these questions and assume that doing so will enable you to pass the exam. Instead, study the text of the book and *use Linux*.

To get the most out of this book, you should read each chapter from start to finish, perform the suggested exercises, and answer the review questions. Even if you're already familiar with a topic, you should skim the chapter; Linux is complex enough that there are often multiple ways to accomplish a task, so you may learn something even if you're already competent in an area.

Conventions Used in This Book

This book uses certain typographic styles in order to help you quickly identify important information and to avoid confusion over the meaning of words such as onscreen prompts. In particular, look for the following styles:

▶ *Italicized text* indicates key terms that are described or defined for the first time in a chapter. (Italics are also used for emphasis.)

▶ A `monospaced` font indicates the contents of configuration files, messages displayed at a text-mode Linux shell prompt, filenames, text-mode command names, and Internet URLs.

▶ *Italicized monospaced text* indicates a variable—information that differs from one system or command run to another, such as the name of a client computer or the name of a user's data file.

▶ **Bold monospaced text** is information that you're to type into the computer, usually at a Linux shell prompt. This text can also be italicized to indicate that you should substitute an appropriate value for your system. When isolated on their own lines, commands are preceded by non-bold monospaced $ or # command prompts, denoting regular user or system administrator use, respectively.

In addition to these text conventions, which can apply to individual words or entire paragraphs, a few conventions highlight segments of text.

A margin note identifies additional information that may be relevant to the principal point of the accompanying paragraph but that isn't critical to its basic understanding. This could be a cross-reference to information in another chapter, an interesting but non-critical minor fact, or a warning about a rare pitfall of a procedure.

As a general rule, margin notes are best read after the paragraphs to which they refer.

SIDEBARS

A sidebar is an extended description of a topic that's related to the main text but that doesn't fit neatly into the flow of the surrounding paragraphs. It may expand on a point to provide added context or suggest an alternative way of doing things from the method emphasized in the main text.

Many chapters of this book describe both GUI and text-mode methods of accomplishing the tasks they describe. Because you're likely to be more familiar with GUI tools, most chapters begin with them; however, in most cases Linux's text-mode tools are more powerful. Furthermore, the Linux Essentials certification covers mainly text-mode tools. Therefore, you should be sure to learn the text-mode tools. As you gain proficiency with Linux, you're likely to find yourself using the text-mode tools more than the GUI tools because of the added flexibility the text-mode tools provide. Furthermore, the GUI tools tend to vary a lot between distributions, whereas the text-mode tools vary much less.

## CHAPTER 1

Selecting an Operating System

The fact that you're reading this book means you want to learn about the Linux operating system (OS). To begin this journey, you must first understand what Linux is and what an OS is. This chapter is therefore devoted to these basic issues. I describe what an OS is, how users interact with an OS, how Linux compares to other OSs with which you may be familiar, and how specific Linux implementations vary. Understanding these issues will help you make your way as you learn about Linux and switch between Linux-based systems and other computers.

- ▶ **What is an OS?**
- ▶ **Investigating user interfaces**
- ▶ **Where does Linux fit in the OS world?**
- ▶ **What is a distribution?**

What Is an OS?

An OS provides all the most fundamental features of a computer, at least from a software point of view. An OS enables you to use the computer's hardware devices, it defines the user interface standards, and it provides basic tools that begin to make the computer useful. Ultimately, many of these features trace their way back to the OS's *kernel*, which is described in more detail next. Other OS features are owed to additional programs that run atop the kernel, as described later in this chapter.

What Is a Kernel?

An OS kernel is a software component that's responsible for managing various low-level features of the computer, including:

- ▶ Interfacing with hardware devices (network adapters, hard disks, and so on)

▶ Allocating memory to individual programs

▶ Allocating CPU time to individual programs

▶ Enabling programs to interact with each other

When you use a program (say, a Web browser), it relies on the kernel for many of its basic functions. The Web browser can only communicate with the outside world by using network functions provided by the kernel. The kernel allocates memory and CPU time to the Web browser, without which it couldn't run. The Web browser may rely on plug-ins to display multimedia content; such programs are launched and interact with the Web browser through kernel services. Similar comments apply to any program you run on a computer, although the details vary from one OS to another and from one program to another.

In sum, the kernel is the software "glue" that holds the computer together. Without a kernel, a modern computer can do very little.

Kernels are not interchangeable; the Linux kernel is different from the Mac OS X kernel or the Windows kernel. Each of these kernels uses a different internal design and provides different software interfaces for programs to use. Thus, each OS is built from the kernel up and uses its own set of programs that further define each OS's features.

Linux uses a kernel called *Linux*—in fact, technically speaking, the word *Linux* refers *only* to the kernel. Other features that you might associate with Linux are provided by non-kernel programs, most of which are available on other platforms, as described shortly, in "What Else Identifies an OS."

A student named Linus Torvalds created the Linux kernel in 1991. Linux has evolved considerably since that time. Today, it runs on a wide variety of CPUs and other hardware. The easiest way to learn about Linux is to use it on a desktop or laptop PC, so that's the type of configuration that's emphasized in this book. The Linux kernel, however, runs on everything from tiny cell phones to powerful supercomputers.

> **Many programs run on multiple kernels, but most need OS-specific tweaks. Programmers create *binaries*—the program files for a particular processor and kernel—for each OS.**

What Else Identifies an OS?

The kernel is at the core of any OS, but it's a component that most users don't directly manipulate. Instead, most users interact with a number of other software components, many of which are closely associated with particular OSs. Such programs include the following:

Certification Objective

Command-line shells   Years ago, users interacted with computers exclusively by typing commands in a program (known as a *shell*) that accepted such commands. The commands would rename files, launch programs, and so on. Although many computer users today don't use text-mode shells, they're still important for intermediate and advanced Linux users, so I describe them in more detail in Chapter 6, "Getting to Know the Command Line," and subsequent chapters rely heavily on your ability to use a text-mode shell. Many different shells are available, and which shells are available and popular differ from one OS to another. In Linux, a shell known as the Bourne Again Shell (bash or Bash) is popular.

Graphical user interfaces   A graphical user interface (GUI) is an improvement on a text-mode shell, at least from the perspective of a beginning user. Instead of using typed commands, GUIs rely on icons, menus, and a mouse pointer. Windows and Mac OS both have their own OS-specific GUIs. Linux relies on a GUI known as the X Window System, or X for short. X is a very basic GUI, so Linux also uses *desktop environment* program suites, such as the GNU Object Model Environment (GNOME) or the K Desktop Environment (KDE), to provide a more complete user experience. It's the differences between a Linux desktop environment and the GUIs in Windows or OS X that will probably strike you most when you first begin using Linux.

Certification Objective

Utility programs   Modern OSs invariably ship with a wide variety of simple utility programs—calculators, calendars, text editors, disk maintenance tools, and so on. These programs differ from one OS to another. Indeed, even the names and methods of launching these programs can differ between OSs. Fortunately, you can usually find the programs you want by perusing menus in the main desktop environment.

Libraries   Unless you're a programmer, you're unlikely to need to work with libraries directly; nonetheless, I include them in this list because they provide critical services to programs. Libraries are collections of programming functions that can be used by a variety of programs. For instance, in Linux most programs rely on a library called `libc`. Other libraries provide features associated with the GUI or that help programs parse options passed to them on the command line. Many libraries exist for Linux, which helps enrich the Linux software landscape.

You can search for Linux equivalents to popular Mac OS X or Windows programs on Web sites such as `http://www.linuxrsp.ru/win-lin-soft/table-eng` or `http://www.linuxalt.com`.

Productivity programs   Major productivity programs—Web browsers, word processors, graphics editors, and so on—are the usual reason for using a computer. Although such programs are often technically separate from the OS, they are sometimes associated with certain OSs. Even when a program is available on many OSs, it may have a different "feel" on each OS because of the different GUIs and other OS-specific features.

In addition to software that runs on an OS, several other features can distinguish between OSs, such as the details of user accounts, rules for naming disk files, and technical details of how the computer starts up. These features are all controlled by software that's part of the OS, of course—sometimes by the kernel and sometimes by non-kernel software.

Investigating User Interfaces

Earlier, I noted the distinction between text-mode and graphical user interfaces. Although most end users favor GUIs because of their ease of use, Linux retains a strong text-mode tradition. Chapter 6 describes Linux's text-mode tools in more detail, and Chapter 4, "Using Common Linux Programs," covers basic principles of Linux GUI operations. It's important that you have some grounding in the basic principles of both text-mode and graphical user interfaces now, since user interface issues crop up from time to time in intervening chapters.

Using a Text-Mode User Interface

Certification
Objective

In the past, and even sometimes today, Linux computers booted in text mode. Once the system had completely booted, the screen would display a simple text-mode login prompt, which might resemble this:

```
Debian GNU/Linux 6.0 essentials tty1

essentials login:
```

The details of such a login prompt vary from one system to another. This example includes several pieces of information:

> ▶ The OS name and version—Debian GNU/Linux 6.0

> ▶ The computer's name—essentials

> ▶ The name of the hardware device being used for the login—tty1

> ▶ The login prompt itself—login:

To log in to such a system, you must type your username at the login: prompt. The system then prompts you for a password, which you must also type. If you entered a valid username and password, the computer is likely to display a login message, followed by a shell prompt:

```
rodsmith@essentials:~$
```

To try a text-mode login, you must first install Linux on a computer. Neither the Linux Essentials exam nor this book covers Linux installation; consult your distribution's documentation to learn more.

If you see a GUI login prompt, you can obtain a text-mode prompt by pressing Ctrl+Alt+F1 or Ctrl+Alt+F2. To return to the GUI login prompt, press Alt+F1 or Alt+F7.

In this book, I omit most of the prompt from example commands when they appear on their own lines. I keep the dollar sign ($) prompt, though, for ordinary user commands. Some commands must be entered as root, which is the Linux administrative user. I change the prompt to a hash mark (#) for such commands, since most Linux distributions make a similar change to their prompts for the root user.

The details of this shell prompt vary from one installation to another, but you can type text-mode commands at the shell prompt. For instance, you could type ls (short for *list*) to see a list of files in the current directory. The most basic commands are shortened by removing vowels, and sometimes consonants, in order to minimize the amount of typing required to execute a command. This has the unfortunate effect of making many commands rather obscure.

Some commands display no information, but most produce some type of output. For instance, the ls command produces a list of files:

```
$ ls
106792c01.doc   f0101.tif
```

This example shows two files in the current directory: 106792c01.doc and f0101.tif. You can use additional commands to manipulate these files, such as cp to copy them or rm to remove (delete) them. Chapter 6 ("Getting to Know the Command Line") and Chapter 7 ("Managing Files") describe some common file manipulation commands.

Some text-mode programs take over the display in order to provide constant updates or to enable you to interact with data in a flexible manner. Figure 1.1, for instance, shows the nano text editor, which is described in more detail in Chapter 11, "Editing Files." Once nano is working, you can use your keyboard's arrow keys to move the cursor around, add text by typing, and so on.

Chapter 13, "Understanding Users and Groups," describes Linux accounts, including the root account, in more detail.

```
  GNU nano 2.2.4              File: parts.txt

# partition table of /dev/sdb
unit: sectors

/dev/sdb1 : start=          63, size=257447873, Id= 7
/dev/sdb2 : start=348336128, size=140060672, Id=83
/dev/sdb3 : start=272781310, size= 75554818, Id= f
/dev/sdb4 : start=257447936, size= 15331328, Id=83, bootable
/dev/sdb5 : start=272781312, size= 16224256, Id=83
/dev/sdb6 : start=289007616, size=  9764864, Id=82
/dev/sdb7 : start=298774528, size= 17745920, Id=83


                         [ Read 10 lines ]
^G Get Help  ^O WriteOut  ^R Read File  ^Y Prev Page  ^K Cut Text   ^C Cur Pos
^X Exit      ^J Justify   ^W Where Is   ^V Next Page  ^U UnCut Text ^T To Spell
```

FIGURE 1.1 Some text-mode programs take over the entire display.

Even if you use a graphical login, you can use a text-mode shell inside a window, known as a *terminal*. Common Linux GUIs provide the ability to launch a terminal program, which provides a shell prompt and the means to run text-mode programs.

Using a Graphical User Interface

Certification Objective

▶

Some Linux GUI login screens don't prompt you for a password until after you've entered a valid username.

Most users are more comfortable with GUIs than with text-mode commands. Thus, many modern Linux systems start up in GUI mode by default, presenting a login screen similar to the one shown in Figure 1.2. You can select your username from a list or type it, followed by typing your password, to log in.

FIGURE 1.2 Graphical login screens on Linux are similar to those for Windows or Mac OS X.

Unlike Windows and Mac OS X, Linux provides a number of desktop environments. Which one you use depends on the specific variety of Linux you're using, what software options you selected at installation time, and your own personal preferences. Common choices include GNOME, KDE, Xfce, and Unity. Many other options are available as well. In Figure 1.2, you can see a selection option for the desktop environment in the lower-left corner of the central dialog box. It reads GNOME in Figure 1.2, meaning that if the item is left unchanged, the computer will launch GNOME when the user logs in.

Linux desktop environments can look quite different from one another, but they all provide similar functionality. Figure 1.3 shows the default KDE on an openSUSE 12.1 installation, with a couple of programs running. Chapter 4 describes common desktop environments and their features in more detail, but for now, you should know that they all provide features such as:

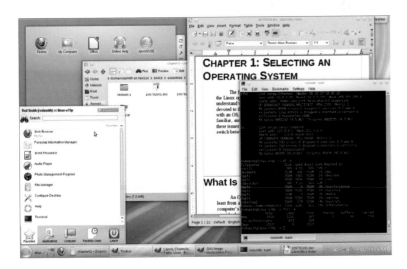

FIGURE 1.3 Linux desktop environments provide the types of GUI controls that most users expect.

Program launchers   You can launch programs by selecting them from menus or lists. Typically, one or more menus exist along the top, bottom, or side of the screen. In Figure 1.3, you can click the openSUSE gecko icon in the bottom-left corner of the screen to produce the menu that appears in that figure.

File managers   Linux provides GUI file managers similar to those in Windows or Mac OS X. A window for one of these is open in the center of Figure 1.3.

Window controls   You can move windows by clicking and dragging their title bars, resize them by clicking and dragging their edges, and so on.

Multiple desktops   Most Linux desktop environments enable you to keep multiple virtual desktops active, each with its own set of programs. This feature is very handy to keep the screen uncluttered while you run many programs simultaneously. Typically, an icon in one of the menus enables you to switch between virtual desktops.

Logout options   You can log out of your Linux session, which enables you to shut down the computer or let another user log in.

Logging out is very important in public computing environments. If you fail to log out, a stranger might come along and use your account for malicious purposes.

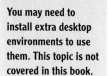

You may need to install extra desktop environments to use them. This topic is not covered in this book.

As you learn more about Linux, you'll discover that its GUI environments are quite flexible. If you find you don't like the environment that's the default for your distribution, you can change it. Although they all provide similar features, some people have strong preferences about desktop environments. Linux gives you a choice in the matter that's not available in Windows or Mac OS X, so feel free to try multiple desktop environments.

Where Does Linux Fit in the OS World?

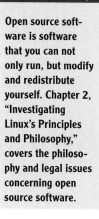

As described later, in "What Is a Distribution?," Linux can be considered a family of OSs. Thus, you can compare one Linux version to another one.

Certification Objective

Open source software is software that you can not only run, but modify and redistribute yourself. Chapter 2, "Investigating Linux's Principles and Philosophy," covers the philosophy and legal issues concerning open source software.

This chapter's title implies a comparison, and as this book is about Linux, the comparison must be to non-Linux OSs. Thus, I compare Linux to three other OSs or OS families: Unix, Mac OS X, and Microsoft Windows.

Comparing Linux to Unix

If you were to attempt to draw a "family tree" of OSs, you would end up scratching your head a lot. This is because OS designers often mimic each other's features, and sometimes even incorporate each other's code into their OSs' workings. The result can be a tangled mess of similarities between OSs, with causes ranging from coincidence to code "borrowing." Attempting to map these influences can be difficult. In the case of Linux and Unix, though, a broad statement is possible: Linux is modeled after Unix.

Unix was created in 1969 at AT&T's Bell Labs. Unix's history is complex and involves multiple *forks* (that is, splitting of the code into two or more independent projects) and even entirely separate code rewrites. Modern Linux systems are, by and large, the product of open source projects that clone Unix programs, or of original open source code projects for Unix generally. These projects include:

The Linux kernel Linus Torvalds created the Linux kernel as a hobby programming project in 1991, but it soon grew to be much more than that. The Linux kernel was designed to be compatible with other Unix kernels, in the sense that it used the same software interfaces in source code. This made using open source programs for other Unix versions with the Linux kernel easy.

The GNU project The GNU's Not Unix (GNU) project is an effort by the Free Software Foundation (FSF) to develop open source replacements for all the core elements of a Unix OS. In 1991, the FSF had already released the most important such tools, with the notable exception of the kernel. (The GNU HURD kernel is now available but is not as popular as the Linux kernel.) Alternatives to the GNU tools include proprietary commercial tools and open source tools developed for the BSD Unix variants. The tools used on a Unix-like OS can influence its overall "flavor," but all of these tool sets are similar enough to give any Unix variety a similar feel compared to a non-Unix OS.

Xorg-X11 The X Window System is the GUI environment for most Unix OSs. Most Linux distributions today use the Xorg-X11 variety of X. As with the basic text-mode tools provided by the GNU project, choice of an X server can affect some features of a Unix-like OS, such as the types of fonts it supports.

Desktop environments GNOME, KDE, Xfce, and other popular open source desktop environments have largely displaced commercial desktop environments even on commercial versions of Unix. Thus, you won't find big differences between Linux and Unix in this area.

Server programs Historically, Unix and Linux have been popular as server OSs—organizations use them to run Web servers, e-mail servers, file servers, and so on. Linux runs the same popular server programs as do commercial Unix versions and the open source BSDs.

User productivity programs In this realm, as in server programs, Linux runs the same software as do other Unix-like OSs. In a few cases, Linux runs more programs, or runs them better. This is mostly because of Linux's popularity and the vast array of hardware drivers that Linux offers. If a program needs advanced video card support, for example, it's more likely to find that support on Linux than on a less popular Unix-like OS.

On the whole, Linux can be thought of as a member of the family of Unix-like OSs. Although Linux is technically *not* a Unix OS, it's similar enough that the differences are unimportant compared to the differences between this family as a whole and other OSs, such as Windows. Because of its popularity, Linux offers better hardware support, at least on commodity PC hardware. Some Unix varieties offer specific features that Linux lacks, though. For instance, the Zettabyte File System (ZFS), available on Solaris, FreeBSD, and some other OSs, provides advanced filesystem features that aren't yet fully implemented in Linux.

GNU is an example of a recursive acronym—an acronym whose expansion includes the acronym itself. This is an example of geek humor.

Mac OS X, described shortly, is a commercial Unix that eschews both X and the desktop environments that run on it in favor of Apple's own GUI.

A ZFS add-on for Linux is available, but it's not fully integrated into the OS. A Linux filesystem known as Btrfs offers many ZFS features, but Btrfs isn't yet complete.

CODE TYPES

Human beings write programs in a form known as *source code*. Although source code can seem arcane to the uninitiated, it's crystal clear compared to the form a program must take for a computer to run it: *binary code*. A program known as a *compiler* translates source code to binary code. (Alternatively, some programming languages rely on an *interpreter*, which converts source code to binary code "on the fly," eliminating the need to compile source code.)

(Continues)

> **CODE TYPES** *(Continued)*
>
> The term *open source* refers to the availability of source code, which is generally withheld from the public in the case of commercial programs and OSs. A programmer with access to a program's source code can fix bugs, add features, and otherwise alter how the program operates.

Comparing Linux to Mac OS X

 Certification Objective

Mac OS X is a commercial Unix-based OS that borrows heavily from the BSDs and discards the usual Unix GUI (namely X) in favor of its own user interface. This makes OS X both very similar to Linux and quite different from it.

You can open an OS X Terminal window and type many of the same commands described in this book to achieve similar ends. If a command described in this book isn't present, you may be able to install it in one way or another. OS X ships with some popular Unix server programs, so you can configure it to work much like Linux or another Unix-like OS as a network server computer.

OS X differs from Linux in its user interface, though. The OS X user interface is known as *Cocoa* from a programming perspective, or *Aqua* from a user's point of view. It includes elements that are roughly equivalent to both X and a desktop environment in Linux. Because Cocoa isn't compatible with X from a programming perspective, applications developed for OS X can't be run directly on Linux (or on other Unix-like OSs), and porting them (that is, modifying the source code and recompiling them) for Linux is a non-trivial undertaking. Thus, native OS X applications seldom make the transition to Linux.

> ▶
>
> **The X in X server is a letter X, but the X in OS X is a Roman numeral (10), denoting the tenth version of Mac OS.**

OS X includes an implementation of X that runs under Aqua. This makes the transfer of GUI Linux and Unix programs to OS X relatively straightforward. The resulting programs don't entirely conform to the Aqua user interface, though. They may have buttons, menus, and other features that look out of place compared to the usual appearance of OS X equivalents.

Apple makes OS X available for its own computers. Its license terms forbid installation on non-Apple hardware, and even aside from licensing issues, installing OS X on non-Apple hardware is a non-trivial undertaking. A variant of OS X, known as iOS, runs on Apple's iPad and iPhone devices, and is equally non-portable to other devices. Thus, OS X is largely limited to Apple hardware. Linux, by contrast, runs on a wide variety of hardware, including most PCs. You can even install Linux on Macintosh computers.

Comparing Linux to Windows

Most desktop and laptop computers today run Microsoft Windows. Thus, if you're considering running Linux, the most likely comparison is to Windows. Broadly speaking, Linux and Windows have similar capabilities; however, there are significant differences in details. These include the following:

Certification
Objective

Licensing   Linux is an open source OS whereas Windows is a proprietary commercial OS. Chapter 2 covers open source issues in greater detail, but for now you should know that open source software gives you greater control over your computer than does proprietary software—at least in theory. In practice, you may need a great deal of expertise to take advantage of open source's benefits. Proprietary software may be preferable if you work for an organization that's only comfortable with the idea of software that's sold in a more traditional way. (Some Linux variants, though, are sold in a similar way, along with service contracts.)

Costs   Many Linux varieties are available free of charge, and so are appealing if you're trying to cut costs. On the other hand, the expertise needed to install and maintain a Linux installation is likely to be greater, and therefore more expensive, than the expertise needed to install and maintain a Windows installation. Different studies on the issue of total cost of ownership of Linux vs. Windows have gone both ways, but most tend to favor Linux.

Hardware compatibility   Most hardware components require OS support, usually in the form of drivers. Most hardware manufacturers provide Windows drivers for their devices, or work with Microsoft to ensure that Windows includes appropriate drivers. Although some manufacturers provide Linux drivers, too, for the most part the Linux community as a whole must supply the necessary drivers. This means that Linux drivers may take a few weeks or even months to appear after a device becomes available. On the other hand, Linux developers tend to maintain drivers for old hardware for much longer than manufacturers continue to support their own old hardware. Thus, a modern Linux may run better than a recent version of Windows on old hardware. Linux also tends to be less resource-intensive, so you can be productive on older hardware when using Linux.

Software availability   Some popular desktop applications, such as Microsoft Office, are available on Windows but not on Linux. Although Linux alternatives, such as OpenOffice.org or LibreOffice, are available, they haven't caught on in the public's mind. In other realms, the situation is reversed. Popular server programs, such as the Apache Web server, were developed first for Linux or Unix.

Although many such servers are available for Windows, they run more efficiently on Linux. If you have a specific program you must run, you may want to research its availability and practicality on any platforms you're considering.

User interfaces   Like Mac OS X, Windows uses its own unique user interface. This fact contributes to poor inter-OS portability. (Tools exist to help bridge the gap, though; X Window System implementations for Windows are available, as are tools for running Windows programs in Linux.) Some users prefer the Windows user interface to any Linux desktop environment, but others prefer a Linux desktop environment.

Configurability   Linux is a much more configurable OS than is Windows. Although both OSs provide means to run specific programs at startup, change user interface themes, and so on, Linux's open source nature means you can tweak any detail you want. Furthermore, you can pick any Linux variant you like to get a head start on setting up the system as you see fit.

Security   Advocates of each OS claim it's more secure than the other. They can do this because they focus on different security issues. Many of the threats to Windows come from viruses, which by and large target Windows and its huge installed user base. Viruses are essentially a non-issue for Linux; in Linux, security threats come mostly from break-ins involving misconfigured servers or untrustworthy local users.

For over a decade, Windows has dominated the desktop arena. In both homes and offices, users have become familiar with Windows and are used to popular Windows applications, such as Microsoft Office. Although Linux *can* be used in such environments, it's a less popular choice for a variety of reasons—its unfamiliarity, the fact that Windows comes pre-installed on most PCs, and the lack of any compelling Linux-only applications for most users.

Unix generally, and Linux in particular, on the other hand, have come to dominate the server market. Linux powers the Web servers, email servers, file servers, and so on that make up the Internet and that many businesses rely on to provide local network services. Thus, most people use Linux daily even if they don't realize it.

In most cases, it's possible to use either Linux or Windows on a computer and have it do an acceptable job. Sometimes, though, specific needs dictate use of one OS or another. You might need to run a particular exotic program, for instance, or your hardware might be too old for a modern Windows or too new for Linux. In other cases, your own or your users' familiarity with one OS or the other may favor its use.

▶

Microsoft is making major changes to its user interface with Windows 8. The new user interface, Metro, works the same on everything from cell phones to desktop computers.

What Is a Distribution?

Up until now, I've described Linux as if it were a single OS, but this isn't really the case. Many different Linux *distributions* are available, each consisting of a Linux kernel along with a set of utilities and configuration files. The result is a complete OS, and two Linux distributions can differ from each other as much as either differs from OS X or even Windows. I therefore describe in more detail what a distribution is, what distributions are popular, and the ways in which distribution maintainers keep their offerings up to date.

Creating a Complete Linux-Based OS

I've already described some of what makes up a Linux OS, but some details need reiteration or elaboration:

Certification
Objective

A Linux kernel   A Linux kernel is at the core of any Linux OS, of course. I've written this item as *a* Linux kernel because the Linux kernel is constantly evolving. Two distributions are likely to use slightly different kernels. Distribution maintainers also often *patch* kernels—that is, they make small changes to fix bugs or add features.

Core Unix tools   Tools such as the GNU tool set, the X Window System, and the utilities used to manage disks are critical to the normal functioning of a Linux system. Most Linux distributions include more or less the same set of such tools, but as with the kernel, they can vary in versions and patches.

Supplemental software   Additional software, such as major server programs, desktop environments, and productivity tools, ships with most Linux distributions. As with core Unix software, most Linux distributions provide similar options for such software. Distributions sometimes provide their own "branding," though, particularly in desktop environment graphics.

Startup scripts   Much of a Linux distribution's "personality" comes from the way it manages its startup process. Linux uses scripts and utilities to launch the dozens of programs that link the computer to a network, present a login prompt, and so on. These scripts and utilities vary between distributions, which means that they have different features and may be configured in different ways.

An installer   Software must be installed to be used, and most Linux distributions provide unique installation software to help you manage this important task. Thus, two distributions may install in very different ways, giving you different options for key features such as disk layouts and initial user account creation.

The UNetbootin tool
(http://unetbootin
.sourceforge.net)
**can copy the files
from a Linux installa-
tion disc image file to
a USB flash drive.**

Typically, Linux distributions are available for download from their Web sites. You can usually download a CD-R or DVD image file that you can then burn to an optical disc. When you boot the resulting disc, the installer runs and you can install the OS. You can sometimes download an image that can be copied to a USB flash drive if your computer lacks an optical drive.

Some Linux installers come complete with all the software you're likely to install. Others come with only minimal software and expect you to have a working Internet connection so that the installer can download additional software. If your computer isn't connected to the Internet, be sure to get the right type of installer.

A Summary of Common Linux Distributions

Certification
Objective

Depending on how you count, there are about a dozen major Linux distributions for desktop, laptop, and small server computers, and hundreds more that serve specialized purposes. Table 1.1 summarizes the features of the most important distributions.

TABLE 1.1 Features of major Linux distributions

Distribution	Availability	Package format	Release cycle	Administrator skill requirements
Arch	Free	pacman	Rolling	Expert
CentOS	Free	RPM	approximately 2-year	Intermediate
Debian	Free	Debian	2-year	Intermediate to Expert
Fedora	Free	RPM	approximately 6-month	Intermediate
Gentoo	Free	ebuild	Rolling	Expert
Mandriva	Free	RPM	1-year	Intermediate
openSUSE	Free	RPM	8-month	Intermediate
Red Hat Enterprise	Commercial	RPM	approximately 2-year	Intermediate

(Continues)

TABLE 1.1 *(Continued)*

Distribution	Availability	Package format	Release cycle	Administrator skill requirements
Slackware	Free	tarballs	Irregular	Expert
SUSE Enterprise	Commercial	RPM	2–3 years	Intermediate
Ubuntu	Free	Debian	6-month	Novice to Intermediate

These features require explanation:

Availability　Most Linux distributions are entirely open source or free software; however, some include proprietary components and are sold for money, typically with a support contract. Red Hat Enterprise Linux (RHEL) and SUSE Enterprise Linux are the two most prominent examples of this type of distribution. Both have completely free cousins. For RHEL, CentOS is a near-clone that omits the proprietary components, and Fedora is an open version that serves as a testbed for technologies that may eventually be included in CentOS. For SUSE Enterprise, openSUSE is a free alternative.

Package format　Most Linux distributions distribute software in *packages*, which are collections of many files in one. Package software maintains a local database of installed files, making upgrades and uninstallations easy. The RPM Package Manager (RPM) system is the most popular one in the Linux world, but Debian packages are very common, too. Other packaging systems work fine but are distribution-specific. Slackware is unusual in that it uses *tarballs* for its packages. These are package files created by the standard `tar` utility, which is used for backing up computers and for distributing source code, among other things. The tarballs that Slackware uses for its packages contain Slackware-specific information to help with package management. Gentoo is unusual because its package system is based on compiling most software from source code. This is time-consuming but enables experienced administrators to tweak compilation options to optimize the packages for their own hardware and software environments.

> Tarballs are similar to the zip files that are common on Windows. Chapter 10, "Searching, Extracting, and Archiving Data," describes how to create and use tarballs.

Release cycle　I describe release cycles in more detail shortly, in "Understanding Release Cycles." As a general rule, distributions with short release cycles aim to provide the latest software possible, whereas those with longer release cycles strive to provide the most stable environments possible. Some try to have it both ways; for instance, Ubuntu releases long-term support (LTS) versions in April of even-numbered years. Its other releases aim to provide the latest software.

Administrator skill requirements   The final column in Table 1.1 provides my personal estimation of the skill level required to administer a distribution. As you can see, I've described most Linux distributions as requiring "intermediate" skill to administer. Some, however, provide less in the way of user-friendly GUI administrative tools, and so require more skill. Ubuntu aims to be particularly easy to use and administer.

> Don't be scared off by the "intermediate" classification of most distributions. This book's purpose is to help you manage the essential features of such distributions.

Most Linux distributions are available for at least two platforms—that is, CPU types: *x*86 (also known as IA32, i386, and several variants) and *x*86-64 (also known as AMD64, EM64T, and *x*64). Until about 2007, *x*86 computers were the most common variety, but more recently, *x*86-64 computers have become the standard. If you have an *x*86-64 computer, you can run either an *x*86 or an *x*86-64 distribution on it, although the latter provides a small speed improvement. More exotic platforms, such as PowerPC, Alpha, and SPARC, are available. Such platforms are mostly restricted to servers and to specialized devices (described shortly).

In addition to the mainstream PC distributions, several others are available that serve more specialized purposes. Some of these run on regular PCs, but others run on their own specialized hardware:

> Android is best known as a cell phone OS, but it can be used on other devices. Some e-book readers, for instance, run Android.

Android   Many cell phones today use a Linux-based OS known as *Android*. Its user interface is similar to that of other smart phones, but underneath lies a Linux kernel and a significant amount of the same Linux infrastructure you'll find on a PC. Such phones don't use X or typical desktop applications, though; instead, they run specialized applications for cell phones.

Network appliances   Many broadband routers, print servers, and other devices you plug into a local network to perform specialized tasks run Linux. You can sometimes replace the standard OS with a customized one if you want to add features to the device. Tomato (`http://www.polarcloud.com/tomato`) and OpenWrt (`https://openwrt.org`) are two examples of such customized Linux distributions. Don't install such software on a whim, though; if done improperly, or on the wrong device, they can render the device useless!

> I recommend you download Parted Magic, or a similar tool, to have on hand in case you run into problems with your main Linux installation.

TiVo   This popular digital video recorder (DVR) uses a Linux kernel and a significant number of standard support programs, along with proprietary drivers and DVR software. Although many people who use them don't realize it, they are Linux-based computers under the surface.

Parted Magic   This distribution, based at `http://partedmagic.com`, is a Linux distribution for PCs that's intended for emergency recovery operations. It runs from a single CD-R and you can use it to access a Linux or Windows hard disk if the main installation won't boot.

Android, Linux-based network appliances, and TiVo are examples of *embedded systems* that use Linux. Such devices typically require little or no administrative work from users, at least not in the way such tasks are described in this book. Instead, these devices have fixed basic configurations and guided setup tools to help inexperienced users set critical basic options, such as network settings and your time zone.

Certification Objective

Understanding Release Cycles

Certification Objective

Table 1.1 summarized the release cycles employed by a number of common Linux distributions. The values cited in that table are the time between releases. For instance, new versions of Ubuntu come out every six months, like clockwork. Most other distributions' release schedules provide some "wiggle room"; if a release date slides a month, that may be acceptable.

After its release, a distribution is typically supported until sometime *after* the next version's release—typically a few months to a year or more. During this support period, the distribution's maintainers provide software updates to fix bugs and security problems. Once the support period has passed, you can continue to use a distribution, but you're on your own—if you need updated software, you'll have to compile it from source code yourself or hope that you can find a compatible binary package from some other source. As a practical matter, therefore, it's generally a good idea to upgrade to the latest version before the support period ends. This fact makes distributions with longer release cycles appealing to businesses, since a longer time between installations minimizes disruptions and costs associated with upgrades.

Two of the distributions in Table 1.1 (Arch and Gentoo) have *rolling* release cycles. Such distributions have no version numbers in the usual sense; instead, upgrades occur in an ongoing manner. Using such a distribution makes it unnecessary to ever do a full upgrade, with all the hassles that creates; however, you'll occasionally have to do a disruptive upgrade of one particular subsystem, such as a major upgrade in your desktop environment.

Prior to the release of a new version, most distributions make pre-release versions available. *Alpha software* is extremely new and very likely to contain serious bugs, while *beta software* is more stable but nonetheless more likely to contain bugs than is the final release software. As a general rule, you should avoid using such software unless you want to contribute to the development effort by reporting bugs or unless you're desperate to have a new feature.

Certification Objective

THE ESSENTIALS AND BEYOND

Linux is a powerful OS that you can use on everything from a cell phone to a supercomputer. At Linux's core is its *kernel*, which manages the computer's hardware. Built atop that are various utilities (many from the GNU project) and user applications. Linux is a clone of the Unix OS, with which it shares many programs. Mac OS X is another Unix OS, although one with a unique user interface. Although Windows shares many features with Unix, it's an entirely different OS, so software compatibility between Linux and Windows is limited. Linux comes in many varieties, known as distributions, each of which has its own unique "flavor." Because of this variety, you can pick a Linux version that best suits your needs, based on its ease of use, release cycle, and other unique features.

SUGGESTED EXERCISES

▶ Make a list of the programs you run as an ordinary user, including everything from a calculator applet to a major office suite. Look for equivalents at `http://www .linuxrsp.ru/win-lin-soft/table-eng` or `http://www.linuxalt.com`. Is there anything you can't find? If so, try a Web search to find an equivalent.

▶ Read more about two or three Linux distributions by perusing their Web pages. Which distribution would you select for running a major Web server? Which distribution sounds most appealing for use by office workers who do word processing and email?

REVIEW QUESTIONS

1. Which of the following is *not* a function of the Linux kernel?

    A. Allocating memory for use by programs

    B. Allocating CPU time for use by programs

    C. Creating menus in GUI programs

    D. Controlling access to the hard disk

    E. Enabling programs to use a network

2. Which of the following is an example of an embedded Linux OS?

    A. Android   D. Debian

    B. SUSE   E. Fedora

    C. CentOS

(Continues)

THE ESSENTIALS AND BEYOND (Continued)

3. Which of the following is a notable difference between Linux and Mac OS X?

    A. Linux can run common GNU programs, whereas OS X cannot.

    B. Linux's GUI is based on the X Window System, whereas OS X's is not.

    C. Linux cannot run on Apple Macintosh hardware, whereas OS X can run only on Apple hardware.

    D. Linux relies heavily on BSD software, whereas OS X uses no BSD software.

    E. Linux supports text-mode commands, but OS X is a GUI-only OS.

4. True or false: The Linux kernel is derived from the BSD kernel.

5. True or false: If you log into a Linux system in graphical mode, you cannot use text-mode commands in that session.

6. True or false: CentOS is a Linux distribution with a long release cycle.

7. A Linux text-mode login prompt reads _____ (one word).

8. A common security problem with Windows that's essentially nonexistent on Linux is _____ .

9. Pre-release software that's likely to contain bugs is known as _____ and _____ .

## CHAPTER 2

Investigating Linux's Principles and Philosophy

You can frequently select a product or technology on purely pragmatic grounds—what OS works well for a given task, which software suite is the least expensive, and so on. Sometimes, though, understanding the principles and philosophy that underlie a technology can be useful, and might even guide your choice. This is true of some Linux users; the open source model of Linux, which I introduced in Chapter 1, "Selecting an Operating System," has implications that can affect how Linux works. Furthermore, some people in the Linux world can become quite passionate about these principles. Whether or not you agree with these people, understanding their point of view can help you appreciate the Linux culture that you'll find in the workplace, online, at conferences, and so on.

This chapter covers these issues, beginning with information on Linux's origins and development over time up to the present. I then describe open source principles and how they can affect the way an open source OS works in the real world. Finally, I describe some of the roles in which Linux can work—as an embedded OS, as a desktop or laptop OS, and as a server OS.

▶ **Linux through the ages**

▶ **Using open source software**

▶ **Understanding OS roles**

Linux through the Ages

Although Linux's birth date of 1991 is recent by most historical standards, in the computer world 20 years is an eternity. Nonetheless, the software and culture in the early 1990s, and even before then, has had quite a legacy on today's software world. After all, what we use today is built atop the foundation created in the past. Thus, looking at how Linux originated will help you to understand Linux as it exists today.

Understanding Linux's Origins

Computers today can be classified in much the same way as was done in 1991, although some details have changed. A notable addition is embedded computers, as in cell phones.

In 1991, as today, computers were classified by their sizes and capabilities. Computers could belong to any of a handful of categories, ranging from desktop personal computers (PCs) to supercomputers. The PC marketplace of 1991 was dominated by *x*86-based computers that are the direct ancestors of today's PCs; however, other types of PCs were available, such as Macintoshes. Such computers generally used different CPUs and ran their own custom OSs.

In 1991, most PCs ran Microsoft's Disk Operating System (MS-DOS, PC-DOS, or DOS). DOS was extremely limited by today's standards; it was a single-tasking OS that didn't take full advantage of the memory or CPUs available at the time. The versions of Microsoft Windows available in 1991 ran on top of DOS. Although Windows helped work around some of DOS's limitations, it didn't fundamentally fix any of them. These early versions of Windows employed *cooperative multitasking*, for instance, in which programs could voluntarily give up CPU time to other processes. The DOS kernel could not wrest control from a program that hogged CPU time.

Unix was not the only multi-user, multitasking OS in 1991. Others, such as Virtual Memory System (VMS), were available. Unix is most relevant to Linux's history, though.

Above the PC level, Unix was a common OS in 1991. Compared to DOS and the Windows of that time, Unix was a sophisticated OS. Unix supported multiple accounts and provided true *preemptive multitasking*, in which the kernel could schedule CPU time for programs, even if the programs didn't voluntarily give up control. These features were practical necessities for many servers and for multi-user computers such as minicomputers and mainframes.

As time has progressed, the capabilities of each class of computer have grown. By most measures, today's PCs have the power of the minicomputers or even the mainframes of 1991. The OSs used on the PCs of 1991 don't scale well to more powerful hardware, and today's PCs are now powerful enough to run the more sophisticated OSs of 1991. For this reason, DOS and its small-computer contemporaries have been largely abandoned in favor of Unix and other alternatives.

Today's versions of Windows are not derived from DOS. Instead, they use a new kernel that shares many design features with VMS.

In 1991, Linus Torvalds was a student at the University of Helsinki, studying computer science. He was interested in learning about both Unix and the capabilities of the new *x*86 computer he'd just purchased. Torvalds began the program that would become the Linux kernel as a low-level terminal emulator—a program to connect to his university's larger computers. As his program grew, he began adding features that turned his terminal program into something that could be better described as an OS kernel. Eventually, he began writing with the goal of creating a Unix-compatible kernel—that is, a kernel that could run the wide range of Unix software that was available at the time.

Unix's history, in turn, stretched back two more decades, to its origin at AT&T in 1969. Because AT&T was at that time a telephone monopoly in the United

States, it was legally forbidden from selling software. Therefore, when its employees created Unix, AT&T basically gave the OS away. Universities were particularly enthusiastic about adopting Unix, and some began modifying it, since AT&T made the source code available. Thus, Unix had a two-decade history of open software development. Most Unix programs were distributed as source code, since Unix ran on a wide variety of hardware platforms—binary programs made for one machine would seldom run on a different machine.

Early on, Linux began to tap into this reservoir of available software. As noted in Chapter 1, early Linux developers were particularly keen on the GNU's Not Unix (GNU) project's software, so Linux quickly accumulated a collection of GNU utilities. Much of this software had been written with workstations and more powerful computers in mind, but because computer hardware kept improving, it ran fine on the x86 PCs of the early 1990s.

Linux quickly acquired a devoted following of developers who saw its potential to bring workstation-class software to the PC. These people worked to improve the Linux kernel, to make the necessary changes in existing Unix programs so that they would work on Linux, and to write Linux-specific support programs. By the mid-1990s, several Linux distributions existed, including some that survive today. (Slackware was released in 1993, and Red Hat in 1995, for example.)

The 386BSD OS was a competing Unix-like OS in the early 1990s. Today it has forked into several related OSs: FreeBSD, NetBSD, OpenBSD, Dragonfly BSD, and PC-BSD.

THE MICROKERNEL DEBATE

Linux is an example of a monolithic kernel, which is a kernel that does everything a kernel is supposed to do in one big process. In 1991, a competing kernel design, known as a microkernel, was all the rage. Microkernels are much smaller than monolithic kernels; they move as many tasks as they can into non-kernel processes and then manage the communications between processes.

Soon after Linux's release, Linus Torvalds engaged in a public debate with Andrew Tanenbaum, the creator of the Minix OS that Torvalds used as an early development platform for Linux. Minix uses a microkernel design, and Tanenbaum considered Linux's monolithic design to be backward.

As a practical matter for an end user, either design works. Linux and the BSD-derived kernels use monolithic designs, whereas modern versions of Windows, the GNU HURD, and Minix are examples of microkernels. Some people still get worked up over this distinction, though.

Seeing Today's Linux World

By the mid-1990s, the most important features of Linux as it exists today had been established. Changes since then have included:

Improvements in the kernel   The Linux kernel has seen massive changes since 1991, when it lacked many of the features we rely on today. Improvements include the addition of networking features, innumerable hardware drivers, support for power management features, and support for many non-*x*86 CPUs.

Improvements in support tools   Just as work has progressed on the Linux kernel, improvements have also been made to the support programs on which it relies—the compilers, shells, GUIs, and so on.

Creation of new support tools   New support tools have emerged over the years. These range from simple and small utilities to big desktop environments. In fact, some of these tools, such as modern desktop environments, are far more obvious to the end user than is the kernel itself.

Creation of new distributions   As noted earlier, Slackware dates to 1993 and Red Hat (the predecessor to Red Hat Enterprise Linux, CentOS, and Fedora) originated in 1995. Other distributions have emerged in the intervening years, and some have been quite important. The Android OS used on smart phones and tablets, for instance, is becoming influential in the early 2010s.

Linux's roots remain very much in the open source software of the 1980s and 1990s. Although a typical desktop or embedded OS user is likely to perceive the OS through the lens of the GUI, much of what happens under the surface happens because of the Linux kernel and open source tools, many of which have existed for decades.

Using Open Source Software

The philosophies that underlie much software development for Linux are different from those that drive most software development for Windows. These differing philosophies affect how you obtain the software, what you can do with it, and how it changes over time. Thus, I describe these principles. I also describe how Linux functions as a sort of "magnet," integrating software from many sources in one place.

Understanding Basic Open Source Principles

Broadly speaking, software can be described as coming in several different forms, each with different expectations about payment, redistribution, and users' rights.

The number of categories varies depending on the depth of analysis and the prejudices of the person doing the categorization, but as a starting point, four categories will do:

Commercial software   Individuals or companies develop commercial software with the intent to sell it for a profit. Developers generally keep the source code for commercial source software secret, which means that users can't normally make changes to the software except to alter configuration settings the software supports. In the past, commercial software was sold in stores or by mail order, but today it's often sold via downloads from the Internet. Redistributing commercial software is generally illegal. Microsoft Windows and Microsoft Office are both common examples of commercial software.

Shareware software   From a legal perspective, *shareware* software is similar to commercial software in that it's copyrighted and the author asks for payment. The difference is that shareware is distributed on the Internet or in other ways and "sold" on an honor system—if you use the software beyond a trial period, you're expected to pay the author. Shareware was common in 1991 and is still available today, but it's much rarer.

Freeware   Freeware, like shareware, is available for free. Unlike shareware authors, though, the authors of freeware don't ask for payment. Sometimes, freeware is a stripped-down version of a more complete shareware or commercial program. Other times, the authors make it available for free to promote another product. Examples include Windows drivers for many hardware devices or the Adobe Reader program for reading Portable Document Format (PDF) files. As with commercial and shareware programs, freeware generally comes without source code.

Open source software   Open source software is defined by a set of ten principles, available at `http://www.opensource.org/docs/osd`. The most important of these principles are the right of the user to redistribute the program, the availability of source code, and the right of the user to make and distribute changed versions of the program. These principles mean that users can alter open source programs to suit their own needs, even in ways or for purposes the original author doesn't support.

Variants within each of these categories exist, as well as hybrids that don't quite fit in any category. For instance, the Open Source Initiative maintains a list of licenses it has approved as fulfilling its criteria (`http://www.opensource.org/licenses`); however, developers sometimes release software using obscure licenses or using licenses that impose conditions that run afoul of one of the more obscure Open Source Initiative rules. Such software is technically not open source, but it might be closer to open source than to another category.

Freeware should not be confused with *free software*, which is closely related to open source software. Chapter 3, "Understanding Software Licensing," describes free software in more detail.

Certification Objective

Chapter 3 covers specific open source licenses in greater detail.

The basic idea behind open source software is that software developed in a transparent manner is likely to be superior to software developed in a closed manner. This superiority (and arguments against it) comes in several ways:

Better code   Exposing source code to the community at large means that it can be reviewed, judged, and improved upon by any interested party. Otherwise obscure bugs might be found and squashed when they might linger and cause problems in a closed-source product. On the other hand, the validity of this claim is not well supported by research, and smaller projects might not gain much in the way of interest from other programmers, so they might not benefit from outside code review.

More flexibility   By providing users with the source code, an open source project gives users the ability to customize the software for their own needs. If users submit changes back to the maintainer, or release them as a new branch of the project, then everybody can benefit from such changes. Of course, critics would argue that this flexibility is only a benefit to those with the necessary skill and time to make such changes, or to those with the money to hire somebody to do it.

Lower cost   Although the open source definition does not forbid sale of software, the redistribution requirements mean that open source software ends up being available free of charge. On the other hand, if you want support you may need to purchase a support contract, which can reduce or eliminate the cost benefits.

Lack of vendor lock-in   The developers of some proprietary products, and particularly very popular ones, can make it difficult for competing products by using proprietary file formats or standards and by not supporting more open standards. Open source tools are less subject to such problems, since they can be modified to support open standards even if they initially don't do so. As a practical matter, though, even proprietary file formats and protocols are usually reverse-engineered, so vendor lock-in usually ends up being a temporary problem rather than a permanent one.

Of course, within the Linux community the general consensus is that each of these factors is a real point in favor of Linux, and of open source software generally; the downsides noted are generally regarded as minor compared to the advantages. In the end, you'll need to make up your own mind on these matters after using different types of software.

This principle is sometimes referred to as "Linus's Law," which was stated by Eric S. Raymond in "The Cathedral and the Bazaar": "Given enough eyeballs, all bugs are shallow."

Linux as a Software Integrator

Since soon after Unix was created, the OS fragmented into a set of loosely affiliated OSs. These OSs were incompatible on the binary level but more or less compatible on the source code level. This is still true today. You can take the same program and compile it for FreeBSD, OS X, and Linux, and it will work the same on all three platforms—but the compiled binaries made for one platform won't work on the others.

There are exceptions to this rule, though. Some programs rely on features that are available on just some Unix-like OSs. Others have quirks that make it impossible to compile them on some OSs. If a program falls into disuse, it may become unusable on newer OSs because it relies on compiler or OS features that have changed. Such problems tend to be ironed out over time, but they do crop up periodically.

Because of Linux's popularity, most open source Unix programs compile and work fine on Linux. Commercial programs for Linux also exist, although most of these are obscure or specialized. In any event, Linux has become an OS that most open source Unix programs must support. This effect is so strong that many projects now target Linux as the primary platform.

Understanding OS Roles

Computers fill many roles in the world, and as computers have become more common and less expensive, those roles have multiplied. Linux can serve as the OS for most of these roles, each of which draws on its own subset of support utilities. Some of these roles also require tweaking the kernel itself. I briefly describe three of these roles: embedded computers, desktop and laptop computers, and server computers.

Understanding Embedded Computers

As noted in Chapter 1, embedded computers are specialized devices that fulfill a specific purpose. Examples include:

Cell phones   Modern cell phones use computers with OSs that range from simple to complex. Linux powers some of these cell phones, usually in the form of Android.

Certification
Objective

Apple, Microsoft, and other vendors provide their own OSs for cell phones.

e-book readers   These devices, like cell phones, are specialized computers and so use an OS to power them. For many current e-book readers, that OS is Linux—either a custom Linux version or Android.

The MythTV package (`http://www` `.mythtv.org`) **can turn an ordinary PC into a Linux-based DVR, although you'll need a TV tuner and other specific hardware to make it work.**

DVRs   Digital video recorders (DVRs), which record TV shows for later viewing, are computers with specialized software. Some of these, including the popular TiVo models, run Linux.

Car computers   Automobiles have included computers for years. These have mostly been tucked out of the way to monitor and control the engine; however, modern cars increasingly come with computers that users more readily identify as being computers. They manage global positioning system (GPS) navigation systems, control the radio, and even provide Internet access.

Appliances   Televisions, refrigerators, and other appliances are increasingly using computers to monitor energy use and for other purposes.

You might also think of tablet computers as falling in this category as well, although they can more closely resemble desktop or laptop computers. The distinction is mainly one of how much control the user has over the OS; embedded devices are designed to be used, but not maintained, by end users. The system administration tasks described in this book are done at the factory or using much simpler and more specialized user interfaces.

Understanding Desktop and Laptop Computers

Certification
Objective

Desktop computers are similar to another class of computer, known as *workstations*. Workstations tend to be more powerful and specialized, and they often run Unix or Linux.

Linux began life on a desktop computer, and although Linux doesn't come close to dominating that market, desktop computers are a good way to begin learning about Linux. Laptop computers are similar to desktop computers from a system administration perspective; both types of computers are often used by a small number of people for productivity tasks, such as word processing, Web browsing, and managing digital photos. For brevity, I'll use the term *desktop* to refer to both types of computer from here on.

Linux software for such tasks is widely available and is quite good, although some people prefer commercial counterparts, such as Microsoft Office or Adobe Photoshop, that aren't available for Linux. This preference for a few specific commercial products is part of why Microsoft Windows continues to dominate the desktop market. Some people have speculated that the open source development model doesn't lend itself to the creation of popular GUI applications because software developers tend to be too technically oriented to fully appreciate the needs of less technically capable users. Without an explicit way to require developers to fulfill these needs, which for-profit companies create, open source software projects lag behind their commercial counterparts in usability. This view is not universally held, though, and at worst, open source projects lag behind their commercial counterparts just a bit.

Specific software that's required on most Linux-based desktop computers includes:

- ▶ The X Window System GUI (X for short)

- ▶ A popular desktop environment, such as GNOME, KDE, Xfce, or Unity

- ▶ A Web browser, such as Mozilla Firefox

- ▶ An email client, such as Mozilla Thunderbird or Evolution

- ▶ A graphics editor, such as the GIMP

- ▶ An office suite, such as OpenOffice.org or the similar LibreOffice

Additional requirements vary depending on the user's needs. For instance, one user might need multimedia editing tools, whereas another might need scientific data analysis software.

Linux distributions such as Fedora and Ubuntu typically install these popular desktop tools by default, or as a group by selecting a single install-time option. These distributions are also designed for relatively easy maintenance, so that users with only modest skill can install the OS and keep it running over time.

Understanding Server Computers

Server computers can be almost identical to desktop computers in terms of their hardware, although servers sometimes require bigger hard disks or better network connections, depending on how they're used. Many popular network server programs were written for Unix or Linux first, making these platforms the best choice for running them. Examples include:

Certification
Objective

- ▶ Web servers, such as Apache

- ▶ Email servers, such as sendmail and Postfix

- ▶ Databases, such as MySQL

- ▶ File servers, such as the Network File System (NFS) or Samba

- ▶ Print servers, such as the Common Unix Printing System (CUPS) or Samba

- ▶ Domain Name System (DNS) servers, such as the Berkeley Internet Name Domain (BIND)

- ▶ Dynamic Host Configuration Protocol (DHCP) servers, such as the Internet Software Consortium's (ISC's) dhcpd

▶ Time servers, such as the Network Time Protocol (NTP)

▶ Remote login servers, such as Secure Shell (SSH) or Virtual Network Computing (VNC)

In a large organization, each of these services may have a distinct associated server computer. It's possible, though, for one computer to run many of these server programs simultaneously.

Most of these servers do not require a GUI, so server computers can do without X, desktop environments, or the typical desktop programs you'll find on a desktop computer. One of Linux's advantages over Windows is that you can run the computer without these elements, and even uninstall them completely. Doing so means that the GUI won't be needlessly consuming system resources such as RAM. Furthermore, if an item such as X isn't running, any security bugs it might harbor become unimportant. Some distributions, such as Debian, Arch, and Gentoo, eschew GUI configuration utilities. This makes these distributions unfriendly to new users, but the reliance on text-mode configuration tools is not a problem to experienced administrators of server computers.

The people who maintain large server computers are generally technically quite proficient and can often contribute directly to the open source server projects they use. This close association between users and programmers can help keep server projects on the cutting edge of what's required in the real world.

Note that the distinction between desktop and server computers is not absolute; a computer can run a mixture of both types of software. For instance, you might configure desktop computers in an office environment to run file server software. This configuration enables users to more easily share their work with others in the office. In a home or small office setting, running other servers on desktop computers can obviate the need to buy specialized hardware to fulfill those roles.

Remote login servers enable users to run desktop-style programs on a computer remotely. Therefore, they're sometimes found even on desktop systems.

THE ESSENTIALS AND BEYOND

Linux's development history is tied to that of Unix and to open source development generally. Open source software is provided with source code and with the right to modify and redistribute the source code. This guarantees your ability to use the software even in ways the original author did not anticipate or support, provided you have the knowledge and time to alter it, or the resources to hire somebody else to do so. These open source principles have led to a great deal of popular software, particularly in the server arena; however, open source developers have been less able to capture the general public's excitement with applications designed for desktop computers.

(Continues)

THE ESSENTIALS AND BEYOND (Continued)

SUGGESTED EXERCISES

· ▶ Read the Features Web page on FreeBSD, `http://www.freebsd.org/features .html`, a competitor to Linux. How would you say it differs from Linux?

▶ Research the features of two or three open source programs that interest you, such as Apache, LibreOffice, and Mozilla Firefox. Do the feature lists seem complete? Are there features missing that are present in commercial counterparts?

REVIEW QUESTIONS

1. What type of multitasking does Linux use?

    A. Preemptive   **D.** Single-tasking

    B. Multi-user   **E.** Single-user

    C. Co-operative

2. Which of the following is a characteristic of all open source software?

    A. The software cannot be sold for a profit; it must be distributed free of charge.

    B. It must be distributed with both source code and binaries.

    C. Users are permitted to redistribute altered versions of the original software.

    D. The software was originally written at a college or university.

    E. The software must be written in an interpreted language that requires no compilation.

3. Which of the following programs is *most* likely to be installed and regularly used on a desktop computer that runs Linux?

    A. Apache   **D.** Evolution

    B. Postfix   **E.** BIND

    C. Android

4. True or false: VMS was a common OS on *x*86 PCs at the time Linux was created.

5. True or false: Some DVRs run Linux.

6. True or false: A Linux computer being used as a server generally does not require X.

7. Linux uses a _____ kernel design, as contrasted with a microkernel design.

8. A type of software that's distributed for free but that requires payment on the "honor system" if a person uses it is called _____.

9. A _____ computer is likely to run a word processor and Web browser.

Understanding Software Licensing

Software is a type of intellectual property (IP), which is governed by copyright laws and, in some countries, patent laws. As a general rule, this makes it illegal to copy software unless you're the software's author. Open source software, however, relies on licenses, which are documents that alter the terms under which the software is released. As described in this chapter, open source licenses grant additional rights to software's users.

Open source software in general owes a great deal to three organizations: the Free Software Foundation (FSF), the Open Source Initiative (OSI), and the Creative Commons. Each organization has a distinct philosophy and role to play in the open source world. There are also numerous specific open source licenses, which I summarize at the end of this chapter, along with ways that businesses can use them.

▶ **Investigating software licenses**

▶ **The Free Software Foundation**

▶ **The Open Source Initiative**

▶ **The Creative Commons**

▶ **Using open source licenses**

Investigating Software Licenses

Copyright law has existed for centuries, and as such, it wasn't designed with software in mind. Nonetheless, copyright law does apply to software, and licenses that software authors apply to their software interact with copyright law to create the specific rights that you have—and *don't* have—to use, modify, and redistribute software. I therefore describe these basic principles, as well as the differences, in broad strokes, between proprietary and open source license terms.

Copyright and Software

Certification Objective

A copyright is, as the name implies, a legally recognized right to create a copy of something. In most countries, if you write a book, take a photograph, or create a computer program, you and you alone have a right to make copies of that book, photograph, or computer program. You can give others a right to make such copies, or even relinquish control of the copyright to somebody else.

Copyright laws vary from one country to another, but most countries are signatories to the Berne Convention, an international treaty that requires countries to recognize each other's copyrights. That is, if Fred writes a book (or opera, or computer program) in the United States, that work will be copyrighted not only in the United States, but also in Iceland, Kenya, the United Kingdom, and other countries that have ratified the treaty.

Because most copyright laws were written long before computers came into being, they frequently don't mesh well with the needs of computers. For instance, copyright laws forbid copying of a work, but a computer program is useless without such copies. Examples of copies that must necessarily be made to run a program, or that are advisable for safety, include:

▶ A copy of the program from an installation medium to a hard disk

▶ A copy of the program from the hard disk to the computer's random access memory (RAM)

▶ A copy of the RAM into swap space

▶ A copy of the RAM into various smaller caches on the motherboard or CPU used to improve performance

▶ One or more backups of the hard disk, to protect against disk failures

Swap space is disk space that serves as an adjunct to RAM. For instance, if RAM fills up, the OS begins to use swap space as if it were RAM.

In the past, such copies were generally ignored, on the principle of *fair use*—that is, exceptions to the otherwise exclusive right to copy a work given to copyright holders. Other examples of fair use include quotes used in reviews or news reports and excerpts used in research or teaching. Today, copyright law explicitly recognizes the need to copy software to use it, at least in the United States.

PATENTS, TRADEMARKS, AND SOFTWARE

Certification
Objective

Copyright is one example of IP, but there are others. One of these is patents. A copyright protects a single creative work, which can be considered an expression of an idea, but a patent protects the *idea* itself. Patents typically apply to inventions, such as the proverbial "better mousetrap."

In the United States, software patents are legal. Although you can't patent an entire program, you can patent the algorithms that the program uses. Such patents are both common and controversial. Some open source programs don't use certain file formats because the algorithms required to use them are patented and the patent-holders have threatened to sue unauthorized users. Critics of software patents contend that most such patents are trivial or obvious—two things that a patented invention must not be. Companies sometimes use software patents as a way to block another company from selling a product, or to demand payment from a company that sells a product. Many companies selling Android-based cell phones have paid fees to patent-holders who have made software patent claims against their products.

In many other countries, software algorithms cannot be patented. Efforts are underway to change the relationships between software and patents—both to make software patentable in countries where it is not and to restrict or eliminate software patents in countries where software can currently be patented.

Trademarks are another type of IP. These are names, logos, and similar identifiers of a specific company or product. Software and the companies that produce it often use trademarks, as do hardware companies. The name *Linux* was trademarked in 1994 by an individual with little real involvement in the Linux community who attempted to charge royalties on the name. After a lawsuit, the trademark was transferred to the Linux Mark Institute (LMI; http://www.linuxfoundation.org/programs/legal/trademark).

As an end user, you're unlikely to need to deal explicitly with software patents or trademarks. The software patent and trademark games are played at the level of corporations. This contrasts with copyright issues, which can affect individuals who violate copyright law. If you work for a company that releases software, though, patent and trademark law could affect you if your software runs afoul of somebody's software patent or trademark. You should consult an attorney if you believe this might be the case.

Using Licenses to Modify Copyright Terms

Although software is subject to copyright law, most software is released with a *license*, which is a document written in legalese that claims to modify the rights granted by copyright law. In most cases, you don't sign such a license, although in some cases you must click a button to accept the license terms. In the past, licenses were sometimes printed on the boxes in which software was distributed. Such licenses are often called *end-user license agreements (EULAs), click-through licenses, shrink-wrap licenses,* or *click-wrap licenses.* Open source software gener-ally comes with a license in a file, often called COPYING.

Software licenses can modify copyright terms by making the terms either more or less restrictive. For example:

▶ The license to Microsoft Windows 7 Home Basic ties the software to a single computer; once you use the software, you cannot move the software to another computer without violating the license terms. This clause represents a restriction compared to copyright law, which applies to the software without explicit reference to the machine on which it's run.

▶ The General Public License (GPL), which is the license used by the Linux kernel, grants you the right to redistribute the software, includ-ing both the source code and binaries. This represents a loosening of the restrictions provided by copyright law.

As a general rule, licenses for proprietary software provide restrictions on what would otherwise be your rights under copyright law, whereas open source licenses grant you additional rights. There can be exceptions to this rule, though; for instance, a *site license* is a license for a proprietary program that grants an organi-zation a right to make a certain number of copies of the program—say, 100 copies of a word processor for all the company's computers.

The Free Software Foundation

The Free Software Foundation (FSF) is a critical force in the open source world. Founded in 1985 by Richard Stallman, the FSF is the driving force behind the GNU's Not Unix (GNU) project described in the previous two chapters. The FSF has a certain philosophy, which I describe next. This philosophy manifests itself in the GPL, which is the FSF's favored software license.

Understanding the FSF Philosophy

The FSF advocates what it calls *free software*, which it defines in terms of freedom to do things you want to do with the software, not the price of the software. A common phrase to make this distinction clear is "free as in speech, not free as in beer." The FSF defines four specific software freedoms:

▶ Freedom to use the software for any purpose

▶ Freedom to examine the source code and modify it as you see fit

▶ Freedom to redistribute the software

▶ Freedom to redistribute your modified software

Certification Objective

◀

Free software, as the FSF defines it, is different from *freeware*. This term generally refers to software that's free of charge, but not necessarily free as in speech.

These freedoms are similar to the principles espoused by the OSI, described shortly; however, there are some important differences in interpretation, also as described shortly. The FSF elaborates on the implications of each of its principles, and their interactions, at `http://www.gnu.org/philosophy/free-sw.html`.

In an ideal world, by the FSF's standards, all software would be free—distributed with source code and all the freedoms just outlined. Some Linux distributions meet this ideal in isolation; however, some distributions include proprietary software. Sometimes this software is freeware, but other times it's a bit of proprietary code that enables the vendor to restrict redistribution and charge money to sell the software. Since free software is not necessarily free of charge, selling it is not a problem from the FSF's point of view, but given the other freedoms, free software's price tends toward zero as it gets passed around.

The point of all this talk of freedom is to empower users—not just developers or companies. If you can modify a program that does *almost* what you want it to do so that it does *exactly* what you want it to do, that fact is a big advantage compared to a proprietary program. If you can then redistribute your modified version of the program, you can help others (assuming they want similar functionality). Thus, the FSF philosophy, when applied, can create a benefit to the wider community.

The FSF philosophy and the licenses it inspires are often referred to as *copyleft*. This is a play on the word *copyright*, reflecting the fact that copyright provisions are used to ensure freedoms that are, in some respects, the exact opposite of what copyright was created to do—that is, to guarantee a freedom of users to copy software, rather than to restrict that right.

Free Software and the GPL

A Linux distribution is a collection of many programs, which may use different individual licenses. No one license takes priority over the others.

The legal expression of the FSF's principles comes in the form of the GPL (sometimes called the *GNU GPL*). Two versions of the GPL are common, version 2 and version 3. (The older version 1 is seldom used anymore.) Both versions of the GPL apply the four freedoms of the FSF philosophy to the licensed software. They also make explicit an implication of those four freedoms, by stating that derivative works must also be released under the GPL. This clause prevents a company from wholly appropriating an open source program. For instance, many companies make Linux distributions, and some use Linux kernels that incorporate bug-fix "patches." These kernels, like the mainstream Linux kernel, are all available under the GPL. No company could legally release a distribution based on a patched Linux kernel and then refuse to make its kernel patches available.

The GPL version 2 (or GPLv2 for short) was released in 1991, and held sway for many years. In 2007, GPLv3 appeared, with the intention of closing what the FSF viewed as loopholes in the GPLv2, particularly with respect to changes in laws and practices since 1991. Specifically, the GPLv3 contains clauses that are intended to combat use of hardware restrictions that limit the FSF's four freedoms and to address issues related to software patents. Many new programs are now being released under the terms of the GPLv3, and many older programs now use the GPLv3 rather than the GPLv2. Some programs have not changed, though. Notable among these is the Linux kernel itself, which still uses the GPLv2. This is an important choice because it means that the Linux kernel can still be used at the heart of devices that are otherwise fairly closed, such as TiVos and Android-based phones. Many such devices use restrictive boot processes to prevent unauthorized kernels from booting—a process that the GPLv3 would forbid.

A variant of the GPL is the Lesser GPL, or LGPL. Developers often use the LGPL with *libraries*, which are collections of code that can be used by other programs. For instance, in Linux libraries implement the features that create dialog boxes and menus. Many GUI programs use these features, and placing them in libraries helps programmers and reduces the size of the programs that use them. The wording of the GPL, however, would require that all the programs that use a GPLed library also be released under the terms of the GPL. This strong requirement motivated the creation of the LGPL, which is similar to the GPL but enables programs that use a library to be released under another license—even a commercial license.

The acronym LGPL used to expand to *Library GPL*, but this was changed in 1999.

Another related license is the GNU Free Documentation License (FDL), which is intended to be used by documentation rather than by programs. The GPL, being written for software, doesn't apply perfectly to static documents, so the FSF created the GNU FDL to fill the gap. A notable user of the FDL is Wikipedia (`http://www.wikipedia.org`); all of its content is available under the terms of the GNU FDL.

The Open Source Initiative

The OSI was founded in 1998 by Bruce Perens and Eric S. Raymond as an umbrella organization for open source software generally. Its philosophy, described in more detail shortly, is similar to that of the FSF but differs in some important details. As a general rule, more software qualifies as open source than qualifies as free (in the way the FSF means), but precisely what qualifies depends on the open source definition and, in a strict sense, on what the OSI has approved in terms of its licenses.

Understanding the Open Source Philosophy

In the 1980s and 1990s, the free software movement gathered momentum in certain circles, including academia and among hobbyists. Businesses, however, were slow to adopt free software. Many who did adopt it did so reluctantly or even unwittingly—system administrators, pressed to perform their duties with minuscule budgets, would quietly install Linux, Apache, Samba, and other free software as a way to avoid having to buy expensive commercial alternatives.

The FSF's advocacy efforts were (and are) based on a strong moral imperative—software *should be free*, in the FSF's view, with "free" defined as described earlier. This approach appeals to some people, but others—particularly businesses that want to make money off of software—find this type of advocacy strange at best and threatening at worst.

For these reasons, the OSI's creators designed their organization as a way to advocate free software. By using a new term—*open source*—and by softening some of the FSF's moral imperatives, the OSI aims to promote open source software in the business world. The difference in tone from the FSF's moral imperative can be seen in the opening statement on the OSI's Web site (`http://www.opensource.org`):

> *Open source is a development method for software that harnesses the power of distributed peer review and transparency of process. The promise of open source is better quality, higher reliability, more flexibility, lower cost, and an end to predatory vendor lock-in.*

 Certification Objective

The biggest philosophical difference between the FSF and the OSI is reflected in a requirement of the GPL: that derived works also be distributed under the GPL. The OSI has certified many licenses as being open source, including the GPL;

however, many of these licenses lack similar restrictions. Software released under such licenses has, in the past, found its way into closed-source products. The OSI does not object to such a path, provided the software was licensed in a way that permits it. The FSF, on the other hand, explicitly forbade such appropriation for proprietary uses in its GPL.

As a general rule, free software in the FSF's sense is also open source software, although some licenses the FSF recognizes as being free have not been approved by the OSI. Many open source licenses do not qualify as free by the FSF's definition, though. Figure 3.1 illustrates this relationship.

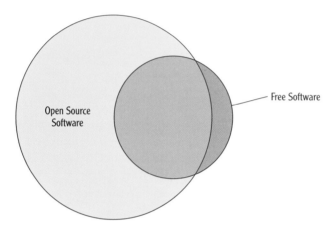

Open Source
Software

Free Software

FIGURE 3.1 Most free software is open source, but a significant amount of open source software is not free.

Certification Objective

Today, there is some tension between free software purists in the FSF's sense and the more pragmatic open source community. For the most part, though, the two share goals that are similar enough that their differences are minor. In fact, two terms, *free and open source software (FOSS)* and *free/libre open source software (FLOSS),* are sometimes used as umbrella terms to explicitly refer to both types of software and development.

Defining Open Source Software

Certification Objective

The open source definition appears at `http://www.opensource.org/docs/osd`. It consists of ten principles, which are (paraphrased):

Free redistribution   The license must permit redistribution, including redistribution as part of a larger work.

▶

The OSI's ten principles were derived from those expressed by the Debian GNU/Linux developers.

Source code availability   The author must make source code available and permit redistribution of both source code and (if applicable) binary code.

Permission to derive works   The license must permit others to modify the software and to distribute such modifications under the same license as the original.

Respect for source code integrity   The license may restrict redistribution of modified source code, but only if patch files may be distributed along with the original source code. The license may require that derived works change the software's name or version number.

Note that the open source definition permits, but does not require, that the license require redistribution under the original license.

No discrimination against persons or groups   The license must not discriminate against any person or group of people.

No discrimination against fields of endeavor   The license must not forbid use of the program in any field, such as in business or by genetics researchers.

Automatic license distribution   The license must apply to anybody who receives the program without needing a separate agreement.

Lack of product specificity   The license must not require that the program be used or distributed as part of a larger program—that is, you may extract a single program from a larger collection and redistribute it alone.

Lack of restrictions on other software   The license must not impose restrictions on other software that's distributed along with the licensed software.

Technology neutrality   The license must not be restricted based on specific technologies or interfaces.

The first three of these principles are the most important, at least in understanding the point of open source technology. The collection as a whole bears a strong resemblance to the FSF's four principles and the extended description of its implications on the FSF's Web page (http://www.gnu.org/philosophy/free-sw.html). As already described, however, there are some differences, particularly with respect to licensing requirements for derived works.

The Creative Commons

The Creative Commons, headquartered at http://creativecommons.org, was founded by Lawrence Lessig. Its goal is to combat what its creators and supporters view as a creative culture that is increasingly tied to permissions granted

Certification
Objective

(or *not* granted) by those who hold copyrights on earlier works. Much of our current culture is derived from earlier cultural works—for instance, *Star Wars* is inspired, in part, by common myths and legends. *Star Wars* itself is copyrighted, however, which limits the rights of current artists to distribute works that are derivative of it, at least without permission.

The Creative Commons promotes its aims by providing six licenses that are designed for various purposes. You can select a license by answering a few questions on the Creative Commons Web site (at `http://creativecommons.org/choose/`), such as whether you want to permit commercial use of your work.

The FSF and the OSI are dedicated to promoting software freedoms. The Creative Commons' goals are broader, though; their licenses are aimed at audio recordings, video recordings, textual works, and so on, not just computer programs. Nonetheless, the Creative Commons as an organization helps promote the types of freedoms that also concern the FSF and the OSI.

Using Open Source Licenses

As an individual user, you might not need to delve too deeply into open source license details. The principles behind the OSI guidelines guarantee that you have the right to use open source programs as you see fit, and even to redistribute those programs. If you're building a business, though, and particularly a business that creates or distributes open source software, you may need to better understand these licenses. Thus, I describe a few of them in more detail and I also describe some of the ways that companies have found to use open source licenses as parts of their business models.

Understanding Open Source Licenses

Every open source license has its own unique characteristics. These are mostly of interest to developers who might want to contribute to a software project, but on occasion they may be important to a system administrator. The major open source licenses include the following:

GNU GPL and LGPL   As noted earlier, the Linux kernel uses the GPLv2, and many other Linux tools use the GPL (either version 2 or version 3). Many Linux libraries use the LGPL.

BSD   The BSD license is used by the open source BSD OSs, and by various software components developed for them. Unlike the GPL, the BSD license allows modifications to be distributed under other licenses. The latest versions of this license are very similar to the MIT license.

Two BSD licenses are common: an older 3-clause and a newer 2-clause. (The 3-clause version is sometimes called the "new" or "revised" license, in reference to a still older version.)

Certification
Objective

MIT   The Massachusetts Institute of Technology (MIT) was the original moving force behind the X Window System (X for short), and the MIT license (sometimes called the X11 license) continues to be used for Xorg-X11—the implementation of X included with all major Linux distributions. The MIT license is unusually short.

Apache   Like the BSD and MIT licenses, the Apache license is an open source license that permits redistribution under the same or another license. If a text file called NOTICE comes with the original work, it must be included in any derived work. This enables the original developer to provide contact or other information, even to users of heavily modified versions of the program.

Certification
Objective

As the name implies, the Apache license originated with the Apache Web browser; however, it's used by many other projects, as well.

Artistic   The Artistic license was originally developed for the Perl programming language, but it has been used with other programs. It's filled with requirements and loopholes for those requirements. Most software that uses the Artistic license is shipped with the stipulation that this license is optional; the user may elect to follow the terms of some other license (usually the GPL) instead.

NPL and MPL   The Netscape Public License (NPL) and Mozilla Public License (MPL) were developed by Netscape when they brought their Netscape Web browser (the parent of the Firefox Web browser) into the open source field. The NPL reserves some rights for the copyright holder, but the MPL is more open.

Certification
Objective

Many additional licenses meet the OSI's requirements. You can find a complete list on the Open Source Initiative Web site, http://www.opensource.org/licenses/.

The details of the various open source licenses are probably not important to most system administrators. You may use and redistribute any open source program as you like. If you modify a program, though, you should be aware of redistribution requirements, particularly if you want to merge two or more programs or distribute a program under a modified license. You should also be aware that some Linux distributions may include software that doesn't qualify as open source. Some of this is commercial software, and some of it falls into some variant category.

Some combinations of open source licenses are *incompatible* with each other, meaning that you can't legally combine the code and release the modified version.

One final concern when describing software licenses is the license for Linux as a whole. When you download a CD-ROM image file or buy a Linux package, the software you obtain uses many different licenses—the GPL, the BSD license, the MIT license, and so on. Most of these licenses are open source, but some aren't. Many distributions ship with a few shareware or not-quite-open-source packages, such as the shareware XV graphics program. Retail packages sometimes include outright commercial software. For this reason, you shouldn't copy a retail Linux package's disc unless you've researched the issue and found that copying is OK. If the distribution vendor provides free-as-in-beer download links, copying is probably OK.

Linux distributions include installation programs, configuration programs, and the like. These tools are usually all that a distribution packager can lay claim to, in terms of copyright. Most distribution maintainers have made their installation and configuration routines available under the GPL or some other open source license, but this isn't always the case. Such details can turn what might seem like an open source OS into something that's not quite fully open source. Debian maintains a policy of using only open source software in its main package set, although it lets freely redistributable but non-open source programs into its "non-free" package set.

Because a complete Linux distribution is composed of components using many different licenses, it's not very useful to speak of a single copyright or license applying to the entire OS. Instead, you should think of a Linux distribution as being a collection of different products that comes with a unifying installation utility. The vast majority of all the programs use one open source license or another, though.

Understanding Open Source Business Models

Certification Objective

Some Linux distributions, such as Debian, are maintained by volunteers or by not-for-profit organizations. Others, such as Red Hat Enterprise Linux, are maintained by a company that expects to make a profit. How, though, can a company make a profit if its core product is available for free on the Internet? Several approaches exist to making money from open source software, including:

Services and support   The product itself can be open source, and even given away for free, while the company sells services and support, such as training and a technical support phone line. For instance, a game might be open source but require a subscription to an online service to provide a full set of features.

Some hardware vendors are reluctant to release open source drivers because doing so necessarily reveals programming information about their hardware, which some vendors are reluctant to do.

Dual licensing   A company can create two versions of the product: One version is completely open source and another adds features that are not available in the open source version. The open source version is then akin to the free samples that supermarkets often provide—it's a way to draw in paying customers.

Multiple products   The open source product may be just one offering from the company, with revenue being generated by other product lines. These other product lines could be other software or some other product, such as manuals.

Open source drivers   A special case of the preceding one is that of hardware vendors, who make money by selling hardware. They might opt to release drivers, or perhaps even hardware-specific applications, as open source as a way to promote their hardware.

Bounties   Users can drive open source creation by offering to pay for new software or new features in existing software. Sites such as FOSSFactory (http://www.fossfactory.org) can help bring together users, each of whom as an individual might not be able to offer enough money to motivate development, to entice programmers to write the desired code.

Donations   Many open source projects accept donations to help fund development. Although this isn't a commercial funding model in the usual sense, it does help fund the operations of organizations such as the FSF.

Beyond these commercial opportunities, of course, a great deal of open source software is developed in academia, by governments, by non-profit organizations, by hobbyists, and so on. Even companies can be motivated to give back changes they make for themselves because hoarding their changes will create more work—if an internal change is not given back to the original author, the change will have to be re-applied with each new release.

THE ESSENTIALS AND BEYOND

Software licensing can be complex, and it's a topic that seldom interests technical people. Nonetheless, license terms can affect how the software community as a whole functions and therefore how software evolves over time. Linux is dominated by a handful of open source licenses, which permit (and sometimes require) that changes remain free. Such licenses typically impose few or no restrictions on how you can use the software. This contrasts with proprietary licenses, which are often loaded with restrictions. Organizations such as the FSF, the OSI, and the Creative Commons promote open source licenses. The OSI in particular tries to convince businesses to adopt open source licenses, advocating business models that employ open source as a way to generate revenue.

SUGGESTED EXERCISES

▶ Look up the GPLv2, GPLv3, and BSD 2-clause licenses. (http://www.opensource.org/licenses/ is a good place to find them all.) Read them and compare them. Which would you use if you were to write an open source program?

▶ Read the OSI mission statement (three paragraphs at the top of its main Web page at http://www.opensource.org) and the "Our Core Work" section of the FSF's "About" page (http://www.fsf.org/about/).

(Continues)

THE ESSENTIALS AND BEYOND *(Continued)*

REVIEW QUESTIONS

1. Which of the following is *not* required in order for software to be certified as open source?

    A. The license must not discriminate against people or groups of people.

    B. The license must not require that the software be distributed as part of a specific product.

    C. The license must require that changes be distributed under the same license.

    D. The program must come with source code, or the author must make it readily available on the Internet.

    E. The license must automatically apply to anybody who acquires the software.

2. Which is true of Linux distributions as a whole?

    A. They're covered by the GPL or the BSD license, depending on the distribution.

    B. Sometimes, they may not be copied because of non-open source software they may contain.

    C. They may be copied only after software using the MIT license is removed.

    D. They all completely conform to the principles of the open source movement.

    E. They all qualify as free software, as the FSF uses the term.

3. Which of the following is a key part of the FSF's philosophy?

    A. Developers should use the latest version of the FSF's GPL.

    B. Users should have the right to modify free software and distribute it under a commercial license.

    C. Developers should write software only for free operating systems such as GNU/Linux.

    D. Users should engage in civil disobedience by copying proprietary software.

    E. Users must have the right to use software as they see fit.

4. True or false: Copyright law governs the distribution of software in most countries.

(Continues)

THE ESSENTIALS AND BEYOND (Continued)

5. True or false: The FSF's free software definition and the OSI's ten principles of open source software both require that users have the ability to examine a program's workings—that is, its source code.

6. True or false: Because their hardware designs are proprietary, hardware vendors cannot release open source drivers for their products.

7. A license created by the FSF and often used for libraries is the _____.

8. An organization devoted to promoting open source-like principles in fields such as video and audio recordings is the _____.

9. The FSF's general principles are summarized by the term _____, which refers to using copyright laws for purposes that are in some ways contrary to copyright's original intent.

## CHAPTER 4

Using Common Linux Programs

This chapter begins a more hands-on look at Linux, as opposed to the more abstract information presented in the previous chapters. This chapter begins with a look at Linux desktop environments, including information on the most common desktop environments and basic use information. If you're using a desktop environment, chances are good that you're doing so in order to run productivity software, so I describe some common productivity packages for Linux. Another major use of a Linux system is as a network server, so I also describe some of the most common server programs you may encounter. Although you might not need to write programs yourself, you may need to compile programs from source code, so you should be familiar with some common Linux programming tools, and I describe these.

▶ **Using a Linux desktop environment**

▶ **Working with productivity software**

▶ **Using server programs**

▶ **Managing programming languages**

Using a Linux Desktop Environment

Chances are your first experience with a working Linux system will involve a *desktop environment*, which is a set of programs that control the screen and provide small utility programs to perform tasks such as manage files. Linux provides several desktop environment options, so if you don't like one you can choose another. In addition to presenting information on available desktop environments, I describe some of the tools you can use to launch programs and manage files.

Choosing a Desktop Environment

Depending on your Linux distribution and installation options, chances are good your system has more than one desktop environment available. The most common desktop environments are:

KDE   The K Desktop Environment (KDE; http://www.kde.org) is one of the most popular desktop environments for Linux. It's the default desktop environment for Mandriva and SUSE. It includes many powerful tools that integrate together very well. It's built using the Qt widget set.

> A *widget set* is a library that handles GUI features such as menus and dialog boxes. Qt and GTK+ are the two most common widget sets on Linux today.

GNOME   The GNU Network Object Model Environment (GNOME; http://www.gnome.org) is KDE's primary rival in the Linux desktop environment arena. Fedora and Debian use it as a default desktop environment. GNOME is built atop the GIMP Tool Kit (GTK+) widget set. Like KDE, GNOME includes many powerful tools that work together. GNOME aims to provide a very easy-to-use desktop environment, and so it provides fewer options than KDE.

LXDE   The Lightweight X11 Desktop Environment (LXDE; http://lxde.org) is, as its full name suggests, intended to consume few resources and therefore work well on old or modest computers.

Unity   Canonical, the publisher of the Ubuntu distribution, released the Unity desktop environment in 2010. Like GNOME, it aims for simplicity as a way of helping users who are inexperienced or who don't want a lot of clutter.

Xfce   This desktop environment, headquartered at http://www.xfce.org, was originally modeled on a commercial desktop environment known as CDE, but it is built using the GTK+ widget set. Xfce provides more configurability than GNOME or Unity, and it aims to consume fewer system resources than most other desktop environments.

Roll-Your-Own   It's possible to build a desktop environment of your own from components you like. At a minimum, you need a window manager (dozens are available; see http://xwinman.org for a partial list), but for the configuration to truly be a desktop environment, you'll need other components, such as a file manager and small productivity tools. All of the components need to be accessible from some sort of menu system.

Unfortunately, it's impossible to give a simple set of rules for when one desktop environment works better than another, although some generalities do apply.

New users who are accustomed to Windows or Mac OS will probably be happiest with KDE; this environment is most like these traditional desktop operating systems' environments. Although they deviate more from the model used by other OSs, GNOME and Unity aim for ease of use and so can be good choices for the inexperienced. Users who are familiar with commercial Unix OSs might give Xfce a try. Xfce and LXDE are good choices on systems that have less than copious RAM or less than blazing CPUs. People who like to customize everything or who have less-capable computers should investigate the roll-your-own approach.

You may want to give two or three desktop environments a try. In most cases, you can install multiple environments using a package manager, as described in Chapter 9, "Using Programs and Processes." Thereafter, you'll see an option to select your desktop environment when you log into the computer, as shown in Figure 4.1, which shows a login screen for a Fedora system. Note the button in the lower-left corner of the login dialog box. It reads GNOME in Figure 4.1, but by clicking it, you can select another desktop environment before you type your password. The details of how you select a desktop environment vary from one system to another, though, so you may need to peruse options on your login screen to find the one you want.

◀

Password selection is extremely important. Chapter 14, "Creating Users and Groups," covers this topic.

FIGURE 4.1 GUI login managers usually provide a selection of environments from which you can choose what to run.

Launching Programs

Certification
Objective

Most desktop environments provide several ways to launch programs. Details vary considerably from one environment to another, but examples include the following:

Desktop menus   Many desktop environments provide menus along a top, bottom, or side edge of the screen. One or more items in these menus can give you access to a preselected set of applications.

Desktop icons   Some desktop environments enable you to place icons in the main area of the desktop. Clicking or double-clicking these icons then launches the applications they represent. This approach generally requires customization, though; few default configurations place applications in the main desktop area.

Panels   Some desktop environments provide panels, typically located on the sides of the screen, in which icons for common applications appear. Unity uses such a configuration by default, as does GNOME 3—although in the case of GNOME 3, the panel appears only when you click the Activities item in the upper-left corner of the screen.

Context menus   You can sometimes right-click in an unused part of the screen to obtain a context menu with a variety of options, which may include the option to run programs.

Searching for programs   Some desktop environments, such as GNOME 3, provide a prominent search feature that you can use to find a program by name. Typically, you type part of a program's name and programs whose names match appear in a list. You can then select the program you want to run from that list.

Certification
Objective

Terminals   You can launch a program called a *terminal*, which provides a text-mode user interface inside a window. You can then run either text-mode or GUI programs by typing their filenames in this window. This approach is covered in more detail in Chapter 6, "Getting to Know the Command Line."

The procedure described here requires that you have a modern video card. If you lack such hardware, GNOME 3 falls back on an older menu-based system for launching programs.

To help clarify some of these methods, a couple of examples are in order. First, consider launching the Firefox Web browser in Fedora 16 using GNOME 3. To do so, you would follow these steps:

1. Click the Activities item in the upper-left corner of the screen. The result is a panel (called Favorites) on the left side of the screen, as shown in Figure 4.2.

FIGURE 4.2 Panels enable you to launch popular programs in GNOME, Unity, and some other desktop environments.

2. Move the mouse over the Firefox icon, which is the topmost icon in Figure 4.2.

3. Click the Firefox icon. After a brief delay, a Firefox window should open.

Several other ways to do this also exist, such as typing the program's name in the search field (visible near the upper-right corner of Figure 4.2) or finding the program in an applications list (accessible by clicking Applications near the top middle-left of Figure 4.2). Because only a handful of programs appear in the GNOME 3 panel, you must either add programs to it or launch programs that the Fedora developers did not include by default in some other way.

For comparison, KDE under openSUSE 12.1 provides several obvious ways to launch Firefox:

▶ By clicking its icon in the Desktop Folder window (visible in the upper-left corner of Figure 4.3).

▶ By clicking its icon near the left side of the panel on the bottom of the screen (again, see Figure 4.3).

▶ By finding it in the Applications list. You can open this list by starting with the Kicker (accessible via the SUSE chameleon icon in the lower-left corner of the screen) and selecting Applications ➢ Internet ➢ Web Browser ➢ Web Browser (Firefox). Figure 4.3 shows the beginning of this selection in progress.

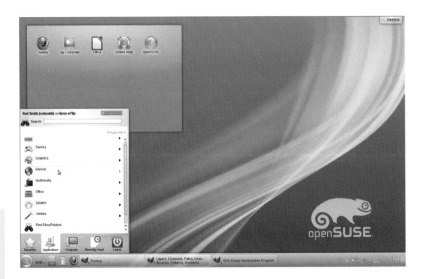

FIGURE 4.3 KDE's desktop interface provides launch methods similar to those available in Windows.

As with GNOME, the widest range of launch options are available for a handful of popular applications such as Firefox. You may need to use the more complex methods, such as locating the program in the Applications list, for less popular programs. You can, however, reconfigure the desktop environment to add programs you use frequently.

Using a File Manager

If you're used to Windows or Mac OS X, you've almost certainly used a *file manager* to manipulate your files. Linux, of course, provides a file manager for this purpose, too—in fact, you have a choice of several, although most of them operate in a similar way. As an example, consider Nautilus, which is GNOME's default file manager. If you were running GNOME 3 on Fedora, the Nautilus icon resembles a filing cabinet in the Favorites panel, as shown in Figure 4.2. Your desktop environment may also launch a file manager when you insert a removable disk, such as a USB flash drive or a CD-ROM or DVD-ROM disc. Figure 4.4 shows Nautilus running on a fresh installation.

Because Nautilus is similar to the file managers in other OSs, chances are you'll be able to use its main features quite easily. A few items do deserve mention:

Locations   Along the left side of the window, you'll see a series of locations. In Figure 4.4, these fall into three categories:

> ▶ The Devices category includes disk partitions that aren't part of your standard installation, including removable disks.

▶ The Computer category is mostly common folders in your own home directory, although File System refers to the entire Linux installation.

▶ The Network category provides access to network resources; however, this may require extra configuration before it works correctly.

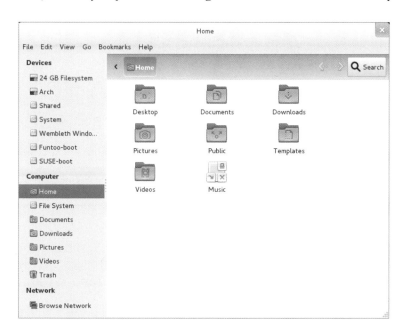

FIGURE 4.4 Nautilus provides a view of your files similar to that in other OSs' file managers.

Home   The Home location refers to your *home directory*—that is, the directory where you store your own user files. Ordinarily, you'll create all of your personal files in your home directory. The default view of Nautilus when you launch it manually is of your home directory, as shown in Figure 4.4, so the right pane shows the files and subdirectories of this directory.

Bookmarks   If you want to change the list of default locations, you can select Edit ➢ Bookmarks from the main menu. The resulting dialog box resembles Figure 4.5. You can remove existing bookmarks or create new ones by entering the path to the directory, giving it a name, and clicking Close. If you add bookmarks, they'll appear in a new section titled Bookmarks.

Document Properties   You can right-click a file and select Properties from the resulting dialog box. This produces a Properties dialog box, as shown in Figure 4.6. The Open With tab enables you to associate a document type with an application.

FIGURE 4.5 You can manage bookmarks to enable quick access to directories that interest you.

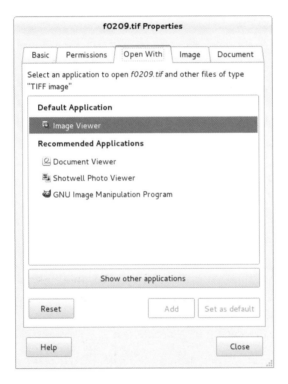

FIGURE 4.6 Nautilus enables you to associate document types with applications.

Working with Productivity Software

The area of productivity software is extremely broad; hundreds, if not thousands, of productivity applications exist, and entire books have been written about many of them. Therefore, in this chapter I can only provide names and brief descriptions of a few of the most important such tools. I begin by providing some tips on how to find a program to perform a task in Linux. I then describe some of the tools in a few common categories, including Web browsers, email clients, office tools, multimedia applications, cloud computing, and mobile applications.

Finding the Right Tool for the Job

Linux provides productivity applications in many broad categories, but if you're not already familiar with the field, you might have a hard time tracking them down. This is particularly true because applications' names don't always clearly identify their purpose.

A few techniques can help you to find suitable applications:

Using desktop menus   You can use the menus or other application display tools on your desktop environment to locate productivity applications. Such tools often categorize applications in helpful ways. For example, the KDE Kicker (shown in Figure 4.3) breaks applications down into categories (Edutainment, Games, Graphics, and so on) and subcategories (Photography and Scanning in the Graphics category, for instance). This can help you track down an application, but only if it's already installed.

Using search features   You may be able to use a search feature, either in a desktop environment or in a Web browser, to locate a suitable application. Typing in a critical word or phrase, such as *office* (in conjunction with *Linux* if you're doing a Web search) may help you locate office applications (word processors, spreadsheets, and so on).

Using tables of equivalents   If you normally use a particular Windows application, you may be able to find a Linux substitute by consulting a table of equivalent applications, such as the ones at `http://www.linuxrsp.ru/win-lin-soft/table-eng` or `http://www.linuxalt.com`.

Using others' expertise   You can ask other people—co-workers, friends, or people in online forums—for help in finding a suitable application. This technique is particularly helpful if you've performed a basic search yourself but found nothing that meets your specific criteria.

Some of these methods, such as using desktop menus, can only find software that's already installed. Other techniques, such as Web searches, can find programs that you don't have installed. You can usually install software with the help of your distribution's packaging system, as described in Chapter 9.

Using a Web Browser

Linux supports a variety of Web browsers, including the following:

Chrome   Google's Chrome browser (http://www.google.com/chrome) aims to be fast and easy to use. Since its introduction in 2008, it's gained rapidly in popularity. Although Chrome is technically a commercial project, it's available free of charge. An open source variant, known as Chromium, is also available.

Certification Objective

Firefox   This program, headquartered at http://www.mozilla.org, is the most popular browser for Linux, and is also quite popular on Windows and Mac OS X. It's a very complete browser, but it can consume a lot of memory, so it may not be the best choice on an older or weaker computer.

Galeon   This program, headquartered at http://galeon.sourceforge.net, is a browser that's officially part of the GNOME Office suite. It's designed as a lightweight GUI Web browser.

Konqueror   This KDE program serves a dual function: It's both a Web browser and a file manager. Konqueror does a good job with most Web pages. It's fairly lightweight, and so is well worth trying, particularly if you use KDE. You can read more at http://www.konqueror.org.

Lynx   Most Web browsers are GUI programs that display text in multiple fonts, show graphics inline, and so on. Lynx (http://lynx.browser.org) is unusual in that it's a text-based Web browser. As such, it's a useful choice if you run Linux in text mode or if you don't want to be bothered with graphics. Lynx is also useful as a test browser when you develop your own Web pages—if a page is readable in Lynx, chances are visually impaired people who browse the Web with speech synthesizers will be able to use your page.

Opera   An unusual commercial entrant in the Linux Web browser sweepstakes, Opera (http://www.opera.com) claims to be unusually fast. Although Opera is commercial, you can download it at no charge.

Notably absent from this list is Microsoft's Internet Explorer, which is extremely popular on Windows. Unfortunately, some Web sites just won't work with anything but Internet Explorer. Other sites are somewhat picky, but they can work with at least one Linux browser. Thus, you should probably install at least two Linux Web browsers.

Certification Objective

Web browsers give users easy access to a world of information—literally! Unfortunately, the Web has a dark side, too. Problems include:

▶ Web sites can log user access data, which can be used in marketing or in other ways you might not like.

> ▶ Much Web-based content is dynamic, meaning that Web sites download small programs (often written in Java) that your Web browser runs. This content might be harmless, but it's increasingly being used to deliver malware.

> ▶ Malicious Web sites can trick users into giving up sensitive data, such as financial information, by pretending to be a trusted site. This technique is known as *phishing*.

> ▶ Most Web sites are not secure—data transferred can be read on intervening computers. Most sensitive sites, such as Internet banking sites and online retailers, now encrypt their sensitive data, but you should be cautious when sending such data.

> ▶ Because of security concerns, passwords used on most Web sites are subject to theft. This can pose a dilemma because it can be hard to remember all your Web site passwords. Many browsers can do this for you, but that stores your passwords on your hard disk, which makes them vulnerable to theft or loss.

◀

Chapter 14, "Creating Users and Groups," describes how to create passwords that are both memorable and hard to guess.

Some of these problems aren't unique to the Web, of course. For instance, most email transfers are insecure, so you shouldn't send sensitive data via email.

Using Email Clients

Email client programs enable you to read and write email messages. Such programs can either access a mailbox on your own computer or, using email network protocols described later, send and receive email with the help of network mail server computers. Common Linux email clients include the following:

Evolution   This program, based at http://projects.gnome.org/evolution/, is a powerful GUI email client. It also includes groupware and scheduling features.

KMail   The KDE project's KMail (http://userbase.kde.org/KMail) is well integrated into that desktop environment, but you can use it even in other desktop environments if you like.

mutt   This is one of several text-based email readers. Despite its text-mode interface, mutt is quite capable. You can read more at http://www.mutt.org.

Thunderbird   This program, based at http://www.mozilla.org/thunderbird/, is an email client that's closely associated with the Firefox Web browser.

Certification
Objective

Email clients work in a similar way in any OS. Typically, you must configure them to know how to send and receive messages—whether to use the local computer's facilities or remote servers. Thereafter, you can read incoming messages and send outgoing messages.

Using Office Tools

Several office tool packages for Linux exist. These packages offer some combination of word processors, spreadsheets, presentation programs, graphics programs, databases, and sometimes other programs. Examples include:

GNOME Office   The applications in GNOME Office are developed independently of each other, but GNOME Office attempts to link them together into a coherent whole. Specific projects within GNOME Office are AbiWord (word processor), Evince (document viewer), Evolution (groupware and email client), Gnumeric (spreadsheet), Inkscape (vector graphics and presentation creation), and Ease (presentation). You can learn more at `http://live.gnome.org/GnomeOffice`.

KOffice   This office suite, based at `http://www.koffice.org`, is loosely associated with the KDE project, although you can use it even if you use another desktop environment. It includes KWrite (word processor), KCells (spreadsheet), Artwork (vector graphics), Showcase (presentation), and Kivio (flowcharting).

LibreOffice   This office suite was created as a *fork* of the older OpenOffice.org suite (described shortly). It's becoming the most popular office suite in Linux. It provides six applications: Writer (word processor), Calc (spreadsheet), Impress (presentation), Base (database), Draw (vector graphics), and Math (equation editor). LibreOffice has a reputation for being a big and slow suite. The speed issue is not a major problem on modern hardware, but on older systems you may want to consider something else. You can read more at `http://www.libreoffice.org`.

OpenOffice.org   Until early 2011, this office suite, based at `http://www.open office.org`, was the most prominent one for Linux. Its corporate sponsor, Oracle, stopped supporting commercial development of the project, which triggered the fork of the LibreOffice project.

Most of these programs support the OpenDocument Format (ODF), which is an open set of file formats that's slowly making inroads as a standard for word processing, spreadsheet, and other office files. Although ODF is intended to enable easy transfer of files across applications, application-specific assumptions often hinder such transfers, especially on complex documents.

Many other programs exist in this space, although many aren't part of office suites. Some are unusual. For instance, LyX (`http://www.lyx.org`) can take the place of a word processor, but it's rather unusual: It's built as a way to create and

A *fork* of a program is when a single project splits into two projects, typically because different groups of developers have diverging goals.

Certification Objective

Certification Objective

edit LaTeX documents, LaTeX being a document format that's popular in computer science, mathematics, and some other technical fields.

Using Multimedia Applications

Linux has an excellent reputation as a workhorse server platform, but until recently, its capacity as a multimedia OS has been lacking. This was largely because of a dearth of applications; however, Linux's multimedia application list has grown considerably in the last decade. Current offerings include the following:

Audacity This program, based at `http://audacity.sourceforge.net`, is an audio editor for Linux, similar to commercial products like Sound Forge for other platforms. You can use it to cut sections from an audio file, equalize volume, remove tape hiss or other noises, apply artificial audio effects, and more.

Certification
Objective

Blender You can use this program to create complex 3-D images, including both stills and animations. You can learn more about Blender at `http://www.blender.org`.

Certification
Objective

The GIMP The GNU Image Manipulation Program (GIMP; `http://www.gimp.org`) is a still image manipulation program similar in broad strokes to Adobe Photoshop. (The GTK+ toolkit, which is the basis of GNOME and many other programs, was originally created for the GIMP.)

Certification
Objective

ImageMagick This is a suite of graphics programs, but with a twist: You typically use the ImageMagick programs from the command line. You can use it to convert file formats, add frames to images, resize images, and so on. You can learn more at `http://www.imagemagick.org`.

Certification
Objective

HandBrake This program provides an easy way to convert between video formats, and particularly into formats that use the efficient H.264 encoding. You can learn more at `http://handbrake.fr`.

MythTV You can turn a regular PC into a digital video recorder (DVR) using this software, which is based at `http://www.mythtv.org`. MythTV uses a client-server model, enabling one recorder to service multiple players on TVs throughout your home.

A few motion pictures that used effects rendered via Linux include *Titanic*, the *Shrek* series, and *Avatar*.

Given this range of multimedia applications, you can use Linux for everything from cropping photos of your 2-year-old's birthday party to rendering the effects for major motion pictures. If you have very special needs, digging a bit may turn up something else—this list is just the start!

Using Linux for Cloud Computing

Cloud computing is the delivery of computer software as a service, typically over the Internet, rather than in the form of applications stored on the user's computer. In most cases, users access cloud computing resources via a Web browser. Thus, in theory Linux can function as a cloud computing client platform—just launch a Web browser on the cloud computing provider and away you go.

In practice, there can sometimes be complications. For instance, a cloud computing provider might require that you use a particular Web browser or have a specific browser plug-in installed. In some cases, it might be impossible to meet these requirements in Linux; however, if the provider supports a wide range of browsers as clients, you shouldn't have problems using cloud computing resources.

Examples of cloud computing include:

▶ Dropbox (`http://www.dropbox.com`), an online file storage and backup service

▶ Google Apps (`http://www.google.com/apps`)

▶ Microsoft Office Web Apps (`http://office2010.microsoft.com/en-us/web-apps/`)

▶ Web-based email, available from many providers

Using Mobile Applications

Although Android is a Linux-based OS, for the most part it runs entirely different applications than do desktop or server implementations of Linux. This is understandable—chances are you wouldn't want to try to write a long document, such as a book, with a cell phone, so many of the features in a big office program such as LibreOffice Write would go to waste on a mobile computing device.

Instead, mobile computing typically focuses on small programs known as *apps*. In the case of Android, you can download apps using an app called Market. (A Web-based version is available at `http://market.android.com`.) Apps typically provide quick and specialized computation, often employing features of the phone. For instance, an app can calculate the calories you've burned while riding a bicycle or retrieve a weather forecast for your area. Both these examples use your phone's global positioning system (GPS) features to identify the phone's (and your!) position.

Although most Linux applications for desktop and server computers are open source and available free of charge, Android apps are often non-free, albeit low in cost. Be sure to check the cost before you download an app!

Using Server Programs

Linux is a powerful OS for running server programs, so it should come as no surprise that you can find a wide variety of server programs for Linux. In the following pages I describe some common server protocols and the programs that use them. I also briefly describe the process of installing and launching servers and provide basic information on server security issues.

Identifying Common Server Protocols and Programs

Networks, including the Internet, function by means of network *protocols*, which are clearly defined descriptions of how two computers should exchange data to achieve some end, such as transferring email or delivering a file to be printed. Most protocols are described in one or more standards documents, known as Request for Comments (RFC) documents, each of which has a number. Typically, one RFC document defines the protocol, and over time additional RFC documents define extensions or modifications of the protocol as they become necessary.

Most network protocols involve transferring data over one or more *ports*, which are numbered resources on a computer. You can think of a port as being something like a telephone extension number—the main number (an Internet Protocol, or IP, address) identifies the computer as a whole and the port number identifies the protocol being used. A server program attaches itself to a port number and receives all incoming requests on that port.

Table 4.1 summarizes some common port numbers, the protocols with which they're associated, and the Linux programs that are often used in conjunction with these protocols. Note that many ports and protocols are associated with more than one program. This is because Linux provides choices for many protocols—you can choose which of several server programs to use for a given protocol, just as you can choose which of several word processors or Web browsers to use.

Android apps are increasingly a source of malware. You can minimize your risk by downloading apps only from Google's own Market source.

The /etc/services **file links common port numbers to short names that are often used in other configuration files.**

TABLE 4.1 Common port numbers and their purposes

Port number	Protocol	Common server program(s)	Explanation
20–21	FTP	oftpd, ProFTPD, Pure-FTPd, vsftpd	The File Transfer Protocol (FTP) is an old protocol for transferring files over a network. It supports both anonymous and password-mediated access. FTP is unusual in that it uses two ports.
22	SSH	OpenSSH	The Secure Shell (SSH) is an encrypted remote access tool. It also supports file transfers and encrypting other protocols.
23	Telnet	telnetd	This is an old unencrypted remote login protocol. It's seldom used today, although its client program, telnet, can be a useful network diagnostic tool.
25	SMTP	Exim, Postfix, qmail, sendmail	The Simple Mail Transfer Protocol (SMTP) is the main protocol for moving email on the Internet. The sender initiates SMTP transfers.
42	DNS	dnsmasq, named	The Domain Name Service (DNS) enables computers to look up an IP address by providing a hostname, or vice-versa. Without it, you'd need to refer to all computers by IP address rather than by name.
67	BOOTP, DHCP	dnsmasq, dhcpd	The Bootstrap Protocol (BOOTP) and its newer cousin, the Dynamic Host Configuration Protocol (DHCP), both enable a computer on a local network to help automatically configure other computers to use a network.

(Continues)

TABLE 4.1 *(Continued)*

Port number	Protocol	Common server program(s)	Explanation
80	HTTP	Apache	The Hypertext Transfer Protocol (HTTP) is the basis of the World Wide Web (WWW, or Web).
109–110	POP2 and POP3	Courier, Cyrus IMAP, Dovecot, UW IMAP	The Post Office Protocol (POP) has gone through several revisions, each with its own port. This protocol enables a recipient to initiate an email transfer, so it's often used as the last leg in email delivery, from a server to the recipient.
118	SQL	MySQL, PostgreSQL	The Structured Query Language (SQL) is a network-enabled database interface language. If you run an SQL server on your network, client computers can access and modify that database.
137–139	SMB/CIFS	Samba	Microsoft uses the Server Message Block (SMB)/Common Internet File System (CIFS) protocols for file and printer sharing, and Samba implements these protocols in Linux.
143, 200	IMAP	Courier, Cyrus IMAP, Dovecot, UW IMAP	The Internet Message Access Protocol (IMAP) is another recipient-initiated email transfer protocol, similar to POP. IMAP makes it easier for recipients to permanently store and manage email on the server computer, though.
389	LDAP	OpenLDAP	The Lightweight Directory Access Protocol (LDAP) is a network protocol for accessing directories, which in this context are a type of database. LDAP is often used to store network login information, among other things.

(Continues)

TABLE 4.1 (Continued)

Port number	Protocol	Common server program(s)	Explanation
443	HTTPS	Apache	This protocol is a secure (encrypted) variant of HTTP.
2049	NFS	NFS	The Network File System (NFS) is a protocol, and a server of the same name, for file sharing between Unix and Unix-like OSs.

Table 4.1 is incomplete; it only summarizes some of the more important protocols and the servers that deliver them. Numerous other protocols and servers exist, many of them for very specialized tasks.

Some protocols are most often used on local networks. For instance, DHCP by its nature is intended to help you manage your own local network by making it easier to configure client computers—just tell the computers to use DHCP and that's it. SMB/CIFS is also usually employed only locally, to enable users to more easily access each other's files and printers. Protocols like HTTP, on the other hand, are generally used on the Internet as a whole, although they can also be used on local networks.

Chapter 17, "Managing Network Connections," describes network configuration in greater detail.

SERVER PROGRAMS AND SERVER COMPUTERS

The term *server* can apply to an entire computer or to a single program running on that computer. When applied to a computer as a whole, the term identifies the purpose of the computer and the fact that it runs one or more server programs. Server computers typically provide services that are used by anywhere from a handful to millions of client computers—that is, the computers that use a server's services.

In the networking world, a server (computer or program) listens for a connection from a client (computer or program) and responds to data transfer requests. Server computers are often—but not always—more powerful than their clients.

When you read the word *server* (or *client*, for that matter), it may refer to either a computer or a program. The context usually makes it clear which meaning is intended, although sometimes this isn't the case—in fact, sometimes

(Continues)

SERVER PROGRAMS AND SERVER COMPUTERS *(Continued)*

the speaker or writer may not know! For instance, somebody might report "the Samba server isn't working." In such a case, you might need to figure out whether it's the Samba server program or something else on the server computer that's causing problems!

Sometimes the client-server lines can get blurred. For instance, in office settings, it's common for many computers to function as file *servers* by running file server software such as Samba or NFS. Such a configuration enables Sam to make his files available to Jill, and for Jill to make her files available to Sam. In this situation, both computers function as both client and server, and run both types of software. In any given exchange, though, only one is the client and one the server.

Installing and Launching Servers

The topic of maintaining server programs is beyond the scope of this book, but you should be aware of the basics of this task. You can install servers in the same way you install other software, as described in Chapter 9.

Once the software is installed, you must launch a server. You do this differently than the way you launch a desktop application. Instead of clicking an icon or menu entry in a GUI, you typically launch a server by configuring the computer to run it automatically whenever it boots. Thereafter, the server program runs in the background, as a *daemon*—that is, as a process that runs unattended.

Most servers run via a startup script, which Linux runs automatically whenever it boots. You can also type the startup script name, usually followed by a keyword such as start or stop, to start or stop the server manually. Traditionally, Linux startup scripts have been stored in /etc/init.d or /etc/rc.d. This location, and the nature of startup scripts, has been changing with recent distributions, although most distributions retain compatibility scripts in these old locations.

Some servers run via a *super server*, such as inetd or xinetd. These server programs run constantly, keeping the servers they manage unloaded except when they're needed. This configuration can minimize the memory impact of running many seldom-used servers. The super server can also function as a security feature; like a doorman, it can keep out the riff-raff.

◄

The word *daemon* derives from Greek mythology; daemons were helpful supernatural beings, just as Unix and Linux daemons are helpful programs.

Securing Servers

Whenever you run a server, you also run the risk of its being compromised and abused. Risks fall into several categories:

▶ Servers can contain bugs that enable outsiders to abuse the software to run programs locally.

▶ You can misconfigure a server, granting outsiders greater access to your system than you'd intended.

▶ Users with accounts and remote access via a server can abuse this trust. This risk is particularly great if combined with a server bug or misconfiguration.

▶ A server can be used as a stepping-stone to attack others, making it appear as if an attack originated from your computer.

▶ Even without breaking into a computer, an attacker can swamp a server with bogus data, thus shutting it down. This technique is called a *denial-of-service (DoS) attack*.

Server security is an extremely complex topic, and details vary from one server to another. For instance, if you run a server such as a remote login server, Samba, or a POP or IMAP email server, you probably want to pay careful attention to password security, since all of these servers rely on passwords. Passwords are unimportant to a DHCP or DNS server, though. Of course, even if a DHCP or DNS server program doesn't use passwords, other server programs running on the same computer might!

Broadly speaking, securing a server involves paying attention to each of the risk factors just outlined. Some specific steps you can take to secure your servers include the following:

▶ You should keep your server programs up-to-date by using your package management tools to upgrade servers whenever upgrades become available. You can also research specific servers to pick ones that have good security reputations.

▶ You should learn enough about server configuration to be sure you can configure your servers properly.

▶ You should remove unused accounts and audit necessary accounts to be sure they use strong passwords.

▶ You can use firewall configurations to restrict outsiders' access to server computers that are intended for internal use only. You can also use firewalls to minimize the risk of one of your computers being used to attack others.

Chapter 14, "Creating Users and Groups," describes how to create strong passwords.

Managing Programming Languages

Many users never need to deal with programming languages; however, basic knowledge of what they are and how they differ from one another is important for Linux users, for a variety of reasons. You might need to install languages for users on systems you manage, or use programming languages yourself to compile software from source code. You might also want or need to learn about programming, particularly if you find a need to modify your computer's configuration at a low level—many of the startup and other tasks are handled by scripts that you can modify yourself.

For these reasons, the rest of this chapter is devoted to presenting basic information on programming languages. I begin by describing the differences between compiled and interpreted languages, which are important to understand so that you can properly handle program files or choose which you want to use. I then provide brief descriptions of some common programming languages so that you can identify and use their source code files or choose which language you want to learn to use.

Choosing a Compiled vs. an Interpreted Language

At their core, computers understand binary codes—numbers that represent operations, such as adding two numbers or choosing which of two actions to take. People, however, are much better at handling words and symbols, such as + or if. Thus, most programming involves writing a program in a symbolic programming language and then translating that symbolic code into the numeric form that computers understand. Dozens, if not hundreds, of such *programming languages* exist, each with its own unique features.

Among high-level languages, two broad categories exist:

Compiled languages   Programmers convert (or *compile*) a program written in a compiled language from the original source code form into the machine code form when writing the program. The compilation process can take some time—typically a few seconds to several hours, depending on the size of the program and the speed of the computer. Compilation can also fail because of errors in the program. When the compilation succeeds, the resulting machine code executes quickly.

Interpreted languages   Programs written in interpreted languages are converted to machine code at the time they're run, by a program known as an *interpreter*. In fact, the conversion happens on a line-by-line basis. That is, the program is never completely converted to machine code; the interpreter figures out what each line does and then does that one thing. This means that interpreted programs run much more slowly than compiled programs. The advantage is that interpreted programs are easier to develop, since you don't need to deal with the compilation process. Interpreted programs are also easy to modify; just open the program file in a text editor and save it back. This feature makes interpreted languages useful for helping with system startup tasks that system administrators might want to change—administrators can make and test changes quickly.

PROGRAMMING IN ASSEMBLY LANGUAGE

In addition to compiled and interpreted languages, another option is *assembly language*. This is a language with a simple one-to-one correspondence between machine code numbers and the symbols the programmer uses. Assembly language is very low-level, which means that a skilled assembly language programmer can produce very compact and efficient programs. Assembly language is not very portable, though; it takes a lot of effort to convert a program written for, say, the *x*86-64 CPU to run on a PowerPC processor. Writing assembly language programs is also harder than writing programs in most higher-level languages. For these reasons, assembly language programs have become rarer as computers have become more powerful; the speed and size advantages of assembly language just aren't very compelling for most purposes in the early 21st century.

In theory, most languages can be implemented in either compiled or interpreted form. In practice, though, most languages are most commonly used in just one form or the other.

Some languages don't fit neatly into either category. See the "Programming in Assembly Language" sidebar for one important exception. Some others fall into an in-between category, such as Java, which is compiled from source code into a platform-independent form that must be interpreted.

Identifying Common Programming Languages

Linux supports a wide range of programming languages, including the following:

Assembly   As noted earlier, this low-level language can produce very efficient programs but is difficult to write and is non-portable. In fact, referring to "assembly" as if it were one language is a bit misleading, since each architecture has its own assembly language.

C This language is arguably the most important compiled language for Linux, since most of the Linux kernel, as well as a huge number of Linux applications, are written in C. C can produce fairly efficient code, but it's also easy to write buggy programs in C because it lacks some error-checking features that are common in many other languages. C source code files typically have filenames that end in .c or .h—the .c files are the main source code files, whereas the .h files are *header* files, which contain short definitions of the functions in the .c files, for reference by other files in a program. A large program can consist of dozens, if not hundreds or thousands, of individual source code files. In Linux, C programs are generally compiled with the gcc program, which is part of the GNU Compiler Collection (GCC) package.

C++ This language is an extension to C that adds *object-oriented* features, meaning that greater emphasis is given to data structures and their interactions than to the procedures used to control the flow of the program. Many complex Linux programs, such as KDE and OpenOffice.org/LibreOffice, are written largely in C++. C++ source code files can have filenames that end in .cc, .cpp, .cxx, or .c++, with header files ending in .h, .hh, .hpp, .hxx, or .h++. In Linux, C++ is generally compiled with the g++ program, which is part of GCC.

Java Java was created by Sun Microsystems (now owned by Oracle) as a cross-platform language that's somewhere between being compiled and interpreted. It's become popular as a language for small applications delivered via Web sites, although some other programs are Java based as well. Java source code usually has a name that ends in .java or .class, whereas Java byte code files usually have names that end in .jar.

Perl This interpreted language is designed for easy manipulation of text, but it's a general-purpose language that can be used for many other tasks as well. Perl programs typically have filenames that end in .pl, .pm, or .t.

PHP The PHP: Hypertext Preprocessor (PHP; a recursive acronym) language was created for use on Web servers in order to generate dynamic content—that is, content that varies depending on the user, the time of day, or some other criterion. PHP is an interpreted language and it requires a PHP-aware Web server, such as Apache. Given such a server and appropriate configuration, a Web site can support user logins, shopping carts, different content based on users' locations, and so on. PHP files most often have names that end in .php, although several variants are common.

Python This interpreted language makes code readability a major goal. It supports (but does not require) object orientation. It's often used for scripting purposes, but it can be used to write more complex programs, too. Python programs often use .py filename extensions, although several variants of this are common, too.

Certification Objective

▶

Chapter 12, "Creating Scripts," covers the basics of creating or modifying Bash scripts.

Shell scripting   Most Linux text-mode shells—the programs that enable entirely keyboard-based use of the computer—provide their own interpreted languages. Of these, the Bourne Again Shell (Bash or bash) is the most common, so Bash scripting is quite common. Many of the files that control the Linux startup process are in fact Bash scripts. Such scripts frequently have no unique filename extension, although some use a .sh extension.

THE ESSENTIALS AND BEYOND

When you're just starting out with Linux, chances are you'll begin by using a desktop environment—the first set of programs you see when you log in. A desktop environment enables you to run more programs, including common productivity tools such as Web browsers, email clients, office utilities, and multimedia applications. If you're configuring a computer as a server, of course, you'll want to run server programs, but you'll do this by editing configuration files rather than launching them from a desktop environment. If you need to do programming, you should be aware of some common Linux programming languages, which enable you to write everything from trivial scripts to huge servers or productivity suites.

SUGGESTED EXERCISES

▶ Try at least two different desktop environments. Use each desktop environment for your normal computing tasks for a day or two so that you can decide which you prefer.

▶ Try at least two different Linux Web browsers. Use each to visit your favorite Web sites. Do you notice differences in speed or how the elements on the page are laid out? Which do you prefer?

REVIEW QUESTIONS

1.   Which of the following are Linux desktop environments? (Select all that apply.)

   A. GTK+

   B. GNOME

   C. KDE

   D. Evolution

   E. Xfce

(Continues)

THE ESSENTIALS AND BEYOND *(Continued)*

2. If you want to enable one Linux computer to access files stored on another Linux computer's hard disk, which of the following network protocols is the best choice?

   A. SMTP   **D.** DNS

   B. NFS   **E.** DHCP

   C. PHP

3. In which of the following languages was most of the Linux kernel written?

   A. Bash shell script   **D.** C++

   B. Java   **E.** Perl

   C. C

4. True or false: OpenOffice.org and LibreOffice are very similar office suites.

5. True or false: Servers can be disrupted by malicious outsiders even if the computer that runs them is never broken into.

6. True or false: Python is generally implemented as an interpreted language.

7. Thunderbird is a(n) _____ program. (Specify the general category of the software.)

8. A Linux server that handles the SMB/CIFS protocol normally runs the _____ software.

9. A program written in a(n) _____ programming language is completely converted to binary form before being run.

## CHAPTER 5

Managing Hardware

Although Linux is software, it relies on hardware to operate. The capabilities and limitations of your hardware will influence the capabilities and limitations of Linux running on that hardware. Therefore, you should know these features for any computer you use extensively or that you plan to buy. This chapter will help you learn about and perform basic management tasks with your hardware. I begin with low-level issues, such as the nature of your central processing unit (CPU) and motherboard. Often overlooked, the power supply can cause problems if it's undersized or misbehaves, so I describe it. Hard disks require special care in their setup, which I briefly describe. A common sticking point in Linux is display issues, since a malfunctioning display prevents any interaction with the computer. Today, most external devices attach via the Universal Serial Bus (USB), so I describe its features. Finally, this chapter covers the common issue of *drivers*, which are software components that control hardware devices.

▶ **Learning about your CPU**

▶ **Identifying motherboard capabilities**

▶ **Sizing your power supply**

▶ **Understanding disk issues**

▶ **Managing displays**

▶ **Handling USB devices**

▶ **Managing drivers**

Learning About Your CPU

Certification
Objective

Your CPU (sometimes called the *processor*) is the "brain" of your computer—it does most of the computer's actual computing. I've mentioned CPUs in earlier

Many devices have more specialized computing circuitry. Most notably, video cards include graphics processing units (GPUs) to do specialized graphics computations.

chapters in reference to distribution availability—to run on a given CPU, most software must be recompiled for that CPU. Thus, it's important that you know enough about the different CPU families to know their strengths and weaknesses and to identify what type of CPU your computer uses.

Understanding CPU Families

CPU manufacturers tend to create product lines by making regular improvements to their products. Improvements range from minor (such as running the CPU at a faster *clock rate*, which is like running an engine at a faster speed) to moderate redesigns to improve speed (which is like shifting gears to get better speed) to radical redesigns (which are like using a bigger or more efficient engine, but one based on the original design). All of these types of changes remain within a single CPU family, so they can run the same code as their predecessors. Still more radical differences exist across CPU families; two CPUs from different families can typically *not* run each other's binary programs, although there are exceptions to this rule, including one very important one that I describe shortly.

On desktop computers, two CPU families are (or were recently) common:

x86   This CPU type originated with Intel's 8086 CPU, but the first model capable of running Linux was the 80386 (also known as the *386*). Development continued with the 80486 (also known as the *486*), the Pentium, and related Intel CPUs, such as the Celeron. AMD, Cyrix, VIA, and others have all released CPUs that are compatible with Intel's designs. Recent AMD names for its *x*86 CPUs include Athlon and Duron. The earliest *x*86 CPUs were 16-bit models, but the model line has been 32-bit since the 80386.

The upcoming section, "Identifying Your CPU," describes how to determine what CPU you've got.

x86-64   Other names for this architecture include *AMD64*, *x64*, and *EM64T*. AMD created the *x*86-64 architecture as a 64-bit extension to the *x*86 architecture. Unusually, *x*86-64 CPUs can run the earlier 32-bit *x*86 code, but when run in 64-bit mode, such CPUs have access to additional features that improve speed. Intel has created its own *x*86-64 CPUs. Both Intel and AMD have used the same product line names for their *x*86-64 CPUs as for their *x*86 CPUs. This fact can make it hard to tell whether you've got a 32-bit *x*86 CPU or a 64-bit *x*86-64 CPU, at least based on the CPU's marketing name. Most desktop and small server computers sold since about 2007 have used *x*86-64 CPUs.

CPU BIT DEPTH

CPUs process data in binary (base 2), meaning that numbers are represented using only two digits—0 and 1. CPUs have limits to the sizes of the numbers they can process, though, and those limits are described in terms of the number of binary digits, or *bits*, that the CPU can handle. A 32-bit CPU, for instance, can process numbers that contain up to 32 binary digits. Expressed as positive integers, this means that numbers can range in size from 0 to $2^{32} - 1$ (4,294,967,295 in the base 10 that people generally use). When dealing with larger numbers, the CPU must combine two or more numbers, which requires extra code.

CPUs with larger bit depths have an advantage when dealing with lots of memory, since memory addresses must fit into the CPU's basic unit size. In particular, a 32-bit CPU has a 4 GiB limit on memory—although some architectures, including *x*86, provide tricks to work around this limit. Greater bit depth does not improve speed per se except when dealing with very large numbers; however, the 64-bit *x*86-64 CPU architecture is faster than its 32-bit *x*86 predecessor for unrelated reasons.

In addition to *x*86 and *x*86-64 CPUs, several other model lines are available. Most of these CPUs are used in embedded applications or in very high-end servers. A couple you might encounter on desktops or small servers are:

PowerPC This CPU, created as a cooperative effort of Apple, IBM, and Motorola, was Apple's CPU of choice between 1994 and 2006, and so is found in Macintoshes of that vintage. Today, it's used in some game consoles, embedded devices, and servers. Both 32- and 64-bit versions of this architecture are available. *PPC* is a common abbreviation for this architecture.

Itanium Intel created the Itanium, or IA-64, architecture as a 64-bit replacement for the *x*86 line; however, it gained little market penetration except in the server field.

Linux can run on PowerPC and Itanium, as well as on other CPU families, such as MIPS and SPARC; however, your choice of distribution is likely to be limited. Because software has to be recompiled and tested on new architectures, it takes effort to prepare a distribution for each architecture, and many distribution maintainers are unwilling or unable to expend this effort for more than *x*86 and *x*86-64.

Debian is available on many architectures, so if you need to support Linux on a wide range of CPUs, using Debian can make sense.

Some high-end motherboards also support multiple CPUs, so you can use, say, two 4-core CPUs to get the performance of an 8-CPU system.

Many CPUs today are *multi-core* models. These CPUs package the circuitry for two or more CPUs into one unit. When plugged into a motherboard, such a CPU looks like multiple CPUs to the OS. The advantage is that Linux can run as many CPU-intensive programs as you have cores and they won't slow each other down significantly by competing for CPU resources.

Identifying Your CPU

If you've got a working Linux system, you can learn a great deal about your CPU by using three text-mode commands:

uname -a   Typing **uname -a** displays basic information on the kernel and the CPU. For instance, one of my systems returns x86_64 AMD Phenom (tm) II X3 700e Processor, among other things, indicating the manufacturer and model number of the CPU.

lscpu   This command returns additional information on about 20 lines of output. Much of this information is highly technical, such as the sizes of *caches* the CPU supports. Some of it's less technical, such as the architecture and the number of CPUs or cores it supports.

cat /proc/cpuinfo   This command returns still more information compared to lscpu. Chances are you won't need this information yourself, but a developer or technician might want some of this information to help debug a problem.

One thing to keep in mind is that modern *x*86-64 CPUs can run software compiled for the older *x*86 architecture. Thus, you might be running a 32-bit Linux distribution on a 64-bit CPU. The output of these commands can be confusing in such cases. For instance, here's part of what lscpu shows on one such system:

```
Architecture:          i686
CPU op-mode(s):        64-bit
```

The Architecture line suggests an *x*86 CPU (i686 being a specific variant of that architecture), but the CPU op-mode(s) line indicates that the CPU supports 64-bit operation. If you have trouble interpreting this output, you might be able to find something by looking up the CPU's model on the manufacturer's Web site; however, manufacturers tend to bury such information in hard-to-read specification sheets, so be prepared to read carefully.

Identifying Motherboard Capabilities

Certification Objective

If the CPU is the computer's brain, the motherboard is the rest of the computer's central nervous system. The motherboard is a large circuit board inside the computer. It's dominated by a *chipset*, which is one or more chips that provide key functionality for the computer—they handle the hard disk interfaces, the USB interfaces, the network devices, and so on. Some chipsets include video circuitry for video cards, although this functionality is sometimes separate, and sometimes it's built into the CPU.

In addition to the chipset, motherboards include plug-in interfaces for key components:

- ▶ One or more slots for the computer's CPU(s)

- ▶ Slots for random access memory (RAM)

- ▶ Slots for plug-in Peripheral Component Interconnect (PCI) or other cards

- ▶ Connectors for Serial Advanced Technology Attachment (SATA) disks, and sometimes for Parallel ATA (PATA) disks

- ▶ Back-panel connectors that provide external interfaces for USB devices, keyboards, monitors, and so on

- ▶ Connectors for additional external devices, such as front-panel USB plugs; such devices are attached via short internal cables

Some motherboards—typically used in larger desktop and server computers—have many connectors for many purposes. Such motherboards are highly expandable but they're physically large enough that they require bulky cases. Other motherboards are much smaller and can be used in compact computers, but such computers aren't as expandable. Laptop computers also have motherboards, which are necessarily of the small variety, with little opportunity for internal expansion.

Most of the connectors on a motherboard are managed by its primary chipset. Some high-end boards provide features beyond those of its primary chipset. Such features require a secondary chipset, such as an extra Ethernet chipset for a second network port or an extra SATA chipset for more or faster hard disk interfaces.

Whether the feature is provided by the main or by a secondary chipset, you can learn about most of the motherboard's features with the lspci command, which shows information on PCI devices. The output looks something like this:

```
$ lspci
00:00.0 Host bridge: Advanced Micro Devices [AMD] RS780 Host Bridge
00:11.0 SATA controller: ATI Technologies Inc SB700/SB800 SATA↵
 Controller [IDE mode]
00:12.0 USB Controller: ATI Technologies Inc SB700/SB800 USB OHCIO↵
 Controller
00:14.1 IDE interface: ATI Technologies Inc SB700/SB800 IDE Controller
00:14.2 Audio device: ATI Technologies Inc SBx00 Azalia (Intel HDA)
```

◀

Motherboards are sometimes referred to as *mainboards*.

◀

I've edited this for brevity.

```
01:05.0 VGA compatible controller: ATI Technologies Inc Radeon HD 3200↵
  Graphics
01:05.1 Audio device: ATI Technologies Inc RS780 Azalia controller
02:00.0 Ethernet controller: Realtek Semiconductor Co., Ltd.↵
  RTL8111/8168B PCI Express Gigabit Ethernet controller (rev 02)
03:06.0 Ethernet controller: Intel Corporation 82559 InBusiness 10/100↵
  (rev 08)
```

You may not understand everything in this output, but you should be able to glean some information from it. For instance, the computer has a number of ATI devices—an SATA controller, a USB controller, a graphics adapter, and so on. Two Ethernet devices are present—one made by Realtek and the other by Intel. Although it's not obvious from this output, the Realtek network adapter is built into the motherboard, whereas the Intel device resides on a plug-in card.

Sizing Your Power Supply

Certification Objective

A computer's power supply takes the alternating current (AC) power from a wall outlet and converts it to the direct current (DC) that your motherboard and everything you plug into it uses. Laptop computers and some small desktop units use power adapter "bricks" that you can put on the floor. Larger desktop computers have internal power supply units. These internal units are larger, both physically and in terms of the amount of power they can deliver.

Every power supply has limits on the amount of DC power it can deliver. This is important because every device you plug into the computer consumes a certain amount of power. If your computer manufacturer cut corners, the power supply may be barely adequate for the computer as delivered. If you add a hard disk or a power-hungry plug-in card, you could exceed the amount of power that the power supply can deliver. The result can be unreliable operation—the computer can crash or behave erratically, perhaps corrupting data or files. Such problems can be hard to distinguish from other problems, such as bad RAM or a failing hard disk.

If you need to replace your power supply, pay attention to its output in watts. You should be able to find the output of your current power supply on a sticker—but you'll need to open your computer first, at least for most desktop systems. Be sure to get a power supply that's rated for at least as many watts as the one you're replacing. Also be sure it will fit—sizes are standardized, but there are a few variants available. In the case of a laptop or a small desktop computer with an external power supply, you must ensure that a replacement provides the right type of connector to the computer. Buying a replacement from the computer's manufacturer is usually the best course of action in this case.

Understanding Disk Issues

Disks are a critical part of most Linux installations. Therefore, I describe three basic disk issues in this chapter: disk hardware interfaces, disk partitioning, and filesystems. I also describe some of the issues surrounding removable disks, including optical (CD-ROM, DVD-ROM, and Blu-ray) discs.

Disk Interfaces

Today, two disk interfaces are common, both of which have already been mentioned:

PATA   This interface was very common in the past, but it's fading in popularity. It features wide 40- or 80-pin cables that transfer several bits of data simultaneously—hence the word *parallel* in the name Parallel ATA (PATA). A PATA cable can have up to three connectors—one for the motherboard or disk controller card and two more for up to two hard disks. Alternative names for PATA (or specific variants of it) include Integrated Device Electronics (IDE) or Enhanced IDE (EIDE). The ATA Packet Interface (ATAPI) standard defines a software interface that helps ATA manage devices other than hard disks. Although in some cases the differences between the technologies described by these variant terms are important, today they're often used synonymously.

SATA   In 2003, a serial version of the ATA protocol was created, hence Serial ATA (SATA). SATA is more or less software compatible with PATA, but it uses thinner cables that can handle just one hard disk per cable. In 2012, SATA is the dominant disk technology on new computers. An external variant, eSATA, provides high-speed connections to external hard disks.

In addition to these technologies, others exist. The Small Computer System Interface (SCSI) is a parallel interface that was once common on servers and high-end interfaces but is less common today. The Serial Attached SCSI (SAS) is a serial variant that's quite similar to SATA. Both of these technologies are important because ATAPI is modeled after SCSI. The Universal Serial Bus (USB) interface is often used for connecting external disks.

Partitioning a Disk

You can think of a hard disk as a set of *sectors*, each of which holds a small amount of data—normally 512 bytes, although some disks have larger sectors. The disk hardware itself does little to help organize data on the disk, aside from providing a means to read and write specific sectors. On-disk data management is left up to

You can install Linux in a *diskless* configuration, in which a Linux computer boots using files stored on a network server.

Certification
Objective

Most modern Linux distributions treat all disks as if they were SCSI disks from a software perspective.

Certification
Objective

the OS. Disk partitions and filesystems are two levels of organization imposed on disks to help manage the data they store.

Partitions are a lot like the drawers in a filing cabinet. Think of a single disk as the main filing cabinet, which is then split up into multiple partitions, much like drawers. This analogy is good as far as it goes, but it has its limits. Unlike filing cabinet drawers, disk partitions can be created in whatever size and quantity are convenient, within the limits of the disk's size. A typical disk has between one and a dozen partitions, although you can create more.

Disk partitions exist to help subdivide the disk into pieces with broadly different purposes, such as partitions for different OSs or for different types of data within an OS. For instance, it's common to create separate partitions for swap space (which is used much like RAM in case you run out of RAM), for user data files, and for the OS itself.

Hard disks and their partitions are frequently represented in diagrams similar to Figure 5.1. This diagram displays partitions as subdivisions of the disk, with partition sizes in the diagram more or less proportional to their true sizes on the disk. Thus, in Figure 5.1 you can see that /boot is tiny compared to /home. As in the figure, partitions are uninterrupted sections of a disk—that is, /home, for instance, is a set of sectors with no other partition carved out of its interior.

> **Some partitioning tools represent their partitions in a vertical stack rather than a horizontal chain. The principle is the same either way.**

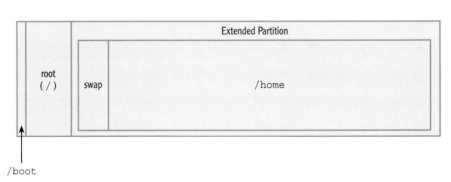

FIGURE 5.1 Disk partitions are often visualized as boxes within a hard disk.

The most common partitioning scheme for x86 and x86-64 computers has gone by various names over the years, including *master boot record (MBR)*, *MS-DOS*, and *BIOS partitioning*. It supports three types of partitions:

Primary   This is the simplest type of partition. A disk can have zero to four primary partitions, one of which may be an extended partition.

Extended This is a special type of primary partition that serves as a placeholder for logical partitions. A disk may have at most one extended partition.

Logical These partitions are contained within an extended partition. In theory, a disk can have billions of logical partitions, thus overcoming the limit of four primary partitions, but in practice you're unlikely to see more than about a dozen of them.

MBR's use of three partition types is awkward and limiting, but inertia has kept it in place for three decades. MBR partitions have a hard limit, though: They can't support disks larger than 2 TiB (tebibytes), assuming 512-byte sectors, which are nearly universal today.

The Globally Unique Identifier (GUID) Partition Table (GPT) is the successor to MBR. GPT supports disks of up to 8 ZiB (zebibytes), which is about 4 billion times as large as MBR's limit. GPT also supports up to 128 partitions by default, with no distinction between primary, extended, and logical partitions. In these respects, GPT is a superior partitioning system to MBR; however, its support varies between OSs. Linux supports both systems quite well. Windows can boot only from MBR when the computer uses the Basic Input/Output System (BIOS), and it can boot only from GPT when the computer is based on the Unified Extensible Firmware Interface (UEFI). Thus, if you dual-boot with Windows, you may need to select your partitioning system with care.

◄

1 TiB is 2^{40} bytes, whereas 1 ZiB is 2^{70} bytes.

MULTI-BYTE UNITS

It's common to use prefixes from the International System of Units (SI units)—*kilo* (*k*), *mega* (*M*), *giga* (*G*), *tera* (*T*), and so on—in conjunction with *byte* (B) to refer to large quantities of storage space, as in kB, MB, and so on. Technically, these units are defined as base-10 values—*kilo* means 1,000, *mega* means 1,000,000, and so on. In computers, though, base-2 values, such as 2^{10} (1024) and 2^{20} (1,048,576), are often more natural, so the SI units have often (but not always) been used to mean these base-2 values. This practice has led to confusion, since it's not always clear whether base-10 or base-2 units are being used.

To resolve this conflict, the Institute of Electrical and Electronics Engineers (IEEE) defined a new set of prefixes as IEEE-1541. Under this system, new units and prefixes describe base-2 values. The first few of these are:

▶ A kibibyte (KiB) is 2^{10} (1024) bytes.

(Continues)

MULTI-BYTE UNITS *(Continued)*

▶ A mebibyte (MiB) is 2^{20} (1,048,576) bytes.

▶ A gibibyte (GiB) is 2^{30} (1,073,741,824) bytes.

▶ A tebibyte (TiB) is 2^{40} (1,099,511,627,776) bytes.

In this book, I use IEEE-1541 units when describing features that are best expressed in this system, such as partition table size limits. Most Linux disk utilities use SI and IEEE-1541 units correctly, but which is used depends on the whim of the programs' authors. Be alert to this difference, particularly when dealing with large numbers—note that a tebibyte is almost 10 percent larger than a terabyte!

Several other partitioning systems exist, but you're unlikely to encounter most of them. One possible exception is the Apple Partition Map (APM), which Apple used on its Macintoshes prior to its switch to Intel CPUs.

When it comes to partitioning a disk, Linux supports three families of tools:

fdisk family   The fdisk, cfdisk, and sfdisk tools are simple text-based partitioning utilities for MBR disks and some more exotic partition table types. These tools work well and provide the means to recover from some disk errors, but their text-based nature can be intimidating to those who are unfamiliar with disk partitioning.

libparted-based tools   Tools based on the libparted library can handle MBR, GPT, and several other partition table types. Some of these tools, such as GNU Parted, are text based, but others, such as GParted, are GUI, and so are likely to be easier for new users to use. Figure 5.2 shows GParted in action. Note how its display mirrors the structure shown in Figure 5.1. Many Linux installers include libparted-based partitioning tools that run during system installation.

GPT fdisk family   The gdisk, cgdisk, and sgdisk tools are modeled after the fdisk family but work with GPT disks. They provide more options for handling GPT than do libparted-based tools, but at the cost of friendliness for new users.

I am the author of the GPT fdisk family of partitioning tools.

If you're working with a pre-installed Linux system, you may not need to partition your disk; however, if you ever replace or install a new hard disk, you'll have to partition it before you can use it. You may also need to partition removable disks, although they generally come from the factory pre-partitioned with one big partition.

To partition a disk, you must know the disk's device filename. In Linux, these filenames are normally /dev/sda, /dev/sdb, and so on, with each disk taking on a new letter. Partitions are numbered starting with 1, so you might refer to /dev/sda2, /dev/sdb6, and so on. When using MBR, partitions 1 through 4 are reserved for primary or extended partitions, whereas logical partitions take numbers 5 and up.

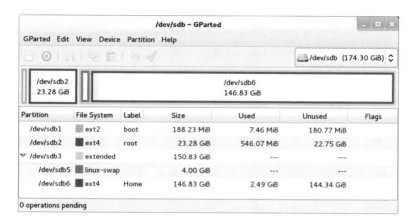

FIGURE 5.2 GParted, like other GUI disk partitioning tools, provides a graphical representation of your partitions.

Understanding Filesystem Issues

Most disk partitions contain filesystems, which are data structures that help the computer organize your directories and files. In Windows, each filesystem receives its own device letter, such as A: and B: for floppy disks, C: for the first hard disk partition (normally the boot partition), and so on. In Linux, by contrast, all filesystems are part of a single directory tree. The main filesystem is referred to as the root (/) filesystem. If a disk has multiple filesystem partitions, each is *mounted* at a *mount point* in the root (/) filesystem—that is, the contents of the additional filesystems are made available at specific directories, such as at /home (which holds users' data files) or /boot (which holds boot files). Several Linux filesystems exist, each with its own unique features:

Ext2fs The Second Extended Filesystem (ext2fs) was popular in the 1990s but is rarely used today because it lacks a *journal*, which is a filesystem feature that speeds filesystem checks after power outages or system crashes. A journal consumes disk space, though, so ext2fs is still useful on small disks. You might want to use it for a separate /boot partition, for instance, since such partitions are rather small. Its Linux filesystem type code is ext2.

The word *filesystem* is sometimes applied to the directory structure as a whole, even if it contains multiple low-level filesystems. Which meaning is intended is usually clear from the context.

The original Extended Filesystem (extfs) was used in the early 1990s but was quickly eclipsed by ext2fs. Extfs is no longer supported.

Ext3fs   The Third Extended Filesystem (ext3fs) is essentially ext2fs with a journal. Until around 2010, it was a very popular filesystem, but ext4fs has taken its place. It supports files of up to 2 TiB and filesystems of up to 16 TiB (ext2fs imposes the same limits). Its Linux type code is ext3.

Ext4fs   The Fourth Extended Filesystem (ext4fs) is a further development of the ext filesystem line. It adds speed improvements and the ability to handle larger files and disks—files may be up to 16 TiB in size, and filesystems may be up to 1 EiB (2^{60} bytes). Linux utilities refer to it as ext4.

> **Current partitioning tools limit ext4 filesystem sizes to 16 TiB; however, this limit will be raised sooner or later.**

ReiserFS   This filesystem, referred to as reiserfs by Linux tools, is similar to ext3fs in features, with an 8 TiB file-size limit and 16 TiB filesystem-size limit. Its best feature is its capacity to make efficient use of disk space with small files—those with sizes measured in the low kibibyte range. ReiserFS development has slowed, but it remains usable.

JFS   IBM developed its Journaled File System (JFS) for its AIX OS, and its code eventually worked its way into Linux. JFS supports maximum file and filesystem sizes of 4 PiB and 32 PiB, respectively (1 PiB is 1024 TiB). JFS is not as popular as many other Linux filesystems. Linux tools use jfs as its type code.

XFS   Silicon Graphics developed the Extents File System (XFS; Linux type code xfs) for its IRIX OS and later donated its code to Linux. XFS supports files of up to 8 EiB and filesystems of up to 16 EiB, making it the choice for *very* big disk arrays. XFS works well with large multimedia and backup files.

Btrfs   This new filesystem (pronounced "butter-eff-ess" or "better-eff-ess") is intended as the next-generation Linux filesystem. It supports files of up to 16 EiB and filesystems of the same size. It also provides a host of advanced features, such as the ability to combine multiple physical disks into a single filesystem. As of early 2012, Btrfs is still experimental, but it may provide the best overall feature mix once it's finished. Its Linux type code is btrfs.

> **It's possible to use several filesystems in a single Linux installation, to take advantage of the benefits of each filesystem for different sets of files.**

If you're planning a new Linux installation, you should consider ext4fs, ReiserFS, or XFS as your filesystems. Currently, ext4fs provides the best overall features and performance, while ReiserFS and XFS are worth considering for volumes that will hold particularly small and large files, respectively. Ext4fs is a good choice for volumes that hold large files, though, so you could use ext4fs for everything and not go far wrong, particularly on a general-purpose computer.

In addition to Linux's native filesystems, the OS supports several other filesystems, some of which are important in certain situations:

FAT　The File Allocation Table (FAT) filesystem was the standard with DOS and Windows through Windows Me. Just about all OSs support it. Its compatibility also makes it a good choice for exchanging data between two OSs that dual-boot on a single computer. Unlike most filesystems, FAT has two Linux type codes: msdos and vfat. Using msdos causes Linux to use the filesystem as DOS did, with short filenames with at most 8 characters plus a 3-character extension (*8.3 filenames*); when you use vfat, Linux supports long filenames on FAT.

FAT's simplicity and widespread support make it a popular filesystem on floppy disks, USB flash drives, cell phones, e-book readers, digital camera media, and so on.

NTFS　Microsoft developed the New Technology File System (NTFS) for Windows NT, and it is the default filesystem for recent versions of Windows. Linux provides a limited read/write NTFS driver, and a full read/write driver is available in the NTFS-3g software (http://www.tuxera.com). You're most likely to encounter it on a Windows boot partition in a dual-boot configuration or on larger removable or external hard disks. Under Linux, the standard kernel driver is known as ntfs, whereas the NTFS-3g driver is called ntfs-3g.

Linux's ntfs driver is based in the kernel, which makes it fast. The ntfs-3g driver, unlike most filesystem drivers, is *not* kernel-based, so it's not as fast.

HFS　Apple used its Hierarchical File System (HFS) in Mac OS through version 9.*x* and still supports it in Mac OS X. You might encounter HFS on some removable media, and particularly on older disks created under pre-X versions of Mac OS. Linux provides full read/write HFS support using its hfs driver.

HFS+　Apple's HFS+, also known as *Mac OS Extended*, is the current filesystem for Mac OS X; you're likely to encounter it on dual-boot Macs and on some removable media created for use with Macs. Linux provides read/write HFS+ support with its hfsplus driver; however, write support is disabled by default on versions of the filesystem that include a journal.

Mac users often use FAT on removable media for compatibility reasons.

ISO-9660　This filesystem is used on optical media, and particularly on CD-ROMs and CD-Rs. It comes in several levels with differing capabilities. Two extensions, *Joliet* and *Rock Ridge*, provide support for long filenames using Windows and Unix standards, respectively. Linux supports all these variants. You should use the iso9660 type code to mount an ISO-9660 disc.

UDF　The Universal Disk Format (UDF) is a filesystem that's intended to replace ISO-9660. It's most commonly found on DVD and Blu-ray media, although it's sometimes used on CD-Rs as well. Its Linux type code is, naturally, udf.

Most non-Linux filesystems lack support for the Unix-style ownership and permissions that Linux uses. Thus, you may need to use special mount options to set ownership and permissions as you want them. Exceptions to this rule include HFS+ and ISO-9660 when Rock Ridge extensions are in use. Rock Ridge discs are generally created with ownership and permissions that enable normal use of the disc, but if you're faced with an HFS+ disk, you may find that the user ID (UID) values don't match those of your Linux users. Thus, you may need to copy data as root, create an account with a matching UID value, or change the ownership of files on the HFS+ disk. (This last option is likely to be undesirable if you plan to use the disk again under Mac OS X.)

To access a filesystem, you must mount it with the `mount` command. For instance, to mount the filesystem on `/dev/sda5` at `/shared`, you would type the following command:

```
# mount /dev/sda5 /shared
```

Alternatively, you can create an entry for the filesystem in the `/etc/fstab` file, which stores information such as the device file, filesystem type, and mount point. When you're done using a filesystem, you can unmount it with the `umount` command, as in **umount /shared**.

The `umount` command's name has just one n.

Using Removable and Optical Disks

Certification Objective

If you insert a removable disk into a computer that's running most modern Linux distributions, the computer will probably detect that fact, mount the disk in a subdirectory of `/media`, and launch a file manager on the disk. This behavior makes the system work in a way that's familiar to users of Windows or Mac OS.

When you're done using the disk, you *must* unmount it before you can safely remove it. Most file managers enable you to do this by right-clicking the entry for the disk in the left-hand pane and selecting an option called Unmount, Eject Volume, or Safely Remove, as shown in Figure 5.3. If you fail to do this, the filesystem may suffer damage.

Some devices, such as optical disc drives, can lock their eject mechanisms to prevent forced removal of the media.

Most removable disks are either unpartitioned or have a single partition. They frequently use FAT, which is a good choice for cross-platform compatibility. If you need to, you can partition USB flash drives and most other removable media.

Optical discs are unusual in that they require their own special filesystems (ISO-9660 or UDF). Although you can mount and unmount these discs just like other disks, you can only read them, not write to them. If you want to create an optical disc on blank media, you must use special software, such as the text-mode `mkisofs`, `cdrecord`, or `growisofs`, or the GUI K3B or X-CD-Roast. These tools create an ISO-9660 filesystem from the files you specify and then burn it to the blank disc. Thereafter, you can mount the disc in the usual way.

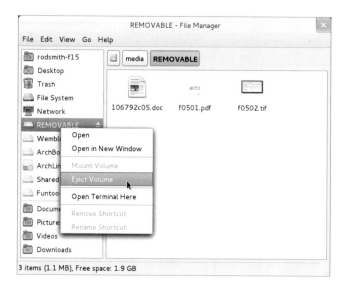

FIGURE 5.3 Linux file managers enable you to unmount removable media.

Managing Displays

Linux provides two display modes: text-mode and GUI. A text-mode display is fairly straightforward and requires little or no management. GUI displays, on the other hand, are more complex. In Linux, the X Window System (or X for short) manages the GUI display. In the next few pages, I describe what X is and how X interacts with common display hardware.

Certification Objective

Understanding the Role of X

Most people don't give much thought to the software behind their computers' displays; it all just works. Of course, behind the scenes the task of managing the display is fairly complex. Just some of the things that the software must do, on any platform, includes:

1. Initialize the video card, including set its resolution

2. Allocate sections of the display to hold windows that belong to particular applications

3. Manage windows that overlap so that only the "topmost" window's contents are displayed

4. Manage a pointer that the user controls via a mouse or similar device

5. Direct user input from a keyboard to whatever application is active

6. Display text and simple shapes within windows, at the request of user programs

7. Provide user interface elements to move and resize windows

8. Manage the interiors of windows, such as displaying menus and scroll bars

Desktop environments include window managers, but window managers without desktop environments are also available.

In Linux, tasks 1 through 6 are handled by X, but task 7 is handled by a program called a *window manager* and task 8 is handled by GUI libraries known as *widget sets*. The font display element of task 6 can be handled by X, but in recent years many programs have begun using a library called Xft for this task. Thus, the overall job of handling the display is broken up across several programs, although X handles most of the low-level tasks.

Modern Linux distributions use a version of X that can detect your hardware—including the video card, monitor, keyboard, and mouse—and configure itself automatically. The result is that the software normally works properly without any explicit configuration. Sometimes, though, this auto-configuration fails. When this happens, you must manually edit the X configuration file, /etc/X11/xorg.conf. If this file is missing, you can generate a sample file by typing the following command (with X *not* running) as root:

Chapter 11, "Editing Files," describes the pico, nano, and Vi text-mode text editors.

```
# Xorg -configure
```

The result is normally a file called /root/xorg.conf.new. You can copy this file to /etc/X11/xorg.conf and begin editing it to suit your needs. This task is complex and is beyond the scope of this book, but knowing the name of the file can help you get started—you can examine the file and locate additional documentation by searching on that name.

Using Common Display Hardware

Certification Objective

Much of the challenge in dealing with video devices is in managing drivers for the video chipsets involved. Most modern computers use one of a handful of video drivers:

▶ nv, nouveau, and nvidia work with NVIDIA video hardware.

▶ ati and fglrx work with AMD/ATI video hardware.

▶ intel works with Intel video hardware.

▶ The fbdev and vesa drivers are generic drivers that work with a wide variety of hardware, but they produce suboptimal performance.

▶ Many older video cards use more obscure drivers.

The nvidia and fglrx drivers are proprietary drivers provided by their manufacturers. Check the manufacturers' Web sites for details, or look for packages that install these drivers. These proprietary drivers provide features that aren't available in their open source counterparts, although the nouveau driver implements some of these features. In this context, video driver "features" translate into improved performance, particularly with respect to 3D graphics and real-time displays (as in playing back video files).

In the past, most video cards connected to monitors using a 15-pin Video Graphics Array (VGA) cable. Today, 29-pin Digital Visual Interface (DVI) cables are quite common. (Figure 5.4 shows both types.) DVI has the advantage of being a digital interface, which can produce a cleaner display on modern liquid crystal display (LCD) monitors.

High Definition Multimedia Interface (HDMI) is another cable type. HDMI and DVI are similar, but HDMI is more common on televisions, whereas DVI is more common on computers.

FIGURE 5.4 VGA connectors (left) were common in years past and are still available today; DVI connectors (right) are common on newer monitors and video cards.

Monitor resolutions are typically measured in terms of horizontal and vertical number of pixels. In the past, resolutions of as low as 640×480 have been common, but today it's rare to use a monitor that has an optimum resolution of lower than 1280×1024 or 1366×768, and resolutions of 1920×1080 or higher are commonplace. You should consult your monitor's manual to determine its optimum resolution. Typically, physically larger monitors have higher resolutions; however, this isn't always true.

Most monitors use an *aspect ratio* of either 4:3 or 16:9, referring to the ratio of the length to the height of the display.

In the best of all possible worlds, Linux will auto-detect your monitor's optimum resolution and set itself to that value whenever you boot the computer. Unfortunately, this sometimes doesn't work. Keyboard/video/mouse (KVM) switch boxes and extension cables can sometimes interfere with this auto-detection, and older monitors might not support the necessary computer/monitor communication. Thus, you may need to crack open your monitor's manual to learn what its optimum resolution is. Look for this information in the features or specifications section; it will probably be called *optimum resolution, maximum resolution,* or something similar. It may also include a refresh rate value, as in *1280×1024 @ 60 Hz* .

In most cases, you can set the resolution using a GUI tool such as the Displays item in GNOME System Settings panel, shown in Figure 5.5. In Figure 5.5, the Resolution button enables you to set the resolution to any desired value. If you can't find the optimum resolution in the list, you may need to perform more advanced adjustments involving the /etc/X11/xorg.conf file—a topic that's beyond the scope of this book. On rare occasion, you may need to upgrade your video card; some cards aren't able to handle the optimum resolutions used by some monitors.

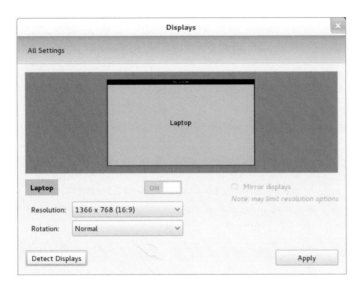

FIGURE 5.5 Most desktop environments provide GUI tools to help you set your display's resolution.

Handling USB Devices

Certification
Objective
Most modern computers use USB as the primary interface for external peripherals. Keyboards, mice, cameras, flash storage, hard disks, network adapters, scanners, printers, and more can all connect via USB. For the most part, USB devices

work in a plug-and-play manner—you plug them in and they work. Some specific caveats include the following:

Human interface devices   X usually takes over keyboards, mice, tablets, and similar devices when you plug them in. If you have problems, you may need to adjust your X configuration by editing /etc/X11/xorg.conf, but this is an advanced topic that's beyond the scope of this book.

Disk storage   I include USB flash drives, external hard disks, and other storage devices in this category. As described earlier, in "Using Removable and Optical Disks," it's critical that you unmount the disk before you unplug its USB cable. Failure to do so can result in data corruption.

Cell phones, cameras, e-book readers, and music players   You can often use these devices like disk devices to transfer photos, music, or other files. You may need to activate an option on the device to make it look like a disk device to the computer, though. When you're done, unmount the device and deactivate its interface mode.

Scanners   Linux uses the Scanner Access Now Easy (SANE; http://www.sane -project.org) software to handle most scanners. A few require obscure or proprietary software, though.

Printers   Most distributions automatically configure suitable printer queues when you plug in a USB printer. If you need to tweak the configuration, try entering **http://localhost:631** in a Web browser on the computer in question. Doing so opens a Web-based printer configuration utility. Some distributions provide distribution-specific printer configuration tools, as well.

Managing Drivers

Most hardware devices require the presence of special software components to be useful. A piece of software that "talks" to hardware is known as a *driver*, so you should know how drivers work in Linux. Several broad classes of drivers exist, so I begin by describing those. Whatever the driver type, you should know how to locate and install drivers for your hardware.

Certification
Objective

Understanding Types of Drivers

Linux requires drivers because different hardware—even two devices that serve very similar purposes, such as two network adapters—can function in very different

▶

In fact, several layers exist between the network hardware and a program like Firefox; the driver is just one of these layers.

ways. That is, the methods required to initialize and use two network adapters may be entirely different. To provide generalized interfaces so that programs like the Firefox Web browser can use any network adapter, the Linux kernel uses drivers as a bridge between the hardware-agnostic kernel interfaces and the hardware itself.

Broadly speaking, drivers can exist in one of two locations:

▶ The kernel

▶ A library or application

Most drivers are kernel based, and in fact a large chunk of the Linux kernel consists of drivers. Kernel drivers handle most of the devices that are internal to the computer's box, such as the hard disks, network interfaces, and USB interfaces. The kernel hosts most drivers because drivers typically require privileged access to hardware, and that's the purpose of the kernel.

Some drivers reside in a library or application. Many of these devices are external to the computer itself. Examples include:

▶ SANE, which handles scanners

▶ Ghostscript, which converts printed output into a form that particular printers can understand

▶ X, which manages the display

X is unusual in that it's a non-kernel element that communicates more or less directly with the video hardware. SANE and Ghostscript, by contrast, both communicate with external hardware devices via interfaces (such as a USB port) that are handled by the kernel. That is, you need at least two drivers to handle such devices. To print to a USB printer, for instance, you use the kernel's USB driver and a Ghostscript printer driver. Ideally, most users will be unaware of this complexity, but you may need to understand it if problems arise.

Locating and Installing Drivers

Most drivers come with the Linux kernel itself, or with the library or application that handles the type of hardware. For instance, most X installations include a set of video drivers so that you can use most video cards. For this reason, it's seldom necessary to track down and install additional drivers for common hardware. There are exceptions; for instance:

New hardware   If your hardware is very new (meaning the model is new, not just that you purchased it recently), it might need drivers that haven't yet made their way into whatever distribution you're using.

Unusual hardware   If you're using very exotic hardware, such as a specialized scientific data-acquisition board, you may need to track down drivers for it.

Proprietary drivers   Some manufacturers provide proprietary drivers for their hardware. For instance, the nvidia and fglrx video drivers (referred to earlier, in "Using Common Display Hardware") can improve the performance of video displays based on NVIDIA or ATI/AMD chipsets, respectively. Some hardware requires proprietary drivers. This is particularly common for some exotic hardware.

Bug fixes   Drivers, like other software, can be buggy. If you run into such a problem, you might want to track down a more recent driver to obtain a bug fix.

One way to obtain a new kernel-based driver is to upgrade the kernel. Note that a kernel upgrade can provide both bug fixes to existing drivers and entirely new drivers. Similarly, upgrading software such as SANE, Ghostscript, or X can upgrade or add new drivers for the devices that such packages handle.

If you're using exotic hardware or need some other hard-to-find driver, your task can be more difficult. You can check with the manufacturer or perform a Web search to try to find drivers.

If you obtain a driver that's not part of the kernel (or software package to handle the device), you should read the instructions that come with the driver. Installation procedures vary quite a bit from one driver to another, so it's impossible to provide a simple step-by-step installation procedure that works in all cases. Some drivers come with installation utilities, but others require you to follow a procedure that involves typing assorted commands. If you're very unlucky, the driver will come in the form of a *kernel patch*. This is a way to add or change files in the main kernel source code package. You must then recompile the kernel—a task that's well beyond the scope of this book.

THE ESSENTIALS AND BEYOND

Software and hardware interact in numerous ways to determine a computer's capabilities. Your CPU is one determinant of your computer's speed, and it also determines what version of Linux you can run. CPUs are mounted on motherboards, which contain other critical circuitry for managing hard disks, displays, and other devices. Your hard disk must be partitioned and prepared with one or more filesystems before it's useful. Video hardware—both the monitor and the video circuitry inside the computer—determine how your desktop environment looks and how fast the computer can move windows and display videos. USB manages most external devices, such as keyboards, mice, and external disks. Software known as drivers manages all these hardware devices.

(Continues)

THE ESSENTIALS AND BEYOND *(Continued)*

SUGGESTED EXERCISES

▶ At a Linux shell prompt, type **uname -a**, **lscpu** , and cat **/proc/cpuinfo**. Compare the output and try to determine your CPU's capabilities. In particular, can it run 64-bit applications, and is your current distribution a 32-bit or 64-bit distribution?

▶ After you've logged into your preferred desktop environment, insert an optical disc, a USB flash drive, or some other removable disk. Does a file browser open up? If not, open one manually and try to find your removable disk. Once you've accessed the disk, unmount it so that you can safely remove it.

REVIEW QUESTIONS

1. Which of the following commands provides the most information about your motherboard's features?

   A. lscpu

   B. Xorg -configure

   C. fdisk -l /dev/sda

   D. lspci

   E. http://localhost:631

2. Why might you want to partition a hard disk? (Select all that apply.)

   A. To install more than one OS on the disk

   B. To use ext4fs rather than ReiserFS

   C. To turn a PATA disk into an SATA disk

   D. To separate filesystem data from swap space

   E. To separate the disk's cache from its main data

3. Which of the following devices is *not* commonly attached via USB?

   A. Video monitors

   B. Keyboards

   C. External hard disks

   D. Printers

   E. Scanners

4. True or false: An EM64T CPU is capable of running a Linux distribution identified as being for the AMD64 CPU.

5. True or false: UDF is a good filesystem to use for a Linux installation on a hard disk.

6. True or false: The Linux kernel includes drivers for various disk controllers, network adapters, and USB interfaces, among other things.

(Continues)

THE ESSENTIALS AND BEYOND (Continued)

7. The *x*86 CPU uses a ____-bit architecture.

8. A computer power supply converts electricity from alternating current to _____. (Two words)

9. The _____ standard is a modern video interface that's commonly used on computer monitors.

## CHAPTER 6

Getting to Know the Command Line

You may think of the command line as an archaic relic from the 1970s, with about as much relevance to computing today as a disco ball. Not so! Although Linux has numerous GUI programs, they're mostly just flashy frontends to underlying text-mode tools. By learning those tools, you'll be able to unlock Linux's true power, enabling you to get your work done more quickly. You'll also be able to manage should the Linux GUI system fail entirely, or should you need to log in and administer the system remotely. Command-line tools can also be scripted, meaning that you can write a simple program that performs a task more quickly or easily than could be done using the standard programs alone. For these reasons, most chapters of this book describe both GUI and command-line ways of getting things done.

To start with command-line operations, you must know how to start one. With that task in hand, you must know how to run programs and manipulate files. You should also be familiar with several labor-saving features of Linux command lines.

▶ **Starting a command line**

▶ **Running programs**

▶ **Manipulating files**

▶ **Using shell features**

Starting a Command Line

A Linux command line, or *shell* as it's more properly called, is a program like any other and must be launched in some way. Three methods are commonly used for this: starting a shell in a GUI window called a *terminal*, logging into the computer in a text-mode console, and logging into the computer remotely using a text-mode login protocol.

▶

Other shells include
tcsh, ksh, and
zsh. **Shell choice is
a matter of personal
preference. If you're
just starting out, it's
best to stick with
Bash simply because
it's popular.**

▶

The word *terminal*
**can also apply to
a tool that handles
text-mode connec-
tions between com-
puters, particularly
over RS-232 serial
lines and modems.
This type of terminal
program is uncom-
mon today.**

**When you use
the administrative
account,** root, **the
prompt normally
ends in a hash mark
(#). Chapter 13,
"Understanding
Users and Groups,"
describes the**
root **account in
more detail.**

▶

The default shell in most Linux distributions is the Bourne-Again Shell (Bash or bash), which is based on an older shell called the Bourne Shell. Other shells are available. Most of these are similar to Bash in broad strokes, although some details differ. Each account specifies its own default shell, so individual users can change their shells if they like. (This is done with account management tools such as usermod, which is described in Chapter 14, "Creating Users and Groups.")

Launching a Terminal

Most Linux distributions provide several terminal programs, although the details depend on your installation options—most desktop environments provide their own terminals, so your choices depend on the desktop environments you installed. (You can run one desktop environment's terminal program within another, if you like.) Most terminal programs include the word *terminal* in their names, although some don't, such as the K Desktop Environment's (KDE's) Konsole and the generic xterm.

The details of how to launch a terminal program differ from one desktop environment to another. You can normally find an entry in your desktop environment's menus, as outlined in Chapter 4, "Using Common Linux Programs." For example, if you're using the popular GNU Network Object Model Environment (GNOME), version 3, you can find the available terminals by following this procedure:

1. Click Activities in the top-left corner of the screen.

2. Click the Applications heading.

3. Select the System Tools filter near the right of the screen, which results in a display similar to the one in Figure 6.1. You should see at least one terminal program, and perhaps more than one. Figure 6.1 shows Konsole, LXTerminal, and two programs called Terminal (GNOME's Terminal and Xfce's Terminal).

4. Select the terminal you want to use and it will launch. Figure 6.2 shows GNOME's Terminal, but you can use another terminal program if you like.

The terminal program shows a prompt—[rodsmith@wembleth ~]$ in Figure 6.2. This example shows the default Fedora prompt, which includes your username, your computer's hostname, your current directory (a tilde, ~, refers to your home directory), and a dollar sign ($). Some of these features are likely to change as you use the shell, as described in subsequent sections of this chapter.

If you're using another distribution, the prompt is likely to differ in details, although most default prompts end in a dollar sign ($) or a greater-than symbol (>) for ordinary user shells.

FIGURE 6.1 A standard Linux installation should provide at least one terminal program.

FIGURE 6.2 GNOME's Terminal program is typical and is dominated by a textual display area.

Most terminal programs provide common features of X programs—you can resize them, close them, select options from menus, and so on. Details depend on the program you're using, though. You may want to peruse the options available on your program's menus so you can set the font to one you like, change the color scheme, and so on.

Most terminal programs support *tabs*, which are similar to the tabs in a Web browser. In most cases, you can open a tab by selecting File ➢ Open Tab in the terminal's menu. Having multiple tabs open is handy because it enables you to run multiple programs simultaneously, work easily in multiple directories, or run programs both as yourself and as `root`. Alternatively, you can run multiple terminal programs to achieve the same ends.

When you're done with a terminal, you can close it like other programs, by selecting File ➢ Close Window from its menu. Alternatively, you can type **exit** at its shell prompt.

Logging Into a Text-Mode Console

At first glance, Linux looks like Windows or Mac OS in that it's a GUI OS. Scratch the surface, though, and you'll find a purely text-mode interface waiting. Linux supports *virtual terminals (VTs)*, which are virtual screens that can hold different types of information—textual or graphical. Most Linux distributions run with six or seven VTs. In CentOS, Fedora, and Red Hat, the first VT typically runs the X Window System, which is Linux's GUI. In most other distributions, X runs in VT 7 or VT 8, leaving VT 1 as a text-mode display. You can switch between VTs by pressing Ctrl+Alt+Fn, where Fn is a function key. (When switching between text-mode VTs, Alt+Fn is sufficient.) Thus, to enable a text-mode console, follow these steps:

1. Press Ctrl+Alt+F2. You'll see a text-mode prompt that reads something like this:

   ```
   Fedora release 16 (Verne)
   Kernel 3.1.0-7.fc16.x86_64 on an x86_64 (tty2)
   wembleth.rodsbooks.com login:
   ```

2. Type your username at this prompt and it will respond with a new prompt:

   ```
   Password:
   ```

3. Type your password here and you'll see a Bash prompt like the one shown in the window in Figure 6.2.

You can switch back and forth between your text-mode login and your X session by using Ctrl+Alt+F*n* keystrokes. You can also initiate multiple text-mode logins and switch between them in the same way. This feature can be handy if you're trying to debug a problem that's related to X.

When you're done with your text-mode session, type **exit** or **logout** to terminate it.

Logging In Remotely

Remote logins must be enabled by running a server program such as the Secure Shell (SSH), and you may find that you can't initiate such a connection by default. Once you've configured SSH to accept remote logins, though, you can use an SSH client program, such as `ssh`, to do the job:

```
$ ssh wembleth
rodsmith@wembleth's password:
```

Once you type your password, you'll be logged in. This example assumes you're using a Linux shell on the client computer. Note that Linux's `ssh` client passes your current username to the server. You can log in using another username by preceding its hostname with your username on the remote system and an at-sign (@), as in **ssh rsmith@wembleth** to log into `wembleth` as `rsmith`. SSH clients for other OSs, including Windows, are available, but their operational details differ.

Other text-mode remote-login programs, such as `telnet` and `rlogin`, exist; however, most of these are older protocols that don't employ encryption and so should be avoided. GUI remote login tools, such as Virtual Network Computing (VNC), are also available. Most of these tools also lack encryption features, although they can be *tunneled* through SSH to add encryption—a topic that's beyond the scope of this book.

Once you've logged in remotely, you can use the computer much as if it were local. Be sure to log out when you're finished by typing **exit** or **logout**.

Running Programs

Once you've opened a terminal or logged in using a text-mode tool, you should know how to use the shell. Bash includes a few built-in commands, but much of what you'll do in a shell involves running other programs. As described in the following sections, you can run text-mode and GUI programs. Sometimes you may want to run a program in the background and yet retain use of the shell for yourself. Another trick in running programs is redirecting input and output, which can be useful in many situations.

Logging out is important, especially on a public computer. It's easy to forget that you used a text-mode shell, so get into the habit of checking this detail.

Certification Objective

Configuring an SSH server is beyond the scope of this book, but you can use an SSH client, as shown here, with any server that's already configured.

Running Text-Mode Programs

Linux stores programs in several locations, including /bin, /usr/bin, and /usr/local/bin. (Programs that are used mainly by root appear in /sbin, /usr/sbin, and /usr/local/sbin as well.) If an executable program appears in one of these directories (which make up the *path*), you can run it simply by typing its name:

```
$ free
              total       used       free     shared    buffers     cached
Mem:        3798016    3759004      39012          0      24800    1117444
-/+ buffers/cache:    2616760    1181256
Swap:       6291452          0    6291452
```

This example command displays information on the computer's use of memory. You needn't be concerned with the details of this command's output, though; just note that the free program displayed information in the same terminal in which it was launched.

You can learn what directories make up the path by typing the following command:

```
$ echo $PATH
```

The result will be a colon-delimited set of directory names, which the shell searches in sequence whenever you type a command that it doesn't handle directly.

Many commands accept *arguments*, which are subcommands or codes that follow the program name. For instance, the cat command, whose name is short for *concatenate*, can quickly display a short text file on the screen:

```
$ cat afile.txt
This is the contents of afile.txt.
```

In this example, cat takes a filename as an argument: afile.txt. Many programs enable you to perform a wide variety of tasks depending on the precise arguments they're given. You can learn about such arguments, and other usage details, by using the Linux manual system. The program to do this is called man, and you pass it the name of the command you want to learn about as an argument, as in **man cat** to learn about cat.

The man command illustrates a feature of some text-mode programs: They can take over the entire terminal from which they're launched. In the case of man, you can scroll up or down in the documentation by using arrow keys, Page Up, Page Down, and so on. Text editors, such as vi, emacs, and nano, use similar features.

▶

I denote commands you should type yourself in bold monospace font, and programs' output in standard monospace font.

▶

Chapter 8, "Getting Help," describes the man page system, and other documentation, in more detail.

Running GUI Programs

You can run GUI programs from a terminal as well as text-based programs; however, this doesn't work if you logged in using a text-mode VT, and it might not work with a remote login even if you're running X locally. You must also know the filename of the program to run it. The filename is usually related to the name you use to launch the program from a desktop's menus, but it's not always identical. For instance, GNOME Terminal's filename is `gnome-terminal`, so that's what you'd need to type to launch another GNOME Terminal in this way.

Some GUI programs produce text-mode output that can be useful in tracking down the source of problems, so launching a program from a terminal window can be a good first step when debugging problems. You might also want to launch programs in this way because it can be quicker than tracking down programs in a desktop environment's menus, or because a program doesn't appear in the environment's menus.

Running Programs in the Background

When you launch a GUI program from a terminal window, the GUI program opens its own window or windows. The terminal window remains open, but will normally become unresponsive. If you want to type more commands in this window, you can do so by selecting it and pressing Ctrl+Z. This *suspends* the program—that is, it's sent to sleep. In its sleeping state, the GUI program won't respond to input or do any work. If you want to use both the GUI program and the terminal from which you launched it, you can type **bg** (short for *background*) in the terminal. Both programs will now be active. Typing **fg** returns the sleeping program to the foreground, enabling it to run but making your shell unresponsive. Note that, in this context, the terms *background* and *foreground* refer to the program's relationship to the shell, not to the position of the program's windows in a "stack" of windows on the screen.

If you know before you launch it that you want to run a program in the background, you can do so by appending an ampersand (&) to the end of the command line, as in:

```
$ gedit afile.txt &
```

This command launches the `gedit` GUI editor on `afile.txt` in the background, enabling you to edit your file and continue to use the shell. This feature is most useful for running GUI programs, but it's sometimes used with text-mode programs, too. A complex number-crunching program, for instance, might be designed to run for several minutes or hours and produce no output. You might therefore want to

> Pressing Ctrl+Z also suspends most text-mode programs, enabling you to use the shell before returning to the program by typing fg.

run it in the background and retain control of your shell. Be aware, however, that if you launch a program in the background and it produces output, that output will continue to appear in your shell, possibly intruding on whatever else you're trying to do with the shell!

Manipulating Files

Much of the work you'll do with a command line involves manipulating files. Thus, knowing the rules for handling files is extremely important. In the next few pages, I describe how to learn what files are on your hard disk, how to change between directories, how to refer to files that aren't in the current directory, and the most common commands for manipulating files.

Obtaining File Listings

Certification Objective

To manipulate files, it's helpful to know what they are. The `ls` command, whose name is short for *list*, provides you with this information. The `ls` command displays the names of files in a directory. If you pass it no options, it shows the files in the current directory; however, you can pass it both options and file or directory specifications. This command supports a huge number of options; consult its man page for details. Table 6.1 summarizes the most important `ls` options.

Certification Objective

TABLE 6.1 Common `ls` options

Option (long form)	Option (short form)	Description
`--all`	`-a`	Normally, `ls` omits files whose names begin with a dot (`.`). These *dot files* (also known as *hidden files*) are often configuration files that aren't usually of interest. Adding this parameter displays dot files.
`--color`	N/A	This option produces a color-coded listing that differentiates directories and other special file types by displaying them in different colors. Some Linux distributions configure their shells to use this option by default.
`--directory`	`-d`	Normally, if you type a directory name as an option, `ls` displays the contents of that directory. The same thing happens if a directory name matches a wildcard. Adding this parameter changes this behavior to list only the directory name, which is sometimes preferable.

(Continues)

TABLE 6.1 *(Continued)*

Option (long form)	Option (short form)	Description
N/A	-l	The ls command normally displays filenames only. The -l parameter (a lowercase *L*) produces a long listing that includes information such as the file's permission string, owner, group, size, and creation date.
--file-type	-p	This option appends an indicator code to the end of each name so you know what type of file it is.
--recursive	-R	The -R or --recursive option causes ls to display directory contents recursively. That is, if the target directory contains a subdirectory, ls displays both the files in the target directory *and* the files in its subdirectory. The result can be a huge listing if a directory has many subdirectories.

You may optionally give ls one or more file or directory names, in which case ls displays information about those files or directories, as in this example:

```
$ ls -p /usr /bin/ls
/bin/ls

/usr:
X11R6/   games/                 include/   man/   src/
bin/     i386-glibc20-linux/    lib/       merge@ tmp@
doc/     i486-linux-libc5/      libexec/   sbin/
etc/     i586-mandrake-linux/   local/     share/
```

This output shows both the /bin/ls program file and the contents of the /usr directory. The latter consists mainly of subdirectories, indicated by a trailing slash (/) when -p is used. By default, ls creates a listing that's sorted by filename, as shown in this example. Note, though, that uppercase letters (as in X11R6) always appear before lowercase letters (as in bin).

One of the most common ls options is -l, which creates a listing like this:

```
$ ls -l t*
-rwxr-xr-x  1 rodsmith users      111 Apr 13 13:48  test
-rw-r--r--  1 rodsmith users   176322 Dec 16 09:34  thttpd-2.20b-1.i686.rpm
-rw-r--r--  1 rodsmith users  1838045 Apr 24 18:52  tomsrtbt-1.7.269.tar.gz
-rw-r--r--  1 rodsmith users  3265021 Apr 22 23:46  tripwire.rpm
```

This output includes permission strings (such as -rwxr-xr-x), ownership (an owner of rodsmith and a group of users for all of these files), file sizes, and file

◄

A trailing at-sign (@) denotes a *symbolic link*, which is a file that points to another file.

▶

Chapter 15, "Setting Ownership and Permissions," covers these topics in detail.

creation dates in addition to the filenames. This example also illustrates the use of the * wildcard, which matches any string—thus, t* matches any filename that begins with t.

Changing Directories

Certification Objective

The cd command changes the current directory in which you're working. Although your current directory doesn't matter for many commands, it does matter when you begin to refer to files. As described in the next section, "Using Absolute and Relative File References," some types of file references depend on your current directory.

When you change your current directory, your shell's prompt may change (depending on your distribution's settings), something like this:

```
[rodsmith@wembleth ~]$ cd /usr/bin
[rodsmith@wembleth bin]$
```

▶

In this book, I shorten most shell prompts to a single character, such as $, when I display commands on their own lines.

Many distributions' default configurations display only the final part of the current directory—bin rather than /usr/bin in the preceding example. If you need to know the complete path to your current location, you can use pwd:

```
$ pwd
/usr/bin
```

Linux uses a slash (/) character as a directory separator. If you're familiar with Windows, you may know that Windows uses a backslash (\) for this purpose. Don't confuse the two! In Linux, a backslash serves as a "quote" or "escape" character to enter otherwise hard-to-specify characters, such as spaces, as part of a filename. Also, realize that a slash isn't a legal character in a Linux filename for this reason.

Using Absolute and Relative File References

▶

Don't confuse the root (/) directory with the /root directory, which is the root user's home directory.

As described in Chapter 5, "Managing Hardware," Linux uses a unified directory tree, which means that all files can be located relative to a single *root* directory, which is often referred to using the slash (/) character. If your disk contains multiple partitions, one of these devices becomes the *root filesystem*, and others are *mounted* at some location within the overall directory tree. The same thing happens when you mount a USB flash drive, DVD, or other removable disk device. The result might resemble Figure 6.3, which shows a subset of the directories found on a typical Linux installation, along with a couple of removable media. Most commonly, removable media appear as subdirectories of the /media directory. Most subdirectories can be split off as separate partitions or even placed on separate disks. In Figure 6.3, the /home directory is on its own partition, but it's accessed in exactly the same way as it would be if it were part of the root (/) partition.

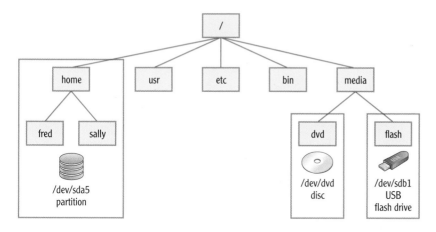

FIGURE 6.3 In Linux, all files are referred to relative to a single root (/) directory.

Files and directories can be referred to in three ways:

Absolute references   These file references are relative to the root (/) directory, as in /home/fred/afile.txt to refer to the afile.txt file in Fred's home directory. Such references always begin with a slash (/) character.

Home directory references   The tilde (~) character refers to the user's home directory. If a filename begins with that character, it's as if the path to the user's home directory were substituted. Thus, for Fred, ~/afile.txt is equivalent to /home/fred/afile.txt.

Relative references   These file references are relative to the current directory. Thus, if Fred is working in his home directory, afile.txt refers to /home/fred/afile.txt. Relative references can include subdirectories, as in somedir/anotherfile.txt. In Linux, every directory includes a special hidden subdirectory, .., which refers to its parent directory. Thus, if Sally is working in /home/sally, she can refer to Fred's afile.txt file as ../fred/afile.txt.

> File permissions can block your access to another user's files, but that's a matter that's described in Chapter 15.

To better understand these concepts, you should try these operations:

1. Launch a new shell, or use an existing one.

2. Type **cd** ~ to change into your home directory.

3. Type **cat /etc/fstab** to view this configuration file using an absolute file reference. Its contents should appear in your terminal.

4. Type **pwd** to view your current directory. It will probably be /home
   /*yourusername*, where *yourusername* is—you guessed it!—your
   username.

5. Type **cat ../../etc/fstab** to view this configuration file using a
   relative file reference. The first .. in this command refers to /home,
   and the second refers to the root (/) directory. (If your home directory is in an unusual location, you may need to adjust the number
   of ../ elements in this command, which is why I had you use pwd to
   find your current directory in the previous step.)

6. Type **cat ~/../../etc/fstab** to view this configuration file using a
   home directory reference.

Of course, steps 5 and 6 use rather awkward file references; in real life, you'd
probably use an absolute file reference to access /etc/fstab from your home
directory. If you were in a subdirectory of /etc, though, typing ../fstab would
be slightly easier than typing /etc/fstab; and typing ~/afile.txt would be
easier than typing the complete path to your home directory.

Using Common File Manipulation Commands

Chapter 7, "Managing Files," describes the most common commands used to
manipulate files in detail, and Chapter 15 describes commands related to file
ownership and permissions. Some of these commands are used in the remain-
der of this chapter, so Table 6.2 summarizes them.

Remember man!
You can use it to
learn about most
Linux commands
and utilities, includ-
ing the common
file manipulation
commands.

TABLE 6.2 Common file manipulation commands

Command	Effect
cat	Displays files on standard output. Two or more files can be specified and output redirected to merge them together.
chgrp	Changes group ownership of a file. Described in more detail in Chapter 15.
chmod	Changes permissions of a file. Described in more detail in Chapter 15.
chown	Changes ownership of a file. Described in more detail in Chapter 15.
cp	Copies a file. Described in more detail in Chapter 7.

(Continues)

TABLE 6.2 *(Continued)*

Command	Effect
echo	Echoes the text you enter on the screen. Although this isn't technically a file command, it can be used with redirection to create or add text to a file.
head	Displays the first few lines of a text file.
less	Displays a file a page at a time.
ln	Creates links to files. Described in more detail in Chapter 7.
ls	Displays files in a directory, as described earlier.
mkdir	Creates a new directory. Described in more detail in Chapter 7.
mv	Moves or renames a file. Described in more detail in Chapter 7.
pwd	Prints the name of the current working directory.
rm	Removes a file. Described in more detail in Chapter 7.
rmdir	Removes a directory. Described in more detail in Chapter 7.
tail	Displays the last few lines of a text file.
wc	Counts characters, words, and lines in a text file. Described in more detail in Chapter 10.

Using Shell Features

Bash includes several features that make using it much easier. I've already described some of these. Many others are beyond the scope of this book. Two, however, deserve attention even in a brief introduction to shells: command completion and command history.

Using Command Completion

Command completion is the hero of everybody who hates typing: It's a way to enter a long command or filename with a minimal number of keystrokes. To

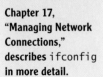

Some of the details of how command completion works vary from one distribution to another.

use command completion, you type part of a command or filename and then press the Tab key. If only one command on the path completes the command, Bash fills in the rest—and likewise when using command completion to refer to files. To illustrate the use of command completion, you can try it out with a few commands:

1. Launch a shell.

2. Type **if** followed by pressing the Tab key. The computer will probably beep or sound a tone. This indicates that your incomplete command could be completed by multiple commands, so you must type more characters. (In some configurations, the computer skips straight to the next step, as if you'd pressed Tab twice.)

3. Press the Tab key again. The shell displays a list of possible completions, such as `if`, `ifconfig`, and `ifdown`.

4. Type **co**, making your command so far **ifco**, and press the Tab key again. The computer will probably complete the command: **ifconfig**. (If it doesn't, another program that completes the command may exist on your computer, so you may need to type another character or two.)

5. Press the Enter key. The computer runs `ifconfig`, which displays information on your network connections.

Chapter 17, "Managing Network Connections," describes `ifconfig` in more detail.

Sometimes, command completion will be able to partially complete a command. For instance, typing **gru** and then pressing Tab is likely to add a single unique character, b; however, several commands begin with `grub`, so you must then add more characters yourself. (These commands deal with the Grand Unified Bootloader, GRUB, which helps Linux to boot.)

Command completion also works with files. For instance, you can type **cat /etc/ser** followed by the Tab key to have Bash complete the filename, and therefore the command, as **cat /etc/services**. (This command shows you the contents of a Linux configuration file.)

Using Command History

Bash remembers the recent commands you've typed, and you can use this fact to save yourself some effort if you need to type a command that's similar to one you've typed recently. In its most basic form, you can use the up arrow key to enter the previous command; pressing the up arrow repeatedly moves backward through earlier and earlier commands. Table 6.3 summarizes some other commonly used keystrokes you can use in the command history—or even when editing new commands.

TABLE 6.3 Bash editing and command history features

Keystroke	Effect
Up arrow	Retrieves the previous entry from the command history.
Left arrow	Moves the cursor left one character.
Right arrow	Moves the cursor right one character.
Ctrl+A	Moves the cursor to the start of the line.
Ctrl+E	Moves the cursor to the end of the line.
Delete key	Deletes the character under the cursor.
Backspace key	Deletes the character to the left of the cursor.
Ctrl+T	Swaps the character under the cursor with the one to the left of the cursor.
Ctrl+X then Ctrl+E	Launches a full-fledged editor on the current command line.
Ctrl+R	Searches for a command. Type a few characters and the shell will locate the latest command to include those characters. You can search for the next-most-recent command to include those characters by pressing Ctrl+R again.

◄

Many of the Bash command editing features are similar to those used by the emacs **text editor.**

As an example of command history in use, try this:

1. Type **cd /tmp** to change to the /tmp directory, in which many programs store temporary files.

2. Type **ls** to see a list of the files in your current directory (/tmp).

3. Press the up arrow key. Your ls command should re-appear.

4. Press the spacebar and type in ~ to make the new command **ls ~**, and then press Enter. You should now see the contents of your home directory.

5. Type **cat /etc/fstab** to see the contents of /etc/fstab, which is a file that defines how disk space is used.

6. Press Ctrl+R. The Bash prompt will change to read (reverse-i-search)`':.

7. Type **1** (without pressing Enter). Your earlier **ls ~** command will appear.

8. Press Ctrl+R again. The command should change to a simple **ls**—the one you entered in step 2.

9. Press Enter. The **ls** command should execute again.

> The Ctrl+R search feature searches on anything you enter on a command line—a command name, a filename, or other command parameters.

Another history feature is the history command. Type **history** to view all the commands in your history, or add a number (as in **history 10**) to view the most recent specified number of commands.

I encourage you to experiment with these features. Tab completion and command history are both powerful tools that can help you avoid a great deal of repetitive typing. Command history can also be a useful memory aid—if you've forgotten the exact name of a file or command you used recently, you might be able to retrieve it by searching on part of the name you *do* remember.

THE ESSENTIALS AND BEYOND

Command lines are powerful tools in Linux; they're the basis on which many of the friendlier GUI tools are built, they can be accessed without the help of a GUI, and they can be scripted. To use the text-mode tools described in other chapters of this book, you should be familiar with the basics of a Linux shell. These include knowing how to start a shell, how to run programs in a shell, how to manipulate files, and how to use a shell's time-saving features.

SUGGESTED EXERCISES

▶ Read the man pages for the following commands: man, less, cat, cd, ls, grep, and su.

▶ Launch a GUI program, such as gedit, with and without a trailing ampersand (&). When you launch it without an ampersand, use Ctrl+Z to put it into the background and see how the program reacts to mouse clicks. Use fg to return it to the foreground, then repeat the process but use bg to run the program in the background. See what happens in your terminal when you exit from the GUI program.

(Continues)

▶ In a shell, type a single letter, such as **m**, and press the Tab key. What happens? What happens if you type a less common letter, such as **z**, and then press Tab?

▶ Experiment with the command history. Use it to search on strings that are part of both command names and filenames you've used. Use the arrow keys and editing features described in Table 6.3 to edit commands you've used previously.

REVIEW QUESTIONS

1.   What keystroke moves the cursor to the start of the line when typing a command in Bash?

   A. Ctrl+A   **D.** Up arrow

   B. Left arrow   **E.** Ctrl+E

   C. Ctrl+T

2.   How can you run a program in the background when launching it from a shell? (Select all that apply.)

   A. Launch the program by typing **start** *command*, where *command* is the command you want to run.

   B. Launch the program by typing **bg** *command*, where *command* is the command you want to run.

   C. Append an ampersand (&) to the end of the command line.

   D. Launch the program normally, type Ctrl+Z in the shell, and then type **bg** in the shell.

   E. Launch the program normally, type Ctrl+Z in the shell, and then type **fg** in the shell.

3.   Which of the following commands, typed at a Bash prompt, returns you to your home directory?

   A. `home`   **D.** `homedir`

   B. `cd /home`   **E.** `cd ~`

   C. `cd homedir`

4.   True or false: The Alt+F2 keystroke, typed in X, brings up a text-mode display you can use to log into Linux.

5.   True or false: The filename `..\upone.txt` refers to the file `upone.txt` in the parent of the current directory.

(Continues)

THE ESSENTIALS AND BEYOND *(Continued)*

6.   True or false: The -r option to ls creates a recursive directory listing.

7.   The _____ command displays the path to the current working directory.

8.   To view all files, including hidden files and directories, in the current directory, you would type **ls** _____.

9.   The _____ command displays text files or can concatenate multiple files together.

## CHAPTER 7

Managing Files

Much of what you do with a computer involves manipulating files. Most obviously, files hold the correspondence, spreadsheets, digital photos, and other documents you create. Files also hold the configuration settings for Linux—information on how to treat the network interfaces, how to access hard disks, and what to do as the computer starts up. Indeed, even access to most hardware devices and kernel settings is ultimately done through files. Thus, knowing how to manage these files is critically important for administering a Linux computer. This chapter begins with a description of the basic text-mode commands for manipulating files. Directories are files, too, so this chapter covers directories, including the commands you can use to create and manipulate them.

▶ **Manipulating files**

▶ **Manipulating directories**

Manipulating Files

If you've used Windows or Mac OS X, chances are you've used a GUI file manager to manipulate files. Such tools are available in Linux, as noted in Chapter 4, "Using Common Linux Programs," and you can certainly use a file manager for many common tasks. Linux's text-mode shells, such as Bash, provide simple but powerful tools for manipulating files, too. These tools can simplify some tasks, such as working with all the files with names that include the string invoice. Thus, you should be familiar with these text-mode commands.

To begin this task, I describe some ways you can create files. With files created, you can copy them from one location to another. You may sometimes want to move or rename files, so I explain how to do so. Linux enables you to create *links*, which are ways to refer to the same file by multiple names. If you never want to use a file again, you can delete it. *Wildcards* provide the means to refer to many files using a compact notation, so I describe them. Finally, I cover the case-sensitive nature of Linux's file manipulation commands.

Creating Files

Chapter 11, "Editing Files," describes how to create text files with the text-mode pico, and nano, and Vi editors.

Certification
Objective

Normally, you create files using the programs that manipulate them. For instance, you might use a graphics program to create a new graphics file. This process varies from one program to another, but GUI programs typically use a menu option called Save or Save As to save a file. Text-mode programs provide similar functionality, but the details of how it's done vary greatly from one program to another.

One program deserves special mention as a way to create files: touch. You can type this program's name followed by the name of a file you want to create, such as **touch newfile.txt** to create an empty file called newfile.txt. Ordinarily, you don't need to do this to create a file of a particular type, since you'll use a specialized program to do the job. Sometimes, though, it's helpful to create an empty file just to have the file itself—for instance, to create a few "scratch" files to test some other command.

A programmer's tool known as make compiles source code if it's new, so programmers sometimes use touch to force make to recompile a source code file.

If you pass touch the name of a file that already exists, touch updates that file's access and modification time stamps to the current date and time. This can be handy if you're using a command that works on files based on their access times and you want the program to treat an old file as if it were new. You might also want to do this if you plan to distribute a collection of files and you want them all to have identical time stamps.

You can use a number of options with touch to modify its behavior. The most important of these are as follows:

Don't create a file   The -c or --no-create option tells touch to not create a new file if one doesn't already exist. Use this option if you want to update time stamps but not accidentally create an empty file, should you mistype a filename.

Set the time to a specific value   You can use -d *string* or --date=*string* to set the date of a file to that represented by the specified string, which can take any number of forms. For instance, **touch -d "July 4 2012" afile.txt** causes the date stamps on afile.txt to be set to July 4, 2012. You can achieve the same effect with -t [[*CC*]*YY*]*MMDDhhmm*[.*ss*], where [[*CC*]*YY*]*MMDDhhmm* [.*ss*] is a date and time in a specific numeric format, such as 201207041223 for 12:23 PM on July 4, 2012.

Consult the man page for touch to learn about its more obscure options.

Copying Files

Certification
Objective

If you're working in a text-mode shell, the cp command copies a file. (Its name is short for *copy*.) Its basic use is to pass it a source filename and a destination filename, a destination directory name, or both. Thus, there are three ways you can use it, as outlined in Table 7.1. Although the example filenames in Table 7.1 suggest that the original file be in your current working directory, this need not be the case; *orig.txt* could include a directory specification, such as /etc/fstab or ../afile.txt.

Chapter 6, "Getting to Know the Command Line," covers various types of absolute and relative directory references.

TABLE 7.1 Examples of the use of **cp**

Example command	Effect
cp *orig.txt new.txt*	Copies *orig.txt* to *new.txt* in the current directory.
cp *orig.txt* /otherdir	Copies orig.txt to the /*otherdir* directory. The copy will be called *orig.txt*.
cp *orig.txt* /otherdir/new.txt	Copies orig.txt to the /*otherdir* directory. The copy will be called *new.txt*.

The critical point to understand is how the destination filename is specified. This can be less than obvious in some cases, since file and directory specifications can look alike. For instance, consider the following command:

```
$ cp outline.pdf ~/publication
```

This command can produce any of three results:

▶ If ~/publication is a directory, the result is a file called ~/publication /outline.pdf.

▶ If ~/publication is a file, the result is that this file will be replaced by the contents of outline.pdf.

▶ If ~/publication doesn't yet exist, the result is a new file, called ~/publication, which is identical to the original outline.pdf.

If you follow a directory name with a slash (/), as in ~/publication/, cp returns an error message if ~/publication doesn't exist or is a regular file.

Keeping these results straight can be confusing if you're new to command-line file copying. Thus, I encourage you to experiment by creating a test directory using mkdir (described later, in "Creating Directories"), creating subdirectories in this directory, and copying files into this test directory tree using all of these methods of referring to files. (This is the type of situation where touch can be handy for creating test files.)

The cp command provides many options that modify its behavior. Some of the more useful options enable you to modify the command's operation in helpful ways:

Force overwrite   The -f or --force option forces the system to overwrite any existing files without prompting.

Use interactive mode   The -i or --interactive option causes cp to ask you before overwriting any existing files.

Chapter 13, "Understanding Users and Groups," describes Linux accounts. Chapter 15, "Setting Ownership and Permissions," describes file permissions.

Preserve ownership and permissions   Normally, a copied file is owned by the user who issues the cp command and uses that account's default permissions. The -p or --preserve option preserves ownership and permissions, if possible.

Perform a recursive copy   If you use the -R or --recursive option and specify a directory as the *source*, the entire directory, including its subdirectories, is copied. Although -r also performs a recursive copy, its behavior with files other than ordinary files and directories is unspecified. Most cp implementations use -r as a synonym for -R, but this behavior isn't guaranteed.

Perform an archive copy   The -a or --archive option is similar to -R, but it also preserves ownership and copies links as is. The -R option copies the files to which symbolic links point rather than the symbolic links themselves. (Links are described in more detail later in this chapter, in "Using Links.")

Perform an update copy   The -u or --update option tells cp to copy the file only if the original is newer than the target or if the target doesn't exist.

This list of cp options is incomplete but covers the most useful options. Consult cp's man page for information about additional cp options.

Moving and Renaming Files

Certification Objective

In a text-mode shell, the same command, mv, is used to both move and rename files and directories. Its use is very similar to that of cp; for instance, if you wanted to move outline.pdf to ~/publication, you would type:

```
$ mv outline.pdf ~/publication
```

Linux uses mv for renaming files because the two operations are identical when the source and destination directories are the same.

If you specify a filename with the destination, the file will be renamed as it's moved. If you specify a filename and the destination directory is the same as the source directory, the file will be renamed but not moved. In other words, mv's effects are much like cp's, except that the new file replaces, rather than supplements, the original.

Behind the scenes, mv does the following:

▶ When the source and target are on the same filesystem, mv rewrites directory entries without actually moving the file's data.

▶ When you move a file from one filesystem to another, mv copies the file and then deletes the original file.

The mv command takes many of the same options as cp does. From the earlier list, --preserve, --recursive, and --archive don't apply to mv, but the others do.

Using Links

Sometimes it's handy to refer to a single file by multiple names. Rather than create several copies of the file, you can create multiple *links* to one file. Linux supports two types of links, both of which are created with the ln command:

Certification
Objective

Hard link A *hard link* is a duplicate directory entry. Both entries point to the same file. Because they work by tying together low-level filesystem data structures, hard links can exist only on a single filesystem. In a hard link scenario, neither filename holds any sort of priority over the other; both tie directly to the file's data structures and data. Type ln *origname linkname*, where *origname* is the original name and *linkname* is the new link's name, to create a hard link.

Symbolic link A *symbolic link* (aka a *soft link*) is a file that refers to another file by name. That is, the symbolic link is a file that holds another file's name, and when you tell a program to read to or write from a symbolic link file, Linux redirects the access to the original file. Because symbolic links work by filename references, they can cross filesystem boundaries. Type ln -s *origname linkname* to create a symbolic link.

Symbolic links are similar to *shortcuts* on the Windows desktop.

You can identify links in long directory listings (using the -l option to ls) in a couple of ways. An example will illustrate this:

```
$ ln report.odt hardlink.odt
$ ln -s report.odt softlink.odt
$ ls -l
total 192
-rw-r--r-- 2 rod users 94720 Jan 10 11:53 hardlink.odt
-rw-r--r-- 2 rod users 94720 Jan 10 11:53 report.odt
lrwxrwxrwx 1 rod users    10 Jan 10 11:54 softlink.odt -> report.odt
```

This example began with a single file, report.odt. The first two commands created two links, a hard link (hardlink.odt) and a symbolic link (softlink.odt). Typing ls -l shows all three files. The original file and the hard link can be identified as links by the presence of the value 2 in the second column of the ls -l output; this column identifies the number of filename entries that point to the file, so a value higher than 1 indicates that a hard link exists. The symbolic link is denoted by an l (a lowercase *L*, not a digit *1*) in the first character of the softlink.odt file's permissions string (lrwxrwxrwx). Furthermore, the symbolic link's filename specification includes an explicit pointer to the linked-to file.

Both types of links are useful for referring to files by multiple names or in multiple directories. For instance, if you write a letter that you send to multiple recipients, you might want to store copies in directories devoted to each recipient. In such a situation, either type of link will probably work fine, but each type has implications. Most importantly, if you use symbolic links, deleting the original file makes the file completely inaccessible; the symbolic links remain but point to a non-existent file. If you use hard links, by contrast, you must delete *all* the copies of the file to delete the file itself. This is because hard links are duplicate directory entries that point to the same file, whereas symbolic links are separate files that refer to the original file by name.

If you modify a file by accessing its soft link, or by any hard-linked name, you should be sure that the program you use will modify the original file. Some programs create a backup of the original file that you can use to recover the original in case you find that your changes were in error. Most editors do this in such a way that the backup is a new file, and write changes to the original file, thus affecting the original file as well as the link. Some programs, though, rename the original file and then write a new file with the changes. If a program does this and you've accessed the file via a link, the linked-to file will be unaffected by your changes. If in doubt, test your program to be sure it does what you expect.

If you want to create a link to a directory, be aware that you can normally do this only via symbolic links. Hard links between directories are potentially dangerous in terms of low-level filesystem data structures, so the ln utility permits only the superuser to create such links. Even then, most filesystems disallow hard links between directories, so in practice even root usually can't create them. Any user can create symbolic links to a directory, though.

Linux installations make use of links (mostly symbolic links) in various places. For instance, system startup scripts are often referred to via symbolic links located in directories dedicated to specific startup conditions, known as *runlevels*. Runlevel management is beyond the scope of this book.

Deleting Files

The rm command deletes files in a text-mode shell. As you might expect, you pass the names of one or more files to this command:

```
$ rm outline.pdf outline.txt
```

This example deletes two files, outline.pdf and outline.txt. If you want to delete an entire directory tree, you can pass rm the -r, -R, or --recursive option along with a directory name:

```
$ rm -r oldstuff/
```

The -i option causes rm to prompt before deleting each file. This is a useful safety measure. You can use the -f (--force) option to override this setting, if -i is configured as the default. Several other options to rm exist; consult its man page to learn about them.

The rm **command's name is (very!) short for** *remove*.

Distributions sometimes set the -i **option by default for** root, **but not for ordinary users.**

It's important to realize that rm does *not* implement any functionality like a file manager's "trash can." Once you delete a file with rm, it's gone, and you can't recover it except by using low-level filesystem tools—a topic that's well beyond the scope of this book. Thus, you should be careful when using rm—and even more careful when using it with its -r option or as root!

Using Wildcards

You can use *wildcards* to refer to files. (Using wildcards is also sometimes called *globbing*.) A wildcard is a symbol or set of symbols that stands in for other characters. Three classes of wildcards are common in Linux:

Certification Objective

? A question mark (?) stands in for a single character. For instance, b??k matches book, balk, buck, or any other four-character filename that begins with b and ends with k.

* An asterisk (*) matches any character or set of characters, including no character. For instance, b*k matches book, balk, and buck just as does b??k. b*k also matches bk, bbk, and backtrack.

Bracketed values Characters enclosed in square brackets ([]) normally match any character in the set. For instance, b[ao][lo]k matches balk and book but not buck. It's also possible to specify a range of values; for instance, b[a-z]ck matches back, buck, and other four-letter filenames of this form whose second character is a lowercase letter. This differs from b?ck—because Linux treats filenames in a case-sensitive way and because ? matches any character (not just any letter), b[a-z]ck doesn't match bAck or b3ck, although b?ck matches both of these filenames.

Wildcards are implemented in the shell and passed to the command you call. For instance, if you type **ls b??k**, and that wildcard matches the three files balk, book, and buck, the result is precisely as if you'd typed **ls balk book buck**.

The way Bash expands wildcards can lead to unexpected, and sometimes undesirable, consequences. For instance, suppose you want to copy two files, specified via a wildcard, to another directory, but you forget to give the destination directory. The cp command will interpret the command as a request to copy the first of the files over the second.

Understanding Case Sensitivity

Linux's native filesystems are case-sensitive, which means that filenames that differ only in case are distinct files. For instance, a single directory can hold files called afile.txt, Afile.txt, and AFILE.TXT, and each is a distinct file. This

Certification Objective

case sensitivity also means that, if you type a filename, you must enter it with the correct case—if a file is called `afile.txt` but you type its name as `Afile.txt`, the program you're using will tell you that the file doesn't exist.

This is different from what happens in Windows or (usually) in Mac OS X, in which filenames that differ only in case are treated identically. This means that, in these OSs, you can't have two files that differ only in case in the same directory, and you can specify a filename using any case variant you like. Windows also creates a short filename (8 characters with an optional 3-character extension) for every file with a longer name, to help out older software that works only with such filenames. Linux doesn't create such alternate filenames.

Case sensitivity is primarily a function of the filesystem, not of the operating system. Thus, if you access a non-Linux filesystem (on a removable disk, a non-Linux partition on a dual-boot computer, or using a network filesystem), you may find that case-insensitive rules will apply. This is particularly likely when accessing File Allocation Table (FAT) and New Technology File System (NTFS) volumes, which are common on Windows computers, external hard disks, and USB flash drives. A further twist on this rule is that many Linux programs, such as Bash, assume case sensitivity even on case-insensitive filesystems. Features such as command completion, described in Chapter 6, "Getting to Know the Command Line," may work only if you use the case in which filenames are recorded, even on case-insensitive filesystems.

Ordinarily, case sensitivity creates few real problems, particularly if you use GUI programs that enable you to point-and-click to select files. You should be aware of these issues, however, when copying files or directories to FAT, NTFS, HFS+, or other case-insensitive filesystems. If a directory you want to copy contains files with names that differ only in case, you'll end up with a disk that contains just one of the offending files.

Manipulating Directories

No doubt you're familiar with the concept of directories, although you may think of them as "folders," since most GUI file managers represent directories using file folder icons. Naturally, Linux provides text-mode commands to manipulate directories. These include directory-specific commands to create and delete directories, as well as use of some of the file-manipulation commands described earlier to manage directories.

> **Apple's Hierarchical File System Plus (HFS+) supports both case-sensitive and case-insensitive variants. Apple uses the case-insensitive mode by default.**

Creating Directories

You can use the mkdir command to create a directory. Ordinarily, you'll use this command by typing the name of one or more directories following the command:

Certification
Objective

```
$ mkdir newdir
$ mkdir dirone newdir/dirtwo
```

The first example creates just one new directory, newdir, which will then reside in the current directory. The second example creates two new directories: dirone and newdir/dirtwo. In this example, mkdir creates dirtwo inside the newdir directory, which was created with the preceding command.

Chapter 6 includes information on how to specify locations other than the current directory, as well as how to change your current directory with the cd command.

In most cases, you'll use mkdir without options, other than the name of a directory, but you can modify its behavior in a few ways:

Set mode   The -m *mode* or --mode=*mode* option causes the new directory to have the specified permission mode, expressed as an octal number. (Chapter 15, "Setting Ownership and Permissions," describes these topics in more detail.)

Create parent directories   Normally, if you specify the creation of a directory within a directory that doesn't exist, mkdir responds with a No such file or directory error and doesn't create the directory. If you include the -p or --parents option, though, mkdir creates the necessary parent directory. For instance, typing **mkdir first/second** returns an error message if first doesn't exist, but typing **mkdir -p first/second** succeeds, creating both first and its subdirectory, second.

Deleting Directories

The rmdir command is the opposite of mkdir; it destroys a directory. To use it, you normally type the command followed by the names of one or more directories you want to delete:

Certification
Objective

```
$ rmdir dirone
$ rmdir newdir/dirtwo newdir
```

These examples delete the three directories created by the mkdir commands shown earlier.

Like mkdir, rmdir supports few options, the most important of which handle these tasks:

Ignore failures on non-empty directories   Normally, if a directory contains files or other directories, rmdir doesn't delete it and returns an error message.

With the `--ignore-fail-on-non-empty` option, `rmdir` still doesn't delete the directory, but it doesn't return an error message.

Delete tree The `-p` or `--parents` option causes `rmdir` to delete an entire directory tree. For instance, typing **`rmdir -p newdir/dirtwo`** causes `rmdir` to delete `newdir/dirtwo`, then `newdir`. You could use this command rather than the second one shown earlier to delete both of these directories.

You should understand that `rmdir` can delete only *empty* directories; if a directory contains any files at all, it won't work. (You can use the `-p` option, however, to delete a set of nested directories, as long as none of them holds any non-directory file.) Of course, in real life you're likely to want to delete directory trees that hold files. In such cases, you can use the `rm` command, described earlier, in "Deleting Files," along with its `-r` (or `-R` or `--recursive`) option:

```
$ rm -r newdir
```

This command deletes `newdir` and any files or subdirectories it might contain. This fact makes `rm` and its `-r` option potentially dangerous, so you should be particularly cautious when using it.

Linux Security Features

When you log in as an ordinary user, you can accidentally delete your own files if you err in your use of `rm` or various other commands. You cannot, however, do serious damage to the Linux installation itself. This is because Unix was designed as a multi-user OS with multi-user security features in mind, and because Linux is a clone of Unix, Linux has inherited these security features. Among these features are the concepts of file ownership and file permissions. You can only delete your own files—or more precisely, you can only delete files if you have write access to the directories in which they reside. You have such access to your own home directory, but not to the directories in which Linux system files reside. Thus, you can't damage these Linux system files.

Chapter 13, "Understanding Users and Groups," covers these concepts in more detail. Chapter 13 also describes how you can acquire the power to administer the computer. With this power comes the ability to damage the system, though, so you should be careful to do so only when necessary.

Managing Directories

Directories are just special files—they're files that hold other files. Thus, you can use most of the file-manipulation tools described elsewhere in this chapter to manipulate directories. There are some caveats, though:

- ▶ You can use touch to update a directory's time stamps, but you can't use touch to create a directory; mkdir handles that task.

- ▶ You can use cp to copy a directory; however, you must use the -r, -R, --recursive, -a, or --archive option to copy the directory and all its contents.

- ▶ You can use mv to move or rename a directory.

- ▶ You can use ln with its -s option to create a symbolic link to a directory. No common Linux filesystem supports hard links to directories, though.

As an example, suppose you have a directory in your home directory called Music/Satchmo, which contains Louis Armstrong music files. You want to reorganize this directory so that the files appear under the performer's last name, but you want to retain access to the files under the name Satchmo, since your music players refer to them this way. You could type the following commands to achieve this goal:

```
$ cd ~/Music
$ mv Satchmo Armstrong
$ ln -s Armstrong Satchmo
```

Alternatively, you could omit the first command and specify the complete path to each of the directories or links in the mv and ln commands. As written, the first two of these commands rename the ~/Music/Satchmo directory to ~/Music/Armstrong. The final command creates a symbolic link, ~/Music/Satchmo, that points to ~/Music/Armstrong.

THE ESSENTIALS AND BEYOND

Much of what you do with a computer qualifies as file management. Thus, you must understand the basic tools for managing files in Linux. These include commands to create, delete, copy, move, and rename files, as well as to create links to files. Directories in Linux are just files that contain other files, so most of the same commands you can use on files also work on directories. Special commands to create and delete directories exist, too.

(Continues)

THE ESSENTIALS AND BEYOND *(Continued)*

SUGGESTED EXERCISES

▶ Create a file with touch (or some other program) and then practice copying it with cp, renaming it with mv, moving it to another directory with mv, and deleting it with rm.

▶ Create a directory with mkdir and then practice using cp, mv, and rm on it, just as with files. Try copying files into it and then try deleting the directory with both rmdir and rm. Do both commands work?

REVIEW QUESTIONS

1. Which of the following commands would you type to rename newfile.txt to afile.txt?

   A. mv newfile.txt afile.txt

   B. cp newfile.txt afile.txt

   C. ln newfile.txt afile.txt

   D. rn newfile.txt afile.txt

   E. touch newfile.txt afile.txt

2. You want to copy a directory, MyFiles, to a USB flash drive that uses the FAT filesystem. The contents of MyFiles are as follows:

   ```
   $ ls -l MyFiles/
   total 276
   -rw-r--r-- 1 jen   users 129840 Nov 8 15:13 contract.odt
   -rw-r--r-- 1 rod   users  42667 Nov 8 15:12 outline.pdf
   -rw-r--r-- 1 sam   users 105979 Nov 8 15:12 Outline.PDF
   ```

   The USB flash drive is mounted at /media/usb, and so you type **cp -a MyFiles/ /media/usb**. What problem will occur when you attempt to copy these files?

   A. The command will fail because it tries to create links.

   B. The MyFiles directory will be copied, but none of its files will be copied.

   C. One file will be missing on the USB flash drive.

   D. One file's name will be changed during the copy.

   E. Everything will be fine; the command will work correctly.

(Continues)

3. You type **mkdir one/two/three** and receive an error message that reads, in part, No such file or directory. What can you do to overcome this problem? (Select all that apply.)

   A. Add the --parents parameter to the mkdir command.

   B. Issue three separate mkdir commands: **mkdir one**, then **mkdir one/two**, and then **mkdir one/two/three**.

   C. Type **touch /bin/mkdir** to be sure the mkdir program file exists.

   D. Type **rmdir one** to clear away the interfering base of the desired new directory tree.

   E. Type **rm -r one** to clear away the entire interfering directory tree.

4. True or false: You can create a symbolic link from one low-level filesystem to another.

5. True or false: You can easily damage your Linux installation by mistyping an rm command when you log into your regular account.

6. True or false: You can set a directory's time stamps with the touch command.

7. You want to copy a file (origfile.txt) to the backups directory, but if a file called origfile.txt exists in the backups directory, you want to go ahead with the copy only if the file in the source location is newer than the one in backups. The command to do this is **cp _____ origfile.txt backups/**.

8. You've typed **rmdir junk** to delete the junk directory, but this command has failed because junk contains word processing files. What command might you type to do the job?

9. Which wildcard character matches any one symbol in a filename?

## CHAPTER 8

Getting Help

We can all use a little help sometimes. When using a computer, the problem is often a simple lapse of memory—you might have forgotten the name of a command, or the details of how to use an option to a command whose name you do remember. For situations like these, modern OSs provide help systems. In Linux, these take several forms. One of the oldest of these is the *manual page* system, often referred to as man pages, after the command you use to read them. A more modern system with similar goals is the info page system. Beyond these two formal documentation systems are additional sources of information, such as tutorials and other manuals provided with the OS, online documentation, and consultation with experts.

▶ **Using man pages**

▶ **Using info pages**

▶ **Finding additional documentation**

Using *man* Pages

Certification Objective

Manual pages describe programs, configuration files, and other features of a Linux installation. Before you consult them, though, you should understand their purpose, and therefore their capabilities and limitations. With that information in mind, you can begin searching for information in the man page system, including searching for man pages by section or by searching for keywords using the whatis or apropos utility. Once you're reading a man page, knowing its structure can help you quickly locate the information you need.

Understanding the Purpose of *man* Pages

Linux man pages can be an extremely helpful resource, but you must understand their purpose and limitations. Unlike the help systems in some OSs, Linux man pages are not supposed to be tutorial in nature; they're intended as quick references to help somebody who's already at least somewhat familiar with a command, configuration file, or other OS feature. They're most useful

The upcoming section, "Finding Additional Documentation," describes how to locate documentation that's more tutorial than man pages.

when you need to know the options to use with a command, the name of an option in a configuration file, or similar details. If you need to learn a new program from scratch, other documentation is often a better choice. Manual pages also vary greatly in quality; some are very good, but others are frustratingly terse, and even occasionally inaccurate. For the most part, they're written by the programmers who wrote the software in question, and programmers seldom place a high priority on user documentation.

In this book, I describe many Linux commands in a tutorial style, but I often omit information on obscure options, subtle program effects, and so on. In principle, man pages should cover such minutiae. This makes man pages an excellent resource to learn more about the commands described in this book, should you need to go further.

Locating *man* Pages by Section Number

The precise man page search order defined by MANSECT varies from one distribution to another, but section 1 is usually searched first, followed by section 8 and then the others.

In the simplest case, you can read a man page by typing **man** followed by the name of a command, configuration file, system call, or other keyword. Each man page falls into one of nine categories, as summarized in Table 8.1. Some keywords lead to entries in multiple sections. In such instances, the man utility returns the entry in the section based on a search order specified by the MANSECT entry in the /etc/man.conf configuration file. You can override this behavior by passing a section number before the keyword. For instance, typing **man passwd** returns information from manual section 1, on the passwd command, but typing **man 5 passwd** returns information from manual section 5, on the /etc/passwd file format. Some man pages have entries in sections with variant numbers that include the suffix p, as in section 1p. These refer to POSIX standard man pages, as opposed to the Linux man pages, which are, for the most part, written by the people who wrote the open source Linux programs the man pages describe.

TABLE 8.1   Manual sections

Section number	Description
1	Executable programs and shell commands
2	System calls provided by the kernel
3	Library calls provided by program libraries
4	Device files (usually stored in /dev)
5	File formats

(Continues)

TABLE 8.1 *(Continued)*

Section number	Description
6	Games
7	Miscellaneous (macro packages, conventions, and so on)
8	System administration commands (programs run mostly or exclusively by `root`)
9	Kernel routines

If you're just starting out with Linux, chances are you'll be most interested in section 1, which is also usually the first section in the man page search order—although section 6 can also be interesting if you have the time to spare! As you move on to more advanced and administrative tasks, you'll find sections 4, 5, and 8 important. Sections 2, 3, and 9 are of most interest to programmers.

Searching for a *man* Page

One of the problems with man pages is that it can be hard to locate help on a topic unless you know the name of the command, system call, or file you want to use. Fortunately, methods of searching the manual database exist and can help lead you to an appropriate man page:

Summary search The whatis command searches summary information contained in man pages for the keyword you specify. The command returns a one-line summary for every matching man page. (This summary is the Name section, described shortly, in "Reading man Pages.") You can then use this information to locate and read the man page you need. This command is most useful for locating all the man pages on a topic. For instance, typing **whatis man** returns lines confirming the existence of the man page entries for man, in various sections.

Thorough search The apropos command performs a more thorough search, of both the Name and Description sections of man pages. The result looks much like the results of a whatis search, except that it's likely to contain many more results. In fact, doing an apropos search on a very common word, such as the, is likely to return so many hits as to make the search useless. A search on a less common word is likely to be more useful. For instance, typing **apropos samba** returns thirteen entries on one of my systems, including those for cupsaddsmb, smbpasswd, and lmhosts—all tools related to the Samba file- and printer-sharing tool.

Details of what man **pages are available vary from one distribution to another. This will affect the results of both** whatis **and** apropos **searches.**

Certification
Objective

Certification
Objective

The -k **option to** man **is equivalent to** apropros. **Thus, you can type either** apropos *keyword* **or man** -k *keyword*.

Reading *man* Pages

The convention for man pages is a succinct style that employs several sections, each of which has a particular purpose. This organization can help you locate the information you need—you might need information that you know is in a particular section, in which case you can quickly scan down to that section. Common sections include the following:

Name   A man page begins with a statement of the command, call, or file that's described, along with a few words of explanation. For instance, the man page for man (section 1) has a Name section that reads man – an interface to the on-line reference manuals.

Synopsis   The synopsis provides a brief description of how a command is used. Optional parameters appear in square brackets, such as [-D]. An ellipsis (. . .) denotes an optional set of repeated elements, such as multiple filenames if a command takes one or more filenames as options. Some commands provide multiple synopsis lines, indicating that certain options are contingent upon others.

Description   The description is an English-language summary of what the command, file, or other element does. The description can vary from a short summary to something many pages in length.

Options   This section expands on the options outlined in the Synopsis section. Typically, each option appears in a list, with a one-paragraph explanation indented just below it.

Files   This section lists files that are associated with the man page's subject. These might be configuration files for a server or other program, related configuration files for a configuration file, or what have you.

See Also   This section provides pointers to related information in the man system, typically with a section number appended. For instance, the man page for fdisk (a disk partitioning tool) refers to the man pages for cfdisk, sfdisk, parted, and several other partitioning tools.

Bugs   Many man pages provide a Bugs section in which the author describes any known bugs or limitations, or states that no known bugs exist.

History   Some man pages provide a summary of the program's history, citing project start dates and major milestones between then and the current version.

This history isn't nearly as comprehensive as the changes file that ships with most programs' source code.

Author   Most man pages end with an Author section, which tells you how to contact the author of the program.

Specific manual pages may contain fewer, more, or different sections than these. For instance, the Synopsis section is typically omitted from man pages on configuration files. Manual pages with particularly verbose descriptions often split the Description section into several parts, each with its own title.

Figure 8.1 shows a typical man page in a terminal window. As you can see, section numbers appear in bold uppercase letters, making it easy to locate relevant sections as you page through the document.

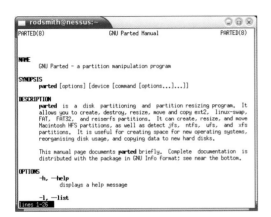

FIGURE 8.1 The formatting of man pages helps you to locate information quickly.

Although man is a text-mode command, GUI variants exist. The xman program, for instance, provides a point-and-click method of browsing through man pages. You can't type a subject on the command line to view it as you would with man, though—you must launch xman and then browse through the manual sections to a specific subject.

Using *less*

Linux's man system uses a program called less to display information. This program is a *pager*, which displays a text file a screen (that is, a page) at a time. You can move forward or backward through the file, move to a specific line, and search for information. Table 8.2 summarizes the most common ways of moving about a document using less.

> By default, man **uses** the less **program to enable you to move back and forth in the document. The upcoming section, "Using** less**," describes this program in detail.**

> **An earlier pager was known as** more, **but** less **adds features. This peculiar name is an example of geek humor.**

Certification
Objective

TABLE 8.2 less file navigation commands

Keystroke	Action
h or H	Displays help on using less.
Page Down, spacebar, Ctrl+V, f, or Ctrl+F	Moves down one screen in the document.
Page Up, Esc+V, b, or Ctrl+B	Moves up one screen in the document.
Down Arrow, Enter, Ctrl+N, e, Ctrl+E, j, or Ctrl+J	Moves down one line in the document.
Up Arrow, y, Ctrl+Y, Ctrl+P, k, or Ctrl+K	Moves up one line in the document.
xg, x<, or x Esc+<	Go to line x in the document—for instance, typing **100g** displays the document's 100th line. If x is omitted, the default is 1.
xG, x>, or x Esc+>	Go to line x in the document. If x is omitted, the default is the last line of the document.
xp or x%	Go to the point x percent through the document—for instance, typing **50p** goes to the document's halfway point.
/$pattern$	Searches forward for *pattern* in the document, starting at the current location. For instance, typing **/BUGS** searches for the string BUGS.
?$pattern$	Performs a backwards search, locating instances of *pattern* before the current location.
n or /	Repeat the previous search.
q or Q or :q or :Q or ZZ	Quits from the less pager.

The notation Esc+V refers to pressing the Esc key followed by the V key.

Table 8.2 presents a small fraction of the commands available in less. To learn more about less, you can read its man page:

1. Log into the computer in text mode or open a terminal window.

2. Type **man less**. This action opens the man page for the less pager.

3. Read the first screen of text. When you reach the last word at the bottom of the screen, press the spacebar key. This moves the display to the next page, so you can continue reading.

4. Press the up arrow key. This moves the display up a single line, which is useful if you need to re-read just a few words from the end of the last page.

5. Press the down arrow key. As you might expect, this moves the display down by one line.

6. Press the Esc key followed by the V key. This moves the display back one page.

7. Press the G key (that is, Shift+G) to move to the end of the man page.

8. Press the g key (that is, G *without* using the Shift key) to move back to the start of the man page.

9. Type **/OPTIONS** to locate the Options section. Chances are your first hits will be to references to this section, rather than to the Options section itself.

10. Repeatedly press the n key until you find the Options section.

11. Press the q key to quit from less, and therefore from reading the man page.

You could use the Page Down key or others noted in Table 8.2 instead of the spacebar, if you prefer. Similar substitutions are possible in subsequent steps.

Some implementations search in a case-sensitive way, but others are case-insensitive. Try searching on options **(in lowercase) to determine which yours is.**

Of course, when you read man pages you aren't likely to use these exact options; you'll use whatever features you need to use to find the content that interests you. The key is to familiarize yourself with a few important features so that you can make effective use of less to read man pages and other documents.

Although less is important for reading man pages, you can also use it to read other text-mode documents, such as README files that come with many programs or plain-text documents that you might find on the Internet or that friends or co-workers give you. To use less in this way, type its name followed by the filename of the file you want to read, as in **less README** to read the README document. You can use all the actions summarized in Table 8.2 (or by less's man page) on documents read in this way, just as you can on man pages.

Using *info* Pages

Certification
Objective

The man page system is ubiquitous on Unix-like OSs, including Linux, but it's also quite old and is therefore limited. Thus, a newer documentation system, known as info pages, is also available. In the next few pages, I describe how info pages fill gaps in the man page system and I describe how to use info pages.

Understanding the Purpose of *info* Pages

The basic design of man pages dates back decades, so it predates some important developments in managing information. Most notably, man pages are not hyperlinked. Although a See Also section is common in man pages, you can't select one of these items to read the relevant man page directly; you must quit from the man system and type a new man command to read the new page. This lack of hyperlinking also makes navigating through a large man page awkward. You can use text searches to locate information you desire, but these often find the wrong text—or if you mistype a string, your search might fail completely.

The goal of info pages is to overcome these problems by supporting hyperlinking. Each info page is known as a *node*, and the info page system as a whole is an interrelated set of nodes, similar to the World Wide Web (WWW or Web) of the Internet. An individual program's documentation may be split up across multiple nodes, which can make each node easier to locate and search—but if you need to search for information and you're not sure in which node it resides, you may need to search multiple nodes.

Nodes are organized on *levels*, which are similar to the levels of organization in a book. This book, for instance, has chapters and two levels of headings within each chapter. Similarly, the info page for a program is likely to have one main node, similar to a chapter, along with multiple nodes at a lower level, similar to chapter headings. Some programs' info pages include further levels to help organize information.

In terms of writing style, info pages are similar to man pages—they are terse but comprehensive descriptions of their topics, intended for people who are already at least broadly familiar with the programs in question. If you're just starting out with a program, other types of documentation (described later, in "Finding Additional Documentation") may be a better choice.

Broadly speaking, programs sponsored by the Free Software Foundation (FSF) use info pages in preference to man pages. Many FSF programs now ship with minimal man pages that point the user to the programs' info pages. Non-FSF programmers have been slower to embrace info pages; many such programs don't ship with info pages at all, and instead rely on traditional man pages.

The info browser can read and display man pages, so using info exclusively can be an effective strategy for reading Linux's standard documentation.

Reading *info* Pages

The usual tool for reading info pages is called info. To use it, you type **info** followed by the topic, as in **info info** to learn about the info system itself. Once you're in the info system, you can use a number of keystrokes, summarized in Table 8.3, to move around a document.

Certification
Objective

TABLE 8.3 info file navigation commands

Keystroke	Action
?	Displays help information.
N	Moves to the next node in a linked series of nodes on a single hierarchical level. This action may be required if the author intended several nodes to be read in a particular sequence.
P	Moves back in a series of nodes on a single hierarchical level. This can be handy if you've moved forward in such a series but find you need to review earlier material.
U	Moves up one level in the node hierarchy.
Arrow keys	Moves the cursor around the screen, enabling you to select node links or scroll the screen.
Page Up, Page Down	These keys scroll up and down within a single node, respectively. (The standard info browser also implements many of the more arcane commands used by less and outlined in Table 8.2.)
Enter	Moves to a new node once you've selected it. Links are indicated by asterisks (*) to the left of their names.
L	Displays the last info page you read. This action can move you up, down, or sideways in the info tree hierarchy.
T	Displays the top page for a topic. Typically this is the page you used to enter the system.
Q	Exits from the info page system.

As an example of info pages in use, try the following:

1. Log into the computer in text mode or open a terminal window.

2. Type **info info**. You should see the top node for the info documentation appear.

3. Read the main page, using the arrow keys or the Page Down keys to view the entire page.

4. Using the arrow keys, select the link to the Expert Info node near the bottom of the main page.

5. Press the Enter key to view the Expert Info node.

6. Press the U key to browse up one level—back to the main node.

7. Browse to the Advanced node.

8. Press the N key to go on to the next node on the current level, which in fact is the Expert Info node.

9. Press the Q key to exit from the info reader.

If you're more comfortable with GUIs than with text-mode tools, you can access info pages with point-and-click tools:

Emacs   The GNU Emacs editor, which is an extremely powerful text editor, provides an info page browser as part of its info package.

tkinfo   This stand-alone program, shown in Figure 8.2, provides a point-and-click interface to the info page system. You can use most of the same keyboard options as with the info browser, but you can also navigate by clicking links or by using the buttons or menu options it provides.

> **Unlike the text-mode info program, neither Emacs' info browser nor tkinfo can display man pages.**

Finding Additional Documentation

Although man pages and info pages are both very useful resources, other documentation is available, too, and is sometimes preferable to these forms of documentation. Broadly speaking, help on Linux can come in three forms: additional documentation on your computer, additional documentation online, and help from experts.

> **Of course, these categories blur together. For instance, documentation might be available online but not on your computer until you install an appropriate package.**

FIGURE 8.2 GUI info page browsers can make this form of documentation accessible to those who are uncomfortable with the command line.

Locating Program Documentation on Your Computer

Most Linux programs ship with their own documentation, even aside from man or info pages. In fact, some programs have so much documentation that it's installed as a separate package, typically with the word documentation or doc in the package name, such as samba-doc.

The most basic and traditional form of program documentation is a file called README, readme.txt, or something similar. Precisely what information this file contains varies greatly from one program to another. For some, the file is so terse it's nearly useless. For others, it's a treasure trove of help. These files are almost always plain text files, so you can read them with less or your favorite text editor.

If you downloaded the program as a source code tarball from the package maintainer's site, the README file typically appears in the main build directory extracted from the tarball. If you installed the program from a binary package file, though,

README **files often contain information on building the package that doesn't apply to binaries provided with a distribution. Distribution maintainers seldom change such information in their** README **files, though.**

Certification
Objective

the README file could be in any of several locations. The most likely places are /usr/doc/*packagename*, /usr/share/doc/*packagename*, and /usr/share/doc/packages/*packagename*, where *packagename* is the name of the package (sometimes including a version number, but more often not).

In addition to or instead of the README file, many programs provide other documentation files. These may include a file that documents the history of the program in fine detail, descriptions of compilation and installation procedures, information on configuration file formats, and so on. Check the source code's build directory or the directory in which you found the README file for other files.

Some larger programs ship with extensive documentation in PostScript, Portable Document Format (PDF), Hypertext Markup Language (HTML), or other formats. Depending on the format and package, you might find a single file or a large collection of files. As with the README files, these files are well worth consulting, particularly if you want to learn to use a package to its fullest.

Some programs rely on configuration files, typically located in the /etc directory, to control their behavior. Although the syntax for configuration files is often arcane, many distributions provide default configuration files that include extensive comments. Details vary from one program to another, but comment lines often begin with hash marks (#). Thus, you may be able to learn enough about a program to adjust its configuration merely by reading the comments in its configuration file.

If you can't find a README or similar file, you can employ a number of tools to help find documentation files:

Chapter 9, "Using Programs and Processes," describes the principles of package management tools.

▶ You can use your distribution's package management system to locate documentation. For instance, on an RPM-based system, you might type **rpm -ql** *apackage* **| grep doc** to locate documentation for *apackage*. Using grep to search for the string doc in the file list is a good trick because documentation directories almost always contain the string doc.

▶ The Linux find command can search your entire directory tree, or a subset of it, for files that match a specified criterion. To search for a file that includes a certain string in its name, for instance, you might type **find /usr/share/doc -name** "**string*", where *string* is the keyword you want to find in a filename. This command searches the /usr/share/doc directory tree, but you can search another directory tree instead. If you search a directory with lots of files and subdirectories, this command can take a long time to complete.

Certification
Objective
▶ The Linux locate command searches a database of filenames that Linux maintains. It can therefore do its job much quicker than find can, but you can't control the part of the computer that the system

searches. Type **locate** followed by the string you want to find, as in **locate parted** to find any files related to the parted disk partitioning tool.

▶ The whereis program searches for files in a restricted set of locations, such as standard binary file directories, library directories, and man page directories. This tool does *not* search user directories or many other locations that are easily searched by find or locate. The whereis utility is a quick way to find program executables and related files like documentation or configuration files. To use it, type **whereis** followed by the name of the command or file, as in **whereis ls** to find the ls binary and related documentation.

Once you've located documentation files, you must know how to read them. The details, of course, depend on the documentation's file format. You can use less to read many files. Most distributions configure less in such a way that it can interpret common file formats, such as HTML, and to automatically decompress files that are stored in compressed format to save disk space. Table 8.4 summarizes common documentation file formats and the programs you can use to read them. Which formats are used varies from one program to another.

If you want to see a formatted text file, such as an HTML file, in uninterpreted form, use the -L option to less, as in less -L file .html.

TABLE 8.4 Common documentation file formats

Filename extension	Description	Programs for reading
.1 through .9	Unix man pages	man, info, less
.gz or .bz2	File compressed with gzip or bzip2	Use gunzip or bunzip2 to uncompress; or use less, which may be able to uncompress the file and read its underlying format
.txt	Plain text	less or any text editor
.html or .htm	HTML	Any Web browser
.odt	OpenDocument Text	OpenOffice.org, LibreOffice, or many other word processors
.pdf	Portable Document Format (PDF)	Adobe Reader, xpdf
.tif, .png, .jpg	Graphics file formats	The GIMP, Eye of GNOME (eog)

Manually uncompressing a file with gunzip or bunzip2 may require writing the uncompressed version to disk, so you may need to copy the file to your home directory.

Locating Program Documentation Online

In addition to the documentation you find on your computer, you can locate documentation on the Internet. Most packages have associated Internet Web sites, which may be referred to in man pages, info pages, README files, or other documentation. Check these pages to look up documentation. Frequently, online documentation ships with the software, so you might be able to find it on your local hard disk; however, sometimes the local documentation is old or sparse compared to what's available online. Of course, if your local documentation is old, your local software may be old, too—try not to use documentation for software that's substantially newer or older than what you're actually using!

Another online resource that's extremely helpful is the Linux Documentation Project (LDP; http://www.tldp.org). The LDP is dedicated to providing more tutorial information than is commonly available with most Linux programs. You'll find several types of information at this site:

HOWTOs   Linux HOWTO documents are short and medium-length tutorial pieces intended to get you up to speed with a topic or technology. In the past, smaller HOWTOs were classified separately, as mini-HOWTOs; however, the distinction between the two types of document has diminished greatly in recent years. HOWTOs have varying focus—some describe particular programs, whereas others are more task-oriented and cover a variety of tools in service to the task. As the name implies, they're generally designed to tell you how to accomplish some goal.

Guides   Guides are longer documents, often described as book-length. (In fact, some of them are available in printed form.) Guides are intended as thorough tutorial or reference works on large programs or general technologies, such as Linux networking as a whole.

Most of the LDP's FAQs are rather out of date. As I write, some have last-update dates as early as 1996, and the most recent were last updated in 2004.

FAQs   A *Frequently Asked Question (FAQ)* is, as the name implies, a question that comes up often—or more precisely, in the sense of the LDP category, that question and an answer to it. LDP FAQs are organized into categories, such as the Linux-RAID FAQ or the WordPerfect on Linux FAQ. Each contains multiple questions and their answers, often grouped in subcategories. If you have a specific question about a program or technology, looking for an appropriate FAQ can be a good place to look first for an answer.

LDP documents vary greatly in their thoroughness and quality. Some (particularly some of the Guides) are incomplete; you can click on a section heading and see an empty page or a comment that the text has yet to be written. (Many LDP documents are hyperlinked on the Web.) Some LDP documents are very recent, but others are outdated, so be sure to check the date of any document before you begin reading—if you don't, you might end up doing something the hard way or in a way that no longer works. Despite these flaws, the LDP can be an excellent resource for learning about specific programs or about Linux generally. The better LDP documents are excellent, and even those of marginal quality often present information that's not obvious from man pages, info pages, or official program documentation.

Most Linux distributions include the LDP documents in one or more special documentation packages. Check your /usr/doc and /usr/share/doc directories for these files. If they're not present, look for likely packages using your package management tools. On the other hand, using the online versions of LDP documents can be desirable because you can be sure they're the latest available. Those that ship with a distribution can be weeks or months out of date by the time you read them.

Consulting Experts

Whatever the issue is that has you looking for documentation, chances are you're not the first person to do so. In some cases you can save yourself a lot of time by asking another person for help. Some specific resources you can use include the following:

Local experts   Whether it's the Linux expert in the next office, a next-door neighbor, or a fellow student, a person who you know and who knows more about Linux than you can be a valuable resource.

Paid consultants   Paying somebody a consulting fee can often be worthwhile to fix a thorny problem, particularly if you're facing a "time is money" situation in which a delay in solving the problem will literally cost money. A Web search will turn up numerous Linux consulting firms.

Some Linux distributions, such as Red Hat Enterprise Linux and SUSE Enterprise Linux, come with support. If you're using such a distribution, you may have already paid for consulting.

Program authors   Many open source authors are happy to answer questions or provide limited support, particularly if your problem is caused by a bug. Bigger projects (including most Linux distributions) have many authors, and these projects often provide Web forums, mailing lists, or Usenet newsgroups to help users and developers communicate.

Web forums, mailing lists, and Usenet newsgroups   These resources differ in format but serve similar purposes: They enable users to communicate with one another and share their expertise. Many distributions have dedicated Web forums; try a Web search on your distribution name and *forum* to find yours. Mailing lists are more common for individual programs. Search the program's main Web site for information on mailing lists. Usenet newsgroups were popular years ago but are less popular today. Nonetheless, they can still be a useful resource. To use them, you can use a *news reader* program, and your Internet service provider (ISP) must provide Usenet access. Alternatively, you can use Google Groups (`http://groups.google.com`).

IRC   Internet Relay Chat (IRC) is a tool for real-time text-mode communication among small groups of people. To use IRC, you need an IRC client program, such as Irssi (`http://www.irssi.org`), BitchX (`http://www.bitchx.com`), or ChatZilla (`http://www.hacksrus.com/~ginda/chatzilla/`). You can then join an IRC *channel*, in which IRC users exchange messages in real time. IRC, like Web forums, mailing lists, and newsgroups, enables users to communicate directly with one another; but IRC can provide quicker solutions to problems.

Web searches   Web search engines index many Internet resources, including man pages, program documentation sites, Web forums, and even IRC channel discussions. Thus, a Web search can provide you with an answer from an expert without your needing to contact the expert directly.

Careful use of these resources can help you with many Linux problems, whether those problems are simply a lack of knowledge on your part, a misconfiguration, a program bug, or some terrible disaster such as a software update that rendered your computer unbootable. Indeed, the problem today is that there's often *too much* information available; sifting through the irrelevant (or just plain bad) information to find the helpful advice can be difficult. To overcome this challenge, being specific can be helpful. You can narrow a Web search by adding keywords that you believe are relevant to the problem but that are uncommon. Words found in error messages can be helpful in this respect. If you post a problem to a Web forum or send a bug report to a program author, be as specific as you can be. Include information on the distribution you're using, the version of the software with which you need help, and specific details about what it's doing. If the program displays error messages, quote them exactly. Such details will help experts zero in on the cause of the problem.

THE ESSENTIALS AND BEYOND

Whether you need to learn more about a program to use it effectively or solve a problem with a misbehaving program, getting help is often necessary. Linux provides several documentation resources for such situations. The first of these is the man page system, which documents most text-mode commands, configuration files, and system calls. The info page system is similar to the man page system, but info pages employ a more

(Continues)

advanced hyperthreaded file format. If you need more tutorial information than the manor info pages provide, you can often obtain help in the form of extended official user manuals, Web pages, HOWTOs, and other documents, both on your computer and on the Internet. Finally, interacting with experts can help resolve a problem, so you can use numerous in-person and online resources, such as people you know, program authors, and Web forums, to get the help that you need.

SUGGESTED EXERCISES

▶ Fully read at least three man pages for common Linux commands, such as ls, cp, cat, or less. What have you learned about these commands that goes beyond the descriptions in this book?

▶ Search /usr/share/doc for documentation on important programs you use frequently, such as the GIMP, Firefox, or GNOME.

▶ Check your distribution's Web site, or do a Web search, to find a Web forum supporting your distribution. Read some of the discussion threads to get a feel for some of the topics that come up.

REVIEW QUESTIONS

1. Which of the following commands is an improved version of more?

    A. grep   **D.** less

    B. html   **E.** man

    C. cat

2. Which of the following statements is a fair comparison of man pages to HOWTO documents?

    A. man pages require Internet access to read; HOWTOs do not.

    B. man pages are a type of printed documentation; HOWTOs are electronic.

    C. man pages describe software from a user's point of view; HOWTOs are programmers' documents.

    D. man pages are brief reference documents; HOWTOs are more tutorial in nature.

    E. man pages use a hyperlinked format, whereas HOWTOs do not.

(Continues)

THE ESSENTIALS AND BEYOND *(Continued)*

3. A user types **whatis less**. What type of output can be expected?

    A. A short one-paragraph description of the purpose of the less command

    B. The complete path to the less command in the Linux filesystem

    C. Summary information from man pages whose Name sections mention less

    D. The complete man page for less, which you would then scroll through with your terminal

    E. The URLs for Web sites with information on the less command

4. True or false: You can force man to display a man page in a specific section of the manual by preceding the search name with the section number, as in **man 5 passwd**.

5. True or false: info pages are a Web-based documentation format.

6. True or false: Linux documentation in the /usr/share/doc directory tree is almost always in OpenDocument Text format.

7. File formats are described in man section _____.

8. Each document in an info page is known as a(n) _____.

9. The _____ command searches a database of filenames, enabling you to quickly identify files whose names match a term you specify.

Using Programs and Processes

Computers are dynamic and multi-purpose machines; they do a variety of jobs using many tools. This chapter describes the ways you can manage these tools. One aspect of this task is installing, uninstalling, and upgrading software packages. Another aspect of software management is in managing programs once they're running. (Running programs are often called *processes*.) Finally, this chapter covers *log files*, which record details of what running programs do—particularly programs that run automatically and in the background.

▶ **Understanding package management**

▶ **Understanding the process hierarchy**

▶ **Identifying running processes**

▶ **Using log files**

Understanding Package Management

Package management is an area of Linux that varies a lot from one distribution to another. Nonetheless, certain principles are common across most Linux distributions, so I describe these principles, followed by some of the basics of the two major Linux package management systems. I then describe how to manage packages using both the RPM Package Management (RPM; a recursive acronym) and Debian package systems.

Linux Package Management Principles

Certification Objective

If you've installed software in Windows, you're likely familiar with the procedure of double-clicking on an installer program, which places all the files associated with a program where they should go. A Windows software installer is similar to a Linux package file, but there are differences. Linux packages have the following characteristics:

▶ Each package is a single file that can be stored on a disk or transmitted over the Internet.

▶ Linux package files, unlike Windows installers, are not programs; packages rely on other programs to do the work of installing the software.

▶ Packages contain *dependency* information—that is, they can tell the packaging software what other packages or individual files must be installed in order for the package to work correctly.

▶ Packages contain version information, so that the packaging software can tell which of two packages is more recent.

▶ Packages contain architecture information to identify the CPU type (*x*86, *x*86-64, PowerPC, and so on) for which they're intended. A separate code identifies packages that are architecture-independent, such as fonts and desktop themes.

▶ *Binary* packages (that is, those that contain executable programs that are CPU-specific) are typically built from *source* packages (which contain source code that a programmer can understand). It's possible to build a new binary package, given the source package, which can be useful in some unusual circumstances.

The package software maintains a database of information about installed packages (the *package database*). This information includes the names and version numbers of all the installed packages, as well as the locations of all the files installed from each package. This information enables the package software to quickly uninstall software, establish whether a new package's dependencies have been met, and determine whether a package you're trying to install has already been installed and, if so, whether the installed version is older than the one you're trying to install.

Understanding Package Systems

As noted earlier, two package systems, RPM and Debian, are common, although others exist as well. These systems differ in various technical details, as well as

---

Many program packages depend on *library* **packages; libraries provide code that can be used by many programs.**

You can compile and install software from source code manually, without using a packaging tool. This advanced topic is beyond the scope of this book.

Certification Objective

Packages can, and frequently do, contain files that will be installed to many directories on the computer. This fact makes tracking package contents critical.

in the commands used to manage packages and in the format of the package files they use. You cannot install a Debian package on an RPM-based system, or vice versa. Indeed, installing a package intended for one distribution on another is a bit risky even when they use the same package type. This is because a non-native package may have dependencies that conflict with the needs of native packages.

Originally, package systems worked locally—that is, to install a package on your computer you would first have to download a package file from the Internet or in some other way. Only then could you use a local command to install the package. This approach, however, can be tedious when a package has many dependencies—you might attempt an installation, find unmet dependencies, download several more packages, find that one or more of *them* has unmet dependencies, and so on. By the time you've tracked down all of these depended-upon packages, you might need to install a dozen or more packages. Thus, modern distributions provide network-enabled tools to help automate the process. These tools rely on network software *repositories*, from which the tools can download packages automatically. The network-enabled tools vary from one distribution to another, particularly among RPM-based distributions.

In practice, then, the process of managing software in Linux involves using text-mode or GUI tools to interface with a software repository. A typical software installation task works something like this:

1. You issue a command to install a program.

2. The software locates dependencies of the specified program and notifies you of any additional software that must be installed.

3. You issue a final approval for software installation (or decide against it, in which case the process stops).

4. The software downloads all the necessary packages.

5. The software installs all the packages.

Upgrading software works in a similar way, although upgrades are less likely to require downloading depended-upon packages. Removing software can be done entirely locally, of course. Many distributions automatically check with their repositories from time to time and notify you when updates are available. Thus, you can keep your system up to date by clicking a few buttons when you're prompted to do so. As an example, Figure 9.1 shows Fedora 16's Software Update utility, which shows a list of available updates.

Table 1.1 in Chapter 1, "Selecting an Operating System," summarizes some features of several popular Linux distributions, including the package system each uses.

Certification Objective

You can configure most distributions to use local media instead of or in addition to Internet repositories.

Immediately after installing a distribution, you may find that a large number of updates are available.

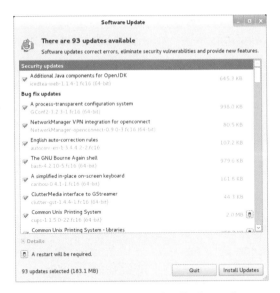

FIGURE 9.1 Most Linux distributions tell you when updates are available for your software.

Package management necessarily involves root access, which is described in more detail in Chapter 13, "Understanding Users and Groups." If you follow the automatic prompts to update your software, you can keep the system up to date by entering the root password, or on some distributions your regular password, when the update software prompts for it.

Managing RPM Systems

RPM-based distributions include Red Hat, Fedora, CentOS, SUSE Enterprise, open-SUSE, and Mandriva. The basic tool for installing software on these distributions is the text-mode rpm command. This program works on local files, though; to use a network repository, you must use another tool, which varies by distribution:

▶ Red Hat, Fedora, and CentOS use the text-mode yum or various GUI front-ends to it, such as Yumex.

▶ SUSE Enterprise and openSUSE use zypper or a GUI front-end such as YaST 2.

▶ Mandriva uses the text-mode urpmi or the GUI Rpmdrake.

Because of the variability between these distributions, particularly for network-enabled updates, providing a complete description of all of these tools is impractical here. Fortunately, the GUI tools are easy to use and accessible. Even the text-mode tools are fairly straightforward, although you may need to consult their man pages to learn the details. Typically, they use logical subcommands, such as install to install a package, as in:

```
# yum install yumex
```

You might use this command to install the GUI Yumex tool on a Red Hat, Fedora, or CentOS system. Similarly, you can remove a specific package by using the remove subcommand or upgrade all of a computer's packages by using upgrade:

```
# yum remove zsh
# yum upgrade
```

These examples upgrade the computer and then remove the zsh package. Both of these commands will produce a number of lines of output, and you may be asked to verify their actions. Consult the man page for yum (or whatever package management software your distribution uses) to learn more about this tool.

If you need to deal with RPM package files directly, you should be aware that they have filename extensions of .rpm. These files also usually include codes for architecture type (such as i386 or x86_64), and often codes for the distribution for which they're intended (such as fc16 for Fedora 16). For instance, samba-3.6.1 -77.fc16.x86_64.rpm is a package file for the samba package, version 3.6.1, release 77, for Fedora 16, on the *x*86-64 platform.

◀

If you want to both upgrade software and remove packages, it's generally best to remove software first. This can obviate some downloads, reducing the upgrade time.

Managing Debian Systems

The Debian GNU/Linux distribution created its own package system, and distributions based on Debian, such as Ubuntu and Mint, use the same system. Atop the basic Debian package system lies the Advanced Package Tool (APT), which provides access to network repositories.

The dpkg command is the lowest-level interface to the Debian package system; it's roughly equivalent to the rpm utility on RPM-based systems. Several tools provide text-mode and graphical interfaces atop dpkg, the most important of these being the text-mode apt-get and the GUI Synaptic. As their names imply, apt-get and Synaptic provide access to network repositories via APT. Figure 9.2 shows Synaptic in use.

Debian package files have names that end in .deb. Like RPM packages, these names typically include codes for the software version and architecture (such as i386 or amd64). For instance, samba_3.6.1-3_amd64.deb is a Debian package file for the samba package, version 3.6.1, revision 3, for AMD64 (*x*86-64) CPUs. You can install such files using dpkg or apt-get, or you can use apt-get to download a package and its dependencies from the Internet, using its install command, as in:

```
# apt-get install samba
```

◀

Third-party implementations of APT for many RPM-based distributions also exist. See http:// apt4rpm.source forge.net for details. At least one RPM-based distribution, PCLinuxOS, uses APT natively.

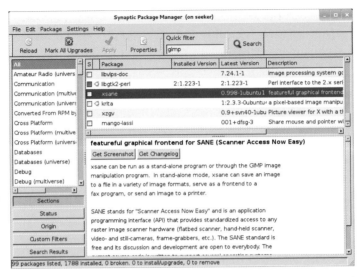

FIGURE 9.2 Synaptic enables you to search for, select, install, and uninstall software on Debian-based systems.

As with RPM packages, you can remove packages or upgrade your computer's software, too:

```
# apt-get remove zsh
# apt-get upgrade
```

APT is a powerful tool, as is the underlying dpkg. You should consult these programs' man pages to learn more about how to use these programs.

Understanding the Process Hierarchy

The Linux *kernel* is the core of a Linux installation. The kernel manages memory, provides software with a way to access the hard disk, doles out CPU time, and performs other critical low-level tasks. The kernel is loaded early in the boot process, and it's the kernel that's responsible for managing every other piece of software on a running Linux computer.

One of the many ways that the kernel imposes order on the potentially chaotic set of running software is to create a sort of hierarchy. When it boots, the kernel runs just one program—normally /sbin/init. The init process is then responsible for starting all the other basic programs that Linux must run, such as the programs that manage logins and always-up servers. Such programs, if launched directly by init, are called its *children*. The children of init can in turn launch their own children. This happens when you log into Linux. The process that launched a given process is called its *parent*.

You can change which program runs as the first process by adding the init= option to your boot loader's kernel option line, as in init=/bin/bash to run bash.

The result of this system is a treelike hierarchy of processes, as illustrated in Figure 9.3. ("Trees" in computer science are often depicted upside down.) Figure 9.3 shows a small subset of the many processes that run on a typical Linux installation: just a few processes associated with a text-mode login, including the `login` tool that manages logins, a couple of `bash` shells, and a few user programs. A working Linux system will likely have dozens or hundreds of running processes. The one on which I'm typing these words has 213 processes going at once!

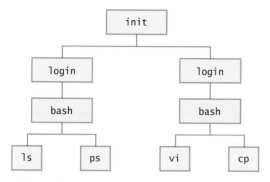

FIGURE 9.3 Linux processes are arranged in a hierarchical tree.

Every process has associated with it a process ID (PID) number. These numbers begin with 1, so `init`'s PID is normally 1. Each process also has a parent process ID (PPID) number, which points to its parent. Many of the tools for managing processes rely on these numbers, and particularly on the PID number.

Identifying Running Processes

Before you can manage processes, you must be able to identify them. The `ps` and `top` utilities can help you identify processes. In either case, you can search for processes in various ways, such as by name or by resource use. You may also want to identify how much memory your processes are consuming, which you can do with the `free` command.

Using *ps* to Identify Processes

The simplest tool for identifying processes is `ps`, which produces a process listing. Listing 9.1 shows an example of `ps` in action. In this example, the `-u` option restricts output to processes owned by the specified user (`rodsmith`), while `--forest` creates a display that shows parent/child relationships.

Certification Objective

Occasionally, a process will terminate but leave behind children. When this happens, `init` "adopts" those child processes.

Internally, the kernel maintains process information in the *process table*. Tools such as `ps` and `top` (described shortly) enable you to view and manipulate this table.

Certification Objective

Listing 9.1: Output of `ps -u rodsmith --forest`

```
$ ps -u rodsmith --forest
  PID TTY          TIME CMD
 2451 pts/3     00:00:00 bash
 2551 pts/3     00:00:00 ps
 2496 ?         00:00:00 kvt
 2498 pts/1     00:00:00 bash
 2505 pts/1     00:00:00  \_ nedit
 2506 ?         00:00:00      \_ csh
 2544 ?         00:00:00          \_ xeyes
19221 ?         00:00:01 dfm
```

Listing 9.2 shows a second example of ps. In this example, the u option adds informational columns, while U rodsmith restricts output to processes owned by rodsmith. The ps command supports a huge number of options (consult its man page for details).

The version of ps **used in most Linux distributions combines features from several earlier** ps **implementations. The result is a huge selection of sometimes redundant options.**

Listing 9.2: Output of `ps u U rodsmith`

```
$ ps u U rodsmith
USER       PID %CPU %MEM   VSZ  RSS TTY      STAT START  TIME COMMAND
rodsmith 19221  0.0  1.5  4484 1984 ?        S    May07  0:01 dfm
rodsmith  2451  0.0  0.8  1856 1048 pts/3    S    16:13  0:00 -bash
rodsmith  2496  0.2  3.2  6232 4124 ?        S    16:17  0:00 /opt/kd
rodsmith  2498  0.0  0.8  1860 1044 pts/1    S    16:17  0:00 bash
rodsmith  2505  0.1  2.6  4784 3332 pts/1    S    16:17  0:00 nedit
rodsmith  2506  0.0  0.7  2124 1012 ?        S    16:17  0:00 /bin/cs
rodsmith  2544  0.0  1.0  2576 1360 ?        S    16:17  0:00 xeyes
rodsmith  2556  0.0  0.7  2588  916 pts/3    R    16:18  0:00 ps u U
```

Given the large number of ps options, different users can have different favorite ways to use the program. I find that typing **ps ax** usually produces the information I want, including PID values and command names (including command-line options) for all the processes on the computer. Adding u (as in **ps aux**) adds usernames, CPU loads, and a few other tidbits. The sheer scope of the information produced, however, can be overwhelming. One way to narrow this scope is to pipe the results through grep, which eliminates lines that don't include the search criterion you specify. For instance, if you want to know the PID number for the gedit process, you can do so like this:

Because ps ax **produces commands with their options, using** grep **to search for a string in the output returns the searched-for command, as well as the** grep **command itself.**

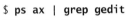

```
$ ps ax | grep gedit
27946 pts/8    Sl      0:00 gedit
27950 pts/8    S+      0:00 grep --colour=auto gedit
```

This command reveals that gedit has a PID value of 27946. This is usually the most important information when you use ps, since you'll use the PID value to change a process's priority or terminate it.

Using *top* to Identify Processes

Although ps can return process priority and CPU use information, the program's output is usually sorted by PID number, and provides information at only a single moment in time. If you want to quickly locate CPU- or memory-hogging processes, or if you want to study how resource use varies over time, another tool is more appropriate: top. This program is essentially an interactive version of ps. Figure 9.4 shows top running in a GNOME Terminal window.

Certification
Objective

```
                                    rodsmith@f15beta:~                      _  □  ×

File  Edit  View  Search  Terminal  Help
top - 17:12:56 up  1:31,  4 users,  load average: 0.12, 0.08, 0.12
Tasks: 148 total,   1 running, 147 sleeping,   0 stopped,   0 zombie
Cpu(s): 10.0%us, 22.3%sy,  0.0%ni, 67.7%id,  0.0%wa,  0.0%hi,  0.0%si,  0.0%st
Mem:   1023448k total,   818456k used,   204992k free,    56068k buffers
Swap:  2031612k total,    58448k used,  1973164k free,   401912k cached

  PID USER      PR  NI  VIRT  RES  SHR S %CPU %MEM    TIME+  COMMAND
 1198 root      20   0  153m  32m 2848 S 14.0  3.3  1:44.88 Xorg
 1960 rodsmith  20   0  723m  25m 9604 S 12.0  2.6  3:59.16 gnome-system-mo
 1701 rodsmith  20   0 1209m  16m 6056 S  1.7  1.7  1:23.24 knotify4
 2142 rodsmith  20   0 53040 7608 1684 S  1.0  0.7  0:03.11 xv
 1693 rodsmith  20   0  624m  10m 5832 S  0.3  1.1  0:04.85 kded4
    1 root      20   0 40244 7520 1616 S  0.0  0.7  0:03.96 systemd
    2 root      20   0     0    0    0 S  0.0  0.0  0:00.00 kthreadd
    3 root      20   0     0    0    0 S  0.0  0.0  0:01.11 ksoftirqd/0
    6 root      RT   0     0    0    0 S  0.0  0.0  0:00.00 migration/0
    7 root       0 -20     0    0    0 S  0.0  0.0  0:00.00 cpuset
    8 root       0 -20     0    0    0 S  0.0  0.0  0:00.00 khelper
    9 root       0 -20     0    0    0 S  0.0  0.0  0:00.00 netns
   10 root      20   0     0    0    0 S  0.0  0.0  0:00.00 sync_supers
   11 root      20   0     0    0    0 S  0.0  0.0  0:00.00 bdi-default
   12 root       0 -20     0    0    0 S  0.0  0.0  0:00.00 kintegrityd
   13 root       0 -20     0    0    0 S  0.0  0.0  0:00.00 kblockd
   14 root       0 -20     0    0    0 S  0.0  0.0  0:00.00 kacpid
```

FIGURE 9.4 The top command shows system summary information and information about the most CPU-intensive processes on a computer.

By default, top sorts its entries by CPU use, and it updates its display every few seconds. You'll need to be familiar with the purposes and normal habits of programs running on *your* system in order to determine if a CPU-hungry application is misbehaving; the legitimate needs of different programs vary so much that it's impossible to give a simple rule for judging when a process is consuming too much CPU time.

You can do more with top than watch it update its display. When it's running, you can enter any of several single-letter commands, some of which prompt you for additional information, as summarized in Table 9.1. Additional commands are described in top's man page.

TABLE 9.1 Common top commands

Command	Description
h or ?	These keystrokes display help information.
k	You can kill a process with this command. The top program will ask for a PID number, and if it's able to kill the process, it will do so.
q	This option quits from top.
r	You can change a process's priority with this command.
s	This command changes the display's update rate, which you'll be asked to enter (in seconds).
P	This command sets the display to sort by CPU usage, which is the default.
M	You can change the display to sort by memory usage with this command.

One of the pieces of information provided by top is the *load average,* which is a measure of the demand for CPU time by applications. In Figure 9.4, you can see three load-average estimates on the top line; these correspond to the current load average and two previous measures. Load averages can be interpreted as follows:

Most computers sold today are multicore models, but single-core models dominated the marketplace prior to about 2006.

▶ A system on which no programs are demanding CPU time has a load average of 0.

▶ A system with one program running a CPU-intensive task has a load average of 1.

▶ Higher load averages on a single-CPU system reflect programs competing for available CPU time.

▶ On a computer with multiple CPUs or CPU cores, load averages can reach the number of CPUs or cores before competition for CPU time begins. For instance, a load average of 4.0 on a system with a 4-core CPU reflects processes demanding exactly as much CPU time as the computer has available.

The w command, described in Chapter 13, can tell you how much CPU time entire terminal sessions are consuming.

The load average can be useful in detecting runaway processes. For instance, if a system normally has a load average of 0.5 but it suddenly gets stuck at a load average of 2.5, a couple of CPU-hogging processes may have *hung*—that is, become unresponsive. Hung processes sometimes needlessly consume a lot of CPU time. You can use top to locate these processes and, if necessary, kill them.

Measuring Memory Use

Processes consume a number of system resources, the most important of these being CPU time and memory. As already noted, top sorts your processes by CPU time by default, so you can identify processes that are consuming the most CPU time. You can press the M key within top to have it sort by memory use, thus identifying the processes that are consuming the most memory. As with CPU time, you can't say that a process is consuming too much memory simply because it's at the top of the list, though; some programs legitimately consume a great deal of memory. Nonetheless, sometimes a program consumes too much memory, either because of inefficient coding or because of a *memory leak*—a type of program bug in which the program requests memory from the kernel and then fails to return it when it's done with the memory. A program with a memory leak consumes increasing amounts of memory, sometimes to the point where it interferes with other programs. As a short-term solution, you can usually terminate the program and launch it again, which resets the program's memory consumption, something like draining a sink that's filled with water from a leaky faucet. The problem will recur, but if the memory leak is small enough, you'll at least be able to get useful work done in the meantime.

If you want to study the computer's overall memory use, the free command is useful. This program generates a report on the computer's total memory status:

Certification Objective

The kernel grants programs access to sets of memory addresses, which the programs can then use. When a program is done, it should release its memory back to the kernel.

```
$ free
             total       used       free     shared    buffers     cached
Mem:       7914888    7734456     180432          0     190656    3244720
-/+ buffers/cache:    4299080    3615808
Swap:      6291452    1030736    5260716
```

The Mem: line reveals total random access memory (RAM) statistics, including the total memory in the computer (minus whatever is used by the motherboard and kernel), the amount of memory used, and the amount of free memory. This example shows that most of the computer's memory is in use. Such a state is normal, since Linux puts otherwise unused memory to use as buffers and caches, which help speed up disk access. Thus, the Mem: line isn't the most useful; instead, you should examine the -/+ buffers/cache: line, which shows the total memory used by the computer's programs. In this example, 4,299,080 KiB of 7,914,888 KiB are in use, leaving 3,615,808 KiB free. In other words, a bit over half the computer's memory is in use by programs, so there should be no memory-related performance problems.

The Swap: line reveals how much *swap space* Linux is using. Swap space is disk space that's set aside as an adjunct to memory. Linux uses swap space when it runs out of RAM, or when it determines that RAM is better used for buffers or caches than to hold currently inactive programs. In this example, 1,030,736 KiB of swap space is in use, with 6,291,452 KiB total, for 5,260,716 free. Swap space use is generally quite low, and if it rises very much, you can suffer performance problems. In the long run, increasing the computer's RAM is generally the best solution to such problems. If you're suffering from performance problems because of excessive swap use and you need immediate relief, terminating some memory-hogging programs can help. Memory leaks, described earlier, can lead to such problems, and terminating the leaking program can restore system performance to normal.

The `free` command supports a number of options, most of which modify its display format. The most useful of these is `-m`, which causes the display to use units of mebibytes (MiB) rather than the default of kibibytes (KiB).

Using Log Files

Many programs that run in the background (that is, daemons) write information about their normal operations to *log files*, which are files that record such notes. Consulting log files can therefore be an important part of diagnosing problems with daemons. The first step in doing this is to locate your log files. In some cases, you may need to tell the program to produce more verbose output to help track down the problem, so I provide some pointers on how to do that. Finally, I describe the kernel ring buffer, which isn't technically a log file but can fill a similar role for kernel information.

Locating Log Files

Certification Objective ▶

Linux stores most log files in the /var/log directory tree. Some log files reside in that directory, but some servers create entire subdirectories in which to store their own log files. Table 9.2 summarizes some common log files on many Linux systems. In addition, many server programs not described in this book add their own log files or subdirectories of /var/log. If you experience problems with such a server, checking its log files can be a good place to start troubleshooting.

Log file details vary between distributions, so some of the files in Table 9.2 may not be present on your system, or the files you find may have different names.

TABLE 9.2 Important log files

Log file	Contents
boot.log	This file summarizes the services that are started late in the boot process via SysV startup scripts.

(Continues)

TABLE 9.2 *(Continued)*

Log file	Contents
cron	This file summarizes processes that are run at regular intervals via the cron daemon. Although this book doesn't cover cron, a problem with it can cause glitches that recur at regular intervals, so you should be aware of it.
cups/	This directory holds log files related to the Linux printing system.
gdm/	This directory holds log files related to the GNOME Display Manager (GDM), which handles GUI logins on many systems.
messages or syslog	This is a general-purpose log file that contains messages from many daemons that lack their own dedicated log files.
secure	You can find security-related messages in this file, including notices of when users employ su, sudo, and similar tools to acquire root privileges.
Xorg.0.log	Information on the most recent startup of the X Window System (X) appears in this log file.

Log files are frequently *rotated*, meaning that the oldest log file is deleted, the latest log file is renamed with a date or number, and a new log file is created. For instance, if it's rotated on December 1, 2012, /var/log/messages will become /var/log/messages-20121201, /var/log/messages-1.gz, or something similar, and a new /var/log/messages will be created. This practice keeps log files from growing out of control.

Most log files are plain text files, so you can check them using any tool that can examine text files, such as less or a text editor. One particularly handy command is tail, which displays the last ten lines of a file (or as many lines as you specify with the -n option). For instance, typing **tail /var/log/messages** shows you the last ten lines of that file.

Note that not all programs log messages. Typically, only daemons do so; ordinary user programs display error messages in other ways—in GUI dialog boxes or in a text-mode terminal. If you think a program should be logging data but you can't find it, consult its documentation. Alternatively, you can use grep to try to find the log file to which the program is sending its messages. For instance, typing **grep sshd /var/log/*** finds the files in which the string sshd (the SSH daemon's name) appears.

◀

Log file rotation occurs late at night, so it won't happen if you shut off your computer. Leave it running overnight periodically to ensure log files are rotated.

**Certification
Objective**

CREATING LOG FILES

Some programs create their own log files; however, most rely on a utility known generically as the *system log daemon* to do this job. This program's process name is generally syslog or syslogd. Like other daemons, it's started during the boot process by the system startup scripts. Several system log daemon packages are available. Some of them provide a separate tool, klog or klogd, to handle logging messages from the kernel separately from ordinary programs.

You can modify the behavior of the log daemon, including adjusting the files to which it logs particular types of messages, by adjusting its configuration file. The name of this file depends on the specific daemon in use, but it's typically /etc/rsyslog.conf or something similar. The details of log file configuration are beyond the scope of this book, but you should be aware that such details can be altered. This fact accounts for much of the distribution-to-distribution variability in log file features.

Once it's running, a log daemon accepts messages from other processes using a technique known as *system messaging*. It then sorts through the messages and directs them to a suitable log file depending on the message's source and a priority code.

Producing More Verbose Log File Entries

Sometimes log files don't provide enough information to pin down the source of a problem. Fortunately, many programs that produce log file output can be configured to produce *more* such output. Unfortunately, doing so can sometimes make it harder to sift through all the entries for the relevant information.

The procedure for increasing the verbosity of log file output varies from one program to another. Typically, you must set an option in the program's configuration file. You should consult the program's documentation to learn how to do this.

Because the kernel ring buffer has a limited size, its earliest entries can be lost if the computer runs for a long time or if something produces many entries.

**Certification
Objective**

Examining the Kernel Ring Buffer

The kernel ring buffer is something like a log file for the kernel; however, unlike other log files, it's stored in memory rather than in a disk file. Like regular log files, its contents continue to change as the computer runs. To examine the kernel ring buffer, you can type **dmesg**. Doing so creates copious output, though, so you'll typically pipe the output through less:

```
$ dmesg | less
```

Alternatively, if you know that the information you want will be associated with a particular string, you can use grep to search for it. For instance, to find kernel ring buffer messages about the first hard disk, /dev/sda, you might type the following:

```
$ dmesg | grep sda
```

Kernel ring buffer messages can be particularly arcane; however, they can also be invaluable in diagnosing hardware and driver problems, since it's the kernel's job to interface with hardware. You might try searching the kernel ring buffer if a hardware device is behaving strangely. Even if you don't understand a message you find, you could try feeding that message into a Web search engine or passing it on to a more knowledgeable colleague for advice.

Some distributions place a copy of the kernel ring buffer when the system first boots in /var/log/dmesg or a similar file. You can consult this file if the computer has been running for long enough for its earliest entries to be lost. If you want to create such a file on a distribution that doesn't do so by default, you can edit the /etc/rc.d/rc.local file and add the following line to its end:

```
dmesg > /var/log/dmesg
```

THE ESSENTIALS AND BEYOND

An operating Linux computer can be thought of as consisting of running programs—that is, processes. Managing processes begins with managing the programs that are installed on the computer, which is a task you can perform with package management tools such as rpm or dpkg. You can learn what processes are running by using tools such as ps and top. Log files can help you learn about the actions of daemons, which may not be able to communicate error messages through the type of text-mode or GUI output that other programs can generate.

SUGGESTED EXERCISES

▶ Is your distribution's software up to date? Locate the option in your desktop environment's menus to run a package manager and check that the system is up to date. A computer running out-of-date software can be vulnerable to bugs and security threats, so keeping your software updated is important!

▶ Type **ps ax | less** and browse through the process list. You might not recognize many of the processes, but some should be familiar. Try using man or a Web search to learn more about some of the processes you don't recognize.

(Continues)

THE ESSENTIALS AND BEYOND *(Continued)*

REVIEW QUESTIONS

1. Which of the following tools is best suited to installing a software package and all its dependencies on a Debian computer?

   A. yum

   B. zypper

   C. dmesg

   D. rpm

   E. apt-get

2. What is the usual name of the first process that the Linux kernel runs, aside from itself?

   A. init

   B. bash

   C. cron

   D. login

   E. grub

3. Where do most log files reside on a Linux computer?

   A. /var/log

   B. /etc/logging

   C. /usr/log

   D. /home/logging

   E. /log/usr

4. True or false: When using suitable commands, you can normally install a program and be sure that all the software on which it depends will also be installed, provided you have an Internet connection.

5. True or false: By default, the first process listed in top is currently consuming the most CPU time.

6. True or false: The dmesg command may produce different output after a computer has been running for weeks than when it first started.

7. Most Linux distributions maintain information on what packages are installed in the _____ _____. (Two words.)

8. You're using bash, and you type **emacs** to launch the emacs editor. In this case, emacs is bash's _____.

9. General system messages are likely to be found in /var/log/messages or /var/log/_____, depending on your distribution.

## CHAPTER 10

Searching, Extracting, and Archiving Data

Although the word "computer" suggests a device for performing mathematical computations, much of a computer's job has more to do with data storage and retrieval than with computation. This chapter covers some of the tools you can use to search, extract, and archive data.

The chapter begins with a look at *regular expressions*, which are a way to describe patterns you might want to look for in data files. You can use regular expressions with many commands, two of which (find and grep) I describe in more detail. This chapter also covers tools that you can use to redirect programs' input and output, which is a useful trick in many situations. Finally, I describe some tools for creating archive files, which can be useful in transferring many files over a network or in creating backups.

► **Using regular expressions**

► **Searching for and extracting data**

► **Redirecting input and output**

► **Archiving data**

Using Regular Expressions

Certification Objective

Documentation sometimes uses the abbreviation *regexp* to refer to a regular expression.

Many Linux programs employ regular expressions, which are tools for expressing patterns in text. Regular expressions are similar in principle to the wildcards that can be used to specify multiple filenames, as described in Chapter 7, "Managing Files." At their simplest, regular expressions can be plain text without adornment. Certain characters are used to denote patterns, though.

Two forms of regular expression are common: basic and extended. Which form you must use depends on the program; some accept just one form, but others can use either type, depending on the options passed to the program. (Some programs use their own minor or major variants on either of these classes of regular expression.) The differences between basic and extended regular expressions are complex and subtle, but the fundamental principles of both are similar.

The simplest type of regular expression is an alphabetic or alphanumeric string, such as HWaddr or Linux3. These regular expressions match any string of the same size or longer that contains the regular expression. For instance, the HWaddr regular expression matches HWaddr, This is the HWaddr, and The HWaddr is unknown. The real strength of regular expressions comes in the use of non-alphanumeric characters, which activate advanced matching rules. The most powerful basic regular expression features include the following:

Bracket expressions   Characters enclosed in square brackets ([]) constitute bracket expressions, which match any one character within the brackets. For instance, the regular expression b[aeiou]g matches the words bag, beg, big, bog, and bug. Including a carat (^) after the opening square bracket matches against any character *except* the ones specified. For instance, b[^aeiou]g matches bbg or bAg but not bag or beg.

Range expressions   A range expression is a variant on a bracket expression. Instead of listing every character that matches, range expressions list the start and end points separated by a dash (-), as in a[2-4]z. This regular expression matches a2z, a3z, and a4z.

Any single character   The dot (.) represents any single character except a newline. For instance, a.z matches a2z, abz, aQz, or any other three-character string that begins with a and ends with z.

Start and end of line   The carat (^) represents the start of a line, and the dollar sign ($) denotes the end of a line.

Repetition   A full or partial regular expression may be followed by a special symbol to denote repetition of the matched item. Specifically, an asterisk (*) denotes zero or more matches. The asterisk is often combined with the dot (as in .*) to specify a match with any substring. For instance, A.*Lincoln matches any string that contains A and Lincoln, in that order—Abe Lincoln and Abraham Lincoln are just two possible matches.

Escaping   If you want to match one of the special characters, such as a dot, you must *escape* it—that is, precede it with a backslash (\). For instance, to match a computer hostname (say, `twain.example.com`), you must escape the dots, as in `twain\.example\.com`.

Extended regular expressions add more features you can use to match in additional ways:

Additional repetition operators   These operators work like an asterisk, but they match only certain numbers of matches. Specifically, a plus sign (+) matches one or more occurrences and a question mark (?) specifies zero or one match.

Multiple possible strings   The vertical bar (|) separates two possible matches; for instance, `car|truck` matches either `car` or `truck`.

Parentheses   Ordinary parentheses (()) surround subexpressions. Parentheses are often used to specify how operators are to be applied; for example, you can put parentheses around a group of words that are concatenated with the vertical bar to ensure that the words are treated as a group, any one of which may match, without involving surrounding parts of the regular expression.

Whether you use basic or extended regular expressions depends on which form the program supports. For programs such as `grep` that support both, you can use either; which you choose is mostly a matter of personal preference. Note that a regular expression that includes characters associated with extended regular expressions will be interpreted differently depending on which type you're using. Thus, it's important to know which type of regular expression a program supports, or how to select which type to use if the program supports both types.

Regular expression rules can be confusing, particularly when you're first introduced to them. Some examples of their use, in the context of the programs that use them, will help. The next section provides such examples, with reference to the `find` and `grep` programs.

Searching for and Extracting Data

Two commands, `grep` and `find`, both use regular expressions and are helpful in locating data. The `grep` utility locates files by scanning their contents. The `grep` program also returns some of the data included in files, which can be useful if you want to extract just a little data from a file or from a program's output. As its name suggests, `find` locates files. It uses surface features, such as the filename and the file's date stamps. Another command, `wc`, provides basic statistics on text files.

> Technically, of these three programs, only `grep` uses regular expressions, although `find` supports pattern matching using a similar mechanism.
>
>

Using *grep*

Certification Objective

The grep command searches for files that contain a specified string and returns the name of the file and (if it's a text file) a line of context for that string. To use grep, you type the command's name, an optional set of options, a regular expression, and an optional filename specification. The grep command supports a large number of options, the most common of which appear in Table 10.1.

> **If you don't specify a filename, grep uses standard input. This can be useful with pipelines, as described shortly, in "Redirecting Input and Output."**

TABLE 10.1 Common grep options

Option (long form)	Option (short form)	Description
--count	-c	Instead of displaying the lines that contain matches to the regular expression, display the number of lines that match.
--file=*file*	-f *file*	This option takes pattern input from the specified file rather than from the command line. The fgrep command is a shortcut for this option.
--ignore-case	-i	You can perform a case-insensitive search, rather than the default case-sensitive search, by using the -i or --ignore-case option.
--recursive	-R or -r	This option searches in the specified directory and all subdirectories rather than simply the specified directory. You can use rgrep rather than specify this option.
--extended-regexp	-E	The grep command uses basic regular expressions by default. To use an extended regular expression, you can pass this option. Alternatively, you can call egrep rather than grep; this variant command uses extended regular expressions by default.

A simple example of grep uses a regular expression with no special components:

```
$ grep -r eth0 /etc/*
```

This example finds all the files in /etc that contain the string eth0 (the identifier for the first Ethernet device on most distributions). Because the example includes the -r option, it searches recursively, so grep searches files in subdirectories of /etc as well as those in /etc itself. For each matching text file, the line that contains the string is printed.

Ramping up a bit, suppose you want to locate all the files in /etc that contain the string eth0 or eth1. You can enter the following command, which uses a bracket expression to specify both variant devices:

```
$ grep eth[01] /etc/*
```

A still more complex example searches all files in /etc that contain the number 127 and, later on the same line, the hostname twain.example.com or localhost. This task requires using several of the regular expression features. Expressed using extended regular expression notation, the command looks like this:

```
$ grep -E "127.*(twain\.example\.com|localhost)" /etc/*
```

This command illustrates another feature you may need to use: shell quoting. Because the shell uses certain characters, such as the vertical bar and the asterisk, for its own purposes, you must enclose certain regular expressions in quotes lest the shell attempt to parse the regular expression as shell commands.

You can use grep in conjunction with commands that produce a lot of output in order to sift through that output for the material that's important to you. (Several examples throughout this book use this technique.) For example, suppose you want to find the process ID (PID) of a running xterm. You can use a pipe to send the result of a ps command through grep:

```
# ps ax | grep xterm
```

The result is a list of all running processes called xterm, along with their PIDs. You can even do this in series, using grep to further restrict the output on some other criterion, which can be useful if the initial pass still produces too much output. For instance, suppose you want to find kernel messages relating to low-speed Universal Serial Bus (USB) devices. As noted in Chapter 9, "Using Programs and Processes," you can use dmesg to review kernel messages, but it produces copious output. You can pass this output through grep to find messages related to USB devices or to messages that include the word low, but either search alone still produces a lot of irrelevant hits. Using grep twice

Ordinary users can't read some files in /etc. Thus, if you type this command as a non-root user, you'll see error messages relating to grep's inability to open files.

Type this command on your computer. It should match at least one file, /etc/hosts. Type it again *without* the -E option to see its operation using basic regular expressions.

The upcoming section, "Redirecting Input and Output," describes pipes in more detail.

in succession successfully limits the output to lines that include both search strings:

```
$ dmesg | grep -i usb | grep low
usb 4-1.1: new low speed USB device number 3 using uhci_hcd
usb 4-1.2.2: new low speed USB device number 5 using uhci_hcd
usb 4-1.2.2: new low speed USB device number 8 using uhci_hcd
```

This differs from using a single grep command with both search terms (using a regular expression such as usb.*low) in that the order in which the search terms appear is important for the single search but not when using grep twice. You can also use different options when you call grep twice, as in the use of -i when searching on usb but not when searching on low in this example.

Using *find*

Certification Objective

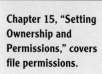

In practice, you must use a pathname or a search criterion with find, **and often both.**

The find utility implements a brute-force approach to finding files. This program finds files by searching through the specified directory tree, checking filenames, file creation dates, and so on to locate the files that match the specified criteria. Because of this method of operation, find tends to be slow, but it's very flexible and is very likely to succeed, assuming the file for which you're searching exists. To use find, type its name, optionally followed by a pathname and a series of options, some of which use specifications that are similar to regular expressions.

You can specify one or more paths in which find should operate; the program will restrict its operations to these paths. The man page for find includes information about its search criteria, but Table 10.2 summarizes common criteria.

Chapter 15, "Setting Ownership and Permissions," covers file permissions.

TABLE 10.2 Common find search criteria

Option	Description
-name *pattern*	You can search for files using their names with this option. Doing so finds files that match the specified *pattern*. This *pattern* is not technically a regular expression, but it does support many regular expression features.
-perm *mode*	If you need to find files that have certain permissions, you can do so by using the -perm *mode* expression. The *mode* may be expressed either symbolically or in octal form. If you precede mode with a +, find locates files in which any of the specified permission bits are set. If you precede *mode* with a -, find locates files in which *all* the specified permission bits are set.

TABLE 10.2 (Continued)

Option	Description
-size *n*	You can search for files based on size with this expression. Normally, *n* is specified in 512-byte blocks, but you can modify this by trailing the value with a letter code, such as *c* for characters (bytes) or k for kilobytes.
-group *name*	This option searches for files that belong to the specified group.
-gid *GID*	This expression searches for files whose group ID (GID) is set to *GID*.
-user *name*	This option searches for files that are owned by the specified user.
-uid *UID*	You can search for files by user ID (UID) number using this option.
-maxdepth *levels*	If you want to search a directory and, perhaps, some limited number of subdirectories, you can use this expression to limit the search.

There are many variant and additional options; find is a very powerful command. As an example of its use, consider the task of finding all C source code files, which normally have names that end in .c, in all users' home directories. If these home directories reside in /home, you might issue the following command:

```
# find /home -name "*.c"
```

The result will be a listing of all the files that match the search criteria.

> If you lack permission to list a directory's contents, find **will return that directory name and the error message** Permission denied.
>
>

Using *wc*

Certification
Objective

A file's size in bytes, as revealed by ls or searched for using find, can be a useful metric. This size value isn't always the most useful one for text files, though. For instance, you might need to know how many words or lines are in a text file—say because you're writing a 1,000-word essay or you want to know how many pages a text document will consume when printed at 52 lines per page. The wc utility provides this information. By default, it displays a count of lines (newline characters, to be precise), words, and bytes for each file you pass it. For instance, you can discover this information for all the files with .txt extensions in your home directory:

```
$ wc ~/*.txt
  1471   1839  71039 /home/rodsmith/500.txt
    31    180   1236 /home/rodsmith/Commands Outputs.txt
  1012   8909  69689 /home/rodsmith/parts.txt
    19     33    383 /home/rodsmith/Problem.txt
     4      4     31 /home/rodsmith/stuff.txt
```

This output reveals that the file 500.txt contains 1,471 lines, 1,839 words, and 71,039 bytes, and provides similar statistics for the remaining files.

You can pass options to limit or expand wc's output, as summarized in Table 10.3. Of the options in Table 10.3, -c, -l, and -w are the defaults, so typing **wc** *file.txt* is equivalent to typing **wc -clw** *file.txt*. The program's man page describes a few more options, but the ones in Table 10.3 are the ones you're most likely to use.

TABLE 10.3 Common wc options

Option (long form)	Option (short form)	Description
--bytes	-c	Displays the file's byte count
--chars	-m	Displays the file's character count
--lines	-l	Displays the file's newline count
--words	-w	Displays the file's word count
--max-line-length	-L	Displays the length of the longest line in the file

Some text files use multi-byte encodings, meaning that one character can consume more than one byte. Thus, -c and -m may not produce identical results, although they often do.

Be aware that wc works correctly on plain text files, but it may produce incorrect or even nonsensical results on formatted text files, such as Hypertext Markup Language (HTML) files or word processor files. You're better off using a word processor or other specialized editor to find the number of words and other statistics for such files.

Redirecting Input and Output

If the output of a program becomes annoying, or if you want to save it for future reference, you can *redirect* it to a file. You can also redirect the input to a program from a file. Although input redirection may sound strange, some programs rely on this feature to enable them to process data, such as raw text files fed through a program that searches the text for patterns. In addition to redirecting output to files or input from files, you can pass one program's output to another one as its input. A related technique involves the xargs command, which enables you to generate command-line options from files or other programs' output.

Using Basic Redirection Operators

Redirection is achieved with the help of *redirection operators*, which are short strings that appear after the command and its arguments. Table 10.4 shows the most common redirection operators. Be aware that output comes in two types:

Certification Objective

Standard output　This is normal program messages.

Standard error　This contains error messages.

◀

TABLE 10.4 Common redirection operators

Having two types of output enables them to be separated so that error messages don't confuse programs that might be expecting certain types of input from another program.

Redirection operator	Effect
>	Creates a new file containing standard output. If the specified file exists, it's overwritten.
>>	Appends standard output to the existing file. If the specified file doesn't exist, it's created.
2>	Creates a new file containing standard error. If the specified file exists, it's overwritten.
2>>	Appends standard error to the existing file. If the specified file doesn't exist, it's created.
&>	Creates a new file containing both standard output and standard error. If the specified file exists, it's overwritten.
<	Sends the contents of the specified file to be used as standard input.
<<	Accepts text on the following lines as standard input.
<>	Causes the specified file to be used for both standard input and standard output.

As an example of redirecting output, consider a grep command to search for information on a particular user in all the configuration files in /etc. Without redirection, such a command might look like this:

```
$ grep david /etc/*
```

This command will return a series of output lines like the following:

```
Binary file /etc/aliases.db matches
/etc/group:wheel:x:10:root,david
/etc/group:audio:x:18:mythtv,david,pulse
/etc/group:cdrom:x:19:haldaemon,david
```

Such output can be quite lengthy, and you might want to peruse it later. To do so, you could redirect the output like this:

```
$ grep david /etc/* > david-in-etc.txt
```

If you then wanted to see the output, you could use cat:

```
$ cat david-in-etc.txt
```

Many programs have options, set on the command line or in configuration files, that affect how verbose their output is. Check a program's man **page to learn about such options.**

In this example you haven't gained anything compared to simply typing **grep david /etc/***, but you might in other cases. For instance, suppose a command is producing copious error messages. You might then redirect standard error to a file and load the file into a text editor so that you can browse through it, search for strings that might be relevant, and so on, even as you attempt to run the command, or a modified version of it, once more.

This example illustrates how standard error and standard output are separate. If you type **grep *david* /etc/*** as a normal user (perhaps substituting your own username for *david*), you're likely to see output such as that shown earlier, specifying the files in which your username appears; however, you're also likely to see error messages, since you lack permission to read some of the files in /etc:

```
grep: /etc/securetty: Permission denied
grep: /etc/shadow: Permission denied
```

The information on the files in which *david* appears is shown via standard output, but the errors are shown via standard error. If you're not interested in the errors, you can redirect them to /dev/null—a device file that serves as a "dumping ground" for data you want to discard:

```
$ grep david /etc/* 2> /dev/null
```

Likewise, if you redirect standard output to a file but do *not* redirect standard error, you'll see the error messages on your screen, but the file you create (such as david-in-etc.txt from the earlier command) will not contain the error messages. You may want to try all the different types of output redirection using **grep** *david* **/etc/*** to get a feel for how they work.

Using Pipes

Another type of redirected output is a *pipe* or *pipeline*. In a pipe, the standard output from one program is redirected as the standard input to a second program. You create a pipe by using a vertical bar (|), which is usually a shifted character above the Enter key, between the two commands. Pipelines can be useful when applied in various ways. For instance, you might pipe the lengthy output of a program through the less pager, which enables you to page up and down through the output, or use grep to search for keywords in the output:

Certification Objective

Chapter 8, "Getting Help," describes the less pager.

```
$ dmesg | grep sda
```

The dmesg command displays messages from the Linux kernel about hardware and other low-level activities. Thus, the result of these two commands is that you'll see any kernel messages that include the string sda—an identifier associated with the first hard disk.

Generating Command Lines

Sometimes you'll find yourself constructing a series of commands that are similar to each other but not similar enough to enable you to use their normal options to substitute a single command. For instance, suppose you want to remove every file in a directory tree with a name that ends in a tilde (~). (This filename convention denotes backup files created by certain text editors.) With a large directory tree, this task can be daunting; the usual file-deletion command (rm, described in more detail in Chapter 7) doesn't provide an option to search for and delete every file in a directory tree that matches such a specific criterion. One command that can do the search part of the job, though, is find, which is described in more detail earlier. If you could combine the output of find to create a series of command lines using rm, the task would be solved. This is precisely the purpose of the xargs command, which builds a command from its standard input. The basic syntax for this command is as follows:

Certification Objective

```
xargs [options] [command [initial-arguments]]
```

The *command* is the command you want to execute, and *initial-arguments* is a list of arguments you want to pass to the command. The *options* are xargs options; they aren't passed to *command*. When you run xargs, it runs *command* once for every word passed to it on standard input, adding that word to the argument list for *command*. If you want to pass multiple options to the command, you can protect them by enclosing the group in quotation marks.

For instance, consider the task of deleting all those backup files, denoted by tilde characters. You can do this by piping the output of find to xargs, which then calls rm:

```
$ find ./ -name "*~" | xargs rm
```

The first part of this command (**find ./ -name** "*~") finds all the files in the current directory (./) or its subdirectories with a name that ends in a tilde (*~). This list is then piped to xargs, which adds each one to its own rm command.

A tool that's similar to xargs in many ways is the backtick (`), which is a character to the left of the 1 key on most keyboards. The backtick is *not* the same as the single quote character ('), which is located to the right of the semicolon (;) on most keyboards.

Text within backticks is treated as a separate command whose results are substituted on the command line. For instance, to delete those backup files, you can type the following command:

```
$ rm `find ./ -name "*~"`
```

Archiving Data

A file archiving tool collects a group of files into a single "package" file that you can easily move around on a single system; back up to a recordable DVD, USB flash drive, tape, or other removable media; or transfer across a network. Linux supports several archiving commands, the most prominent being tar and zip. In addition to understanding these commands, you should be familiar with the consequences of using compression with them.

Another archive program, cpio, is sometimes used in Linux. It's similar in principle to tar, but different in operational details.

Using *tar*

The tar program's name stands for "tape archiver." Despite this fact, you can use tar to archive data to your hard disk or other media, not just to tapes. In fact, *tarballs* (archive files created by tar and typically compressed with gzip or bzip2) are often used for transferring multiple files between computers in one step, such as when distributing source code.

The tar program is a complex package with many options, but most of what you'll do with the utility can be covered with a few common commands. Table 10.5 lists the primary tar commands, and Table 10.6 lists the qualifiers that modify what the commands do. Whenever you run tar, you use exactly one command, and you usually use at least one qualifier.

TABLE 10.5 tar commands

Command	Abbreviation	Description
--create	c	Creates an archive
--concatenate	A	Appends tar files to an archive
--append	r	Appends non-tar files to an archive
--update	u	Appends files that are newer than those in an archive
--diff or --compare	d	Compares an archive to files on disk
--list	t	Lists an archive's contents
--extract or --get	x	Extracts files from an archive

◄

Unlike most single-letter program options in Linux, you can use single-letter tar commands and qualifiers without a leading dash (-).

TABLE 10.6 tar qualifiers

Qualifier	Abbreviation	Description
--directory *dir*	C	Changes to directory dir before performing operations
--file [*host:*]*file*	f	Uses the file called file on the computer called host as the archive file
--listed-incremental *file*	g	Performs an incremental backup or restore, using file as a list of previously archived files
--one-file-system	(none)	Backs up or restores only one filesystem (partition)
--multi-volume	M	Creates or extracts a multi-tape archive
--tape-length N	L	Changes tapes after N kilobytes

(Continues)

TABLE 10.6 *(Continued)*

Qualifier	Abbreviation	Description
--same-permissions	p	Preserves all protection information
--absolute-paths	P	Retains the leading / on filenames
--verbose	v	Lists all files read or extracted; when used with --list, displays file sizes, ownership, and time stamps
--verify	W	Verifies the archive after writing it
--exclude *file*	(none)	Excludes *file* from the archive
--exclude-from *file*	X	Excludes files listed in *file* from the archive
--gzip or --ungzip	z	Processes an archive through gzip
--bzip2	j (some older versions used I or y)	Processes an archive through bzip2
--xz	J	Processes an archive through xz

Of the commands listed in Table 10.5, the most commonly used are --create, --extract, and --list. The most useful qualifiers from Table 10.6 are --file, --listed-incremental, --one-file-system, --same-permissions, --gzip, --bzip2, --xz, and --verbose. If you fail to specify a filename with the --file qualifier, tar will attempt to use a default device, which is often (but not always) a tape device file.

As an example, consider archiving and compressing the my-work subdirectory of your home directory to a USB flash drive mounted at /media/flash. The following command will do the trick:

```
$ tar cvfz /media/flash/my-work.tgz ~/my-work
```

If you then transfer this drive to another system, mount it at /media/usb, and want to extract the archive, you can do so with another command:

```
$ tar xvfz /media/usb/my-work.tgz
```

> The tar utility preserves Linux's ownership and permission information, even when the archive is stored on a filesystem that doesn't support such metadata.

This command creates a subdirectory called my-work in the current working directory and populates it with the files from the archive. If you don't know what's in an archive, it's a good practice to examine it with the --list command before extracting its contents. Although common practice creates tarballs that store files within a single subdirectory, sometimes tarballs drop many files in the current working directory, which can make them difficult to track down if you run the command in a directory that already has many files.

Using Compression

In Linux, the gzip, bzip2, and xz programs all compress individual files. For instance, you might compress a large graphics file like this:

```
$ bzip2 biggraphics.tiff
```

The result is a file with a name like the original but with the addition of a new filename extension to identify it as a compressed format. In this specific case, the result would be biggraphics.tiff.bz2. Most graphics programs won't read files compressed in this way, though. To use a file that's been compressed, you must uncompress it with a matching program. Table 10.7 summarizes the compression programs, their matching uncompression programs, and the filename extensions they create. As a general rule, gzip provides the least compression and xz the most.

◄

Once you've compressed a text file, you won't be able to search it with grep without first uncompressing it. The zgrep variant can search files compressed with gzip, though.

T A B L E   1 0 . 7 Compression and uncompression programs and filename extensions

Compression program	Uncompression program	Filename extension
gzip	gunzip	.gz
bzip2	bunzip2	.bz2
xz	unxz	.xz

The tar program provides explicit support for all three of these compression standards, and compressed tarballs often have their own unique filename extensions (.tgz, .tbz or .tb2, and .txz for tarballs compressed with gzip, bzip2, and xz, respectively). Using two extensions on tarballs, as in archive.tar.bz2, is also common. When you compress a tarball, even by using the -z, -j, or -J option to tar, the compression program works on the tarball with all its files rather than to the individual files within the tarball. This can improve the compression ratio compared to compressing individual files and then bundling them together, but it makes it harder to extract data from a file if it becomes damaged.

Compression works better with some file types than with others. Typically, plain text files compress extremely well, binary program files compress moderately well, and pre-compressed data (such as most video file formats) compress poorly or may even expand in size when compressed again. You should be aware of this fact to know whether to apply compression to your archives. For instance, if you back up a Linux installation, which consists of program and configuration files, without user data, the result is likely to consume about half the space it does on your hard disk. On the other hand, if you want to back up a directory containing MP3 audio files or JPEG graphics, both of which are pre-compressed, you're better off not applying compression.

The gzip, bzip2, and xz compression programs all apply *lossless* compression, meaning that the data recovered by uncompressing the file is identical to what went into it. Some graphics, audio, and audio-visual file formats apply *lossy* compression, in which some data are discarded. When done properly and at low to moderate levels of compression, you'll be hard-pressed to notice the loss, since the algorithms discard data that humans have a difficult time perceiving. When a user applies lossy algorithms aggressively, though, we do notice the effect. Lossy compression tools should never be used on program files, system configuration files, or most user data files; any loss in such files could be disastrous. That's why tar supports only lossless compression tools.

Using *zip*

Outside of the Unix and Linux world, the zip file format is a common one that fills a role similar to a compressed tarball. Linux provides the zip command to create zip files and the unzip utility to extract files from a zip archive. Zip files typically have filename extensions of .zip.

In most cases, you can create a zip archive by passing the utility the name of a target zip file followed by a filename list:

```
$ zip newzip.zip afile.txt figure.tif
```

This command creates the newzip.zip file, which holds the afile.txt and figure.tif files. (The original files remain on your disk.) In some cases you'll need to use options to zip to achieve the desired results. Table 10.8 summarizes the most important zip options; however, the program supports many more. Consult its man page for details.

TABLE 10.8 Common zip options

Option (long form)	Option (short form)	Description
N/A	-0 through -9	Sets the amount of compression; -0 applies no compression, -1 applies minimal (but fast) compression, and so on through -9, which applies maximal (but slow) compression.
--delete	-d	Deletes the specified files from the archive file.
--encrypt	-e	Encrypts the archive with a password. (zip prompts you for this password.)
--freshen	-f	Updates files in an archive if they've changed since the original archive's creation.
--fix or --fixfix	-F or -FF	Performs repairs on a damaged archive file. The --fix/-F option performs minimal repairs, whereas --fixfix/-FF is more thorough.
--filesync	-FS	Updates files in an archive if they've changed since the original archive's creation and deletes files from the archive if they've been deleted on the filesystem.
--grow	-g	Appends files to an existing archive file.
--help	-h or -?	Displays basic help information.
--move	-m	Moves files into the zip archive; that is, the original files are deleted.
--recurse-paths	-r	Includes files and subdirectories inside directories you specify.
--split-size *size*	-s *size*	Creates a potentially multi-file archive, with each file no larger than *size* bytes. (A k, m, g, or t can be appended to the size to specify larger units.)

(Continues)

TABLE 10.8 *(Continued)*

Option (long form)	Option (short form)	Description
--exclude *files*	-x *files*	Excludes the specified files.
--symlinks	-y	Includes symbolic links as such. (Ordinarily, zip includes the linked-to files.)

Of the options in Table 10.8, the -r option is probably the most important, at least if you want to compress an entire directory tree. If you fail to use this option, your archive will contain no subdirectories. Given the speed of modern CPUs, using -9 on a regular basis also makes sense.

To uncompress and extract files in a zip archive file, you can use the unzip program:

```
$ unzip anarchive.zip
```

Zip files typically contain "loose" files in the main directory, so you should generally extract zip archives in an empty subdirectory you create for this purpose.

This example uncompresses the files in the anarchive.zip file into the current directory. Like zip, unzip supports a large number of options, the most important of which appear in Table 10.9.

TABLE 10.9 Common unzip options

Option	Description
-f	Freshens files from the archive; that is, extracts only those files that exist on the main filesystem and that are newer in the archive than on the main filesystem
-l	Lists files in the archive but does not extract them
-p	Extracts files to a pipeline
-t	Tests the integrity of files in the archive
-u	Updates files; similar to -f, but also extracts files that don't exist on the filesystem

(Continues)

TABLE 10.9 *(Continued)*

Option	Description
-v	Lists files in the archive in a more verbose format than -l does
-L	Converts filenames to lowercase if they originated on an uppercase-only OS, such as DOS
-n	Never overwrites existing files
-o	Overwrites existing files without prompting

As a general rule, using unzip without any options except for the input file-name works well; however, you might want to use one or more of its options on occasion. The -l option is particularly useful for examining the archive's contents without extracting it.

THE ESSENTIALS AND BEYOND

Managing your files often requires locating them, and tools such as grep and find help you with this task. The grep utility in particular makes use of regular expressions, which provide a way to describe patterns you might want to find in files or in the output of another program. You can redirect such output into grep (or other programs or files) using redirection operators, and many Linux command-line tools and techniques rely on such redirection. The tar and zip programs both enable you to create archive files that hold many other files. In fact, the tarballs that tar creates are a common means of distributing source code and even binary programs between Linux computers.

SUGGESTED EXERCISES

▶ Use find and grep to locate files in your own directory and on the Linux computer at large. For instance, try locating references to your own username in configuration files in /etc.

▶ Use gzip, bzip2, and xz to compress a couple instances of files of various types, such as text files and digital photos. What file types compress well? Which compression tool works best for each file type?

(Continues)

THE ESSENTIALS AND BEYOND *(Continued)*

REVIEW QUESTIONS

1. Which of the following commands will print lines from the file `world.txt` that contain matches to changes and changed?

   A. `grep change[ds] world.txt`

   B. `tar change[d-s] world.txt`

   C. `find "change'd|s'" world.txt`

   D. `cat world.txt changes changed`

   E. `find change[^ds] world.txt`

2. Which of the following redirection operators appends a program's standard output to an existing file, without overwriting that file's original contents?

   A. `|`   **D.** `>`

   B. `2>`   **E.** `>>`

   C. `&>`

3. You've received a tarball called `data79.tar` from a colleague, but you want to check the names of the files it contains before extracting them. Which of the following commands would you use to do this?

   A. `tar uvf data79.tar`   **D.** `tar tvf data79.tar`

   B. `tar cvf data79.tar`   **E.** `tar Avf data79.tar`

   C. `tar xvf data79.tar`

4. True or false: The regular expression `Linu[^x].*lds` matches the string `Linus Torvalds`.

5. True or false: The `find` command enables you to locate files based on their sizes.

6. True or false: To compress files archived with `zip`, you must use an external compression program such as `gzip` or `bzip2` in a pipeline with `zip`.

7. The character that represents the start of a line in a regular expression is

   _____.

8. Complete the following command to redirect both standard output and standard error from the `bigprog` program to the file `out.txt`.

   ```
   $ bigprog ____ out.txt
   ```

9. The gzip, bzip2, and xz programs all perform _____ compression, in which the decompressed data exactly match the original pre-compression data.

## CHAPTER 11

Editing Files

Computer documents come in many forms, but one of the most basic and flexible is text files. Because of their importance and ubiquity, you must be able to edit text files. This chapter covers this task, with an emphasis on the simple text-mode pico, nano, and Vi editors. I begin by describing some of the roles that text files play. I then describe how to select a text editor. To edit text files, of course, you must be able to start the editor, either on an existing document or to create a new one. The pico and nano editors are quite similar to each other, so I describe their operation together, followed by Vi, which is a much more unusual editor by modern standards. I conclude this chapter with a look at conventions used in configuration files and common formatted text files—two types of text files you'll probably have to edit sooner or later.

▶ **Understanding the role of text files**

▶ **Choosing an editor**

▶ **Launching an editor**

▶ **Editing files with** pico **or** nano

▶ **Editing files with Vi**

▶ **Using configuration file conventions**

▶ **Editing formatted text files**

Understanding the Role of Text Files

A text editor enables you to edit documents that are stored in a plain text format—typically using the American Standard Code for Information Interchange (ASCII), but such files increasingly use Unicode formats to support additional characters. These formats store text documents that, by themselves, include no special formatting or embedded features. That is, text files can't include graphics, use multiple fonts, emphasize words by italicizing them, or use other features that you probably associate with word processors. (As described shortly, though, markup tools provide a partial exception to this rule.)

ASCII AND UNICODE

ASCII dates to the 1960s. It's a 7-bit code, meaning that it supports a maximum of 2^7, or 128, characters. (In practice, ASCII uses 8 bits, so an extra 128 characters are available. These encode various **control characters** or are used in ASCII extensions.) Combined with the fact that it was created to encode the letters used in English, digits, and symbols, ASCII's limited character count makes it rather unhelpful for many non-English languages—there just aren't enough characters available to handle all the characters for all non-English languages.

Over the years, extensions to and variants of ASCII have been used to support additional characters and alphabets that ASCII doesn't support. One way to do this is to use a **code page** to specify, essentially, an alphabet. Each code page specifies a variant of ASCII that's suitable for a particular alphabet. For instance, code page 866 encodes Cyrillic (the alphabet used by Russian and most other Slavic languages). The problem with code pages is that you can generally use only one code page at a time.

Unicode is a more modern approach. It provides a much larger character set, enabling the encoding of any alphabet in common use on Earth, including the huge logographic writing systems used in languages such as Chinese and Japanese. The problem is that Unicode requires many more bits, and several ways to encode it efficiently exist. Fortunately, these Unicode Transformation Format (UTF) schemes are limited in number compared to code pages. Some, such as UTF-8, map the first characters in the same way ASCII does, so an ASCII file is also a valid UTF-8 file. Many text editors today handle UTF-8 (or other Unicode formats) automatically, so you can use a text editor to write text files in any language you like. You may still need to set localization options to tell Linux what sort of keyboard you use and what code page to use by default for programs that still rely on code pages.

Text files encode the ends of lines using one or two special ASCII characters. End-of-line encoding differs between Unix (or Linux) and Windows, but most programs can handle either method.

▶

Formatted text files encode special formatting using unique character sequences. Although you can edit such files with a text editor, specialized editors also exist for many such file types.

▶

Text files consist of lines, which can vary in length from 0 characters to the file's entire size. Frequently, line lengths end at 80 characters or less to make viewing and printing the files easier on conventional terminals and printers, which often have 80-character line-length limits.

Text files can hold any number of types of data. Some of these you might want to create or edit as an ordinary user, and others are important for administering a Linux system. The main file types include the following:

▶ Human language files

▶ Programming language files

▶ Formatted text files

▶ Program and system configuration files

▶ Program log files

Some files contain elements of multiple categories. E-mail, for instance, can be stored in text files. An e-mail file consists largely of human language, but e-mail messages include *headers*, which describe the origin and destination computers, along with information on how the message traveled from one site to the other, which is similar to formatted text or log file data.

Choosing an Editor

All Linux distributions ship with many text editors. Broadly speaking, text editors fall into one of two categories: text-mode and GUI. Beginners are generally more comfortable with GUI editors, and they can be more convenient to use even for experts. Sometimes, though, the X Window System (X for short) doesn't start properly, so you may have to use a text-mode editor. Thus, I recommend that you familiarize yourself with at least one text-mode editor. Some popular text-mode editors include the following:

Vi This editor is a Unix staple. It's small and is usually installed by default, so you can be fairly certain it's present on any Linux computer. It is, however, strange by modern standards; it uses multiple editing *modes*, and you must switch between them to accomplish various tasks. Many longtime Unix and Linux administrators like Vi for its flexibility, power, and small size.

emacs This editor is another Unix staple. It's a big editor with lots of features, so it's less likely to be installed by default, particularly on small emergency systems. Its operating model is more like those of text editors with which novices are familiar, but its commands can seem rather odd.

pico Several small editors are modeled after emacs but omit many of its advanced features in an effort to simplify the editor. One of these editors is pico, which originated as part of the pine e-mail package.

nano This editor is a clone of pico that adds extra features. Many distributions install nano by default.

Of the preceding editors, nano is probably the best one to start with; it's common enough that you're likely to find it already installed on your system, and its method of operation is less idiosyncratic than that of Vi. Although emacs is a capable editor, it's less likely to be installed by default, which can be a drawback,

Unlike Unix and Linux, many Windows configuration and log files use binary formats, necessitating the use of specialized utilities to manage them.

Most Linux distributions use a version of Vi called Vi Improved, or Vim; you can still launch it by typing vi.

Bash's text-editing commands are modeled on those of emacs, so learning emacs can improve your ability to manage Bash.

Some distributions provide pico and some don't. Some don't provide pico, but cause nano to launch when you use the pico command.

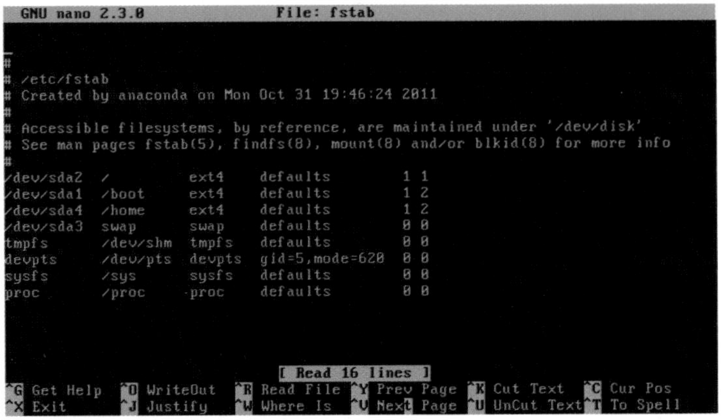

particularly when using an emergency recovery system. For the most part, pico works just like nano, but because nano adds to pico's features, nano is a more capable editor. Figure 11.1 shows nano in operation within a text-mode login session, editing a file called fstab.

FIGURE 11.1 The nano editor enables you to edit a text file in text mode.

As with text-mode editors, several GUI editors are available, including the following:

emacs   This editor is both a text-mode editor and a GUI editor. The GUI features of emacs, however, are sometimes a bit odd; for instance, the scroll bar to move through the file appears on the left side of the window rather than the more common right side.

gedit   The GNU Network Object Model Environment (GNOME) desktop environment has an associated text editor known as gedit. It's a fairly typical text editor, and it's often installed by default.

KWrite and Kate   Just as gedit is associated with GNOME, KWrite and Kate are editors that are associated with the K Desktop Environment (KDE). KWrite is slightly more sophisticated than gedit, and Kate adds some more features, but neither is nearly as powerful as emacs.

NEdit   This editor is not tied to any particular desktop environment, but it's also unlikely to be installed by default. It's similar in power to KWrite.

For a new Linux user, any of these is a good starting GUI editor; all offer the basic features you need for light text file editing. Which you choose may depend on which is installed by default on your system. In the long term, you should probably try a variety of editors to find the one you like best.

Launching an Editor

If you're comfortable with a GUI desktop environment, you can launch a GUI text editor using the desktop environment's menu system or by using a file manager to browse to a file you want to edit and double-clicking that file. This approach works well for files that you own, but if you need to edit system files, you're likely to lack permissions to save changes if you launch a text editor in this way.

Another approach to launching a text editor is to do so from the command line. You can do this as a normal user or as root, so you can edit text files that you own as well as system files. You can also select the editor you want to use—you just need to know its filename, which you type to launch the editor:

```
$ nano
```

This example launches nano. When it opens, you'll see a display like that shown in Figure 11.1, but the bulk of the window or text-mode console will be empty, since you didn't specify a filename. Instead, the center of the top line will read New Buffer. You can begin typing your file. When you save the file (as described later, in "Saving Your Changes from nano"), nano will ask for a filename. Alternatively, you can provide a filename when you launch the program:

```
$ nano great_american_novel.txt
```

This example opens the great_american_novel.txt file and displays it. If the file doesn't exist, nano displays New File near the bottom of the display, where Read 16 lines appears in Figure 11.1. If you mistype the filename, nano will show an empty file, so if you see an empty file instead of the file you were expecting to see, you may have mistyped the filename. If you see Warning: no write permission in the third line from the bottom, this means that you've loaded a file that you have no permission to write. You'll need to run nano as root or modify file permissions, as described in Chapter 15, "Setting Ownership and Permissions," if you want to save the file.

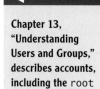

Chapter 13, "Understanding Users and Groups," describes accounts, including the root account, in more detail.

Editing Files with *pico* or *nano*

Certification Objective

If you're familiar with text-mode text editors, you should have few problems learning pico or nano. If you've only used GUI editors to edit text, though, you'll have to learn a few conventions about how to use the keyboard. You must move about the document using the keyboard rather than the mouse, for instance. You can insert, replace, and delete text much as you do in a GUI text editor or word processor.

Using Text Editor Conventions

Every text editor has its own conventions for information it displays on the screen, how to manipulate text, and so on. Most text-mode text editors are similar up to a point—for instance, one or more lines at the top or bottom of the display typically show summary information or brief command prompts. Figure 11.1 shows this information for nano, which includes:

The title bar   The first line of the display is the title bar. This line includes nano's version number, the name of the file being edited, and the modification status.

The status bar   The third line from the bottom of the display is reserved for status information and interactions with the user. This line will prompt you for information such as a filename to write when you save your document or terms you want to find in the document when you perform a search operation.

The shortcut list   The bottom two lines of the editor show a summary of some of the most common operations, along with the keystrokes that trigger them.

A carat (^) preceding a letter refers to a control character. In this book, I indicate such key combinations with "Ctrl+" rather than a carat.

In addition to control characters, nano uses *meta* characters to activate some functions. These key combinations use the Esc key followed by another key. In nano's documentation, meta sequences are denoted by M-*k*, where *k* is a key. In this book, I use Esc rather than M to prefix a meta key combination. For instance, Figure 11.1 describes M-? as the key sequence to move to the last line of the document. Note that these are distinct keystrokes, unlike Ctrl key sequences; that is, you would press Esc, release it, and *then* press the question mark (?) key, including its Shift modifier, to move to the last line of the document.

Exploring Basic *nano* Text-Editing Procedures

You can use pico instead of nano if you prefer; it works almost identically for this task.

As a method of learning nano, consider the task of editing /etc/fstab to add a new disk to the computer. (Don't worry too much about this file's purpose or format; I'm simply using it as a concrete example for demonstrating the editor.) Listing 11.1 shows the original /etc/fstab file used in this example. If you want to follow along, enter it using a text editor with which you're already familiar, and save it to a file on your disk. Alternatively, copy /etc/fstab from your own system to your home directory and use it, but be aware that it won't be identical to the one shown in Listing 11.1. Don't edit your *real* /etc/fstab file as a learning exercise; a mistake could render your system unbootable the next time you reboot. Instead, work on a copy of this file.

Listing 11.1: Sample /etc/fstab file

```
/dev/sda2  /        ext4    defaults        1 1
/dev/sda1  /boot    ext4    defaults        1 2
/dev/sda4  /home    ext4    defaults        1 2
/dev/sda3  swap     swap    defaults        0 0
tmpfs      /dev/shm tmpfs   defaults        0 0
devpts     /dev/pts devpts  gid=5,mode=620  0 0
sysfs      /sys     sysfs   defaults        0 0
proc       /proc    proc    defaults        0 0
```

The first step to using nano is to launch it and have it load the file. In this example, type **nano fstab** while in the directory holding the file. The result should resemble Figure 11.1 (shown earlier), which illustrates nano editing Listing 11.1 but with some comments at the start of the file.

You can add a new entry to fstab in a couple of ways. The first way is to create a new empty line and type an entry manually. You can do so as follows:

1. Press the down arrow key repeatedly until the cursor appears over the t in tmpfs.

2. Press the Enter key. This action opens a new line between the /dev/sda3 line and the tmpfs line.

3. Press the up arrow key once to reposition the cursor on the empty new line.

4. Type the following new line:

```
/dev/sdb1  /home2    ext4    defaults        0 0
```

A second way of creating a new entry demonstrates how to cut and paste text in the editor:

1. Move the cursor to the beginning of the /dev/sdb1 line you've just created by using the arrow keys; you should see the cursor resting on the / in /dev/sdb1.

2. Press Esc-6. This keystroke copies the line on which the cursor resides into a cut/copy buffer.

3. Press Ctrl+U. This keystroke pastes the contents of the cut/copy buffer into the file in the current location.

4. Use the arrow keys to move the cursor to the right of /dev/sdb1.

◄ Comments and other configuration file conventions are described later, in "Using Configuration File Conventions."

◄ Alternatively, Ctrl+K *cuts* text, meaning that it's removed from the file and copied to the buffer. This is useful to move lines to a new location in the file.

You can make more extensive changes to the fstab file, if you like, but be sure to work from a *copy* of the file!

5. Press the Backspace key once and then press the 2 key to change /dev/sdb1 to /dev/sdb2.

6. Use the arrow keys to move the cursor to the left of /home2.

7. Press the Backspace key once and then press the 3 key to change /home2 to /home3.

The result of these changes is a new line, very similar to the one you added earlier:

```
/dev/sdb2   /home3    ext4     defaults        0 0
```

You can make additional changes in a similar way. Although nano lacks a GUI, most of its principles are the same as the ones in GUI text editors and word processors; you just need to know the keystroke to activate the feature you want. Pressing Ctrl+G produces a help listing that summarizes the program's features, which can be handy as you get to know the editor.

Some additional features you might want to use include the following:

Move to the start or end of the file   You can use the arrow keys, Page Up, Page Down, Home, and End to move the cursor around in ways that are common to other editors. To move to the start of the file, press Esc-\; and to move to the end of the file, press Esc-/.

Copy or move multiple lines   If you need to copy or move multiple consecutive lines, you can repeat the Esc-6 or Ctrl+K operation; nano retains all the lines you copy or cut, so that when you press Ctrl+U, all of them will be pasted back.

Insert a file   Pressing Ctrl+R or F5 enables you to insert another file in the current one, at the cursor's current position.

Search for a string   Pressing Ctrl+W or F6 activates a search feature. When activated, nano prompts you for a search term. Type it, followed by the Enter key, and nano finds the next instance of that search term in the file. When you press Ctrl+W or F6 again, the default search term is the last one used, so you can search repeatedly for the same term by pressing Ctrl+W or F6 followed by Enter for each search operation. Alternatively, Esc-W or F16 repeats the last search.

Replace a string   You can replace one string with another by pressing Ctrl+\, Esc-R, or F14. The program prompts you to enter a search term and the term you want to replace it. The search then commences, and nano asks you to verify each replacement. If you want to replace *all* the occurrences without prompting, you can press the A key at the first prompt.

Saving Your Changes from *nano*

Once you've made changes to a text file, of course, you probably want to save them. One way to do this is with the Ctrl+O option. (That's a letter O, not a digit 0.) When you press this key, nano asks:

```
Write Selection to File:
```

Ordinarily, the prompt will include the file's original name, so you can press the Enter key to save the file using that name. If you want to use a different name, though, you can delete the old one and type a new name. If you launched nano without specifying a filename, you can type one at this prompt.

Another way to save the file is to press Ctrl+X. This command exits from nano, but if you've modified the file, it produces the following prompt:

```
Save modified buffer (ANSWERING "No" WILL DESTROY CHANGES) ?
```

Type **y** at this prompt to save the file. The program then shows you the filename prompt that you'd have seen if you'd pressed Ctrl+O, so you can change the filename if you like. Once nano saves the file, it terminates.

Editing Files with Vi

Vi was the first full-screen text editor written for Unix. It's designed to be small and simple. Vi is small enough to fit on tiny, floppy-based emergency boot systems. For this reason alone, Vi is worth learning; you may need to use it in an emergency recovery situation. Vi is, however, a bit strange, particularly if you're used to GUI text editors. To use Vi, you should first understand the three modes in which it operates. Once you understand those modes, you can begin learning about the text-editing procedures Vi implements. You'll also examine how to save files and exit Vi.

Certification Objective

◄

Most Linux distributions ship with a variant of Vi known as Vim, or "Vi Improved." The information presented here applies to both Vi and Vim.

Understanding Vi Modes

At any given moment, Vi is running in one of three modes:

Command mode   This mode accepts commands, which are usually entered as single letters. For instance, i and a both enter insert mode, although in somewhat different ways, as described shortly, and o opens a line below the current one.

Ex mode   To manipulate files (including saving your current file and running outside programs), you use ex mode. You enter ex mode from command mode by typing a colon (:), typically directly followed by the name of the ex-mode command you want to use. After you run the ex-mode command, Vi returns automatically to command mode.

Insert mode   You enter text in insert mode. Most keystrokes result in text appearing on the screen. One important exception is the Esc key, which exits insert mode and returns to command mode.

If you're not sure what mode Vi is in, press the Esc key. Doing so returns you to command mode, from which you can reenter insert mode, if necessary.

Unfortunately, terminology surrounding Vi modes is inconsistent at best. For instance, command mode is sometimes referred to as normal mode, and insert mode is sometimes called edit mode or entry mode. Ex mode often isn't described as a mode at all, but is referred to as *colon commands*.

Exploring Basic Vi Text-Editing Procedures

As a method of learning Vi, consider the task of editing /etc/fstab to add a new hard disk—the same task described earlier, in "Exploring Basic nano Text-Editing Procedures," with respect to nano. Listing 11.1 (in that earlier section) shows the original /etc/fstab file used in this example. If you want to follow along, enter it using a text editor with which you're already familiar, and save it to a file on your disk. Don't edit your *real* /etc/fstab file as a learning exercise; a mistake could render your system unbootable the next time you reboot. Instead, work on a copy of this file.

The first step to using Vi is to launch it and have it load the file. In this example, type **vi fstab** while in the directory holding the file. The result should resemble Figure 11.2, which shows Vi displaying the original file in a text session. Although not shown in Figure 11.2, some systems display a line of tildes (~) down the left side of the screen to indicate the end of the file. The bottom line shows the status of the last command—an implicit file load command that loaded 16 lines and 611 characters (16L, 611C) from the fstab file.

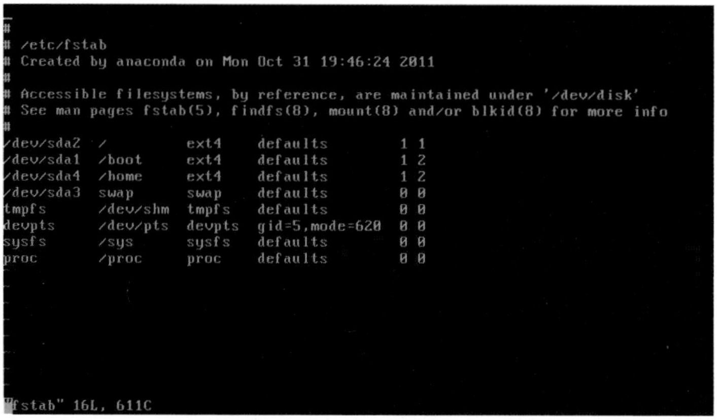

FIGURE 11.2 The last line of a Vi display is a status line that shows messages from the program.

As with nano, you can add a new entry to fstab using Vi either by typing it in its entirety or by duplicating an existing line and then modifying one copy. To do it the first way, follow these steps:

1. Move the cursor to the beginning of the /dev/sda3 lines by using the arrow keys.

2. Press the O (letter O, not number 0) key. This opens a new line immediately below the current line, moves the cursor to that line, and enters insert mode.

3. Type a new entry, such as the following:

   ```
   /dev/sdb1  /home2    ext4    defaults        0 0
   ```

4. Press the Esc key to return to command mode.

To practice making changes by modifying an existing entry, follow these steps:

1. Move the cursor to the beginning of the /dev/sdb1 line you just created by using the arrow keys, if necessary; you should see the cursor resting on the first / of /dev/sdb1.

2. You must now *yank* one line of text. This term is used much as *copy* is used in most text editors—you copy the text to a buffer from which you can later paste it back into the file. To yank text, you use the yy command, preceded by the number of lines you want to yank. Thus, type **1yy** (*do not* press the Enter key, though). The dd command works much like yy, but it deletes the lines as well as copying them to a buffer. Both yy and dd are special cases of the y and d commands, respectively, which yank or delete text in amounts specified by the next character, as in dw to delete the next word.

3. Move the cursor to the line *before* the one where you want the new line to appear.

4. Type **p** (again, without pressing the Enter key). Vi pastes the contents of the buffer starting on the line after the cursor. The file should now have two identical /dev/sdb1 lines. The cursor should be resting at the start of the second one. If you want to paste the text into the document starting on the line *before* the cursor, use an uppercase P command.

5. Move the cursor to the 1 in /dev/sdb1 on the line you've just pasted. You're about to begin customizing this line.

6. Until now, you've operated Vi in command mode. You can use any of several commands to enter insert mode. At this point, the most appropriate is R, which enters insert mode so that it's configured for

text replacement rather than insertion. If you prefer to insert text rather than overwrite it, you can use i or a (the latter advances the cursor one space, which is sometimes useful at the end of a line). For the purposes of these instructions, type **R** to enter insert mode. You should see -- REPLACE -- appear in the status line.

7. Type 2 to change /dev/sdb1 to /dev/sdb2.

8. Use the arrow keys to move the cursor to the 2 in /home2. You must modify this mount point name.

9. Type 3 to change /home2 to /home3.

10. Exit insert mode by pressing the Esc key.

11. Save the file and quit by typing **:wq**. This is an ex-mode command, as described shortly. (The ZZ command is equivalent to :wq.)

> ▶
>
> **You can make more extensive changes to the** fstab **file, if you like, but be sure to work from a** *copy* **of the file!**

Many additional commands are available that you may want to use in some situations. Here are some of the highlights:

Change case   Suppose you need to change the case of a word in a file. Instead of entering insert mode and retyping the word, you can use the tilde (~) key in command mode to change the case. Position the cursor on the first character you want to change, and press ~ repeatedly until the task is done.

Undo   To undo any change, type **u** in command mode.

Open text   In command mode, typing **o** (a lowercase letter O) opens text—that is, it inserts a new line immediately below the current one and enters insert mode on that line.

Search   To search forward for text in a file, type **/** in command mode, followed immediately by the text you want to locate. Typing **?** searches backward rather than forward.

Change text   The c command changes text from within command mode. You invoke it much like the d or y command, as in cw to change the next word or cc to change an entire line.

Go to a line   The G key brings you to a line that you specify. The H key "homes" the cursor—that is, it moves the cursor to the top line of the screen. The L key brings the key to the bottom line of the screen.

Replace globally   To replace all occurrences of one string with another, type **:%s/*original*/*replacement***, where *original* is the original string and *replacement* is its replacement. Change % to a starting line number, comma, and ending line number to perform this change on a small range of lines.

Vi offers a great deal more depth than is presented here; the editor is quite capable, and some Linux users are very attached to it. Entire books have been written about Vi. Consult one of these, or a Vi Web page like `http://www.vim.org`, for more information.

Saving Your Changes from Vi

To save changes to a file, type **:w** from command mode. This enters ex mode and runs the w ex-mode command, which writes the file using whatever filename you specified when you launched Vi. Related commands enable other functions:

Edit a new file   The :e command edits a new file. For instance, **:e /etc/inittab** loads /etc/inittab for editing. Vi won't load a new file unless the existing one has been saved since its last change or unless you follow :e with an exclamation mark (!).

Include an existing file   The :r command includes the contents of an old file in an existing one.

Execute an external command   The ex-mode command :! executes the external command that you specify. For instance, typing **:!ls** runs ls, enabling you to see what files are present in the current directory.

Quit   Use the :q command to quit the program. As with :e, this command won't work unless changes have been saved or you append an exclamation mark to the command (as in :q!).

You can combine ex commands such as these to perform multiple actions in sequence. For instance, typing **:wq** writes changes and then quits from Vi.

Using Configuration File Conventions

Most Linux system configuration files reside in the /etc directory tree, but your user configuration files reside in your home directory, usually in files or subdirectories with names that begin with a dot (.), such as .bashrc, which is the Bash configuration file. Configuration file formats vary from one program to another. Therefore, whether you want to edit a system configuration file or a personal configuration file, you're well advised to consult the documentation for the program in question. There are, however, some features that are common to many configuration files.

One common purpose for configuration files is to set certain program features to particular values. For instance, you might want to tell a mail server program

The Bash configuration file is actually a *shell script*—that is, a program. Chapter 12, "Creating Scripts," describes how to create and edit Bash scripts.

to send outgoing mail to another computer, or you might want to tell a GUI program about its window's height and width. Most configuration files do this by setting a named *variable* to a *value*, by placing both on the same line, sometimes with an equal sign between them. For instance, the main Postfix mail server configuration file (`/etc/postfix/main.cf`) uses an equal sign to set the `relayhost` variable to a value, as in:

```
relayhost = franklin.pangaea.edu
```

The `relayhost` variable, when set, tells Postfix to relay outgoing mail through the named system—`franklin.pangaea.edu`, in this example. Another example is the `/etc/ntp.conf` file, which holds data for the Network Time Protocol (NTP) daemon, which synchronizes your computer's clock with other computers' clocks. You can specify an outside clock source with the `server` variable:

```
server tardis.example.com
```

This line tells NTP to use `tardis.example.com` as a time source. Whether or not a configuration file requires an equal sign is a design decision of the program's author. Some configuration files use still more complex formats, but assigning values to variables is quite common in configuration files.

The `/etc/fstab` file used earlier as an example file doesn't really set variables in either of these ways, but it does link various types of data together, one set per line. The information includes the device filename for a partition, its mount point, its filesystem, and its mount options. Such collections are common in configuration files, but the details differ. For instance, `/etc/fstab` separates elements with *whitespace*—that is, spaces or tabs. Some other files use other separating characters, such as the colon (`:`) that separates user account information in the `/etc/passwd`, `/etc/shadow`, and `/etc/group` files. (Chapter 13 describes these files in more detail.)

Another common feature of configuration files is *comments*—that is, English (or other natural language) text that describes the purpose of a file, a block of lines, or even a single line. Typically, comments begin with one or more special characters. The comment then continues until the end of the line or, sometimes, until another character or set of characters terminates the comment.

The single most common comment character in configuration files is a hash mark (#), which is used to begin a comment. Such comments typically end with the end of the line on which they appear. For instance, the `/etc/ntp.conf` file might include the following lines:

```
# You do need to talk to an NTP server or two (or three).
# server wells.pangaea.edu
server tardis.example.com
```

▶

Don't be too concerned with Postfix or NTP configuration specifically; I merely used them as convenient examples.

The first line is a comment that describes the purpose of the following lines. The second line illustrates an important secondary use of comments: By adding the comment character to the start of the line, you disable it. Thus, the wells .pangaea.edu computer is not configured as an NTP server. Commenting out configuration file entries in this way is useful when you're testing a setup—perhaps you suspect problems with wells.pangaea.edu, so you comment its entry out as a temporary measure. You can easily uncomment the line by removing the hash mark and the following space.

Some servers use other characters or strings to denote comments. For instance, the sendmail e-mail server uses the string dnl to denote comments. If you're examining an unfamiliar configuration file, you should keep an eye out for comments. Even if you don't know the usual comment character used in the file, you can usually figure it out by spotting plain English text in the file.

Knowing these two conventions alone (variable assignment and comments) can help you determine what a configuration file is doing, and therefore enable you to change how it works.

> **Some programs provide default configuration files that have quite wordy comments. Such files can help you figure out how to adjust the program's configuration.**

Editing Formatted Text Files

As noted earlier, in "Understanding the Role of Text Files," formatted text files use ASCII or Unicode formats, in conjunction with conventions for a layout language, to describe text that's more complex than ASCII or Unicode alone can handle. A common formatted text file format is the Hypertext Markup Language (HTML), which is used on the Web—most Web pages use HTML.

Although a full tutorial on how to edit HTML, or any other formatted text file, is beyond the scope of this book, you may want to take a quick look at this type of file so that you can at least begin to understand it, and perhaps make small changes to such files. To that end, Listing 11.2 shows a simple HTML file.

Listing 11.2: A sample HTML file

```
<!DOCTYPE HTML PUBLIC "-//W3C//DTD HTML 4.01 Transitional//EN"
"http://www.w3.org/TR/html4/loose.dtd">
<HTML>
<HEAD>
<TITLE>Linux Essentials</TITLE>
</HEAD>
<BODY BGCOLOR="#FFFFFF" TEXT="#000000">
<CENTER><H1 ALIGN="CENTER">Linux Essentials</H1></CENTER>
<P>The <I>Linux Essentials</I> book covers the essential
tools for using Linux!</P>
</BODY>
</HTML>
```

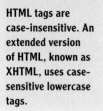

HTML tags are case-insensitive. An extended version of HTML, known as XHTML, uses case-sensitive lowercase tags.

In HTML, most formatting information appears in angle brackets (<>). These *tags* are usually paired, with the ending tag carrying the same name as the beginning one, except that the ending tag's name includes a slash (/). For instance, <P> begins a paragraph and </P> ends it. Likewise, <I> begins italic text and </I> ends it.

In Listing 11.2, the first line identifies the version of HTML the document uses. This enables the Web browser to adjust the way it handles the file. The <HTML> tag begins the bulk of the document. The <HEAD> and <BODY> tags identify two key parts of the document—the header that normally appears in a Web browser's title bar and the main body of the document.

Some opening tags include additional information. For instance, the <BODY> tag in Listing 11.2 specifies the background color (BGCOLOR="#FFFFFF") and text color (TEXT="#000000").

The purpose of describing this is not to make you experts on HTML—it's to point out that you can often parse and even edit formatted text files with minimal knowledge. For instance, you can change the text in the body of Listing 11.2, add new paragraphs by mimicking the way the first one is specified, and so on. If you make a mistake, though, the results can be strange. For instance, if you type Listing 11.2 into a text editor, save it, and point a Web browser to the file, you can see what it looks like as a Web page. If you neglect to type the </I> tag in the paragraph, though, all the text after the book's title will be italicized. If you were to enter another paragraph after the first one, it would be italicized, too! The Web browser will keep on italicizing text until it encounters a </I> tag.

THE ESSENTIALS AND BEYOND

Plain text files, which encode text using ASCII or Unicode, are important on most computer platforms, but they're particularly important on Linux. This is because many of Linux's configuration files use plain text formats, so understanding how to use an editor, such as pico, nano, or Vi, to edit these files enables you to edit a wide variety of configuration files. You should also understand the conventions used by certain configuration file formats, such as common features of configuration files and formatted text files. Even a basic understanding of what you're likely to find will help you edit such files when the need arises.

SUGGESTED EXERCISES

▶ Launch nano to create a new file and type in a complete paragraph from this chapter. Proofread the text and correct any typos you find. (If you found none, congratulations! Now create a few "errors" and correct them.)

(Continues)

THE ESSENTIALS AND BEYOND (Continued)

▶ Type Listing 11.2 into Vi and save it. Point a Web browser at the file (for instance, by typing **file:///home/*yourusername*/sample.html** into a Web browser's address field, if you saved it as ~/sample.html). Add a new paragraph by cutting and pasting the existing paragraph and changing the text. Reload the file to see how your Web browser renders it.

REVIEW QUESTIONS

1. Which type of file is nano *least* likely to be useful for examining or editing?

    A. A /var/log/messages log file

    B. An HTML Web page file

    C. An e-mail message saved from an e-mail client

    D. A LibreOffice word processing document

    E. An /etc/X11/xorg.conf configuration file

2. Which keystrokes invoke the pico or nano search function? (Select all that apply.)

    A. F3   **D.** Ctrl+F

    B. F6   **E.** Ctrl+W

    C. Esc-S

3. How would you remove two lines of text from a file using Vi?

    A. In command mode, position the cursor on the first line and type **2dd**.

    B. In command mode, position the cursor on the last line and type **2yy**.

    C. In insert mode, position the cursor at the start of the first line, hold down the Shift key while pressing the Down arrow key twice, and press the Delete key on the keyboard.

    D. In insert mode, position the cursor at the start of the first line and press Ctrl+K twice.

    E. Select the text with the mouse and then select File ➢ Delete from the menu.

4. True or false: Unicode is useful for encoding most European languages but not Asian languages.

(Continues)

THE ESSENTIALS AND BEYOND *(Continued)*

5. True or false: GUI text editors for ASCII are superior to text-mode ASCII text editors because the GUI editors support underlining, italics, and multiple fonts.

6. True or false: Many (but not all) configuration files use a hash mark (#) to identify comment lines.

7. ASCII supports _____ unique characters.

8. Three keystrokes that can initiate a search-and-replace operation in nano are F14, _____, and _____.

9. While in Vi's command mode, you can type _____ to undo a change.

## CHAPTER 12

Creating Scripts

A script is a program written in an interpreted language, typically associated with a shell or other program whose primary purpose is something other than as an interpreted language. In Linux, many scripts are *shell scripts*, which are associated with Bash or another shell. (If you're familiar with *batch files* in DOS or Windows, scripts serve a similar purpose.) You can write shell scripts to help automate tedious repetitive tasks or to perform new and complex tasks. Many of Linux's startup functions are performed by scripts, so mastering scripting will help you manage the startup process.

This chapter covers Bash shell scripts, beginning with the task of creating a new script file. I then describe several important scripting features that help you to perform progressively more complex scripting tasks.

▶ **Beginning a shell script**

▶ **Using commands**

▶ **Using arguments**

▶ **Using variables**

▶ **Using conditional expressions**

▶ **Using loops**

▶ **Using functions**

▶ **Setting the script's exit value**

LEARNING MORE

Like any programming task, shell scripting can be quite complex. Consequently, this chapter barely scratches the surface of what you can accomplish through shell scripting. Consult a book on the topic, such as Cameron Newham's *Learning the Bash Shell, 3rd Edition* (O'Reilly, 2005) or Richard Blum's *Linux Command Line and Shell Scripting Bible* (Wiley, 2008), for more information.

Beginning a Shell Script

Shell scripts are plain-text files, so you create them in text editors such as Vi, nano, or pico, as described in Chapter 11, "Editing Files." A shell script begins with a line that identifies the shell that's used to run it, such as the following:

```
#!/bin/bash
```

The first two characters are a special code that tells the Linux kernel that this is a script and to use the rest of the line as a pathname to the program that's to interpret the script. (This line is sometimes called the *shebang, hashbang, hashpling,* or *pound bang* line.) Shell scripting languages use a hash mark (#) as a comment character, so the script utility ignores this line, although the kernel doesn't. On most systems, /bin/sh is a symbolic link that points to /bin/bash, but it can point to some other shell. Specifying the script as using /bin/sh guarantees that any Linux system will have a shell program to run the script, but if the script uses any features specific to a particular shell, you should specify that shell instead—for instance, use /bin/bash or /bin/tcsh instead of /bin/sh.

When you're done writing the shell script, you should modify it so that it's executable. You do this with the chmod command, which is described in more detail in Chapter 15, "Setting Ownership and Permissions." For now know that you use the a+x option to add execute permissions for all users. For instance, to make a file called my-script executable, you should issue the following command:

```
$ chmod a+x my-script
```

You'll then be able to execute the script by typing its name, possibly preceded by ./ to tell Linux to run the script in the current directory rather than searching the current path. If you fail to make the script executable, you can still run the script by running the shell program followed by the script name (as in **bash my-script**), but it's generally better to make the script executable. If the script is one you run regularly, you may want to move it to a location on your path, such as /usr/local/bin. When you do that, you won't have to type the complete path or move to the script's directory to execute it; you can just type **my-script**.

Using Commands

One of the most basic features of shell scripts is the ability to run commands. You can use both commands that are built into the shell and external commands—that is, you can run other programs as commands. Most of the commands you type in a shell prompt are external commands—they're programs located in /bin, /usr/bin, and other directories on your path. You can run such programs, as well as internal commands, by including their names in the script. You can also specify parameters to such programs in a script. For instance, suppose you want a script that launches two xterm windows and the KMail mail reader program. Listing 12.1 presents a shell script that accomplishes this goal.

Listing 12.1: A simple script that launches three programs

```
#!/bin/bash
/usr/bin/xterm &
/usr/bin/xterm &
/usr/bin/kmail &
```

Aside from the first line that identifies it as a script, the script looks just like the commands you might type to accomplish the task manually, except for one fact: The script lists the complete paths to each program. This is usually not strictly necessary, but listing the complete path ensures that the script will find the programs even if the PATH environment variable changes. On the other hand, if the program files move (say, because you upgrade the package from which they're installed and the packager decides to move them), scripts that use complete paths will break. If a script produces a No such file or directory error for a command, typing **which** *command*, where *command* is the offending command, should help you locate it.

Each program-launch line in Listing 12.1 ends in an ampersand (&). This character tells the shell to go on to the next line without waiting for the first to finish. If you omit the ampersands in Listing 12.1, the effect will be that the first xterm will open but the second won't open until the first is closed. Likewise, KMail won't start until the second xterm terminates.

Although launching several programs from one script can save time in startup scripts and some other situations, scripts are also frequently used to run a series of programs that manipulate data in some way. Such scripts typically do *not* include the ampersands at the ends of the commands because one command must run after another or may even rely on output from the first. A comprehensive list of such commands is impossible because you can run any program you can install in Linux as a command in a script—even another script. A few commands that are commonly used in scripts include the following:

Normal file manipulation commands   The file manipulation commands, such as ls, mv, cp, and rm, are often used in scripts. You can use these commands to help automate repetitive file maintenance tasks.

Fedora plans to rearrange its directory tree starting with Fedora 17. Once this is done, most program files will reside in /usr/bin.

grep   This command is described in Chapter 10, "Searching, Extracting, and Archiving Data." It locates files that contain the string you specify, or displays the lines that contain those strings in a single file.

find   Where grep searches for patterns within the contents of files, find does so based on filenames, ownership, and similar characteristics. Chapter 10 covers this command.

cut   This command extracts text from fields in a file. It's frequently used to extract variable information from a file whose contents are highly patterned. To use it, you pass it one or more options that specify what information you want, followed by one or more filenames. For instance, users' home directories appear in the sixth colon-delimited field of the /etc/passwd file. You can therefore type **cut -f 6 -d ":" /etc/passwd** to extract this information. The same command in a script will extract this information, which you'll probably save to a variable or pass to a subsequent command.

sed   This program provides many of the capabilities of a conventional text editor (such as search-and-replace operations) but via commands that can be typed at a command prompt or entered in a script.

Certification
Objective

echo   Sometimes a script must provide a message to the user; echo is the tool to accomplish this goal. You can pass various options to echo or just a string to be shown to the user. For instance, echo "Press the Enter key" causes a script to display the specified string. You can also use echo to display the value of variables (described later, in "Using Variables").

**Chapter 10 describes
input redirection.**

mail   The mail command can be used to send e-mail from within a script. Pass it the -s *subject* parameter to specify a subject line, and give it an e-mail address as the last argument. If it's used at the command line, you then type a message and terminate it with a Ctrl+D keystroke. If it's used from a script, you might omit the subject entirely or pass it an external file as the message using input redirection. You might want to use this command to send mail to the superuser about the actions of a startup script or a script that runs on an automated basis.

Many of these commands are extremely complex, and completely describing them is beyond the scope of this chapter. You can consult these commands' man pages for more information. A few of them are described elsewhere in this book, as noted in their descriptions.

Even if you have a full grasp of how to use some key external commands, simply executing commands as you might when typing them at a command prompt is of limited utility. Many administrative tasks require you to modify what you type at a command, or even what commands you enter, depending on information from other commands. For this reason, scripting languages include additional features to help you make your scripts useful.

Using Arguments

Variables can help you expand the utility of scripts. A variable is a placeholder in a script for a value that will be determined when the script runs. Variables' values can be passed as parameters to a script, generated internally to a script, or extracted from a script's environment. (An *environment* is a set of variables that any program can access. The environment includes things like the current directory and the search path for running programs.)

Certification
Objective

Variables that are passed to the script are frequently called *parameters* or *arguments*. They're represented in the script by a dollar sign ($) followed by a number from 0 up—$0 stands for the name of the script, $1 is the first parameter to the script, $2 is the second parameter, and so on. To understand how this might be useful, consider the task of adding a user. As described in Chapter 14, "Creating Users and Groups," creating an account for a new user typically involves running at least two commands—useradd and passwd. You may also need to run additional site-specific commands, such as commands that create unusual user-owned directories aside from the user's home directory.

As an example of how a script with an argument variable can help in such situations, consider Listing 12.2. This script creates an account and changes the account's password (the script prompts you to enter the password when you run the script). It creates a directory in the /shared directory tree corresponding to the account, and it sets a symbolic link to that directory from the new user's home directory. It also adjusts ownership and permissions in a way that may be useful, depending on your system's ownership and permissions policies.

Listing 12.2: A script that reduces account-creation tedium

```
#!/bin/bash
useradd -m $1
passwd $1
mkdir -p /shared/$1
chown $1.users /shared/$1
chmod 775 /shared/$1
ln -s /shared/$1 /home/$1/shared
chown $1.users /home/$1/shared
```

If you use Listing 12.2, you need to type only three things: the script name with the desired username and the password (twice). For instance, if the script is called mkuser, you can use it like this:

```
# mkuser ajones
Changing password for user ajones
New password:
Retype new password:
passwd: all authentication tokens updated successfully
```

Most of the script's programs operate silently unless they encounter problems, so the interaction (including typing the passwords, which don't echo to the screen) is a result of just the `passwd` command. In effect, Listing 12.2's script replaces seven lines of commands with one. Every one of those lines uses the username, so by running this script, you also reduce the chance of a typo causing problems.

Using Variables

Certification Objective

Another type of variable is assigned within scripts—for instance, such variables can be set from the output of a command. These variables are also identified by leading dollar signs, but they're typically given names that at least begin with a letter, such as $Addr or $Name. (When values are assigned to variables, the dollar sign is omitted, as illustrated shortly.) You can then use these variables in conjunction with normal commands as if they were command parameters, but the value of the variable is passed to the command.

For instance, consider Listing 12.3, which checks to see if the computer's router is up with the help of the `ping` utility. This script uses two variables. The first is $ip, which is extracted from the output of `route` using the `grep`, `tr`, and `cut` commands. When you're assigning a value to a variable from the output of a command, that command should be enclosed in backtick characters (`` ` ``), which appear on the same key as the tilde (~) on most keyboards. These are *not* ordinary single quotes, which appear on the same key as the regular quote character (") on most keyboards. The second variable, $ping, simply points to the `ping` program. It can just as easily be omitted, with subsequent uses of $ping replaced by the full path to the program or simply by `ping` (relying on the $PATH environment variable to find the program). Variables like this are sometimes used to make it easier to modify the script in the future. For instance, if you move the `ping` program, you need to modify only one line of the script. Variables can also be used in conjunction with conditionals to ensure that the script works on more systems—for instance, if `ping` were called something else on some systems.

In addition to several commands, the `ip=` line uses backticks (`` ` ``) to assign the output of that command chain to `ip`. Chapter 10 describes this technique.

▶

Listing 12.3: Script demonstrating assignment and use of variables

```
#!/bin/bash
ip=`route -n | grep UG | tr -s " " | cut -f 2 -d " "`
ping="/bin/ping"
echo "Checking to see if $ip is up..."
$ping -c 5 $ip
```

In practice, you use Listing 12.3 by typing the script's name. The result should be the message Checking to see if *192.168.1.1* is up (with

192.168.1.1 replaced by the computer's default gateway system) and the output from the ping command, which should attempt to send five packets to the router. If the router is up and is configured to respond to pings, you'll see five return packets and summary information, similar to the following:

```
$ routercheck
Checking to see if 192.168.1.1 is up...
PING 192.168.1.1 (192.168.1.1) 56(84) bytes of data.
64 bytes from 192.168.1.1: icmp_seq=1 ttl=63 time=23.0 ms
64 bytes from 192.168.1.1: icmp_seq=2 ttl=63 time=0.176 ms
64 bytes from 192.168.1.1: icmp_seq=3 ttl=63 time=0.214 ms
64 bytes from 192.168.1.1: icmp_seq=4 ttl=63 time=0.204 ms
64 bytes from 192.168.1.1: icmp_seq=5 ttl=63 time=0.191 ms

--- 192.168.1.1 ping statistics ---
5 packets transmitted, 5 received, 0% packet loss, time 4001ms
rtt min/avg/max/mdev = 0.176/4.758/23.005/9.123 ms
```

If the router is down, you'll see error messages to the effect that the host was unreachable.

Listing 12.3 is of limited practical use and contains bugs. For instance, the script identifies the computer's gateway merely by the presence of the string UG in the router's output line from route. If a computer has two routers defined, this won't work correctly, and the result is likely to be a script that misbehaves. The purpose of Listing 12.3 is to illustrate how variables can be assigned and used, not to be a flawless working script.

Scripts like Listing 12.3, which obtain information from running one or more commands, are useful in configuring features that rely on system-specific information or information that varies with time. You can use a similar approach to obtain the current hostname (using the hostname command), the current time (using date), the total time the computer's been running (using uptime), free disk space (using df), and so on. When combined with conditional expressions (described shortly), variables become even more powerful because then your script can perform one action when one condition is met and another in some other case. For instance, a script that installs software can check free disk space and abort the installation if insufficient disk space is available.

In addition to assigning variables with the assignment operator (=), you can read variables from standard input using read, as in read response to read input for subsequent access as $response. This method of variable assignment is useful for scripts that must interact with users. For instance, instead of reading the username from the command line, Listing 12.2 may be modified to prompt the user for the username. Listing 12.4 shows the result. To use this script, you type its name *without* typing a username on the command line. The

Certification Objective

script will then prompt for a username, and after you enter one, the script will attempt to create an account with that name.

Listing 12.4: Modified version of Listing 12.2 that employs user interaction

```
#!/bin/bash
echo -n "Enter a username: "
read name
useradd -m $name
passwd $name
mkdir -p /shared/$name
chown $name.users /shared/$name
chmod 775 /shared/$name
ln -s /shared/$name /home/$name/shared
chown $name.users /home/$name/shared
```

One special type of variable is an environment variable, which is assigned and accessed just like a shell script variable. The difference is that the script or command that sets an environment variable uses Bash's export command to make the value of the variable accessible to programs launched from the shell or shell script that made the assignment. In other words, you can set an environment variable in one script and use it in another script that the first script launches. Environment variables are most often set in shell startup scripts, but the scripts you use can access them. For instance, if your script calls X programs, it might check for the presence of a valid $DISPLAY environment variable and abort if it finds that this variable isn't set. By convention, environment variable names are all uppercase, whereas non-environment shell script variables are all lowercase or mixed case.

One special variable deserves mention: $?. This variable holds the *exit status* (or *return value*) of the most recently executed command. Most programs return a value of 0 when they terminate normally and return another value to specify errors. You can display this value with echo or use it in a conditional expression (described next) to have your script perform special error handling.

Consult a program's man page to learn the meanings of its return values.

Using Conditional Expressions

Certification Objective

Scripting languages support several types of *conditional expressions*. These enable a script to perform one of several actions contingent on some condition—typically the value of a variable. One common command that uses conditional expressions is if, which allows the system to take one of two actions depending on whether some condition is true. The if keyword's conditional expression appears in brackets after the if keyword and can take many forms.

For instance, -f *file* is true if *file* exists and is a regular file; -s *file* is true if *file* exists and has a size greater than 0; and *string1* == *string2* is true if the two strings have the same values.

Conditionals may be combined together with the logical and (&&) or logical or (||) operators. When conditionals are combined with &&, both sides of the operator must be true for the condition as a whole to be true. When || is used, if either side of the operator is true, the condition as a whole is true.

Certification
Objective

To better understand the use of conditionals, consider the following code fragment:

```
if [ -s /tmp/tempstuff ]
    then
        echo "/tmp/tempstuff found; aborting!"
        exit
fi
```

This fragment causes the script to exit if the file /tmp/tempstuff is present. The then keyword marks the beginning of a series of lines that execute only if the conditional is true, and fi (if backward) marks the end of the if block. Such code may be useful if the script creates and then later deletes this file, because its presence indicates that a previous run of the script didn't succeed or is still underway.

An alternative form for a conditional expression uses the test keyword rather than square brackets around the conditional:

Certification
Objective

```
if test -s /tmp/tempstuff
```

You can also test a command's return value by using the command as the condition:

```
if [ command ]
    then
        additional-commands
fi
```

In this example, the *additional-commands* will be run only if *command* completes successfully. If *command* returns an error code, the *additional-commands* won't be run.

Conditional expressions may be expanded by use of the else clause:

```
if [ conditional-expression ]
    then
        commands
    else
        other-commands
fi
```

Code of this form causes either *commands* or *other-commands* to execute, depending on the evaluation of *conditional-expression*. This is useful if *something* should happen in a part of the program, but precisely what should happen depends on some condition. For instance, you may want to launch one of two different file archiving programs depending on a user's input.

Certification Objective

What do you do if more than two outcomes are possible—for instance, if a user may provide any one of four possible inputs? You can nest several if/then/else clauses, but this gets awkward quickly. A cleaner approach is to use case:

```
case word in
    pattern1) command(s) ;;
    pattern2) command(s) ;;
    ...
esac
```

Certification Objective

For a case statement, a *word* is likely to be a variable, and each *pattern* is a possible value of that variable. The patterns can be expanded much like filenames, using the same wildcards and expansion rules (* to stand for any string, for instance). You can match an arbitrary number of patterns in this way. Each set of commands must end with a double semicolon (;;), and the case statement as a whole ends in the string esac (case backward).

Upon execution, bash executes the commands associated with the first pattern to match the *word*. Execution then jumps to the line following the esac statement; any intervening commands don't execute. If no patterns match the word, no code within the case statement executes. If you want to have a default condition, use * as the final *pattern*; this pattern matches any *word*, so its commands will execute if no other *pattern* matches.

Filename expansion using asterisks (*), question marks (?), and so on is sometimes called *globbing*.

Using Loops

The aplay command is a basic audio file player. On some systems, you may need to use play or some other command instead of aplay.

Conditional expressions are sometimes used in *loops*. Loops are structures that tell the script to perform the same task repeatedly until some condition is met (or until some condition is no longer met). For instance, Listing 12.5 shows a loop that plays all the .wav audio files in a directory.

Listing 12.5: A script that executes a command on every matching file in a directory

```
#!/bin/bash
for d in `ls *.wav` ; do
    aplay $d
done
```

The for loop as used here executes once for every item in the list generated by ls *.wav. Each of those items (filenames) is assigned in turn to the $d variable and so is passed to the aplay command.

The seq command can be useful in creating for loops (and in other ways, too): This command generates a list of numbers starting from its first argument and continuing to its last one. For instance, typing **seq 1 10** generates 10 lines, each with a number between 1 and 10. You can use a for loop beginning for x in `seq 1 10` to have the loop execute 10 times, with the value of x incrementing with each iteration. If you pass just one parameter to seq, it interprets that number as an ending point, with the starting point being 1. If you pass three values to seq, it interprets them as a starting value, an increment amount, and an ending value.

Another type of loop is the while loop, which executes for as long as its condition is true. The basic form of this loop type is like this:

Certification
Objective

```
while [ condition ]
do
    commands
done
```

The until loop is similar in form, but it continues execution for as long as its condition is *false*—that is, until the condition becomes true.

Using Functions

A *function* is a part of a script that performs a specific sub-task and that can be called by name from other parts of the script. Functions are defined by placing parentheses after the function name and enclosing the lines that make up the function within curly braces:

```
myfn() {
    commands
}
```

The keyword function may optionally precede the function name. In either event, the function is called by name as if it were an ordinary internal or external command.

Functions are very useful in helping to create modular scripts. For instance, if your script needs to perform half a dozen distinct computations, you can place each computation in a function and then call them all in sequence. Listing 12.6 demonstrates the use of functions in a simple program that copies a file but aborts with an error message if the target file already exists. This script accepts a target and a destination filename and must pass those filenames to the functions.

Listing 12.6: A script demonstrating the use of functions

```
#/bin/bash

doit() {
    cp $1 $2
}

function check() {
  if [ -s $2 ]
     then
         echo "Target file exists! Exiting!"
         exit
    fi
}

check $1 $2
doit $1 $2
```

If you enter Listing 12.6 and call it safercp, you can use it like this, assuming the file original.txt exists and dest.txt doesn't:

```
$ ./safercp original.txt dest.txt
$ ./safercp original.txt dest.txt
Target file exists! Exiting!
```

The first run of the script succeeded because dest.txt didn't exist. On the second run, though, the destination file did exist, so the script terminated with the error message.

Note that the functions aren't run directly and in the order in which they appear in the script. They're run only when called in the main body of the script—which in Listing 12.6 consists of just two lines, each corresponding to one function call, at the very end of the script.

Setting the Script's Exit Value

Certification
Objective

Ordinarily, a script's return value is the same as the last command the script called—that is, the script returns $?. You can control the exit value, however, or exit from the script at any point, by using the exit command. Used without any options, exit causes immediate termination of the script, with the usual exit value of $?. This can be useful in error handling or in aborting an ongoing operation for any reason—if the script detects an error or if the user selects an option to terminate, you can call exit to quit.

If you pass a numeric value between 0 and 255 to exit, the script terminates and returns the specified value as the script's own exit value. You can use this feature to signal errors to other scripts that might call your own script. You may have to include extra code to keep track of the causes of abnormal termination, though. For instance, you might set aside a variable (say, $termcause) to hold the cause of the script's termination. Set it to 0 at the start of the script and then, if the script detects a problem that will cause termination, reset $termcause to some non-0 value. (You can use any numeric codes you like; there's no set meaning for such codes.) On exit, be sure to pass $termcause to exit:

```
exit $termcause
```

THE ESSENTIALS AND BEYOND

Serious Linux users and administrators must have at least a basic understanding of shell scripts. Many configuration and startup files are in fact shell scripts, and being able to read them, and perhaps modify them, will help you administer your system. Being able to create new shell scripts is also important, because doing so will help you simplify tedious tasks and create site-specific tools by gluing together multiple programs to accomplish your goals.

SUGGESTED EXERCISES

▶ Write a script that copies a file by prompting the user to enter the source and destination filenames rather than by accepting them as arguments on the command line, as cp does.

▶ Some text editors leave backup files with filenames that end in tildes (~). Write a script that, when you pass it a directory name as an argument, locates all such files in that directory. The script should then ask the user whether to delete each file individually and do so if and only if the user responds by typing **Y**.

REVIEW QUESTIONS

1. After using a text editor to create a shell script, what step should you take before trying to use the script by typing its name?

   A. Set one or more executable bits using chmod.

   B. Copy the script to the /usr/bin/scripts directory.

   C. Compile the script by typing **bash *scriptname***, where *scriptname* is the script's name.

   D. Run a virus checker on the script to be sure it contains no viruses.

   E. Run a spell checker on the script to ensure it contains no bugs.

(Continues)

THE ESSENTIALS AND BEYOND *(Continued)*

2. Describe the effect of the following short script, cp1, if it's called as **cp1 big.c big.cc**:

   ```
   #!/bin/bash
   cp $2 $1
   ```

   A. It has the same effect as the cp command—copying the contents of big.c to big.cc.

   B. It compiles the C program big.c and calls the result big.cc.

   C. It copies the contents of big.cc to big.c, eliminating the old big.c.

   D. It converts the C program big.c into a C++ program called big.cc.

   E. The script's first line is invalid, so it won't work.

3. What is the purpose of conditional expressions in shell scripts?

   A. They prevent scripts from executing if license conditions aren't met.

   B. They display information about the script's computer environment.

   C. They enable the script to take different actions in response to variable data.

   D. They enable scripts to learn in a manner reminiscent of Pavlovian conditioning.

   E. They cause scripts to run only at specified times of day.

4. True or false: A user types **myscript laser.txt** to run a script called myscript. Within myscript, the $0 variable holds the value laser.txt.

5. True or false: Valid looping statements in Bash include for, while, and until.

6. True or false: The following script launches three simultaneous instances of the terminal program.

   ```
   #!/bin/bash
   terminal
   terminal
   terminal
   ```

7. You've written a simple shell script that does nothing but launch programs. In order to ensure that the script works with most user shells, what should its first line read?

8. What command can you use to display prompts for a user in a shell script?

9. What Bash scripting command can you use to control the program flow based on a variable that can take many values (such as all the letters of the alphabet)?

## CHAPTER 13

Understanding Users and Groups

Linux is a multi-user OS, meaning that it provides features to help multiple individuals use the computer. Collectively, these features constitute *accounts*. Previous chapters of this book have referred to accounts in passing but haven't covered them in detail. This chapter changes that; it describes important account principles and a few commands you can use to begin investigating accounts. Related to accounts are *groups*, which are collections of accounts that can be given special permissions on the computer, so this chapter also describes groups. One account, known as root, has special privileges on the computer. You use this account to perform most system administration tasks, so you should understand this account before you tackle the administrative tasks described in the last few chapters of this book.

▶ **Understanding accounts**

▶ **Using account tools**

▶ **Working as** root

Understanding Accounts

Accounts enable multiple users to share a single computer without causing each other too much trouble. They also enable system administrators to track who is using system resources and, sometimes, who is doing things they shouldn't be doing. Thus, account features help users use a computer and administrators administer it. Understanding these features is the basis for enabling you to manage accounts.

Some account features help you identify accounts and the files and resources associated with them. Knowing how to use these features will help you track down account-related problems and manage users of a computer.

> ▶
>
> Even a single-user workstation uses multiple accounts. Such a computer may have just one *user account*, but several *system accounts* help keep the computer running.

Understanding Account Features

Certification Objective Most account features are defined in the /etc/passwd file, which consists of colon-delimited lines, with each line defining a single account. An entry might resemble the following:

```
luke:x:1003:100:Luke Jones:/home/luke:/bin/bash
```

The information contained in the fields of this line includes the following:

Username An account's username is its most salient feature to humans. Most Linux account usernames consist of lowercase letters, and occasionally numbers, as in luke or thx1138. Underscores (_) and dashes (-) are also valid characters in Linux usernames, as are dollar signs ($) at the end.

Password User accounts are normally protected by a password, which is required to log into the computer. Direct login to most system accounts is disabled, so they lack passwords. (The root account is an important exception; it has a password in most distributions.) The password field in the /etc/passwd file usually contains an x, which is a code meaning that the password is stored in /etc/shadow, as described shortly.

Some distributions number user accounts starting at 500 rather than 1,000.

UID In reality, the username is just a label that the computer displays to us numerically challenged humans. The computer uses a user identification (UID) number to track accounts. UID numbers begin with 0 (which refers to the root account) and can range as high as 4,294,967,295 on modern Linux systems. In most distributions, user accounts are numbered 1,000 and above, with lower numbers reserved for system accounts.

File ownership and permissions are described in Chapter 15, "Setting Ownership and Permissions."

GID Accounts are tied to one or more *groups*, which are similar to accounts in many ways; however, a group is a collection of accounts. One of the primary purposes of groups is to enable users to give certain users access to their files, while preventing others from accessing them. Each account is tied directly to a primary group via a group ID (GID) number (100 in the preceding example). Accounts can be tied to other groups by inclusion in the group's definition, as described in Chapter 14, "Creating Users and Groups."

Comment field The *comment field* normally holds the user's full name (Luke Jones in this example), although this field can hold other information instead of or in addition to the user's name.

Home directory User accounts, and some system accounts, have *home directories*. A home directory is an account's "home base." Normally, ownership of an account's home directory belongs to the account. Certain tools and procedures make it easy for users to access their home directories; for instance, the tilde (~) refers to a user's home directory when used at the start of a filename.

Default shell   A default text-mode shell is associated with every account. In Linux, this shell is normally Bash (/bin/bash), but individual users can change this if they like. Most non-root system accounts set the default shell to /sbin/nologin as an added security measure—this program displays a message stating that the account is not available. Using /bin/false works in a similar way, although without the explanatory message.

Although you might guess by its name that /etc/passwd holds password information, this isn't normally the case today, although it was many years ago. For historical reasons, /etc/passwd must be readable by all users, so storing passwords there, even in encrypted form, is risky. Thus, passwords today are stored in another file, /etc/shadow, that ordinary users can't read. This file associates an encrypted password, as well as other information, with an account. This information can disable an account after a period of time or if the user doesn't change the password within a given period of time. A typical /etc/shadow entry looks like this:

```
luke:$1$E/moFkeT5UnTQ:15369:0:-1:7:-1:-1:
```

The meaning of each colon-delimited field on this line is as follows:

Username   Each line begins with the username. Note that the UID is *not* used in /etc/shadow; the username links entries in this file to those in /etc/passwd.

Password   The password is stored in encrypted form, so it bears no obvious resemblance to the actual password. An asterisk (*) or exclamation mark (!) denotes an account with no password (that is, the account doesn't accept logins—it's locked). This is common for accounts used by the system itself.

Last password change   The next field (15369 in this example) is the date of the last password change. This date is stored as the number of days since January 1, 1970.

Days until a change is allowed   The next field (0 in this example) is the number of days before a password change is allowed.

Days before a change is required   This field is the number of days after the last password change before another password change is required.

Days of warning before password expiration   If your system is configured to expire passwords, you may set it to warn the user when an expiration date is approaching. A value of 7, as in the preceding example, is typical.

Days between expiration and deactivation   Linux allows for a gap between the expiration of an account and its complete deactivation. An expired account either can't be used or requires that the user change the password immediately

◄

Passwords are stored using a *hash*, which is a one-way type of encryption. When a user types a password, it's hashed, and if the hashes match, access is granted.

◄

If you've forgotten the root password, you can boot with an emergency disc and copy the contents of a password field for an account whose password you do remember.

after logging in. In either case, its password remains intact. A deactivated account's password is erased, and the account can't be used until it's reactivated by the system administrator.

Expiration date   This field shows the date on which the account will expire. As with the last password change date, the date is expressed as the number of days since January 1, 1970.

Special flag   This field is reserved for future use and normally isn't used or contains a meaningless value. This field is empty in the preceding example.

For fields relating to day counts, a value of -1 or 99999 typically indicates that the relevant feature has been disabled. The /etc/shadow values are generally best left to modification through commands such as usermod (described in Chapter 14, "Creating Users and Groups") and chage. Understanding the format of the file enables you to review its contents or to replace the root password by cutting-and-pasting using an emergency disc, should you forget it.

The /etc/shadow file is normally stored with very restrictive permissions, such as rw------- (600), with ownership by root. (Precise permissions vary from one distribution to another, though.) This fact is critical to the shadow password system's utility because it keeps non-root users from reading the file and obtaining the password list, even in an encrypted form. By contrast, /etc/passwd must be readable by ordinary users and usually has rw-r--r-- (644) permissions. If you manually modify /etc/shadow, be sure it has the correct permissions when you're done.

It's important to realize that an account isn't a single entity like a program binary file. Account information is scattered across several configuration files, such as /etc/passwd, /etc/shadow, /etc/group, and possibly in other configuration files that refer to accounts. User files reside in the user's home directory and perhaps elsewhere. Thus, managing accounts can require doing more than just editing a file or two—although in the case of system accounts, that may be enough. For this reason, various utilities exist to help create, manage, and delete accounts, as described in the rest of this chapter and in Chapter 14.

> ▶
>
> **Examples of user files stored outside of the user's home directory include e-mail in** /var/ spool/mail **and temporary files in** /tmp.

Identifying Accounts

One way to identify user accounts is to use a GUI tool for account management. Such tools vary from one distribution to another, though. One example is the User Accounts tool in the System Settings control panel on a Fedora system. Accessing this option produces a window similar to the one shown in Figure 13.1.

This tool shows only user accounts, not system accounts. It enables changing a few features, such as a user's password, by clicking on them, but its usefulness as an account management tool is limited. Ordinary users, however, can reach it fairly easily and can use it to change their passwords. As an administrator, you can use this tool to quickly verify what accounts are active.

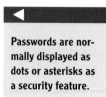

Passwords are normally displayed as dots or asterisks as a security feature.

FIGURE 13.1 The User Accounts tool in System Settings provides minimal account information.

You can identify all of a computer's accounts by viewing the contents of the /etc/passwd file with cat or less or by loading the file in a text editor. Doing so will reveal all the accounts, including both system and user accounts.

Alternatively, if you're searching for information on a specific account, you can use grep to find it in /etc/passwd, as in **grep Jones /etc/passwd** to find information on any account that's tied to a user with the name Jones. (This specific example assumes that the string Jones appears in the passwd file, of course.)

An alternative that's similar to perusing /etc/passwd is to type **getent passwd**. This command retrieves entries from certain administrative databases, including the account database. In most cases, typing **getent passwd** produces results that are identical to typing **cat /etc/passwd**; however, sometimes the two aren't identical. The /etc/passwd file defines only local user accounts. It's possible to configure Linux to use a network account database to define some or all of its accounts. If you use such a configuration, typing **getent passwd** returns both local accounts and accounts defined on the network server.

NETWORK ACCOUNT DATABASES

Many networks employ network account databases. Such systems include the Network Information System (NIS), an update to this system called NIS+, the Lightweight Directory Access Protocol (LDAP), Kerberos realms, Windows NT 4.0 domains, and Active Directory (AD) domains. All of these systems move account database management onto a single centralized computer (often with one or more backup systems). The advantage of this approach to account maintenance is that users and administrators need not deal with maintaining accounts independently on multiple computers. A single account database can handle accounts on dozens (or even hundreds or thousands) of different computers, greatly simplifying day-to-day administrative tasks and simplifying users' lives. Using such a system, though, means that most user accounts won't appear in /etc/passwd and /etc/shadow, and groups may not appear in /etc/group (described shortly, in "Understanding Groups"). These files will still hold information on local system accounts and groups, though.

Linux can participate in these systems. In fact, some distributions provide options to enable such support at OS installation time. Typically, you must know the name or IP address of the server that hosts the network account database, and you must know what protocol that system uses. You may also need a password or some other protocol-specific information, and the server may need to be configured to accept accesses from the Linux system you're configuring.

Activating use of such network account databases after installing Linux is a complex topic that is not covered in this book. Such systems often alter the behavior of tools such as passwd and usermod (described in Chapter 14) in subtle or not-so-subtle ways. If you need to use such a system, you'll have to consult documentation specific to the service you intend to use. My book *Linux in a Windows World* (O'Reilly, 2005) covers this topic for Windows NT 4.0 domains, LDAP, and Kerberos; and Mark Minasi and Dan York's *Linux for Windows Administrators* (Sybex, 2002) covers this topic for Windows NT 4.0 domains and NIS.

Understanding Groups

Certification
Objective

As noted earlier, groups are collections of accounts that are defined in the /etc/group file. Like /etc/passwd, /etc/group consists of a series of colon-delimited lines, each of which defines a single group. An example looks like this:

```
users:x:100:games,sally
```

The fields in /etc/group are:

Group name   The first field, users in the preceding example, is the name of the group. You use it with most commands that access or manipulate group data.

Password   Groups, like users, can have passwords. A value of x means that the password is defined elsewhere, and an empty password field means the group has no password.

GID   Linux uses GID values, like UID values, internally. Translation to and from group names is done for the benefit of users and administrators.

User list   You can specify users who belong to the group in a comma-delimited list at the end of the /etc/group line.

> The use of group passwords is an advanced topic that's beyond the scope of this book.

It's important to recognize that users can be identified as members of a group in either of two ways:

► By specifying the group's GID in users' individual /etc/passwd entries. Because /etc/passwd only has room for one GID value, only one group can be defined in this way. This is the user's primary (or default) group.

► By specifying usernames in the user list in the /etc/group file. A single user can appear multiple times in /etc/group, and a single group can have multiple users associated with it in this way. If a user is associated with a group in this way but not via the user's /etc/passwd entry, this group association is secondary.

When you create new files, those files will be associated with your current group. When you log in, your current group is set to your primary group. If you want to create files that are associated with another group to which you belong, you can use the newgrp command, as in:

```
$ newgrp project1
```

This command makes project1 your current group, so that files you create will be associated with that group. Group ownership of files is important in file security, which is described in more detail in Chapter 15, "Setting Ownership and Permissions."

Using Account Tools

A few commands can help you learn about the users and groups on your computer. Most notably, the whoami and id utilities can tell you about your own identity, and the who and w utilities can give you information about who is currently using the computer.

Discovering Your Own Identity

If you've been using su to change your effective user ID, or if you maintain multiple accounts for yourself and you don't recall which one you used to log in, you might become confused about your current status. In such a case, the whoami command can come in handy: It displays your effective user ID:

```
$ whoami
luke
```

Certification Objective

This example reveals that the current account is luke. If you need more information, you can use the id utility:

```
$ id
uid=1003(luke) gid=100(users) groups=100(users),16(cron),18(audio)
```

This example shows information on both users and groups:

▶ Your user ID and username—uid=1003(luke) in this example

▶ Your current group—gid=100(users) in this example

▶ All your group memberships—the entries following groups= in this example

The id command displays both the numeric UID or GID values and the associated names. The current group is the one that's active, either by default or because you used the newgrp command.

You can limit id's output by specifying a number of options, as summarized in Table 13.1. In addition, you can specify a username, as in **id sally**, to obtain information on that user rather than on yourself.

TABLE 13.1 Options for id

Long option	Short option	Effect
--group	-g	Displays only the effective group ID
--groups	-G	Displays all the groups to which you belong
--user	-u	Displays only the user data
--name	-n	Used in conjunction with -g, -G, or -u, displays only the name not the UID or GID
--real	-r	Used in conjunction with -g, -G, or -u, displays only the UID or GID, not the name

Learning Who's Online

Linux permits multiple users to access the computer simultaneously. Most often, this is done by means of remote access servers such as the Secure Shell (SSH); however, you can use Linux's virtual terminal (VT) feature to log in multiple times using a single keyboard and monitor. Sometimes you might want to know who is using the computer. You might do this before shutting down the computer, for instance, to ensure you don't inconvenience another user.

To learn who is online, you can use a command known as who:

**Certification
Objective**

```
$ who
luke      :0              2012-03-06 13:27
luke      pts/0           2012-03-06 15:16 (:0.0)
sally     pts/7           2012-03-07 13:00 (callisto)
rod       pts/9           2012-03-07 13:22 (remote.example.org)
```

This example shows four logins—two by luke, one by sally, and one by rod. Information provided in the default output includes:

Username   The first column of who's output shows the username.

Terminal identifier   The second column of who's output shows a code associated with the terminal. In this example, luke's first login shows :0 as this identifier, which means it's a local GUI (X) login. The remaining logins all have terminal identifiers of the form pts/#, indicating text sessions. A text session can be a terminal launched in X, a text-mode console login, or a remote login via SSH or some other protocol.

> ◄
>
> **Text-mode sessions can also be indicated by codes of the form tty#.**

Login date and time   who displays the date and time of each login. Thus, you can see that luke's X session began almost one full day before rod logged in.

Remote host   The final column of who's output, if present, shows the login source. Console logins (including both text-mode and X-based logins) don't include a source. A source of the form :# or :#.#, as in luke's second session, indicate a terminal opened in X. A hostname or IP address, as in sally's and rod's sessions, indicates remote access from the specified computer.

You can obtain additional information, most of which is obscure or specialized, by passing options to who. One that's more likely than others to be useful is --count (or -q), which produces a more compact summary of the data:

```
$ who -q
luke luke sally rod
# users=4
```

This output includes just the usernames and a line specifying the total number of sessions. (That number counts one user with multiple logins multiple times.) For information on additional who options, consult its man page.

An alternative to who is w, which is similar to who but produces somewhat more verbose output:

```
$ w
 12:36:40 up 37 days, 45 min,  3 users,  load average: 0.00, 0.02, 0.05
 USER   TTY    LOGIN@   IDLE   JCPU   PCPU WHAT
 luke   :0     06Mar12 40:23   0.01s  0.01s -bash
 luke   pts/0  06Mar12 40.00s  0.01s  0.01s nano
 sally  pts/7  13:00    20:37m 0.00s  0.00s -bash
 rod    pts/9  13:22    2:50   12:44m 0.00s /bin/sh /etc/xdg/xfce4/xinitrc
```

As you can see, w displays much of the same information as who, including the terminal identifier (TTY) and login time (in a different format). In addition, w displays some further information:

▶ The session's idle time tells you how long it's been since the user has interacted with this session. This information can help you identify sessions that the user may have abandoned.

▶ The JCPU column identifies the total amount of CPU time associated with the session. This can be useful debugging information if the computer has become sluggish because of out-of-control processes.

▶ The PCPU column identifies the total amount of CPU time associated with the current process running in the session. Again, this information can help you track down out-of-control processes.

▶ The WHAT column tells you what program the session is running.

Some configurations also display a FROM column, which shows a remote hostname. Using the -f option toggles this option on or off. A few other options can eliminate or modify w's output. Consult the program's man page for details.

Working as *root*

Linux is modeled after Unix, which was designed as a multi-user OS. In principle, you can have thousands of accounts on a single Unix (or Linux) computer. One user, though, needs extraordinary power in order to manage the features of the computer as a whole. This is the root user, also known as the *superuser* or the *administrator*. Knowing why root exists, how to do things as root, and how to use root privileges safely is important for managing a Linux system.

Why Work as *root*?

Most people use computers to do ordinary day-to-day computer tasks—browse the Web, write letters, manage a music collection, and so on. These activities are known collectively as *user tasks*, and they don't require special privileges. As just noted, a Linux computer can have many user accounts, and the users can use the computer from these user accounts (also known as *unprivileged accounts* or *unprivileged users*) to perform such user tasks.

Certification Objective

The root account, on the other hand, exists to enable you to perform *administrative tasks*. These tasks include installing new software, preparing a new disk for use in the computer, and managing ordinary user accounts. Such tasks require access to system files that ordinary users need not modify, or sometimes even read.

Certification Objective

To facilitate performing these tasks, root can read and write every file on the computer. Since Linux relies on files to store system settings, this effectively gives root the power to change any detail of the OS's operation, which is the point of having a superuser account. If the computer is a workstation that's used by just one individual, you might wonder why the distinction between root and the user account is necessary. The explanation is that the power of the root account can lead to accidental damage. For instance, take the rm command. If you mistype an rm command as an ordinary user, you can accidentally delete your own files but not system files. Make the same mistake as root, however, and you can delete system files, perhaps making the computer unbootable. Thus, you should be cautious when using the root account—a topic I'll come back to shortly, in "Using root Privileges Safely."

Acquiring *root* Privileges

When you need to perform a command-line task that requires root privileges, you can do so in any of three ways:

Log in as root You can log in directly as root at a text-mode shell or by using a remote login tool such as SSH. You can even log into GUI mode as root on some Linux distributions, although some distributions disallow this by default because it's very dangerous.

Use su The su command enables you to change your identity within a shell. Type **su *username*** to change your identity to that of the specified *username*. If you omit *username*, root is assumed, so typing **su** enables you to effectively become root. You must, however, know the password for the target account for

Certification Objective

▶

su **stands for**
switch user **or**
substitute user.

this command to work. After you acquire `root` privileges in this way, you can type as many commands as `root` as you like. When you're done, type **exit** to relinquish your superuser status. You can also use su to run a single command as root by using the -c option, as in **su -c *command*** to run *command* as root. If you use a dash (-) within the command, as in **su -** or **su - luke**, the program opens a login session, which runs the target user's login scripts. This can be important because these scripts often set environment variables that can be important for that user, such as $PATH.

Certification
Objective

Use sudo   The sudo command is similar to su, but it works for just one command at a time, which you type after sudo, similar to using su -c. For instance, typing **sudo cat /etc/shadow** enables you to see the contents of the /etc/ shadow file, which is not readable by ordinary users. You must type either your own password or the root password, depending on the sudo configuration, when you use this program. (When using su -c, you must always type the root password.) The next command you type will be executed using your ordinary account privileges. By default, most distributions permit only users who are members of the wheel group to use sudo. Some distributions, such as Ubuntu, rely heavily on sudo and don't permit direct root logins by default.

If you acquire root privileges by logging in directly as root or by using su, your shell prompt will change:

```
[luke@wembleth ~]$ su
Password:
[root@wembleth luke]#
```

To use root **com-**
mands in Ubuntu,
you must either
precede them
with sudo **(as in**
sudo cat /etc/
shadow**) or type**
sudo su **to acquire**
a longer-lasting
root **shell.**

In this example, the username has changed from luke to root; the directory has changed from ~ to luke (since for root, ~ refers to /root, not /home/luke); and the last character of the prompt has changed from a dollar sign ($) to a hash mark (#). Because I use just the last character of the prompt for most examples printed on their own lines in this book, such examples implicitly specify whether a command requires root privileges by the prompt used. For instance, consider accessing the /etc/shadow file mentioned earlier:

```
# cat /etc/shadow
```

▶

The use of the hash mark prompt indicates that you *must* type this command as root.

Some of this book's chapters describe both GUI and text-mode methods of system administration. How, then, can you administer Linux in GUI mode if you must use the text-mode su (or sudo) command to acquire root privileges? One way is to launch a GUI administrative tool from a shell in which you've already used su. This approach works but is a bit inelegant if you're more comfortable with a GUI than with a command line. Most distributions, therefore, provide an alternative: You can launch administrative tools from the computer's desktop menus and the GUI tools will then prompt you for the root password, as shown in Figure 13.2. If you type the password correctly, the program will launch. The result is similar to that of launching the program from a shell using sudo—it runs as root, but without making anything else run as root.

If you're a member of the wheel group, most distributions prompt you for your own password rather than the root password when using such tools.

FIGURE 13.2 When you launch an administrative tool from a GUI, Linux asks you for a password.

SETTING THE *ROOT* PASSWORD

If you're using your own computer, you may already know or have the root password, since most distributions prompt you to enter the root password when you install the system. Some distributions, such as openSUSE, set the root password to be identical to the first user account's password by default. Ubuntu doesn't set a root password at all; instead, Ubuntu's security model favors the use of sudo or GUI equivalents.

If you've forgotten the root password, you can recover or reset it in several ways, such as:

▶ You can type **sudo passwd root** to reset the root password. As described in Chapter 14, passwd is the tool to set an account's password, and so this command will reset the root password. Used in this way, sudo will prompt you for a password (you should type your user password) followed by two prompts for a new root password. This method will work, however, only if you're an authorized user of sudo on your system.

(Continues)

SETTING THE *ROOT* PASSWORD *(Continued)*

▶ Reboot into an emergency system, such as Parted Magic (http://partedmagic.com), and mount your regular installation's root filesystem. You can then locate its /etc/shadow file (it will be located at another mount point, such as /mnt/local/etc/shadow) and load it into a text editor. Locate the entry for an account whose password you know and copy the second colon-delimited entry from that line into the equivalent space for the root account. Passwords are stored in an encrypted form, so you won't recognize the password you copy and paste in this way. After you save your changes, reboot and log into the root account. Once you've logged in, change the root password to something unique.

If you're using a school's or employer's computer, you should either refrain from attempting to perform tasks as root or obtain the root password through authorized channels. If you've been hired as a system administrator, your employer should provide this information, or specify another way to perform maintenance (such as using sudo). If you aren't the computer's official administrator, attempting to perform root tasks on it may be grounds for dismissal. In fact, you might even be sued or imprisoned for breaking into a computer without authorization!

Using *root* Privileges Safely

As already described, root power is dangerous. For instance, preparing a disk requires creating a filesystem on the disk. This topic is not covered in detail in this book, but you should know that you can create a filesystem with mkfs, which takes a partition identifier as an option. Suppose that you want to create a new filesystem on /dev/sda3, so you quickly type a command:

> Note that emergency systems, such as Parted Magic, typically run all your commands as root, so be careful when using them!

```
# mkfs /dev/sda2
```

Did you catch the error? The command specifies /dev/sda2 rather than /dev/sda3. If /dev/sda2 held important data (such as your Linux installation or your /home directory), this mistake could be absolutely disastrous.

This is just one example of the trouble that improper use of root can cause. Others include intruders gaining root access to your computer; unintended changes to configuration files; damage to some (even if not all) of the computer's system files; and changes to ownership or permissions on ordinary user files, rendering them inaccessible to their true owners. Thus, I recommend you take the following precautions whenever you need root access:

▶ Ask yourself if you really need root access. Sometimes there's a way to achieve a goal without superuser privileges or by using those privileges in a more limited way than you'd originally planned. For instance, you might find that only root can write to a removable disk. Such a problem can usually be overcome by adjusting permissions on the disk in one way or another, thus limiting the use of root.

▶ Before pressing the Enter key after typing any command as root (or clicking any confirmation button in a GUI program running as root), take your hands *off* the keyboard and mouse, look over the command, and verify that it's correct in every respect. A simple typo can cause a world of pain. This step has saved me from disaster more than once!

▶ Never run a suspicious program as root. On multi-user systems, unscrupulous users can try to trick administrators into running programs that will do nasty things or give the attacker root privileges. Programs downloaded from random Internet sites could in principle be designed to compromise your security, and such programs are much more dangerous when run as root.

▶ Use root privileges for as brief a period as possible. If you need to type just one or two commands as root, do so and then type **exit** in the root shell to log out or return to your normal privileges. Alternatively, use sudo to run the commands. It's easy to overlook the fact that you're using a root shell and therefore type commands as root that don't need that privilege. Every command typed as root is a risk.

▶ Never leave a root shell accessible to others. If you're performing root maintenance tasks and are called away, type **exit** in your root shell before leaving the computer.

▶ Be careful with the root password. Don't share the password with others, and be cautious about typing it in a public area or when others might be looking over your shoulder. If you're using Linux professionally, your employer may have guidelines concerning who may have root access to a computer. Learn and obey those rules. Be sure to select a strong root password, too.

If a program asks for your or the root password and it's not an administrative program you trust, be suspicious! Research the program before giving it your password!

Chapter 14 describes how to select a strong password.

Following these rules of thumb can help keep you from damaging your computer or giving somebody else root access to the computer.

THE ESSENTIALS AND BEYOND

Accounts are critical to Linux's normal functioning. Ordinarily, most of the tasks you perform on a Linux computer require the privileges of a normal user, so you'll use your own user account to handle these tasks. You can use tools like whoami, id, who, and w to identify your normal account and to determine who else might be using the computer. Occasionally, you'll need to perform administrative tasks that require additional privileges. To acquire such privileges, you must use the root account, which can read and write any ordinary file, access hardware in a low-level way, reconfigure the network, and perform other tasks that ordinary users aren't allowed to do. Because root is so powerful, you should use that power sparingly and be extremely careful when you do use it, lest a typo or other accident cause serious problems.

SUGGESTED EXERCISES

▶ Type **whoami** followed by **id** to review your ordinary user account status. Chances are the id command will reveal that you're a member of a number of groups. Perform a Web search to learn what each one does.

▶ Read the /etc/passwd file or type **getent passwd** to review what accounts are defined on the computer. Are there ordinary user accounts (those with UIDs above 500 or 1,000, depending on your distribution) other than your own? Try performing a Web search to learn the purpose of a few of the system accounts (those with UIDs below 500 or 1,000, depending on your distribution).

REVIEW QUESTIONS

1. What is the purpose of the system account with a UID of 0?

   A. It's the system administration account.

   B. It's the account for the first ordinary user.

   C. Nothing; UID 0 is left intentionally undefined.

   D. It varies from one distribution to another.

   E. It's a low-privilege account that's used as a default by some servers.

2. What type of information will you find in /etc/passwd for ordinary user accounts? (Select all that apply.)

   A. A user ID (UID) number

   B. A complete listing of every group to which the user belongs

   C. The path to the account's home directory

   D. The path to the account's default GUI desktop environment

   E. The path to the account's default text-mode shell

(Continues)

THE ESSENTIALS AND BEYOND *(Continued)*

3. You want to run the command `iptables -L` as root, but you're logged in as an ordinary user. Which of the following commands will do the job, assuming the system is configured to give you root access via the appropriate command?

   A. `sudo iptables -L`

   B. `root iptables -L`

   C. `passwd iptables -L`

   D. `su iptables -L`

   E. `admin iptables -L`

4. True or false: whoami provides more information than id.

5. True or false: Linux stores information on its groups in the /etc/groups file.

6. True or false: As a general rule, you should employ extra care when running programs as root.

7. The file that associates usernames with UID numbers in Linux is _____. (Provide the complete path to the file.)

8. To learn who is currently logged into the computer and what programs they're currently running, you can type _____.

9. UIDs below 500 or 1,000 (depending on the distribution) are reserved for use by _____ accounts.

Creating Users and Groups

Linux is a multi-user OS, meaning that a single Linux computer can support many users, each with a unique account. With this capability comes the need to manage users' accounts, and this chapter covers the procedures you'll use to do so. The chapter begins with information on how to create accounts. With accounts created, I then show you how to modify those accounts and, when necessary, delete them. Finally, groups are similar to accounts in many ways, so I also describe how to create and manage groups.

▶ **Creating new accounts**

▶ **Modifying accounts**

▶ **Deleting accounts**

▶ **Managing groups**

Creating New Accounts

In many environments, the task of adding accounts is quite common. Large businesses frequently hire new employees, universities see new students enrolling, and so on. Thus, you must know how to create new accounts. Before covering the mechanics of creating accounts, I describe the important issues of deciding how to use groups and selecting a good password. I then explain how to create accounts using both GUI and text-mode tools.

Deciding on a Group Strategy

As described in Chapter 13, "Understanding Users and Groups," Linux groups are collections of users. You can use groups to control who can access particular files. As will be described in Chapter 15, "Setting Ownership and Permissions," individuals can change the group affiliations and group permissions of their own files. Thus, the way you use groups can influence your computer's overall security strategy. Two approaches are common:

User groups   Each user can have an associated group; for instance, the user luke can have a group called luke. This user can then set group ownership on his files to luke or set group permissions to whatever is desired, and the system administrator can add users to the luke group. Thereafter, members of the luke group may access files in this group using the permissions determined by the user luke. This approach emphasizes controlling access to individual users' files.

By default, some distributions employ a user groups strategy and others use a project groups strategy. In the latter case, most users are in a group called users by default.

Project groups   In this method, you create groups based on work projects, departmental affiliations, or other real-world groupings of users. For instance, you might have a group called sales for users in the sales department. Members of this group who want to share files with others in this group would assign group ownership and permissions appropriately and store files in an agreed-upon location. This approach works best when the computer is used by a large number of people who collaborate in easily defined groups.

These two approaches are not mutually exclusive; you can mix and match, or create your own approach. You should also realize that users can be members of multiple groups. In fact, this is required for the user groups approach to work at all—otherwise, groups are redundant with accounts.

If you use the project group approach, you should think about which group should be a new user's primary group. This is the group that will be assigned group ownership of the user's files by default.

Selecting a Good Password

Be sure to follow the advice in this section yourself, especially for the root password!

When you create an account, you should normally create a password for it. Sometimes, the user can type the password when the account is created. Other times, though, you'll need to select a password the user should then use. In such cases, you should instruct the user to change the password as soon as possible. In either case, you should educate users about how to select a good password.

Poor but common passwords include those based on the following:

▶ The names of family members, friends, and pets

▶ Favorite books, movies, television shows, or the characters in any of these

▶ Telephone numbers, street addresses, or Social Security numbers

▶ Any other meaningful personal information

> ▶ Any single word that's found in a dictionary (in *any* language)

> ▶ Any simple keyboard or alphanumeric combination, such as qwerty or 123456

The best possible passwords are random collections of letters, digits, and punctuation. Unfortunately, such passwords are difficult to remember. A reasonable compromise is to build a password in two steps:

1. Choose a base that's easy to remember but difficult to guess.

2. Modify that base in ways that increase the difficulty of guessing the password.

One approach to building a base is to use two or more *unrelated* words, such as *bun* and *pen*. You can then merge these two words (bunpen). Another approach, and one that's arguably better than the first, is to use the first letters of a phrase that's meaningful to the user. For instance, the first letters of "yesterday I went to the dentist" become yiwttd. In both cases, the base should not be a word in any language. As a general rule, the longer the password, the better.

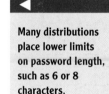

Many distributions place lower limits on password length, such as 6 or 8 characters.

With the base in hand, it's time to modify it to create a password. The user should apply at least a couple of several possible modifications:

Adding numbers or punctuation   One important change is to insert random numbers or punctuation in the base. This step might yield, for instance, bu3npe&n or y#i9wttd. As a general rule, add at least two symbols or numbers.

Mixing case   Linux uses case-sensitive passwords, so jumbling the case of letters can improve security. Applying this rule might produce Bu3nPE&n and y#i9WttD, for instance.

Reversing order   A change that's very weak by itself but that can add somewhat to security when used in conjunction with the others is to reverse the order of some or all letters. You might apply this to just one word of a two-word base. This could yield Bu3nn&EP and DttW9i#y, for instance.

Grow the haystack   A would-be intruder's task of discovering a password has been likened to finding a needle in a haystack. One way to make this task harder is to increase the size of the haystack. In password terms, this means making a password larger. You can do this by using larger words or phrases, of course, but this can make a password harder to remember and type. Even a size increase that simply repeats a single character can be helpful. Thus, you might turn the passwords into Bu3nn&EPiiiiiiiiiii or Dtt::::::::::W9i#y.

Your best tool for getting users to pick good passwords is to educate them. Here are some insights to share with users:

▶ Passwords can be guessed by malicious individuals who know them or even who target them and look up personal information in telephone books, on Web pages, and so on.

▶ Although Linux encrypts its passwords internally, programs exist that feed entire dictionaries through Linux's password encryption algorithms for comparison to encrypted passwords. If a match is found, the password has been found.

▶ User accounts might be used as a first step toward compromising the entire computer or as a launching point for attacks on other computers.

▶ Users should *never* reveal their passwords to others, even people claiming to be system administrators—this is a common scam, but real system administrators don't need users' passwords.

▶ The same password should not be used on multiple systems because doing so quickly turns a compromised account on one computer into a compromised account on all of them.

▶ Writing passwords down or emailing them are both risky practices. Writing a password on a sticky note stuck to the computer's monitor is particularly risky.

Telling your users these things will help them understand the reasons for your concern, and it's likely to help motivate at least some of them to pick good passwords.

Spam e-mails sometimes try to trick users into revealing passwords by claiming that an email, banking, or other account has been deactivated or compromised.

DON'T USE THESE PASSWORDS!

If you do a Web search on *worst passwords* or a similar phrase, you'll quickly discover Web sites that list the most common and most easily guessed passwords that security researchers have uncovered. Details vary from one survey to another, but in one 2011 study (http://www.splashdata.com/press/PR111121.htm), the top 10 most common passwords were:

1. password
2. 123456
3. 12345678

(Continues)

> **Don't Use These Passwords!** *(Continued)*
>
> **4.** qwerty
>
> **5.** abc123
>
> **6.** monkey
>
> **7.** 1234567
>
> **8.** letmein
>
> **9.** trustno1
>
> **10.** dragon
>
> Such passwords are easily discovered by brute-force password-guessing programs and are included in collections of passwords distributed on the Internet. Using such a password is barely better than using no password at all. Do yourself a favor and use a better one!

Creating Accounts Using GUI Tools

Now that you have some idea of what type of group policy you want to use and how to create a good password, you can begin creating accounts. The easiest way to do this is with the help of a GUI tool; however, such tools vary from one Linux distribution to another. The most important variation is in how you access these tools. For instance:

▶ In Fedora 16, you can type **system-config-users** as root at a shell prompt to launch the User Manager utility. Alternatively, you can use a more limited System Settings utility similar to the one in Ubuntu.

▶ In openSUSE 12.1, you can launch the YaST configuration tool and open the User and Group Management tool within YaST.

▶ In Ubuntu 11.10, you can open the System Settings utility in the desktop environment and then click on the User Accounts option. Before you make changes, you must click the padlock icon and enter your password.

As an example of a GUI user management tool, Figure 14.1 shows Fedora's User Manager utility, which provides more features than the User Accounts utility that's part of the System Settings tool. You'll be better able to adjust account options with a more complete tool such as User Manager than with a simple tool such as User Accounts.

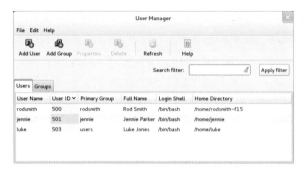

FIGURE 14.1 The User Manager utility provides many options for creating and managing accounts.

To add a user with User Manager, follow these steps:

1. Click Add User. The result is the Add New User dialog box shown in Figure 14.2.

FIGURE 14.2 You can enter all of the basic account information with the Add New User dialog box.

2. Type the username in the User Name field. This is what the user will type at Linux login prompts.

3. Type the user's full name in the Full Name field. This entry is stored in the comment field of /etc/passwd and is displayed in various tools; for instance, it appears in the upper-right corner of the screen when the user logs into GNOME.

4. Type the password twice, once in the Password field and again in the Confirm Password field.

5. In most cases, you can click OK, since the default values for the remaining options are usually fine. (The Home Directory field will be filled in based on the username you enter.) You can, however, customize the login shell, home directory location, and other features before clicking OK.

The new account will appear in the User Manager list. You can subsequently modify it or delete it, as described later in this chapter, should the need arise.

If the user is present when you create the account, you can have the user type the password at this point.

Creating Accounts from the Shell

With any distribution, you use the useradd utility to create an account from the command line. To use this utility, you type its name and the username you want to associate with a new account. You may also include options between useradd and the username, as summarized in Table 14.1.

Certification Objective

You can call useradd as adduser if you prefer; both command names are equivalent.

TABLE 14.1 Options for useradd

Option name	Option abbreviation	Effect
--comment *comment*	-c	This parameter specifies the comment field for the user. (GUI tools generally describe this as the "full name.")
--home *home-dir*	-d	You specify the account's home directory with this parameter. It defaults to /home/*username*.
--expiredate *expire-date*	-e	You set the date on which the account will be disabled, expressed in the form *YYYY-MM-DD*, with this option. The default is for an account that does not expire.
--inactive *inactive-days*	-f	This parameter sets the number of days after a password expires, after which the account becomes completely disabled. A value of –1 disables this feature and is the default.

(Continues)

TABLE 14.1 *(Continued)*

Option name	Option abbreviation	Effect
--gid *default-group*	-g	You set the name or GID of the user's default group with this option. The default for this value is a new group named after the user.
--groups *group[,...]*	-G	This parameter sets the names or GIDs of groups to which the user belongs. More than one may be specified by separating them with commas.
--create-home	-m	When this option is included, user-add creates a home directory for the user. This option is enabled by default.
--skel *skeleton-dir*	-k	Normally, default user configuration files are copied from /etc/skel, but you may specify another template directory with this option, which is valid only in conjunction with -m.
None	-M	This option forces the system to *not* automatically create a home directory.
--shell *shell*	-s	You set the name of the user's default login shell with this option. The default is /bin/bash.
--uid *UID*	-u	This parameter creates an account with the specified user ID value (*UID*).
--non-unique	-o	This parameter enables a single UID number to be reused; this option is passed when creating the second or subsequent account that reuses a UID.

(Continues)

TABLE 14.1 *(Continued)*

Option name	Option abbreviation	Effect
`--system`	`-r`	This parameter specifies the creation of a system account. `useradd` doesn't create a home directory for system accounts, and gives them UID values below 100.
`--no-user-group`	`-N`	This option disables creation of a group for the user.

Some of these options aren't readily accessible when creating accounts using GUI tools, but the details differ from one GUI utility to another. In some cases, options can be set in a GUI utility *after* the account has been created, but not when creating it.

A complete `useradd` command, including setting a few options, looks like this:

```
# useradd -e 2012-12-31 -u 1012 pamela
```

The `useradd` command supports additional options; consult its man page for details.

This example creates an account with a username `pamela` and a UID of 1012. The account expires on December 31, 2012. After that date, the user will be unable to log into the account, although her files won't be deleted, and `root` will be able to reactivate the account.

When you create an account with `useradd`, it will be in a *locked* state—the user will not be able to log in. To unlock it, you must use the `passwd` command, as described next, in "Modifying Accounts."

Behind the scenes, `useradd` (or by extension its GUI front-ends) modifies the contents of /etc/passwd, /etc/shadow, and /etc/group, all of which are described in detail in Chapter 13, "Understanding Users and Groups." If you use `--create-home` or `-m`, or if this option is used by default, the program creates a home directory and copies files from /etc/skel to that location. Creating an account will also usually create a *mail spool file*, in which the user's incoming e-mail will be stored. (This file may go unused on many desktop systems, but it can be very important if you run mail server software on the computer.) Thus, you can see that `useradd` makes quite a few modifications to your computer's files and directories in creating the account.

You might want to specify a UID to keep these values synchronized across computers that share files with the Network File System (NFS), which identifies file ownership via UIDs.

Modifying Accounts

As you've just learned, you can specify many options that affect accounts, such as giving an account a specific UID number, when creating an account. Sometimes, though, it's necessary to change account options after an account has been created. Fortunately, Linux provides both GUI and text-mode tools to help you do this. Before delving into operational details of these tools, though, you should understand when you might want to make changes to accounts, and know how to check whether a user is currently logged in.

Deciding When to Modify Accounts

In an ideal world, you'll create your accounts perfectly every time; however, sometimes this isn't possible. You might lack information that's necessary to create a perfectly tuned account (such as the length of time an employee will be with a company), or your needs might change after the account has been created. Some common specific causes of account changes include (but are by no means limited to) the following:

▶ A user might forget a password. The system administrator can change the password for any account without knowing the original password, so system administrators frequently have to help out users with faulty memories.

▶ Group affiliations may need to change because of restructuring of collaborative arrangements.

▶ Account expiration data may need to be updated. A student might enroll for another semester, for instance. Sometimes an expired account must be re-enabled.

▶ UID numbers may need to be synchronized with other computers, in order to facilitate file sharing across computers or for other reasons.

▶ On occasion a username may need to be changed—for instance, if a user marries and your site policy uses last names in the username.

▶ Users' home directories might change because you've added disk space and need to move some users' home directories to a new location.

When working in a GUI, all of the preceding changes can be handled from User Manager. When working in a text-mode shell, though, you'll need to master a few different programs to handle this range of account modifications.

Checking for Logged-in Users

Be aware that some account changes are potentially quite disruptive if the user is logged in at the moment you perform them. Changing the username and home directory, in particular, are likely to cause problems. Thus, you should make such changes only when the user is logged out. Several tools can help you check who's using the computer, and thus avoid problems:

who This utility, described in Chapter 13, produces a list of users who are currently logged into the computer, along with some details of their login sessions, such as their terminal identifiers and login dates.

w This command is similar to who in broad strokes, but it provides different details. Most notably, it identifies the program that's currently running in each session.

last This program produces a list of recent login sessions, including their starting and ending times, or a notice that the user is still logged in:

```
$ last
jennie   tty3         Sun Jan  8 12:43    still logged in
jennie   tty3         Sun Jan  8 12:43 - 12:43  (00:00)
jennie   tty2         Sun Jan  8 12:36    still logged in
jennie   tty2         Sun Jan  8 12:36 - 12:36  (00:00)
```

One notable limitation of last is that it includes only text-mode logins. This makes its utility for identifying users who are currently using the computer rather limited, since such users are likely to be logged in using a GUI session.

Certification Objective

Modifying Accounts Using GUI Tools

As with adding accounts, the procedure for modifying accounts using GUI tools varies from one tool to another. Most GUI tools provide similar options, although some are more complete than others. In this section, I describe how to modify accounts using Fedora's User Manager, which you can launch by typing **system-config-users** in a terminal window.

To make such changes, you should click the account and then either select File ➤ Properties from the menu or click the Properties icon in the toolbar. The result is a dialog box similar to the one shown in Figure 14.3. This dialog box presents account properties. Each of the four tabs provides access to particular types of data:

User Data As shown in Figure 14.3, you can adjust the account's username, the comment field (identified as Full Name), the password, the home directory,

> **If you launch User Manager as an ordinary user, you'll have to authenticate yourself by typing your or the root password, depending on your configuration.**
>
>

> **The User Manager program does *not* rename or move the user's home directory on the disk; you must do this manually with mv.**
>
>

and the user's login shell. If you type a weak password, the program warns you of this fact and asks for confirmation before accepting it.

FIGURE 14.3 The User Properties dialog box enables you to edit a wide variety of account properties.

Account Info   This tab provides two options: You can enable or disable account expiration (including setting an expiration date if you enable it), and you can lock or unlock the password.

> Locking an account's password prevents logins but doesn't completely disable the account.

Password Info   This tab enables you to set password expiration data. This information is distinct from account expiration data in that an expired account becomes completely disabled, whereas an expired password can be reset by the user, at least for a while. You can set various change values, such as the number of days after a change before the user must change the password again. You can also set an option to force the user to change the password on the next login. (This option will be cleared once this happens.)

Groups   This tab presents a complete list of groups on the computer. Check the box next to any group to which you want the user to belong. You can also set the user's primary group, but only to a group to which the user already belongs.

> If you want to add the user to an entirely new group, you must first create the new group, as described in the section "Managing Groups."

Users can change their own passwords by using GUI options in their desktop environments. For instance, in GNOME, selecting the My Account item from the menu that appears when they click their names in the upper-right corner of the screen produces the User Accounts dialog box, shown in Figure 14.4. Clicking the dots in the Password field produces a dialog box in which the user can type a new password. Administrators can also use this tool to add and modify accounts, but it's much less powerful than User Manager in this role.

FIGURE 14.4 The User Accounts window enables users to change their own passwords.

Modifying Accounts from the Shell

One of the most frequent account modifications is to change a user's password, either as part of account creation or because a user has forgotten the password. You can make this change with the passwd program. Ordinary users can type this command name alone to change their own passwords, but not other users' passwords. The superuser, however, can pass a username to the command to change any account's password:

```
# passwd pamela
Changing password for user pamela.
New password:
Retype new password:
passwd: all authentication tokens updated successfully.
```

As a security measure, the password you type does not echo to the screen as you type it. If the passwords you type don't match, the program refuses to accept your change and prompts you again for a fresh pair of passwords. The program also checks the strength of the password and refuses to accept one that it deems to be too weak.

You can handle most other account modifications using the usermod program. This command works much like useradd, but instead of creating a new account, it modifies an existing one. Table 14.2 summarizes the most important usermod options.

Certification
Objective

In addition to setting passwords, the passwd utility enables you to adjust password expiration and aging options. Consult its man page for details.

Certification
Objective

TABLE 14.2 Options for usermod

Option name	Option abbreviation	Effect
--append	-a	Used with --groups (-G), causes the specified groups to be added to, rather than replace, the existing set of groups for the user.
--comment *comment*	-c	This parameter specifies the comment field for the user. (GUI tools generally describe this as the "full name.")
--home *home-dir*	-d	You specify the account's home directory with this parameter. It defaults to /home/*username*.
--expiredate *expire-date*	-e	You set the date on which the account will be disabled, expressed in the form *YYYY-MM-DD*, with this option. The default is for an account that does not expire.
--inactive *inactive-days*	-f	This parameter sets the number of days after a password expires, after which the account becomes completely disabled. A value of -1 disables this feature and is the default.
--gid *default-group*	-g	You set the name or GID of the user's default group with this option. The default for this value is a new group named after the user.
--groups *group[,...]*	-G	This parameter sets the names or GIDs of groups to which the user belongs. More than one may be specified by separating them with commas.
--login *username*	-l	Changes the account's username to the specified value.

(Continues)

TABLE 14.2 *(Continued)*

Option name	Option abbreviation	Effect
--lock	-L	Locks the account's password, preventing logins.
--move-home	-m	When this option is included with --home (-d), usermod moves the user's existing home directory to the new location.
--shell *shell*	-s	You set the name of the user's default login shell with this option.
--uid *UID*	-u	This parameter changes the account's UID number to the specified value.
--non-unique	-o	This parameter enables a single UID number to be reused (use it in conjunction with --uid/-u).
--unlock	-U	This option unlocks a locked account password.

Many usermod **options are identical to** useradd **options.**

For example, consider the following use of usermod:

```
# usermod -u 1072 -m -d /home2/luke luke
```

This command makes three changes to the luke account:

▶ It changes the UID value to 1072.

▶ It changes the account's home directory to /home2/luke.

▶ It moves the contents of the account's original home directory to its new location.

You might issue a command like this one if you were migrating user accounts to an NFS server mounted at /home2. Such a change might require a new home directory location and a change in the UID value to match that used on the NFS server.

You should be careful when making changes to the UID value because, although usermod changes the UID values of files in common locations such as the user's home directory and e-mail files, it can miss user files in unusual locations.

If you need to make group changes that require adding new groups, consult the upcoming section "Managing Groups" for information on that topic.

The --move-home **(-m) option will be quick when the move is on a single low-level filesystem but potentially slow when it crosses filesystem boundaries.**

Deleting Accounts

Deleting accounts can sometimes be as important as adding or modifying them. Unused accounts can consume disk space. More important, they can be abused, either by their former owners or by others who might be able to break into an account if it has a weak password. Thus, you should routinely delete unused accounts. Before you do so, though, you should understand what happens when you delete an account and decide precisely how to do it, lest you create problems by deleting an account in an inappropriate way. With that knowledge in hand, you can delete accounts using either GUI or text-mode tools.

Avoiding Account-Deletion Pitfalls

Deleting an account may sound simple enough, but a mistake can cause problems, either immediately or in the future. In addition to obvious issues such as accidentally deleting the wrong account, you should consider two factors:

Consider archiving a deleted account's home directory to a long-term backup medium. This will enable you to recover the files should they become valuable in the future.

User file preservation   One of the reasons I mentioned for deleting accounts was to regain the disk space consumed by the account. Recovering this disk space, however, can sometimes be the *wrong* thing to do. Users' files might be extremely valuable, either to the users themselves or to the organization that owns the computer. Thus, you should carefully consider whether to delete the user's home directory or do something else with it, such as move it into another user's home directory and change permissions on the files it contains. The same is true of the user's mail queue (normally stored in /var/spool/mail/*username*, where *username* is the username).

UID and GID reuse   When an account is deleted, the account's UID and GID become available for reuse. In many cases these numbers will not be reused, since Linux assigns these values based on the highest current value. Thus, if you delete any but the highest-numbered current user, the user's old UID and GID numbers won't be reused unless intervening accounts are also deleted. Nonetheless, such deletions can happen, or you might override the default values. If a UID is reused, any files previously owned by the old user will suddenly appear to be owned by the new user. This might cause no problems, but it might cause confusion about who created the files. In some cases, it could even cause suspicion of wrongdoing to fall on the new user, if the old files contain information the new user shouldn't have or if they reside in directories to which the new user shouldn't have access.

If you want to avoid any chance of confusion or claims of misbehavior falling on new users because of UID or GID reuse, you can use the find command to locate all files with particular UID or GID values, using the -uid and -gid options, as in:

```
# find / -uid 1004
```

This example finds all files on the computer with a UID of 1004. (Searching on a GID works the same way but using the -gid option.) You can then reassign ownership of these files using chown or delete them. Ordinarily, you'd issue this command only after deleting or reassigning ownership of the user's home directory, since that directory will probably contain far too many matching files.

You can issue this command as a non-root user, but it will return errors and it may miss some files. Thus, it's best to do this as root.

Deleting Accounts Using GUI Tools

As with other account management tasks, using a GUI is fairly intuitive, but details vary from one distribution to another. As an example, to delete an account from Fedora's User Manager (system-config-user), select the account and then either click Delete in the toolbar or select Edit ➢ Delete from the menu. The result is a confirmation dialog box similar to the one shown in Figure 14.5. Check or uncheck the box to delete the user's home directory, as you see fit and, if you're certain of the action, click Yes. The account will be immediately deleted.

If the user has many files and if you opt to delete those files, the deletion operation may take several seconds, or even minutes, to complete.

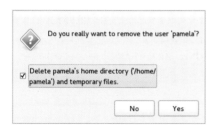

FIGURE 14.5 When you delete an account with User Manager, you may optionally delete the user's home directory.

If the user is currently logged in, User Manager will complain about this fact in the confirmation dialog box. You'll still be able to delete the account, but the user won't be immediately logged out.

Deleting Accounts from the Shell

The userdel command deletes accounts from a text-mode shell. In its simplest form, you pass it a username and nothing more:

Certification Objective

```
# userdel pamela
```

The program doesn't prompt you for confirmation; it just deletes the account. It does not, however, delete the user's home directory by default. To have it do so, pass it the --remove (-r) option.

If the user is currently logged in, userdel notifies you of that fact and does nothing. You can pass it the --force (-f) option to delete the account despite the fact that it's in use. To both force account deletion and remove the user's files, you can pass both options:

```
# userdel -rf pamela
userdel: user pamela is currently logged in
```

The program still complains about the user being logged in, but it deletes the account and files just the same.

Managing Groups

In many respects, groups are analogous to accounts. They're defined in similar files and managed with similar utilities. Groups are also tied to accounts in that accounts include group definitions. Until now, I've assumed you'll be using standard groups or the groups that are defined as part of account creation. Sometimes, though, you need to create, delete, or modify groups for specific purposes, such as if you use a project group strategy. As with account management, you can do this using either GUI or text-mode tools.

Managing Groups Using GUI Tools

If you want to manage system groups as well as user groups, select Edit ➢ Preferences and, in the resulting dialog box, uncheck Hide System Users And Groups.

Many GUI account maintenance tools, such as Fedora's User Manager (system-config-user), provide group management tools that are analogous to the user management tools described throughout this chapter. Referring to Figure 14.1, you'll see that the User Manager window includes both Users and Groups tabs. To manage groups, click the Groups tab. This produces a display resembling Figure 14.6.

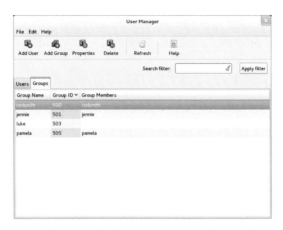

FIGURE 14.6 The User Manager utility enables you to manage groups as well as users.

You can add, modify, and delete groups in a manner that's closely analogous to adding, modifying, and deleting accounts. The number of options available is much smaller, though; for instance, when adding a group, you can specify only its name and GID. Groups don't have home directories, login shells, and so on. You might, of course, want specific users to be members of your new group from the start. To do so, follow these steps:

1. Create a group by clicking Add Group and specifying the group name in the resulting dialog box.

2. Select the group, click Properties, and select the Group Users tab. The result is the Group Properties dialog box shown in Figure 14.7.

FIGURE 14.7 You can add users to a group using the Group Properties dialog box.

3. The Group Users tab contains an alphabetized list of users; locate the users who should be members of the group, select them, and click OK.

Alternatively, you can manage group membership by altering each user's group membership individually, as described earlier in "Modifying Accounts."

Managing Groups from the Shell

You can create groups from the shell using the groupadd command, which works much like useradd for users but takes a smaller set of options, the most important of which appear in Table 14.3. Consult the program's man page for information on more obscure options.

Certification
Objective

TABLE 14.3 Options for groupadd

Option name	Option abbreviation	Effect
--gid *GID*	-g	You can provide a specific GID with this parameter. If you omit it, groupadd uses the next available GID.
--non-unique	-o	Normally, the GID you specify must be unused by other groups, but the -o parameter overrides this behavior, enabling you to create multiple groups that share one GID.
--system	-r	This parameter instructs groupadd to create a system group, which is one with a GID of less than 500 or 1,000, depending on the distribution. Non-system groups are normally used as user private groups.
--force	-f	Normally, if you try to create a group that already exists, groupadd returns an error message. This parameter suppresses that error message.

To modify existing groups, you have three options:

▶ The usermod command includes the --groups (-G) option to alter group membership on a user-by-user basis. You can use this feature to adjust who is a member of particular groups.

▶ You can use the groupmod command. You can use the --gid (-g) and --non-unique (-o) options from Table 14.3 with this command, as well as --new-name *name* (-n *name*), which changes the group's name. You cannot, however, change group membership with groupmod.

▶ You can directly edit the /etc/group file, which stores the group definition. This option is sometimes handy if you want to add several users to a new group; however, it's a bit risky, since a stray keypress could damage the file.

Deleting groups from the shell entails use of the groupdel command, which takes a group name as a single option, as in **groupdel gingko** to delete the gingko group.

THE *WHEEL* GROUP

Linux distributions invariably provide several groups by default. One of these, wheel, is particularly important for system administration because members of the wheel group are granted certain special administrative privileges, such as the right to use the sudo command. Some distributions enable you to add your primary user account to the wheel group when you install the OS. Often, this phrasing is not used; instead, the installer asks if you want to add the account to the "administrators group" or some similar term.

You can change users who are members of the wheel group in the ways described here. When using the User Manager, though, you must uncheck the Hide System Users And Groups option in order to see wheel in the list of groups. If you're using another GUI tool, you may need to look for an analogous option.

THE ESSENTIALS AND BEYOND

In a GUI environment, you can perform most common account maintenance tasks with GUI tools, which enable you to add, modify, and delete accounts by selecting options from menus and lists. Some operations, however, require you to use command-line tools such as useradd, usermod, userdel, and passwd. (The groupadd, groupmod, and groupdel commands provide analogous functionality for groups.) Even if you don't need to use the more obscure features provided by the text-mode tools, they can be quicker to use than the GUI tools once you're familiar with them.

SUGGESTED EXERCISES

▶ Create a test account using User Manager (or another GUI tool provided by your distribution) and then log into the account you've created to verify that it's working as you expected.

▶ Do the same using useradd, but do *not* use passwd to set its password. Were you able to log in? Use passwd and try logging in again.

(Continues)

THE ESSENTIALS AND BEYOND (Continued)

REVIEW QUESTIONS

1. What would a Linux system administrator type to remove the nemo account and its home directory?

   A. `userdel nemo`

   B. `userdel -f nemo`

   C. `userdel -r nemo`

   D. `rm /home/nemo`

   E. `rm -r /home/nemo`

2. Of the following, which is the *best* password?

   A. `LinusTorvalds`

   B. `uB2op%4q****************`

   C. `123456`

   D. `password`

   E. `peanutbuttersandwich`

3. Describe the effect of the following command, assuming it completes successfully:

   `# groupadd henry`

   A. It creates a new group called `henry`.

   B. It adds the user `henry` to the current default group.

   C. It imports group information from the file called `henry`.

   D. It changes the user's default group to `henry`.

   E. It adds the group `henry` to the user's list of groups.

4. True or false: User accounts have higher UID numbers than do system accounts.

5. True or false: Command-line users should normally use `usermod` to change their passwords.

6. True or false: After deleting an account, files formerly owned by the deleted account may remain on the computer.

7. You want to create an account for a new user, using the username `theo` and giving the user a UID of 1926. The command to do this is **useradd** _____.

8. You want to change the username of a user from `e1211` to `emilyn`, without altering anything else about the account. To do so, you would type _____.

9. To create a system account, you must pass the _____ option to `groupadd`.

## CHAPTER 15

Setting Ownership and Permissions

As a multi-user OS, Linux provides tools to help you secure your files against unwanted access—after all, you wouldn't want another user to accidentally (or intentionally) read personal files or even delete your files! Linux handles these tasks through two features of files and directories: their *ownership* and their *permissions*. Every file has an associated owner (that is, an account with which it's linked), and also an associated group. Three sets of permissions define what the file's owner, members of the file's group, and all other users can do with the file. Thus, ownership and permissions are intertwined, although you use different text-mode commands to manipulate them. (GUI tools often combine the two, as described in this chapter.)

▶ **Setting ownership**

▶ **Setting permissions**

> The *set user ID (SUID)* and *set group ID (SGID)* permission bits, described in Chapter 16, "Navigating the Linux Filesystem," can modify the account and group associated with a program.
>
> ▶

Setting Ownership

Linux's security model is based on that of Unix, which was designed as a multi-user OS. This security model therefore assumes the presence of multiple users on the computer, and provides the means to associate individual files with the users who create them—that is, files have *owners*. You should thoroughly understand this concept, and with that understanding, you can change a file's ownership, using either a GUI file manager or a text-mode shell.

Ownership also applies to running programs (that is, *processes*). Most programs you run are tied to the account you used to launch them. This identity, in conjunction with the file's ownership and permissions, determines whether a program may modify a file.

Understanding Ownership

Chapter 13, "Understanding Users and Groups," and Chapter 14, "Creating Users and Groups," described Linux's system of accounts. These accounts are the basis of file ownership. Specifically, every file has an owner—an account with which it's associated. This association occurs by means of the account's *user ID (UID)* number. Every file is also associated with a *group* by means of a *group ID (GID)* number.

As described later, in the section "Setting Permissions," access to the file is controlled by means of permissions that can be set independently for the file's owner, the file's group, and all other users of the computer. As root, you can change the owner and group of any file. The file's owner can also change the file's group, but only to a group to which the user belongs.

The same principles of ownership apply to directories as apply to files: directories have owners and groups. These can be changed by root or, to a more limited extent, by the directory's owner.

CROSS-INSTALLATION UIDs AND GIDs

You may use multiple Linux installations, either dual-booting on one computer or installed on multiple computers. If so, and if you transfer files from one installation to another, you may find that the ownership of files seems to change as you move them around. The same thing can happen with non-Linux Unix-like OSs, such as Mac OS X. The reason is that the filesystems for these OSs store ownership and group information using UID and GID numbers, and a single user or group can have different UID or GID numbers on different computers, even if the name associated with the account or group is identical.

This problem is most likely to occur when using native Linux or Unix filesystems to transfer data, including both disk-based filesystems (such as Linux's ext2fs or Mac OS X's HFS+) or the Network File System (NFS) for remote file access. This problem is less likely to occur if you use a non-Linux/Unix filesystem, such as the File Allocation Table (FAT) or the New Technology File System (NTFS) for disks, or the Server Message Block/Common Internet File System (SMB/CIFS; handled by Samba in Linux) for network access.

If you run into this problem, several solutions exist, but many of them are beyond the scope of this book. One you can use, though, is to change the UID or GID mappings on one or more installations so that they all match. Chapter 14 describes how to change a user's UID number with usermod, and to change a group's GID number with groupmod. When transferring data via removable disks, using FAT or NTFS can be a simple solution, provided you don't need to preserve Unix-style permissions on the files.

Setting Ownership in a File Manager

As described in Chapter 4, "Using Common Linux Programs," a *file manager* enables you to manipulate files. You're probably familiar with file managers in Windows or Mac OS X. Linux's ownership and permissions are different from those of Windows, though, so you may want to know how to check on, and perhaps change, ownership features using a Linux file manager. As noted in Chapter 4, you have a choice of several file managers in Linux. Most are similar in broad strokes but differ in some details. In this section, I use Nautilus, the GNU Network Object Model Environment (GNOME) file manager, as an example.

If you want to change the file's owner, you must run Nautilus as root, but you can change the file's group to any group to which you belong as an ordinary user. The procedure to perform this task as root is as follows:

1. Launch a terminal window.

2. In the terminal window, type **su** to acquire root privileges.

3. In the terminal window, type **nautilus** to launch Nautilus. You can optionally include the path to the directory in which you want Nautilus to start up. If you don't include a path, Nautilus will begin by displaying the contents of the /root directory.

4. Locate the file whose ownership you want to adjust and right-click it.

5. In the resulting menu, select Properties. The result is a Properties dialog box.

6. In the Properties dialog box, click the Permissions tab. The result resembles Figure 15.1.

7. To change the file's owner, select a new owner in the Owner field. This action is possible only if you run Nautilus as root.

8. To change the file's group, select a new group in the Group field. If you run Nautilus as an ordinary user, you will be able to select any group to which you belong, but if you run Nautilus as root, you will be able to select any group.

9. When you've adjusted the features you want to change, click Close.

If you want to change a file's group but not its owner, and if you're a member of the target group, you can launch Nautilus as an ordinary user. You can then pick up the preceding procedure at step 4.

If you're using Ubuntu, you may instead need to use sudo **to launch Nautilus.**

The /root **directory is the** root **account's home directory.**

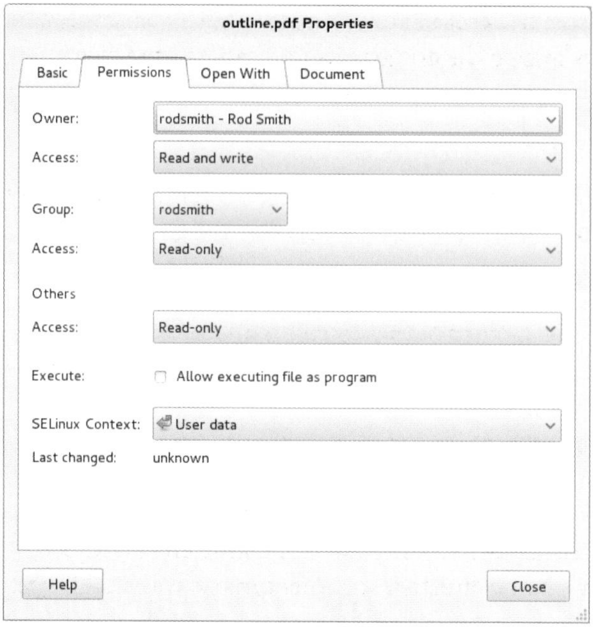

FIGURE 15.1 Linux file managers give you access to the file's ownership and permission metadata.

You should be *extremely* cautious about running Nautilus as root. If you forget you're running this program as root, you can easily create new files as root, which will require additional root-privilege actions to correct by changing file ownership. It's also easy to accidentally delete critical system files as root that you could not delete as an ordinary user. For these reasons, I recommend that you use a text-mode shell to adjust file ownership. The change in the prompt makes it easier to notice you're running as root, and if you're used to using a GUI, you're less likely to launch additional programs as root from a text-mode shell than from Nautilus.

Setting Ownership in a Shell

Certification Objective ▶

The command to change the ownership of a file in the preferred text-mode manner is chown. In its most basic form, you pass it the name of a file followed by a username:

```
# chown bob targetfile.odf
```

> The chown command's name stands for *change owner*.

This example gives ownership of targetfile.odf to bob. You can change the file's principal owner and its group with a single command by separating the owner and group with a colon (:):

```
# chown bob:users targetfile.odf
```

This example gives ownership of `targetfile.odf` to bob and associates the file with the `users` group. To change the group without changing the owner, you can omit the owner, leaving the colon and group name:

```
$ chown :users targetfile.odf
```

Alternatively, you can use the `chgrp` command, which works in the same way but changes *only* the group and does not require the colon before the group name:

```
$ chgrp users targetfile.odf
```

Note that the commands used to change the owner require `root` privileges, whereas you can change the group as an ordinary user—but only if you own the file and belong to the target group.

The `chown` and `chgrp` commands both support a number of options that modify what they do. The most useful of these is `-R` (or `--recursive`), which causes a change in ownership of all the files in an entire directory tree. For instance, suppose that the user mary has left a company, and an existing employee, bob, must access her files. If mary's home directory was /home/mary, you might type:

```
# chown -R bob /home/mary
```

This command gives bob ownership of the /home/mary directory, all the files in the /home/mary directory, including all its subdirectories, the files in the subdirectories, and so on. To make the transition a bit easier for bob, you might also want to move mary's former home directory into bob's home directory.

Setting Permissions

File ownership is meaningless without some way to specify what particular users can do with their own or other users' files. That's where permissions enter the picture. Linux's permission structure is modeled after that of Unix, and it requires a bit of explanation before you tackle the issue. Once you understand the basics, you can begin modifying permissions, using either a GUI file manager or a text-mode shell. You can also set default permissions for new files you create.

Understanding Permissions

To understand Unix (and hence Linux) permissions, you may want to begin with the display created by the `ls` command, which lists the files in a directory, in conjunction with its `-l` option, which creates a long directory listing that

▶

Chapter 6, "Getting to Know the Command Line," introduced the ls command, and describes additional ls options.

includes files' permissions. For instance, to see a long listing of the file test, you might type:

```
$ ls -l test
-rwxr-xr-x  1 rodsmith users     111 Apr 13 13:48  test
```

This line consists of several sections, which provide assorted pieces of information on the file:

Permissions   The first column (-rwxr-xr-x in this example) is the file's permissions, which are of interest at the moment.

▶

Chapter 7, "Managing Files," describes links in more detail.

Number of links   The next column (1 in this example) shows the number of hard links to the file—that is, the number of unique filenames that may be used to access the file.

Username   The next column (rodsmith in this example) identifies the file's owner by username.

Group name   The file's group (users in this example) appears next.

File size   This example file's size is quite small—111 bytes.

Time stamp   The time stamp (Apr 13 13:48 in this example) identifies the time the file was last modified.

Filename   Finally, ls -l shows the file's name—test in this example.

The string that begins this output (-rwxr-xr-x in this example) is a symbolic representation of the permissions string. Figure 15.2 shows how this string is broken into four parts:

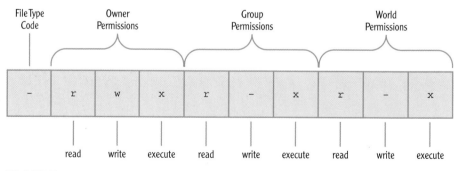

Most of the files you'll manipulate are normal files, directories, and symbolic links.

FIGURE 15.2 A symbolic representation of file permissions is broken into four parts.

The file type code   The first character is the file type code, which represents the file's type, as summarized in Table 15.1. This type character is sometimes omitted from descriptions when the file type is not relevant or when it's identified in some other way.

Owner permissions These permissions determine what the file's owner can do with the file.

Group permissions These permissions determine what members of the file's group (who aren't its owner) can do with the file.

World (or "other") permissions These permissions determine what users who aren't the file's owner or members of its group can do with the file

TABLE 15.1 Linux file type codes

Code	Name	Meaning
–	Normal data file	May be text, an executable program, graphics, compressed data, or just about any other type of data.
d	Directory	Disk directories are files, but they contain filenames and pointers to those named files' data structures.
l	Symbolic link	The file contains the name of another file or directory. When Linux accesses the symbolic link, it tries to read the linked-to file.
p	Named pipe	A pipe enables two running Linux programs to communicate with each other in a one-way fashion.
s	Socket	A socket is similar to a named pipe, but it permits network and bidirectional links.
b	Block device	A file that corresponds to a hardware device to and from which data is transferred in blocks of more than one byte. Disk devices (hard disks, floppies, CD-ROMs, and so on) are common block devices.
c	Character device	A file that corresponds to a hardware device to and from which data is transferred in units of one byte. Examples include parallel and RS-232 serial port devices.

Setting the execute bit on a nonprogram file doesn't turn it into a program, of course; it just indicates that a user may run a file that is a program.

In each of the three sets of permissions, the string identifies the presence or absence of each of three types of access: read, write, and execute. Read and write permissions are fairly self-explanatory. If the execute permission is present, it means that the file may be run as a program. The absence of the permission is denoted by a dash (–) in the permission string. The presence of the permission is indicated by the letter r for read, w for write, or x for execute.

Thus, the example permission string -rwxr-xr-x means that the file is a normal data file and that its owner, members of the file's group, and all other users can read and execute the file. Only the file's owner has write permission to the file.

Another representation of permissions is possible. It's compact but a bit confusing: It takes each of the three permissions groupings of the permission string (omitting the file type code) and converts it into a number from 0 to 7 (that is, a *base 8* or *octal* number). The result is a three-digit octal number. Each number is constructed by starting with a value of 0 and then:

▶ Adding 4 if read permissions are present

▶ Adding 2 if write permissions are present

▶ Adding 1 if execute permissions are present

The resulting three-digit code represents permissions for the owner, the group, and the world. Table 15.2 shows some examples of common permissions and their meanings.

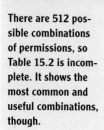

These procedures actually involve binary numbers and logical, not arithmetic, operations. The arithmetic description is easier to understand, though.

There are 512 possible combinations of permissions, so Table 15.2 is incomplete. It shows the most common and useful combinations, though.

T A B L E   1 5 . 2 Example permissions and their interpretations

Permission string	Octal code	Meaning
rwxrwxrwx	777	Read, write, and execute permissions for all users.
rwxr-xr-x	755	Read and execute permission for all users. The file's owner also has write permission.
rwxr-x---	750	Read and execute permission for the owner and group. The file's owner also has write permission. Other users have no access to the file.
rwx------	700	Read, write, and execute permissions for the file's owner only; all others have no access.
rw-rw-rw-	666	Read and write permissions for all users. No execute permissions for anybody.
rw-rw-r--	664	Read and write permissions for the owner and group. Read-only permission for all others.

(Continues)

TABLE 15.2 *(Continued)*

Permission string	Octal code	Meaning
rw-rw----	660	Read and write permissions for the owner and group. No world permissions.
rw-r--r--	644	Read and write permissions for the owner. Read-only permission for all others.
rw-r-----	640	Read and write permissions for the owner, and read-only permission for the group. No permission for others.
rw-------	600	Read and write permissions for the owner. No permission for anybody else.
r--------	400	Read permission for the owner. No permission for anybody else.

Several special cases apply to permissions:

Directory execute bits   Directories use the execute bit to grant permission to search the directory. This is a highly desirable characteristic for directories, so you'll almost always find the execute bit set when the read bit is set.

Directory write permissions   Directories are files that are interpreted in a special way. As such, if a user can write to a directory, that user can create, delete, or rename files in the directory, even if the user isn't the owner of those files and does not have permission to write to those files.

Symbolic links   Permissions on symbolic links are always 777 (rwxrwxrwx, or lrwxrwxrwx, to include the file type code). This access applies only to the link file itself, not to the linked-to file. In other words, all users can read the contents of the link to discover the name of the file to which it points, but the permissions on the linked-to file determine its file access. Changing the permissions on a symbolic link affects the linked-to file.

root   Many of the permission rules don't apply to root. The superuser can read or write any file on the computer—even files that grant access to nobody (that is, those that have 000 permissions). The superuser still needs an execute bit set to run a program file.

◄

The usual rules for writing to directories can be modified with the *sticky bit*, which is described in Chapter 16.

Setting Permissions in a File Manager

The procedure for setting permissions in a file manager is similar to that for setting the ownership of a file:

Details vary in other file managers, but the principles are the same as those described here.

▶ You normally adjust these settings using the same dialog box used to adjust ownership, such as the Nautilus dialog box shown earlier in Figure 15.1.

▶ You don't need to be root to adjust the permissions of files you own.

▶ You should use root access for this job only on files you don't own.

As seen in Figure 15.1, there are three Access items, associated with the Owner, the Group, and Others:

▶ The Owner item provides two options: Read-Only and Read and Write.

▶ The Group and Others items both provide Read-Only and Read and Write plus the None option. You can use these options to set the read and write permission bits on your file.

Nautilus requires setting the execute bit separately, by checking the Allow Executing File As Program box. This check box sets all three execute permission bits; you can't control execute permission more precisely with Nautilus. You also can't adjust the execute permissions on directories with Nautilus.

Setting Permissions in a Shell

Certification Objective

In a text-mode shell, you can use chmod to change permissions. This command is rather complex, mostly because of the complex ways that permissions may be changed. You can specify the permissions in two forms: as an octal number or in a symbolic form, which is a set of codes related to the string representation of the permissions.

The chmod command's name stands for *change mode*, *mode* being another name for permissions.

The octal representation of the mode is the same as that described earlier and summarized in Table 15.2. For instance, to change permissions on report.tex to rw-r--r--, you can issue the following command:

```
$ chmod 644 report.tex
```

A symbolic mode, by contrast, consists of three components:

▶ A code indicating the permission set you want to modify—u for the user (that is, the owner), g for the group, o for other users, and a for all permissions

▶ A symbol indicating whether you want to add (+), delete (-), or set the mode equal to (=) the stated value

▶ A code specifying what the permission should be, such as the common r, w, or x symbols, or various others for more advanced operations

Using symbolic modes with chmod can be confusing, so I don't describe them fully here; however, you should be familiar with a few common types of use, as summarized in Table 15.3. Symbolic modes are more flexible than octal modes because you can specify symbolic modes that modify existing permissions, such as adding or removing execute permissions without affecting other permissions. You can also set only the user, group, or world permissions without affecting the others. With octal modes, you must set all three permission bits equal to a value that you specify.

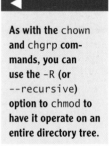

As with the chown and chgrp commands, you can use the -R (or --recursive) option to chmod to have it operate on an entire directory tree.

TABLE 15.3 Examples of symbolic permissions with chmod

Command	Initial permissions	End permissions
chmod a+x bigprogram	rw-r--r--	rwxr-xr-x
chmod ug=rw report.tex	r--------	rw-rw----
chmod o-rwx bigprogram	rwxrwxr-x	rwxrwx---
chmod g-w,o-rw report.tex	rw-rw-rw-	rw-r-----

Setting the umask

The *user mask*, or *umask*, determines the default permissions for new files. The umask is the value that is *removed* from 666 (rw-rw-rw-) permissions when creating new files, or from 777 (rwxrwxrwx) when creating new directories. For instance, if the umask is 022, then files will be created with 644 permissions by default, and new directories will have 755 permissions. Note that the removal operation is not a simple subtraction but a bitwise removal. That is, a 7 value in a umask removes the corresponding rwx permissions; but for files, for which the starting point is rw-, the result is --- (0), not –1 (which is meaningless).

You can adjust the umask with the umask command, which takes the umask value, as in **umask 022**. Typically, this command appears in a system configuration file, such as /etc/profile, or in a user configuration file, such as ~/.bashrc.

THE ESSENTIALS AND BEYOND

File security is important on a multi-user OS such as Linux, and one of the pieces of the puzzle of security is ownership. In Linux, every file has one owner and one associated group. The superuser can set the owner with chown, and either the superuser or the file's owner can set the file's group with chown or chgrp. By itself, ownership is useless, so Linux supports the concept of file permissions, which control which other users can access a file, and in what ways. You can set permissions with the chmod utility. You can view ownership, permissions, and some additional file features using the -1 option to the ls command.

SUGGESTED EXERCISES

▶ As root, copy a file that you created as an ordinary user, placing the copy in your ordinary user home directory. Using your normal account, try to edit the file with a text editor and save your changes. What happens? Try to delete that file with the rm command. What happens?

▶ Create a scratch file as an ordinary user. As root, use chown and chmod to experiment with different types of ownership and permissions to discover when you can read and write the file using your normal login account.

▶ Use the ls -1 command to view the ownership and permissions of files in your home directory, in /usr/bin (where many program files reside), and in /etc (where most system configuration files reside). What are the implications of the different ownership and permissions you see for who can read, write, and execute these files?

REVIEW QUESTIONS

1. What command would you type (as root) to change the ownership of somefile .txt from ralph to tony?

   A. chown ralph:tony somefile.txt

   B. chmod somefile.txt tony

   C. chown somefile.txt tony

   D. chown tony somefile.txt

   E. chmod tony somefile.txt

(Continues)

THE ESSENTIALS AND BEYOND *(Continued)*

2. Typing `ls -ld wonderjaye` reveals a symbolic file mode of `drwxr-xr-x`. Which of the following are true? (Select all that apply.)

A. wonderjaye is a symbolic link.

B. wonderjaye is an executable program.

C. wonderjaye is a directory.

D. wonderjaye may be read by all users of the system.

E. wonderjaye may be written by any member of the file's group.

3. Which of the following commands can you use to change a file's group?

A. groupadd   **D.** ls

B. groupmod   **E.** chown

C. chmod

4. True or false: A file with permissions of 755 can be read by any user on the computer, assuming all users can read the directory in which it resides.

5. True or false: Only root may use the chmod command.

6. True or false: Only root may change a file's ownership with chown.

7. What option causes chown to change ownership on an entire directory tree?

8. What three-character symbolic string represents read and execute permission but no write permission?

9. What symbolic representation can you pass to chmod to give all users execute access to a file, without affecting other permissions?

## CHAPTER 16

Navigating the Linux Filesystem

Several earlier chapters in this book have alluded to the way files are organized on a Linux computer, and have even described some specifics—for instance, that /home is a directory that holds users' home directories. This chapter goes into more detail on this topic. First up is a description of some of the key Linux directories, including their names and purposes. I also describe some special permission bits you can set on files and directories to affect the way Linux treats them. Such attributes can enable you to hide files from view or alter the usual permissions rules in ways that can be helpful for shared user directories.

▶ **Understanding where things go**

▶ **Using special permission bits and file features**

Understanding Where Things Go

▶

The term *filesystem* can refer to low-level data structures or to the organization of files and directories on the computer. In this chapter, the latter meaning is most common.

As described in Chapter 6, "Getting to Know the Command Line," Linux uses a unified directory tree—that is, every partition, removable disk, network file share, and other disk or disk-like storage device is accessible as a directory in a single directory tree (or *filesystem*). This filesystem is structured—certain directories have certain specific purposes, whether the directories exist as regular subdirectories on one partition or are separate devices that are mounted off the root (/) device. Understanding the purpose of the main directories will help you locate files and avoid making disastrous mistakes. Before delving into those specifics, you should understand the distinction between user files and system files.

User Files vs. System Files

To understand the distinction between user files and system files, you should recall that Linux is a multi-user OS. In principle, a single computer can host thousands of users. Consider such a computer—perhaps a mainframe at a university or a large business or a cloud computing server. The vast majority of this computer's thousands of users will be unfamiliar with the details of Linux system administration—they want only to use their word processors, e-mail clients, and other user applications. Such users don't need to deal with system configuration files. Indeed, giving them access to such files—especially write access—could be disastrous. On a computer with 1,000 users, each of whom can change the system configuration, *somebody* will make a change that will bring down the computer, whether through ignorance or malice.

Of course, the issues involved in protecting the computer from its users are just a special case of more general user account issues—on that 1,000-user computer, you probably don't want users to be able to read and write each others' files except in limited ways. Thus, as described in Chapter 13, "Understanding Users and Groups" and Chapter 15, "Setting Ownership and Permissions," you can set permissions on files to prevent unauthorized access.

Certification
Objective

System files are files that control how the computer operates—they include:

▶ System startup scripts that launch servers and other important daemons

▶ Program files, both binary files and scripts

▶ Program support files, such as fonts and icons

▶ Configuration files that define how the system works (network configuration settings, disk layout information, and so on)

▶ Configuration files for most servers and other daemons

▶ Data storage for system programs, such as the database that describes what programs are installed

▶ System log files, which record normal system activity

Chapter 9, "Using
Programs and
Processes,"
describes package
management.

Obviously, non-technical users should not be able to alter system files, except perhaps indirectly. (Log files record activities such as login attempts, for instance.) Users must be able to read some types of system files, such as the fonts and icons they use, but some system files should be protected even from read access. Users should not be able to read the /etc/shadow file because it holds encrypted passwords, for instance.

To achieve the goal of restricting ordinary users' access to system files, they are normally owned by root or by another system account that has a more limited purpose. For instance, many server programs rely on their own specific system accounts. System files can then be protected from unwanted access by setting permissions in some appropriate way, depending on their specific needs. Ordinary users are then unable to write to most system files, protecting them from harm. Because root can read and write any file, you must acquire root privileges to perform most system maintenance tasks.

Immediately after installing Linux, most of the files it contains are system files, and most of the directories and subdirectories on a fresh Linux installation are system directories. As described shortly, a few directories, such as /home and /tmp, are set aside for user files, although even these are structured or configured in such a way as to prevent problems with multi-user access.

The distinction between system files and user files exists even on single-user Linux computers such as your personal laptop computer. This may seem strange or frustrating; after all, if you're the only user, and if you have root access, why bother with the distinction between system files and user files? The answer is that it provides a layer of protection against accidental or malicious damage. If a typo, a bug, or malware would, say, delete all the files on the computer, the damage is contained if this action is performed as a normal user rather than as root—a normal user *can't* delete all the files on the computer. Thus, the distinction between these two account types (and, by extension, these two classes of files) is useful even on a single-user computer.

Users' home directories traditionally reside in /home, whereas /tmp is accessible to all users and holds temporary files.

The Filesystem Hierarchy Standard

Although every Linux distribution has its own unique way of doing certain things, their developers all recognize the need for some standardization in the layout of their directories. For instance, programs should be able to consistently locate key system configuration files in the same places on all distributions. If this weren't the case, programs that rely on such features would become more complex and might not work on all distributions. In order to address this need, the *Filesystem Hierarchy Standard* (FHS) was created. Even aside from Linux, some Unix-like OSs also follow the FHS to one degree or another.

The FHS evolved from an earlier Linux-only standard, the *Filesystem Standard* (FSSTND).

One important distinction made by the FHS is that between *shareable files* and *unshareable files*. Shareable files may be reasonably shared between computers, such as user data files and program binary files. (Of course, you don't *need* to share such files, but you *may* do so.) If files are shared, they're normally shared through a Network File System (NFS) server. Unshareable files contain system-specific information, such as configuration files. For instance, you're not likely to want to share a server's configuration file between computers.

A second important distinction made by the FHS is that between *static files* and *variable files*. The former don't normally change except through direct intervention by the system administrator. Most program executables are good examples of static files. Variable files may be changed by users, automated scripts, servers, or the like. For instance, users' home directories and mail queues are composed of variable files.

The FHS tries to isolate each directory into one cell of this 2 × 2 (shareable/unshareable × static/variable) matrix. Figure 16.1 illustrates these relationships. Some directories contain subdirectories in multiple cells, but in these cases, the FHS tries to specify the status of particular subdirectories. For instance, /var is variable, and it contains some shareable and some unshareable subdirectories, as shown in Figure 16.1.

	Shareable	Unshareable
Static	/usr /opt	/etc /boot
Variable	/home /var/mail	/var/run /var/lock

FIGURE 16.1 The FHS attempts to fit each important directory in one cell of a 2 × 2 matrix.

The FHS comes in numbered versions. Version 2.3, the latest version as I write, was released in January 2004. The URL for FHS's official Web page is `http://www.pathname.com/fhs/`.

Important Directories and Their Contents

The FHS defines the names and purposes of many directories and subdirectories on a Linux system. Table 16.1 summarizes the most important of these. Most of these directories are system directories, the main exceptions being /home, /tmp, /mnt, and /media.

The FHS has been stable for years. Fedora is planning changes for Fedora 17 that will violate or require changes to the FHS.

Certification Objective

TABLE 16.1 Important Linux directories, according to the FHS

Directory	Purpose
/	The root directory; all files appear in this directory or subdirectories of it.
/etc	Holds system configuration files.
/boot	Holds important boot files, such as the Linux kernel, the initial RAM disk, and often boot loader configuration files.

(Continues)

TABLE 16.1 (Continued)

Directory	Purpose
/bin	Holds program files that are critical for normal operation and that ordinary users may run.
/sbin	Holds program files that are critical for normal operation and that ordinary users seldom run.
/lib	Holds libraries—code used by many other programs—that are critical for basic system operation.
/usr	Holds programs and data used in normal system operation but that aren't critical for a bare-bones boot of the system. This directory is split into subdirectories that mirror parts of the root organization—/usr/bin, /usr/sbin, /usr/lib, and so on.
/home	Holds users' home directories. Separating this directory into its own low-level filesystem effectively isolates most user data from the OS, which can be useful if you want to re-install the OS without losing user data.
/root	The root user's home directory. Note that this is different from /, which is pronounced *root*.
/var	Holds miscellaneous transient files, such as log files and print spool files. One subdirectory of /var, /var/tmp, deserves special mention. Like /tmp (described next), /var/tmp holds temporary files. These files should *not* be deleted when the computer reboots.
/tmp	Holds temporary files, often including temporary files created by user programs. Such files may theoretically be deleted when the computer reboots, although in practice many distributions don't do this.
/mnt	The traditional mount point for removable media; sometimes split into subdirectories for each mounted filesystem.
/media	The new mount point for removable media; typically split into subdirectories for each mounted filesystem.
/dev	Holds *device files*, which provide low-level access to hardware.

As an ordinary user, you will create most of your files in your home directory, which is normally a subdirectory of /home. You might also access removable media mounted at /media, and perhaps network resources that might be mounted

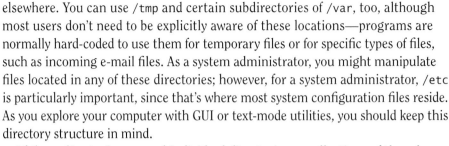

Ordinary users can't write to most system directories, such as /usr. Thus, you can't damage your installation by checking out these directories—*if* you're running as an ordinary user!

See the sidebar, "Fedora 17 and the FHS," for information on changes Fedora is planning to where it stores program files.

Certification Objective

elsewhere. You can use /tmp and certain subdirectories of /var, too, although most users don't need to be explicitly aware of these locations—programs are normally hard-coded to use them for temporary files or for specific types of files, such as incoming e-mail files. As a system administrator, you might manipulate files located in any of these directories; however, for a system administrator, /etc is particularly important, since that's where most system configuration files reside. As you explore your computer with GUI or text-mode utilities, you should keep this directory structure in mind.

Of these directories, several individual directories or collections of them bear special attention:

The configuration directory   The /etc directory holds most system configuration files. Previous chapters have referred to several such files, such as /etc/fstab (which defines where partitions are mounted) and /etc/passwd (which is the primary account definition file). Many more exist. Indeed, you'll find subdirectories in /etc to house multiple configuration files for complex subsystems and servers, such as /etc/X11 (for the X Window System) and /etc/samba (for the Samba file server).

Executable directories   Program files reside mainly in /sbin, /bin, /usr/sbin, and /usr/bin. (Additional directories can house program files on some systems. Most notably, /usr/local/sbin and /usr/local/bin hold locally compiled programs.)

Library directories   *Libraries* are collections of programming functions that can be useful to many programs. They're stored in separate files to save disk space and RAM when programs run, and enable easy updates to library files without re-installing all the programs that rely on them. In Linux, most libraries reside in /lib and /usr/lib, although some can reside elsewhere (such as /usr/local/lib) on some systems.

If you've administered Windows computers, you should be aware of an important difference between Windows and Linux: In Windows, it's common for a program binary, its configuration files, and all its support files to reside in a single directory tree that belongs to the program, such as C:\Program Files\ SomeProgram. In Linux, by contrast, most of a program's key files are likely to reside in standard locations that are shared with other programs, and to be scattered about. For instance, the program's executable might be in /usr/bin, related libraries in /usr/lib, configuration files in /etc or in users' home directories, and so on. This works well in Linux because Linux's packaging systems, described in Chapter 9, keep track of where a package's many files go, enabling you to easily delete or upgrade a package. The Linux system has the advantage of simplifying the *path*, which is the list of directories in which program files reside. (Paths also exist for libraries and man pages.) If you're used to looking for files in program-specific locations, though, adjusting to the Linux system can be awkward. The key is to use your package system to identify where a package's files reside; for instance, typing **rpm -ql** *someprogram* shows where every file in the *someprogram* package resides on an RPM-based system.

The package system does not manage user configuration files, so they can linger after you delete a program. This causes no harm aside from the disk space consumed.

FEDORA 17 AND THE FHS

Fedora's developers have announced that they intend to fold the contents of several directories together—for instance, to combine /bin, /sbin, /usr /bin, and /usr/sbin into a single directory (/usr/bin). Such a change is a violation of the FHS, but whether it will cause any problems remains to be seen. (Fedora 17 is not yet available as of this writing.)

Using Special Permission Bits and File Features

When you investigate the Linux directory tree, you will encounter certain file types that require special attention. Sometimes you may just want to be aware of how these files are handled, since they deviate from what you might expect based on the information presented in earlier chapters. In other cases, you may need to adjust how you use ls or other commands to deal with these files and directories. These special cases include the "sticky bit," hiding files from view, obtaining long listings of directories, and using special execute permissions.

Using Sticky Bits

Consider the following commands, typed on a system with a few files and sub-directories laid out in a particular way:

Certification
Objective

```
$ whoami
kirk
$ ls -l
total 0
drwxrwxrwx 2 root root 80 Dec 14 17:58 subdir
$ ls -l subdir/
total 2350
-rw-r----- 1 root root 2404268 Dec 14 17:59 f1701.tif
```

These commands establish the current configuration: The effective user ID is kirk and the current directory has one subdirectory, called subdir, which root owns but to which kirk, like all the system's users, has full read/write access. This subdirectory has one file, f1701.tif, which is owned by root and to which kirk has no access. You can verify that kirk can't write to the file by attempting to do so with the touch command:

```
$ touch subdir/f1701.tif
touch: cannot touch `subdir/f1701.tif': Permission denied
```

This error message verifies that kirk could not write to subdir/f1701.tif. The file, you might think, is safe from tampering. Not so fast! Try this:

```
$ rm subdir/f1701.tif
$ ls -l subdir/
total 0
```

The rm command returned no error message, and a subsequent check of subdir verifies that it's now empty—in other words, kirk could delete the file even without write permission to it! This may seem like a bug—after all, if you can't write to a file, you might think you shouldn't be able to delete it. Recall, however, that directories are just a special type of file, one that holds other files' names and pointers to their lower-level data structures. Thus, modifying a file requires write access to the file, but creating or deleting a file requires write access to the *directory in which it resides*. In this example, kirk has write access to the subdir directory, but not to the f1701.tif file within that directory. Thus, kirk can delete the file but not modify it. This result is not a bug; it's just a counter-intuitive feature.

Although Linux filesystems were designed to work this way, such behavior is not always desirable. The way to create a more intuitive result is to use a *sticky bit*, which is a special filesystem flag that alters this behavior. With the sticky bit set on a directory, Linux will only permit you to delete a file if you own either it or the containing directory; write permission to the containing directory is not enough. You can set the sticky bit with chown, in either of two ways:

Using an octal code   By prefixing the 3-digit octal code described in Chapter 15 with another digit, you can set any of three special permission bits, one of which is the sticky bit. The code for the sticky bit is 1, so you would use an octal code that begins with 1, such as 1755, to set the sticky bit. Specifying a value of 0, as in 0755, removes the sticky bit.

Using a symbolic code   Pass the symbolic code t for the world permissions, as in **chmod o+t subdir**, to set the sticky bit on subdir. You can remove the sticky bit in a similar way by using a minus sign, as in **chmod o-t subdir**.

Chapter 15 describes the basics of chown.

Other odd numbers will set the sticky bit, too, but will also set additional special permission bits, which are described shortly, in "Using Special Execute Permissions."

Restoring the file and setting the sticky bit enables you to see the effect:

```
$ ls -l
total 0
drwxrwxrwt 2 root root 80 Dec 14 18:25 subdir
$ ls -l subdir/
total 304
-rw-r--r-- 1 root root 2404268 Dec 14 18:25 f1701.tif
$ rm subdir/f1701.tif
rm: cannot remove `subdir/f1701.tif': Operation not permitted
```

In this example, although kirk still has full read/write access to subdir, kirk cannot delete another user's files in that directory.

You can identify a directory with the sticky bit set by a small change in the symbolic mode shown by ls -l: The world execute bit is shown as a t rather than an x. In this example, the result is that subdir's permission appears as drwxrwxrwt rather than drwxrwxrwx.

The sticky bit is particularly important for directories that are shared by many users. It's a standard feature on /tmp and /var/tmp, for instance, since many users store temporary files in these directories, and you wouldn't want one user to be able to delete another's temporary files. If you want users who collaborate on a project to be able to write files into each others' home directories, you might want to consider setting the sticky bit on those home directories, or on the sub-directories in which users are sharing files.

◀

If you delete /tmp **or** /var/tmp **and need to re-create it, be sure to set the sticky bit on your new replacement directory!**

Using Special Execute Permissions

As described in Chapter 15, the execute permission bit enables you to identify program files as such. Linux then enables you to run these programs. Such files run using your own credentials, which is generally a good thing—associating running processes with specific users is a key part of Linux's security model. Occasionally, though, programs need to run with elevated privileges. For instance, the passwd program, which sets users' passwords, must run as root to write, and in some cases to read, the configuration files it handles. Thus, if users are to change their own passwords, passwd must have root privileges even when ordinary users run it.

To accomplish this task, two special permission bits exist, similar to the sticky bit described earlier:

Certification
Objective

Set user ID (SUID) The *set user ID* (SUID) option tells Linux to run the program with the permissions of whoever owns the file rather than with the permissions of the user who runs the program. For instance, if a file is owned by root and has its SUID bit set, the program runs with root privileges and can therefore read any file on the computer. Some servers and other system programs run this way, which is often called SUID root. SUID programs are indicated by an s in the owner's execute bit position in the permission string, as in rwsr-xr-x.

Set group ID (SGID)   The *set group ID* (SGID) option is similar to the SUID option, but it sets the group of the running program to the group of the file. It's indicated by an s in the group execute bit position in the permission string, as in rwxr-sr-x.

You can set these bits using chmod:

Using an octal code   In the leading digit of a 4-digit octal code, set the leading value to 4 to set the SUID bit, to 2 to set the SGID bit, or to 6 to set both bits. For instance, 4755 sets the SUID bit, but not the SGID bit, on an executable file.

Using a symbolic code   Use the s symbolic code, in conjunction with u to specify the SGID bit, g to specify the SGID bit, or both to set both bits. For instance, typing **chmod u+s myprog** sets the SUID bit on myprog, whereas **chmod ug-s myprog** removes both the SUID bit and the SGID bit.

Ordinarily, you don't need to set or remove these bits; when necessary, the package management program sets these bits correctly when you install or upgrade a program. You might need to alter these bits if they've been mistakenly set or removed on files. In some cases you might want or need to adjust these values on program files that you compile from source code or if you need to modify the way a program works. Be very cautious when doing so, though. If you set the SUID or SGID bit on a garden-variety program, it will run with increased privileges. If the program contains bugs, those bugs will then be able to do more damage. If you accidentally remove these permissions, the results can be just as bad—programs like passwd, sudo, and su all rely on their SUID bits being set, so removing this feature can cause them to stop working.

Hiding Files from View

Certification
Objective

If you're used to Windows, you may be familiar with the concept of a *hidden bit*, which hides files from view in file managers, by the Windows DIR command, and in most programs. If you're looking for something analogous in Linux, you won't find it, at least not in the form of a dedicated filesystem feature. Instead, Linux uses a file-naming convention to hide files from view: Most tools, such as ls, hide files and directories from view if their names begin with a dot (.). Thus, ls shows the file afile.txt, but not .afile.txt. Most file managers and dialog boxes that deal with files also hide such *dot files*, as they're commonly called; however, this practice is not universal.

Many user programs take advantage of this feature to keep their configuration files from cluttering your display. For instance, ~/.bashrc is a Bash user configuration file, Evolution's configuration files go in the ~/.evolution directory, and ~/.fonts.conf holds user-specific font configuration information.

You can view dot files in various ways depending on the program in question. Some GUI tools have a check box you can set in their configuration options to force the program to display such files. At the command line, you can use the -a option to ls:

```
$ ls -l
total 0
drwxrwxrwt 2 root root 80 Dec 14 18:25 subdir
$ ls -la
total 305
drwxr-xr-x 3 kirk users    104 Dec 14 18:44 .
drwxr-xr-x 3 kirk users    528 Dec 14 18:21 ..
-rw-r--r-- 1 kirk users 309580 Dec 14 18:44 .f1701.tif
drwxrwxrwt 2 root root     80 Dec 14 18:25 subdir
```

This example shows the hidden file, .f1701.tif, in the current directory. It also shows two hidden directory files. The first, ., refers to the current directory. The second, .., refers to the parent directory.

Note that renaming a file so that it begins with a dot will hide it, but this action will also make the file inaccessible to any program that uses the original filename. That is, if you rename f1701.tif to .f1701.tif, and if another program or file refers to the file as f1701.tif, that reference will no longer work. You *must* include the leading dot in any reference to the hidden file.

Certification Objective

Recall from Chapter 6 that .. is a relative directory reference. This hidden entry is why it works.

Viewing Directories

Chapter 6 introduced the ls command, including many of its options. One of these deserves elaboration at this point: -d. If you're working in a directory that holds many subdirectories, and if you use a wildcard with ls that matches one or more subdirectories, you may get an unexpected result: The output will show the files in the matched subdirectories, rather than the information on the subdirectories themselves. For instance, starting in a directory with two subdirectories, subdir1 and subdir2:

Certification Objective

```
$ ls -l subdir*
subdir1:
total 304
-rw-r--r-- 1 kirk users 309580 Dec 14 18:54 f1701.tif

subdir2:
```

```
total 84
-rw-r--r-- 1 kirk users 86016 Dec 14 18:54 106792c17.doc
```

If instead you want information on the subdirectories, rather than the contents of those subdirectories, you can include the -d option:

```
$ ls -ld subdir*
drwxr-xr-x 2 kirk users 80 Dec 14 18:54 subdir1
drwxr-xr-x 2 kirk users 80 Dec 14 18:54 subdir2
```

THE ESSENTIALS AND BEYOND

Linux's directory tree places files in particular locations according to their function—program binaries, libraries, configuration files, user files, and so on. Knowing where these files reside will help you locate them—say, to find configuration files. When you go looking for files, you should be aware of some tools and filesystem features that can be useful—or confusing, if you're not aware of them. Sticky bits, hidden ("dot") files, the -d option to ls, and SUID and SGID features can all be important when you view or modify files, and especially system files.

SUGGESTED EXERCISES

▶ Examine the names of configuration files in /etc and try to find matching program files in /bin, /sbin, /usr/bin, and /usr/sbin. Examine the configuration files with less or a text editor and read their man pages. (Don't do this for *all* the configuration files in /etc, though—that would take forever! A couple will suffice.)

▶ Experiment with the sticky bit on a "scratch" directory. Using your regular account and either another regular account or the root account, set the ownership and sticky bit on the scratch directory in different ways and test whether you can delete and modify files in the directory.

REVIEW QUESTIONS

1. What types of files are you likely to find in /usr/lib, according to the FHS?

    A. Liberty files   **D.** Library files

    B. Liberated files   **E.** Liberal files

    C. Libra files

(Continues)

THE ESSENTIALS AND BEYOND (Continued)

2. You want to discover the sizes of several dot files in a directory. Which of the following commands might you use to do this?

   A. `ls -la`   **D.** `ls -d`

   B. `ls -p`   **E.** `ls -ld`

   C. `ls -R`

3. When should programs be configured SUID `root`?

   A. At all times; this permission is required for executable programs.

   B. Whenever a program should be able to access a device file.

   C. Only when they require `root` privileges to do their job.

   D. Whenever the program must be able to access an account's user ID (UID) number.

   E. Never; this permission is a severe security risk.

4. True or false: Print spool files are stored in a subdirectory of `/var`.

5. True or false: On a properly configured Linux system, any user can delete any file from `/tmp`.

6. True or false: If you hide a file in Linux by making it a dot file, you must change any existing references to that file in configuration files if those references are to continue working.

7. Typically, optical discs and USB flash drives are mounted in subdirectories of `/mnt` or _____.

8. Temporary files that are guaranteed to *not* be deleted during a reboot reside in

   _____.

9. You want to set the sticky bit on an existing directory, `subdir`, without otherwise altering its permissions. To do so, you should type **chmod** _____ **subdir**.

## CHAPTER 17

Managing Network Connections

Networking is a critical part of modern computing. Fortunately, most Linux distributions can often create a network connection automatically; however, sometimes this process doesn't work, or you may need to tweak the connection or debug problems when they occur. This chapter therefore covers network configuration.

I begin by describing some basic network features that you must understand to properly manage your network configuration. I then describe the process of configuring a network connection. A few tests will help you track down and correct problems, so I explain them in case you run into difficulties. Finally, I explore the dark side to networking: the undesirables of the Internet and how to keep them out of your computer.

▶ **Understanding network features**

▶ **Configuring a network connection**

▶ **Testing your network connection**

▶ **Protecting your system from the bad guys**

Understanding Network Features

Networking involves numerous protocols and technologies that interact in complex ways. Although modern networks and OSs make it easy for users to set up their computers, at least compared to 10 or 20 years ago, doing anything but the simplest configuration requires understanding the key networking protocols and technologies. To begin, I present the following mini-glossary of networking terms:

Certification Objective

DNS   The *Domain Name System (DNS)* is a global network of servers that translate between *hostnames* and *IP addresses* (both described shortly). Most

> **Other means of name resolution exist but are impractical for handling more than a few dozen computers.**

computers are configured to use a *DNS server*, which is a server that performs DNS lookups.

DHCP   The *Dynamic Host Configuration Protocol (DHCP)* is a way for most computers on a network to obtain configuration information from another computer (the *DHCP server*) on the network. DHCP is the key to today's easy network configuration. It's described in more detail shortly, in the section "Deciding Whether to Use DHCP."

> **Other methods of wired networking exist, but most are either obsolete or are used in very high-speed, long-distance, or other capacities.**

Ethernet   This is the wired network hardware that's most often used today. Ethernet comes in several varieties, the most common of which use cables that resemble telephone wires but with broader plugs. Common speeds range from 10 megabits per second (Mbps) to 1 gigabit per second (Gbps, or *gigabit Ethernet*), although faster speeds are available.

Hostname   This is a name that a computer uses for the benefit of humans. Hostnames consist of a computer portion and a network portion. For instance, in lunokhod.luna.edu, lunokhod is the machine name and luna.edu is the network name.

Internet   Used generically (with a lowercase *i*), the word *internet* refers to a network of networks, connected via *routers* (described shortly). With a capital *I*, the word *Internet* refers to the globe-spanning network with which you're no doubt familiar. The Internet is the largest internet ever created.

Certification Objective

IP address   An *Internet Protocol (IP) address* is a number that's assigned to a computer for network addressing purposes. You can think of an IP address as being like a street address or telephone number. Computers communicate with each other via IP addresses. In the past, four-byte *IPv4* addresses have dominated; however, the pool of IPv4 addresses has recently been depleted, so many new installations now use 16-byte *IPv6* addresses. IP addresses are broken down into two parts: a machine portion and a network portion. The network portion may be used in routing (see *router*), whereas the machine portion identifies a computer on a given network. This breakdown into machine and network addresses is accomplished via a *network mask*, as described next.

Network mask   A *network mask* (*mask* or *netmask* for short) is a way to distinguish between the network and machine portions of an IP address. The netmask defines the individual bits of an IP address that belong to each part of the address. This can be done by giving each bit of the machine address a binary 1 value and expressing the result as a number (such as 255.255.0.0 or 255.255.255.0) for an IPv4 address or by specifying the number of bits in the machine portion of the address (as in 16 or 24).

Router   A *router* (also known as a *gateway*) connects two or more networks together. Your desktop or server computer is likely to connect directly to a handful of other computers, including a router. The router links to another network, which in turn links to another, and so on. To contact a computer on another network, your computer communicates through the router. Homes and small businesses often use small *broadband routers* to connect to the Internet. Such devices perform routing and have built-in DNS, DHCP, and other useful servers.

TCP/IP   The *Transmission Control Protocol/Internet Protocol (TCP/IP)* is a set of standards that underlie most modern network communications at the software level.

Wi-Fi   This term applies to the most common forms of wireless networking, more properly known as *IEEE 802.11*. Several variants are available that differ in speed. The section "Creating a Wi-Fi Connection," later in this chapter, describes Wi-Fi configuration in more detail.

The process of creating a network connection is one of assigning the computer an IP address and an associated netmask. Using the IP address, the computer can communicate with other computers on the local network—that is, anything that doesn't require a router as an intermediary. In most cases, you'll want to tell the computer about the network's router so that it can communicate with computers on other network segments (often including the entire Internet). Giving your computer the IP address of a DNS server will enable you to specify computer hostnames rather than IP addresses, which is a highly desirable feature. Thus, these four features—the IP address, the netmask, the router's IP address, and the DNS server's IP address—constitute the basic network configuration features.

In most cases, DHCP can dish out these four features. This can make network configuration fairly automatic, as you'll see in this chapter. If your network doesn't support DHCP, though, you'll need to contact your network's administrator to obtain the critical configuration information. In some cases, you'll need still more information. For instance, if you're using Wi-Fi, you'll need to know the Wi-Fi network's name and perhaps its password.

Certification
Objective

Several alternatives to TCP/IP exist, such as AppleTalk, NetBEUI, and IPX/ SPX. TCP/IP, however, is the most common network protocol, and the one that underlies the Internet.

Configuring a Network Connection

In most cases, your network connection will come up automatically (or very nearly so). Sometimes, though, you'll have to manually adjust the configuration, or simply activate it. If available, automatic configuration is handled via DHCP, so I begin by describing it in more detail. I then cover a topic that's applicable to only some systems: configuring Wi-Fi. If you use it, you must configure Wi-Fi before setting other network options. Once Wi-Fi is configured, the rest of the network setup procedure is much like that for wired networks. I then provide an example of using GUI tools for network configuration; these tools are easy to use and can handle most situations. Finally, I cover text-based configuration tools, which provide a great deal of power that you might need to use in certain settings.

Deciding Whether to Use DHCP

As noted earlier, a computer requires, at a minimum, two pieces of information to connect to a typical network: an IP address and a netmask. IP addresses for a router and a DNS server are practical necessities on most networks, although in some cases you can do without one or both. Some networks require additional configuration details.

DHCP can deliver information even to computers without an IP address by using lower-level addressing methods.

Configuring every computer on a large network with all of this information can be time-consuming. Worse, it can lead to problems caused by human errors, such as typos in IP addresses. For this reason, most networks provide a DHCP server, which can provide this information to other computers.

Depending on the configuration of the server, DHCP can be used to deliver IP addresses in one of two ways:

- ▶ In a fixed way so that each computer receives the same IP address every time it boots

- ▶ Dynamically so that a single computer might receive different IP addresses on different boots

If you're configuring a home or small office network with a broadband router, the router almost certainly includes a DHCP server that you can use. Consult its documentation for details.

Which is used is a policy detail for your network administrator. You needn't be concerned with it, except to know that a computer configured via DHCP isn't necessarily guaranteed to receive the same IP address on each boot. This fact can have important implications. For instance, it's generally easiest and most reliable to configure a server computer if it has a fixed IP address. Thus, as a matter of policy, server computers are often configured *without* using DHCP, even if workstations on the same network use DHCP. This isn't always the case, though—as already noted, DHCP can deliver a fixed address to some or all computers, so the DHCP server's administrator can configure a network's servers in this way.

As a practical matter, unless you're configuring your own small private network, you should ask your network administrator whether to use DHCP for a new computer. If the answer is *no*, you should ask for an IP address, the netmask, the router's IP address, and the DNS server's IP address.

Creating a Wi-Fi Connection

Wi-Fi connections are most often used on laptop and smaller portable computers, since using such devices without a physical network cable is often desirable. Some desktop computers, though, have Wi-Fi capabilities, and you may want to use them.

Before proceeding further, be aware that you must have access to a Wi-Fi network. If you're configuring a computer to connect to a broadband router that you've purchased and set up, consult the router's documentation to learn how to locate the router's critical information, such as the *service set identifier* (SSID; that is, the Wi-Fi network's name, which may be distinct from the TCP/IP network's name) and the password it uses. If you're trying to connect to a business network or a public network, consult the network administrator to obtain this information.

Whatever the computer type, the easiest method of configuring your Wi-Fi connection is to use the GUI. Details of how to do this vary from one distribution to another. As an example, consider doing the task in Fedora:

1. Open the System Settings tool by clicking your name in the upper-right corner of the desktop and selecting System Settings from the resulting menu or by typing **gnome-control-center** at a shell prompt.

2. Click the Network item in the System Settings Hardware section.

3. Click Wireless in the list on the left side of the Network window. The window will change to resemble Figure 17.1.

FIGURE 17.1 You can adjust the most common network settings from the Network item in the System Settings menu.

The procedure described here is equivalent to plugging an Ethernet cable into an Ethernet port. This procedure might or might not set up TCP/IP options.

If you don't see a Wireless option, you may lack Linux drivers for your Wi-Fi hardware. Consult the sidebar "Obtaining Wi-Fi Drivers" for advice on resolving this problem.

4. Click the inverted caret to the right of the Network Name field to access a pull-down menu with a list of networks.

5. Select your network from the list. If the network requires authentication, a dialog box like the one shown in Figure 17.2 will appear.

6. Type your network's password in the Password field, and then click Connect.

Authentication required by wireless network

Passwords or encryption keys are required to access the wireless network 'MyHome'.

Wireless security: WPA & WPA2 Personal

Password: ■■■■■■■■

☐ Show password

Cancel   Connect

FIGURE 17.2 If your Wi-Fi network requires authentication, you must enter a password before you can begin using it.

The word Disconnected in the Network window (Figure 17.1) should change to read Connecting, followed by Connected. Depending on your network's configuration, you may also see an IP address, the default route, and the DNS server's IP address appear in the window. If so, the computer is now completely configured for network access—the utility has automatically performed the tasks described in the section "Using a Network Configuration GUI," later in this chapter. If not, though, you may need to perform additional configuration tasks, such as manually setting an IP address. It's also possible that the Wi-Fi connection has failed.

WI-FI SECURITY

Because Wi-Fi data are carried over radio waves, it's easy for the transmissions to be intercepted. Somebody sitting in a car outside of a building can often gain access to a Wi-Fi network, which poses three problems:

▶ An intruder can intercept data passing over the network, possibly gaining access to sensitive files, acquiring credit card numbers, and so on.

(Continues)

WI-FI SECURITY *(Continued)*

▶ An intruder may be able to launch attacks on your computers from behind any firewall you maintain to protect yourself from outsiders.

▶ An intruder can use your network access to attack other computers or to conduct illegal activities such as pirating movies, music, or software. This not only consumes your network bandwidth, but if the activities are detected, *you* will fall under suspicion!

For these reasons, you should secure any Wi-Fi network you manage. Three security levels are available (four if you count none at all):

WEP   The Wired Equivalent Privacy (WEP) is a very weak encryption protocol. Methods of breaking into a WEP-encrypted network are well known, making this method essentially worthless.

WPA   Wi-Fi Protected Access (WPA) security provides improved encryption and authentication tools compared to WEP.

WPA2   WPA2 is WPA's replacement, and it provides still more improvements in encryption and authentication.

Several variants on each of these encryption methods are available. For instance, WPA and WPA2 provide both *personal* and *enterprise* options, the latter requiring a more complex setup with a dedicated authentication server. Typically, you set the encryption method in a broadband router or wireless access point (WAP). Clients then detect the method in use and present appropriate options, such as the password prompt shown earlier in Figure 17.2.

Public Wi-Fi connections might not use any of these protocols. You can use such connections, but be aware that any data you send or receive might be visible to others.

> You might use `iwlist` scan to locate public Wi-Fi networks in a coffee shop or hotel, followed by an `iwconfig` command to connect to a network you've found.

The GUI method of establishing a Wi-Fi connection is almost always the easiest method to use. If you need to fine-tune the connection, though, you can use various tools to probe for and manage Wi-Fi links. Here are the two most important of these tools:

`iwlist`   This command can identify nearby Wi-Fi networks. Type `iwlist scan` or `iwlist scanning` as root to obtain a list of nearby networks. This command produces a great deal of technical data, though. You're probably most interested in the network names, which appear in the output following the string ESSID, so typing `iwlist scan | grep ESSID` will pare down the output.

iwconfig   This utility connects and disconnects you from specific networks. It uses many options, and you may need to study its man page to fully understand it. In most cases, though, typing something like **iwconfig wlan0 essid** *NoWires* **channel** *1* **mode** *Managed* **key** *s:N1mP7mHNw* will do the trick. This example connects to the *NoWires* network running on channel *1* using the password *N1mP7mHNw*.

Obtaining Wi-Fi Drivers

Unfortunately, Linux driver support for Wi-Fi hardware is fairly weak. If you don't see your Wi-Fi hardware when you try to configure it, you may need to track down suitable drivers. You can begin this task with a tool called lspci, which is described in Chapter 5, "Managing Hardware." Type this command with no options to see a list of available hardware and search that list for a wireless network adapter. For instance, my own laptop's lspci output includes the following line:

```
03:00.0 Network controller: Realtek Semiconductor Co., Ltd.⤶
  RTL8191SEvB Wireless LAN Controller (rev 10)
```

This line identifies the Wi-Fi adapter as a Realtek RTL8191SEvB. A search on Realtek's Web site turns up a driver; however, this driver has to be compiled locally, which is a topic that's beyond the scope of this book. You also might not be lucky enough to find a driver in this way.

An alternative to using a native Linux driver is to use a Windows driver. This unusual option is possible using a package called ndiswrapper (http://ndiswrapper.sourceforge.net), which enables you to install Windows Wi-Fi drivers in Linux. Unfortunately, not all distributions provide ndiswrapper in their standard package sets, but you can usually find a binary package in an add-on repository. Similar functionality is provided by the Linuxant DriverLoader software (http://www.linuxant.com/driverloader/), which is less popular than ndiswrapper but is still worth considering.

If all other options fail, you may need to buy new networking hardware. Many USB Wi-Fi adapters are available, but you should research them to find one that has good Linux support. You can also replace the built-in adapters on some laptops.

Using a Network Configuration GUI

If you've configured a Wi-Fi link but it hasn't obtained an IP address, or if you need to set up a wired network connection, you'll have to set up the TCP/IP networking options. You can do this via text-mode tools, as described later, in "Using Text-Based Tools," or you can use GUI tools. The latter option is easier for new users, but the GUI tools vary from one distribution to another. As an example, the procedure for configuring Fedora using GUI tools is as follows:

1. Open the System Settings tool by clicking your name in the upper-right corner of the desktop and selecting System Settings from the resulting menu or by typing **gnome-control-center** at a shell prompt.

2. Click the Network item in the System Settings Hardware section.

3. Select the network device from the list on the left side of the window. The result should resemble Figure 17.3; however, this figure shows a properly configured network link that has no obvious problems. If your network link isn't working, it might read Disconnected rather than Connected or it might otherwise show significantly different information.

4. Click Options to adjust your network settings.

FIGURE 17.3 Network connections usually set themselves up automatically, but sometimes they don't.

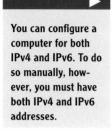

You can configure a computer for both IPv4 and IPv6. To do so manually, however, you must have both IPv4 and IPv6 addresses.

5. Select the IPv4 Settings or IPv6 Settings tab, depending on whether your network uses IPv4 or IPv6. The result resembles Figure 17.4, which shows a partially configured manual IPv4 setup.

FIGURE 17.4 You can set key TCP/IP features after clicking Options in the Network window.

6. Select the connection method using the Method button. The Automatic (DHCP) and Manual options are the most common, but a few more obscure options are available, too. You can disable a network connection by selecting Disabled.

7. If you're using DHCP, you can type your computer's DHCP client ID in the DHCP Client ID field. Some networks use this information to assign the computer a hostname or a fixed IP address. If your network administrator hasn't given you this information, you can leave this field blank.

8. To perform manual configuration, select Manual in the Method button and enter the remaining information. You enter an IP address, netmask, and router address by clicking the Add button, whereupon suitable fields in the Addresses section of the dialog box become available.

9. When you're done making changes, click Save.

If all goes well, your Network dialog box should change to show an IP address, subnet mask, default route, and DNS server address—although some networks omit some of these items.

Using Text-Based Tools

Although the GUI network configuration tools are easy to use and work well most of the time, sometimes you must use a more flexible set of text-based tools. These tools include the following:

ifconfig   This program brings up or shuts down a network connection by associating an IP address and network mask to a piece of network hardware.

Certification Objective

route   This program adjusts the computer's *routing table*, which determines through which network device specific network packets are sent.

Certification Objective

/etc/resolv.conf   This file contains the IP addresses of up to three DNS servers as well as the name of the computer's Internet domain and of other domains that should be searched when the user omits a domain name from a hostname.

Certification Objective

A DHCP client   A DHCP client program, such as dhclient or dhcpcd, can often configure a network connection automatically. You simply type the program's name, perhaps followed by a network device name.

Don't confuse dhcpcd, **a DHCP client, with** dhcpd, **a DHCP server.**

Distribution-specific network scripts   The ifconfig, route, and DHCP client programs produce temporary changes to the computer's network configuration. If you want to make permanent changes, you must store your settings in a configuration file. The name and format of this file varies from one distribution to another. For instance, in Fedora it's /etc/sysconfig/network-scripts/ifcfg-*netname*, where *netname* is the name of the network device; in Debian or Ubuntu, it's /etc/network/interfaces.

The ifconfig and route commands are both quite complex; however, their basic use is fairly straightforward. Suppose you want to assign the IP address 192.168.29.39/24 to the eth0 network device and tell it to use 192.168.29.1 as the router. The following two commands would do the trick:

```
# ifconfig eth0 up 192.168.29.39 netmask 255.255.255.0
# route add default gw 192.168.29.1
```

You can instead take down a connection by using down rather than up with ifconfig, delete routes by using del rather than add with route, and so on. Consult these programs' man pages for details.

Some distributions use dhclient **by default, but others use** dhcpcd**. If you don't know which to use, try both.**

If your network uses DHCP, you can type **dhclient** *netname* or **dhcpcd** *netname* to bring up the *netname* interface and configure it using DHCP. Manually typing this command can be handy if you're trying to debug a network problem related to DHCP or if your network's DHCP configuration has changed and temporarily broken connectivity for some computers.

NETWORK DEVICE NAMES

Traditionally, Linux has given the first Ethernet device a name of eth0 and subsequent devices names of eth1 and so on. Similarly, Wi-Fi devices have acquired names of the form wlan0 and up. Fedora, however, has begun deviating from this scheme, starting with version 15. This makes it harder to predict the device names of Ethernet devices from one computer to another. The goal is to make the device names more stable between reboots on computers with multiple network interfaces. Such systems are often routers or servers with multiple network links, and they typically require specific configurations on specific interfaces. If the device name changes from one boot to another—which can happen if network cards happen to be discovered in different order on different boots—problems can ensue.

You can learn your network device names by typing ifconfig with no options. (You can even do this as a normal user.) The result includes one or more blocks of output like the following:

```
em1    Link encap:Ethernet  HWaddr 00:26:6C:36:C8:58
       inet addr:172.24.21.11  Bcast:172.24.21.255 ↵
Mask:255.255.255.0
       inet6 addr: fe80::226:6cff:fe36:c858/64 Scope:Link
       UP BROADCAST RUNNING MULTICAST  MTU:1500  Metric:1
       RX packets:15962 errors:0 dropped:0 overruns:0 ↵
frame:0
       TX packets:9150 errors:0 dropped:0 overruns:0 ↵
carrier:0
       collisions:0 txqueuelen:1000
       RX bytes:22295082 (21.2 MiB)  TX bytes:2050687 (1.9 ↵
MiB)
       Interrupt:45
```

(Continues)

NETWORK DEVICE NAMES *(Continued)*

In this example, em1 is the device name—it prominently begins this block of output. The name lo refers to a *loopback device*, which is used for certain local access procedures, so you can ignore it if you want to find your network hardware's device name.

If you're configuring your network settings manually, you should enter your DNS name server data and your network name into /etc/resolv.conf. A sample of this file appears in Listing 17.1.

Listing 17.1: A sample /etc/resolv.conf configuration file

```
domain luna.edu
search example.com example.org
nameserver 192.168.1.2
nameserver 10.78.102.1
nameserver 10.78.221.1
```

Three keywords identify DNS resolution features in /etc/resolv.conf:

domain   You identify your computer's default domain name on this line. The primary effect is that the computer searches for hostnames without domain names in this domain. For example, in Listing 17.1, if you specify a hostname of lunokhod, the computer will find the IP address of lunokhod.luna.edu.

search   You can have the computer search for hostnames in additional domains by specifying them on a search line, with domains separated by spaces or tabs. You can specify up to six domains in this way. Be aware, however, that adding domains to the search path is likely to slow down hostname lookup.

nameserver   This keyword identifies DNS server computers by IP address. You can specify multiple servers by including multiple nameserver lines, up to the maximum of three.

If you want to manually adjust your permanent network configuration, you can do so by editing the network configuration file, such as /etc/sysconfig/network-scripts/ifcfg-*netname* on a Fedora system. Listing 17.2 shows a sample of this file.

◄

/etc/resolv
.conf **supports additional keywords, but they're seldom used. Consult its** man **page for details.**

Listing 17.2: A sample network configuration file

```
DEVICE="em1"
BOOTPROTO="static"
IPADDR=192.168.29.39
NETMASK=255.255.255.0
NETWORK=192.168.29.0
BROADCAST=192.168.29.255
GATEWAY=192.168.29.1
ONBOOT=yes
NM_CONTROLLED="yes"
HWADDR=00:26:6C:36:C8:58
TYPE=Ethernet
DEFROUTE=yes
PEERDNS=yes
PEERROUTES=yes
IPV4_FAILURE_FATAL=yes
IPV6INIT=no
NAME="System em1"
UUID=1dad842d-1912-ef5a-a43a-bc238fb267e7
```

Some of these options have purposes that you can figure out based on their names, and you can adjust as necessary. If you don't understand an option, it's best to leave it alone. Some specific features you may want to attend to include the following:

▶ If you want to use DHCP, change the BOOTPROTO line to read BOOTPROTO="dhcp" rather than BOOTPROTO="static" and remove the lines from IPADDR through GATEWAY.

▶ If you want to keep the network link from starting up automatically when the computer boots, change ONBOOT to no. Users will then have to manually activate the network whenever they want to use it.

▶ The NETWORK and BROADCAST options are both derived from the IP address (IPADDR) and netmask (NETMASK). The NETWORK address is the network portion of the IP address but with binary 0 values substituted for the host-specific part of the IP address. The BROADCAST address is similar, but it substitutes binary 1 values for the host-specific part of the address.

Forcing users to start their network connections can limit the computer's use of network resources, such as IP addresses if your network uses DHCP.

If you're running Debian, Ubuntu, or some other distribution that uses a different network configuration file, you'll have to track down that file and modify it. The format may vary from the file shown in Listing 17.2, too, although the entries you must change are usually fairly obvious. If in doubt, consult distribution-specific documentation.

The ifup and ifdown commands bring up or take down a network connection based on the settings in your configuration file. Thus, after you change these settings, you may want to type **ifdown** *netname* followed by **ifup** *netname*. The result should be a network link that reflects the new settings. Be aware, however, that this procedure may disconnect network clients and servers.

Testing Your Network Connection

In most cases, your network connection will work fine from the moment you start it. Sometimes, though, you may need to diagnose problems, either because you can't get the connection to work at all or because a formerly working connection has stopped working. In the following pages, I describe several types of network tests: checking your routing table, testing basic connectivity, testing to locate where a break in connectivity has occurred, testing DNS functioning, and testing the network's status.

Checking Your Routing Table

Earlier, I described using the route command to set the default route on a computer. You can check that your route is sensible by using the same command. In most cases, typing **route** alone will do the job:

Certification
Objective

```
$ route
Kernel IP routing table
Destination   Gateway        Genmask        Flags Metric Ref  Use Iface
192.168.29.0  *              255.255.255.0  U     0      0      0 eth0
127.0.0.0     *              255.0.0.0      U     0      0      0 lo
default       192.168.29.1   0.0.0.0        UG    0      0      0 eth0
```

This shows that data destined for 192.168.29.0 (that is, any computer with an IP address between 192.168.29.1 and 192.168.29.254) goes directly over eth0. The 127.0.0.0 network is a special interface that "loops back" to the originating computer. Linux uses this for some internal networking purposes. The last line shows the default route, which describes what to do with everything that doesn't match any other entry in the routing table. This line identifies the default route's gateway system as 192.168.29.1. If it's missing or misconfigured, some or all traffic destined for external networks, such as the Internet, won't make it beyond your local network segment.

◄

The routing table of a typical workstation or even server is quite simple and can be automatically configured. Network routers often require complex routing tables, though.

Testing Basic Connectivity

The most basic network test is ping, which sends a simple network packet to the system you name (via IP address or hostname) and waits for a reply. In Linux,

Certification
Objective

ping continues sending packets once every second or so until you interrupt it with a Ctrl+C keystroke. You can instead specify a limited number of tests via the -c *num* option. Here's an example of its output:

```
$ ping -c 4 nessus
PING nessus.example.com (192.168.1.2) 56(84) bytes of data.
64 bytes from nessus.example.com (192.168.1.2): icmp_req=1 ttl=64⏎
 time=0.607 ms
64 bytes from nessus.example.com (192.168.1.2): icmp_req=2 ttl=64⏎
 time=0.147 ms
64 bytes from nessus.example.com (192.168.1.2): icmp_req=3 ttl=64⏎
 time=0.145 ms
64 bytes from nessus.example.com (192.168.1.2): icmp_req=4 ttl=64⏎
 time=0.283 ms

--- nessus.example.com ping statistics ---
4 packets transmitted, 4 received, 0% packet loss, time 3001ms
rtt min/avg/max/mdev = 0.145/0.295/0.607/0.189 ms
```

This command sent four packets and waited for their return, which occurred quite quickly (in an average of 0.295 ms) because the target system was on the local network. A few common problem patterns can help you diagnose where a network problem resides:

▶ If you can ping local systems but not remote systems, the problem is probably in your router or in an improper router specification.

▶ If you can ping by IP address but not by name, the problem is most likely with your DNS server or DNS configuration.

▶ If you can't ping at all, even by IP address, then you probably have a fundamental configuration problem.

Finding Breaks in Connectivity

A step up from ping is the traceroute command, which sends a series of three test packets to each computer between your system and a specified target system. Listing 17.3 shows a sample of traceroute's output.

Listing 17.3: A sample traceroute output

```
$ traceroute -n 10.1.0.43
traceroute to 10.1.0.43 (10.1.0.43), 30 hops max, 52 byte packets
 1  192.168.1.2  1.021 ms  36.519 ms  0.971 ms
 2  10.10.88.1  17.250 ms  9.959 ms  9.637 ms
 3  10.9.8.173  8.799 ms  19.501 ms  10.884 ms
 4  10.9.8.133  21.059 ms  9.231 ms  103.068 ms
```

```
5  10.9.14.9   8.554 ms   12.982 ms   10.029 ms
6  10.1.0.44   10.273 ms   9.987 ms   11.215 ms
7  10.1.0.43   16.360 ms   *   8.102 ms
```

The -n option to this command tells it to display target computers' IP addresses rather than their hostnames. This can speed up the process a bit, particularly if you're having DNS problems, and it can sometimes make the output easier to read—but you may want to know the hostnames of problem systems because they can help you pinpoint who's responsible for a problem.

The output of traceroute can be diagnostic in several ways:

- ▶ Typically, times increase with increasing hop numbers. This is normal, and aside from some variability in the example output, you can see this pattern in Listing 17.3.

- ▶ Variable times on a single hop can indicate that a router is overloaded or that some other intermittent issue is causing variability in the times. You can see this factor at play in several hops in Listing 17.3, and particularly in hops 1 and 4. Such issues may result in variable performance but should not cause network sessions to time out or otherwise fail completely.

- ▶ Sometimes a response to a packet is never received. This condition is indicated by an asterisk (*) in a time field, as in the second packet for hop 7 in Listing 17.3.

- ▶ A dramatic jump in times can indicate a great physical distance between routers. Ignoring the middle time of 36.519 ms in the first hop of Listing 17.3, you can see such a jump in the change from hop 1 to hop 2. In the case of Listing 17.3, this indicates the link from the local network to the Internet service provider's network. Even bigger jumps in time are common on intercontinental links. Such jumps are not necessarily signs of misconfiguration that needs to be fixed, but they can influence network performance, particularly for highly interactive protocols such as remote login tools or network-enabled gaming.

◀

Some routers block all traceroute **data. If your** trace-route **output contains nothing but asterisks past a certain point, you may have run into such a system.**

Among other things, traceroute is helpful in determining whether a problem in network connectivity exists in a network for which you're responsible. For instance, the variability in the first hop of Listing 17.3 could indicate a problem on the local network, but the lost packet associated with the final destination most likely is not a local problem. If the trouble link is within your jurisdiction, you can check the status of the problem system, nearby systems, and the network segment in general.

Testing DNS

DNS problems can cause networking to fail almost as badly as can a physically cut cable. Because both people and many network tools rely on hostnames, if DNS resolution doesn't work, the network becomes nearly useless.

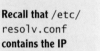

Certification
Objective

▶

The nslookup **program is** *deprecated,* **meaning that developers plan to eventually remove it from common use, but it's available at the moment.**

You can test your network's DNS server by using a number of tools, such as host, dig, and nslookup. These tools are similar in many ways, and they all enable you to look up a hostname by typing the command's name followed by a hostname:

```
$ host www.sybex.com
www.sybex.com has address 208.215.179.220
```

This example shows normal name resolution. In this case, the hostname links directly to just one IP address. In some cases, you may find notices about aliases or multiple IP addresses. This is also normal, at least for some sites. If the command takes a long time to respond or complains about a timeout or an inability to reach servers, though, it means that your computer's DNS configuration is wrong.

▶

Recall that /etc/ resolv.conf **contains the IP addresses of your network's DNS servers. They're identified on** nameserver **lines.**

You can add the IP address of a specific DNS server, as in **host www.whitehouse .gov 192.168.39.7** to test the 192.168.39.7 server. If your computer is configured to use multiple DNS servers, you can test each one individually in this way. Perhaps one is unreliable or incorrect, in which case you might want to remove it from your configuration. Be aware, though, that if you remove a DNS server from /etc/resolv.conf on a computer that's configured via DHCP, your change will eventually be undone by DHCP. If this is a recurring problem, you should probably consult your network administrator.

Although host is a useful tool for performing basic hostname lookups, the dig utility (or the deprecated nslookup) can perform more complex queries and can return more information about a hostname, domain, or IP address. This makes dig a useful tool for advanced network diagnostics, but at the cost of ease of use; it's harder for a novice to interpret dig's output.

Checking Your Network Status

Certification
Objective

Another useful diagnostic tool is netstat. This is something of a Swiss Army knife of network tools because it can be used in place of several others, depending on the parameters it's passed. It can also return information that's not easily obtained in other ways. Some examples include the following:

Interface information   Pass netstat the --interface or -i parameter to obtain information about your network interfaces similar to what ifconfig returns. (Some versions of netstat return information in the same format, but others lay out the information differently.)

Routing information You can use the --route or -r parameter to obtain a routing table listing similar to what the route command displays.

Masquerade information Pass netstat the --masquerade or -M parameter to obtain information about connections mediated by Linux's Network Address Translation (NAT) features, which often go by the name *IP masquerading*. NAT enables a Linux router to "hide" a network behind a single IP address. This can be a good way to stretch limited IPv4 addresses.

Program use Some versions of netstat support the --program (or -p) parameter, which attempts to provide information about the programs that are using network connections. This attempt isn't always successful, but it often is, so you can see what programs are making outside connections.

Open ports When used with various other parameters, or without any parameters at all, netstat returns information about open ports and the systems to which they connect.

All connections The --all or -a option is used in conjunction with others. It causes netstat to display information about the ports that server programs open to listen for network connections, in addition to already-open connections.

Keep in mind that netstat is a powerful tool, and its options and output aren't entirely consistent from one distribution to another. You may want to peruse its man page and experiment with netstat to learn what it can do.

Small broadband routers use NAT. If you have such a device, chances are your desktop and laptop systems needn't be configured to do so themselves.

Protecting Your System from the Bad Guys

Networks provide many useful features for their users. Unfortunately, they also provide many risks. Network security is a complex topic, and I can provide only a few basic tips to help you prevent your system from being compromised. Here are some of the most important things you can do:

Shut down unused servers. Linux's major security vulnerabilities aren't in worms and viruses, as they are with Windows; in Linux, the risks center around outsiders breaking into your computer by abusing server programs that you run. Therefore, it's important that you don't run servers unnecessarily. Some distributions automatically install and run servers, such as the Secure Shell (SSH), the Apache Web server, or a mail server such as sendmail or Postfix. The most thorough way to remove a server is to uninstall it using your package system (described in Chapter 9, "Using Programs and Processes")—but you must issue the command to *uninstall* the relevant package rather than to install it.

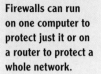

Firewalls can run on one computer to protect just it or on a router to protect a whole network.

Enable a firewall. A *firewall* is a program or system setting that polices network transactions, allowing or disallowing them based on programmed criteria. Most Linux distributions enable firewalls by default, but you may want to adjust their settings for your specific needs.

Use good passwords. Chapter 14, "Creating Users and Groups," describes how to select a good password. If your computer runs a login server of any type, setting a good password can minimize the risk of an outsider breaking in by guessing your password.

Be suspicious. You should be suspicious of untrusted sources of data. *Phishing* (attempting to extract sensitive data from users by posing as some trusted individual or organization) and similar attacks can dupe individuals into giving up passwords, financial data, and so on. Although malicious software (or *malware*) for Linux is rare, it would be easy to produce. You're best off sticking to official software sources and remembering that e-mails, Web sites, and other communications can be faked.

Keep your software up to date. Chapter 9 describes the package management tools you can use to keep your system up to date. It's best to regularly check your system for software updates, since many such updates fix security bugs—problems that can be exploited by outsiders or by legitimate but malicious users to take over your computer.

THE ESSENTIALS AND BEYOND

Networking is integral to today's computers, and Linux provides excellent networking capabilities. In most cases, your computer will detect your network and configure itself automatically; however, sometimes you must manually create an advanced configuration or override an incorrect automatic configuration. You may also need to test your network configuration to determine where a problem lies—in an IP address setting, in a DNS configuration, or elsewhere. Unfortunately, networks can be abused as well as used, so you must remain vigilant against those who would break into your computer and use it for their own purposes. A few steps, such as keeping your software updated, can greatly minimize the risks.

SUGGESTED EXERCISES

▶ On a small private network that you control or in a lab environment under the supervision of an instructor, reconfigure a computer that normally uses DHCP to use its assigned IP address in a static fashion. Test the connection, and then switch back to DHCP.

(Continues)

THE ESSENTIALS AND BEYOND *(Continued)*

Do not perform this test on a work or school network that's used for normal purposes; misconfiguration of a computer's IP address can cause problems for other computers.

▶ Back up your /etc/resolv.conf file and then edit the original so that its nameserver lines point to computers that don't run DNS servers. Test your network configuration by attempting to access remote servers using ping, a Web browser, and other utilities. Observe the types of failures that result. When you're done, restore the original file.

REVIEW QUESTIONS

1. You want to set up a computer on a local network via a static TCP/IP configuration, but you lack a gateway address. Which of the following is true?

   A. Because the gateway address is necessary, no TCP/IP networking functions will work.

   B. TCP/IP networking will function, but you'll be unable to convert hostnames to IP addresses, and vice versa.

   C. You'll be able to communicate with machines on your local network segment but not with other systems.

   D. The computer won't be able to tell which other computers are local and which are remote.

   E. You'll be able to use the computer as a network server system, but not as a network client.

2. Which of the following types of information are returned by typing **ifconfig eth0**? (Select all that apply.)

   A. The names of programs that are using eth0

   B. The IP address assigned to eth0

   C. The hardware address of eth0

   D. The hostname associated with eth0

   E. The gateway with which eth0 communicates

(Continues)

THE ESSENTIALS AND BEYOND *(Continued)*

3. The ping utility responds normally when you use it with an IP address but not when you use it with a hostname that you're positive corresponds to this IP address. What might cause this problem? (Select all that apply.)

   A. The route between your computer and its DNS server may be incorrect.

   B. The target computer may be configured to ignore packets from ping.

   C. The DNS configuration on the target system may be broken.

   D. Your computer's hostname may be set incorrectly.

   E. Your computer's DNS configuration may be broken.

4. True or false: IPv4 addresses are four bytes in length.

5. True or false: The /etc/resolv.conf file tells the computer whether to use DHCP for its network configuration.

6. True or false: You can check the current status of your routing table by typing **route** at a shell prompt.

7. The _____ program serves as a multi-purpose network tool; it can do many of the same things as ifconfig, route, and several others.

8. The traditional name for the first Ethernet interface in Linux (but not in recent versions of Fedora) is _____.

9. A _____ is a program or system configuration that blocks or enables network access to, from, or through a computer based on criteria you specify.

Answers to Review Questions

Chapter 1

1. **C** GUI programs create menus with the help of a library that's designed for this purpose; this is not a function of the Linux kernel. Thus, option C is a non-kernel function, and is correct. The kernel allocates memory and CPU time, and it also controls access to disk and network hardware, so options A, B, D, and E all describe kernel functions and are incorrect.

2. **A** Android is used on cell phones and other small portable devices, and as such it qualifies as an embedded OS, making option A correct. SUSE, CentOS, Debian, and Fedora are all examples of distributions intended mainly for use on desktop, laptop, and server computers; these do not qualify as embedded OSs, so options B, C, D, and E are all incorrect.

3. **B** Linux's GUI is based on the X Window System. Although OS X provides an X implementation, its primary GUI is Apple's proprietary product. Thus, option B is correct. Option A is incorrect because both Linux and OS X can run most GNU programs. Option C is incorrect because Linux can run on both Apple Macintosh and commodity PC hardware. Option D is incorrect because OS X includes many BSD utilities in its standard form. Furthermore, most Linux distributions use GNU utilities rather than their BSD equivalents, although you can use BSD utilities in Linux if you prefer. Option E is incorrect because both Linux and OS X support text-mode commands, although OS X makes it hard to use these commands in anything but its GUI Terminal application.

4. **False** The Linux kernel was intended as a "from-scratch" project to create a new Unix-like kernel. Although there are influences and similarities, the two kernels are largely independent of each other.

5. **False** Programs known as *terminals* enable entry of text-mode commands once you've logged into Linux in GUI mode. You can also switch between multiple *virtual terminals* by using keystrokes such as Ctrl+Alt+F2.

6. **True** CentOS's release cycle is approximately 2 years, which is long by the standards of Linux distributions, some of which have release cycles of just 6 months.

7. **login:**

8. **viruses**

9. **alpha and beta**

Chapter 2

1. **A** Linux's multitasking is preemptive, meaning that the kernel can give CPU time to any process as it sees fit, potentially interrupting (or preempting) other processes. Thus, option A is correct. Linux is a multi-user OS, but *multi-user* is not a type of multitasking, so option B is incorrect. In a co-operative multitasking OS, applications must voluntarily give up CPU time to each other. Although Linux programs can signal the OS that they don't need CPU time, Linux doesn't rely exclusively on this method, so option C is incorrect. A single-tasking OS can run just one process at a time, so option D is incorrect. A single-user OS can support just one user at a time. Such OSs can be either single-tasking or multitasking, and in the latter case, could use either co-operative or preemptive multitasking. Thus, option E is incorrect.

2. **C** The open source definition includes ten points, one of which is that users may modify the original code and redistribute the altered version. Thus, option C is correct. Although as a practical matter all open source software is available at no charge, nothing in the open source definition forbids selling it. In practice, many organizations and individuals *do* sell open source software, either as a convenience (such as DVD-ROMs with Linux distributions for those with slow Internet connections) or in value-added arrangements (such as Red Hat Enterprise Linux, which bundles open source software with a support contract). Thus, option A is incorrect. The open source definition requires distribution of source code, but does not require distribution of binaries. Thus, option B is incorrect. Although some open source software, including the Linux kernel, began life in academia, this is not true of all open source software, so option D is incorrect. The open source definition does not specify that either an interpreted or a compiled language be used, and in fact both have been used to write open source software, so option E is incorrect.

3. **D** Evolution is an e-mail reader program. Such programs are common on desktop computers, so option D is correct. Apache is a Web server, Postfix is an e-mail server, and the Berkeley Internet Name Domain (BIND) is a Domain Name System (DNS) server. Such servers are much less likely to be installed on desktop computers than are client programs such as Evolution, so options A, B, and E are all incorrect. Android is the name of a Linux distribution for cell phones and tablets, so option C is incorrect.

4. **False** VMS was an OS for minicomputers and mainframes when Linux was created. On *x*86 computers, DOS was the dominant OS in 1991.

5. **True** Digital video recorders (DVRs) are specialized computers for recording TV shows. Some commercial DVRs, such as TiVos, run Linux natively. DVR software for standard PCs, such as MythTV, which runs under Linux, also exists.

6. **True** Most server programs do not require the X Window System (X) GUI, so server computer administrators often disable X or even remove it entirely to save disk space and memory and to minimize the risk of security problems.

7. **monolithic**

8. **shareware**

9. **desktop**

Chapter 3

1. **C** The open source definition specifies that users be able to distribute changes, but it doesn't require that the license require distribution under the terms of the same license. Thus, option C does not describe an open source requirement, and so is the correct answer. Options A, B, D, and E all paraphrase actual open source license term requirements.

2. **B** Some distributions (particularly "Enterprise" versions that are sold for money) include software that is neither open source nor even freely redistributable, so option B is correct. Distributions as a whole use many licenses, not just one, so option A is incorrect. The MIT license is one of several open source licenses; such software is not an impediment to copying a distribution, so option C is incorrect. Although some distributions, such as Debian, aim to make their main systems fully open source compliant, not all do this, so option D is incorrect. Likewise, not all distributions are composed completely of free software as the FSF uses the term.

3. **E** Option E paraphrases one of the four key points in the FSF's philosophy, and so is correct. Contrary to option A, the FSF's philosophy does not mandate use of the GPL, much less its most recent version, although the GPL is the FSF's preferred license. Option B is contrary to the FSF's position, which is that free software should remain free; however, this option is compatible with the OSI's philosophy. Although the FSF advocates free software and free OSs, option C is not an explicit part of their philosophy and so is incorrect. Although the FSF wants to see a world dominated by free software, they do *not* advocate software piracy, so option D is incorrect.

4. **True** Courts and laws explicitly recognize computer software as being creative works that are governed by copyright law. In some countries, patent laws also apply to software, although this is not globally true.

5. **True** This principle is at the heart of both the free software and the open source software definitions.

6. **False** Hardware vendors often do release open source drivers for their products. One caveat is that the release of open source drivers necessarily renders some programming interfaces for the hardware open, which some hardware vendors are reluctant to do.

7. **LGPL (or Lesser GPL, or Lesser General Public License)**

8. **Creative Commons**

9. **copyleft**

Chapter 4

1. **B, C, E** GNOME, KDE, and Xfce are all Linux desktop environments, so options B, C, and E are all correct. (Others include LXDE and Unity.) The GIMP Tool Kit (GTK+) is a GUI programming library. Although GNOME and Xfce are both built atop GTK+, it's not a desktop environment, so option A is incorrect. Evolution is a Linux e-mail client, not a desktop environment, so option D is incorrect.

2. **B** The Network File System (NFS) was designed for exactly the task described in the question (although for Unix generally, not just Linux), so option B is correct. The Simple Mail Transfer Protocol (SMTP) is a protocol that enables one computer to send e-mail messages to another computer, so it's a poor choice for achieving the stated goal, and option A is incorrect. The PHP: Hypertext Processor (PHP) language is used to generate dynamic content for Web pages, so option C is incorrect. The Domain Name System (DNS) is a protocol for delivering the mappings between hostnames and IP addresses to computers, so it won't easily achieve the stated goals, making option D incorrect. The Dynamic Host Configuration Protocol (DHCP) enables one computer to provide network configuration information to another one over a network link, so option E is incorrect.

3. **C** The main language for the Linux kernel is C, so option C is correct. Although Bash shell scripts control much of the Linux startup process, these scripts are not part of the kernel, so option A is incorrect. Java is a popular language for Web-based applications, but it's not used in the Linux kernel, so option B is incorrect. C++ is a derivative of C that adds object-oriented features to the language, but the Linux kernel uses regular C, not C++, so option D is incorrect. Perl is a popular interpreted language, particularly for tasks that involve processing text, but it's not the language of the Linux kernel, so option E is incorrect.

4. **True** LibreOffice forked from OpenOffice.org in 2011. Although there are some small differences, the two are still nearly identical, and will likely remain quite similar for years.

5. **True** A denial-of-service (DoS) attack can disrupt a server's operation by directing an overwhelming quantity of bogus data at the server program, or even just the computer on which it runs. This is true even if the server is impeccably managed.

6. **True** Python, like Perl, PHP, and shell languages, is interpreted. This contrasts with C and C++, which are two common compiled languages, and with Java, which is somewhere in-between.

7. **e-mail client**

8. **Samba**

9. **compiled**

Chapter 5

1. **D** The lspci command displays information on PCI devices. Since many motherboard features appear to Linux as PCI devices, option D provides a great deal of information on your motherboard, and so is correct. Option A's lscpu command provides information on the CPU, which means that it provides little direct information on the motherboard, so option A is incorrect. The Xorg program is the Linux X server, and option B creates a new X configuration file. This file might provide hints about video hardware on the motherboard, but option D provides better and more information, so option B is incorrect. The fdisk utility can partition a disk, and the command in option C displays information on how /dev/sda is partitioned. This information has nothing to do with the motherboard's features, though, so option C is incorrect. You can enter http://localhost:631 in a Web browser to configure your printer, but even if you do this, you'll gain no information about your motherboard's features, so option E is incorrect.

2. **A, D** Disk partitioning enables you to separate data of different types into different parts of a disk. Examples of reasons to do this include installing multiple OSs and separating filesystem data from swap space. Thus, options A and D are both correct. Filesystem choice (ext4fs vs. ReiserFS) has nothing to do with partitioning, unless you want to use one filesystem for one partition and the other on another partition, so option B is incorrect. The Parallel Advanced Technology Attachment (PATA) and Serial ATA (SATA) interfaces are hardware standards; you can't turn a PATA disk into an SATA disk by partitioning the disk, so option C is incorrect. Hard disks have caches to improve performance, but partitioning the disk does not separate the disk's cache from the bulk of the disk's data, so option E is incorrect.

3. **A** Video monitors normally attach to the video circuitry built into a computer's motherboard or to a separate video card, so option A is correct. Keyboards, external hard disks, printers, and scanners all commonly connect to a computer via USB, although alternative interfaces exist for all of these devices.

4. **True** Most CPU families have multiple names. *EM64T* is one name that Intel has used for its implementation of the *x86-64* architecture, and AMD64 is one of AMD's names for the same architecture. Thus, the two names identify the same architecture, and an AMD64 Linux distribution will run on an EM64T CPU.

5. **False** The Universal Disk Format (UDF) is a filesystem that's used primarily on optical discs, not on hard disks. Using it for a Linux installation on a hard disk would be awkward or impossible. Linux-specific filesystems (ext2fs, ext3fs, ext4fs, ReiserFS, JFS, XFS, and Btrfs) are the only practical choices for Linux installations on a hard disk.

6. **True** In Linux, most drivers, including those specified, are provided as part of the kernel. Some other drivers, such as those for video cards under X, printers, and scanners, exist outside the kernel, although these may also rely on kernel drivers to do their work.

7. **32**

8. **direct current**

9. **Digital Visual Interface (DVI)**

Chapter 6

1. **A** The Ctrl+A keystroke moves the cursor to the start of the line when editing a command in Bash, so option A is correct. The left arrow key moves a single character to the left, Ctrl+T transposes two characters, the up arrow moves up one item in the history, and Ctrl+E moves to the end of the line.

2. **C, D** Options C and D both describe ways to run a program in the background from a shell, so options C and D are both correct. Neither start nor bg is a command that launches a program in the background. The fg command returns a program to the foreground, meaning that the shell will go back to sleep, which isn't what the question specified.

3. **E** Because the cd command changes the current directory and a tilde (~) refers to your home directory, option E does as the question specifies, and so is correct. Neither home nor homedir is a standard Linux or Bash command, so options A and D are both incorrect. Option B sets the current directory to /home, which is a directory that probably holds your home directory, but it is not your home directory itself, so option B is incorrect. Option C sets the current directory to the homedir subdirectory of the current directory, if it exists. Since this is almost certainly not your home directory, this option is incorrect.

4. **False** When in X, Ctrl must be added to the VT-switching keystroke, so the correct keystroke should be Ctrl+Alt+F2 (or other function keys, through F6).

5. **False** In Linux, a slash (/), not a backslash (\), is the directory separator; a backslash "quotes" the following character, so `..\upone.txt` refers to the file `..upone.txt` in the current directory. Specifying `../upone.txt` (with a slash rather than a backslash) refers to `upone.txt` in the parent directory.

6. **False** You can obtain a recursive directory listing from `ls` by using either `--recursive` or `-R`, but a lowercase `-r` does not have this effect.

7. **pwd**

8. **-a**

9. **cat**

Chapter 7

1. **A** The `mv` command moves or renames a file, so option A is correct. The `cp` command copies a file, so option B is incorrect. The `ln` command creates a link between two files, so option C is incorrect. Option D's `rn` command is fictitious, so this option is incorrect. The `touch` command creates a new file or adjusts the time stamps on an existing file, so option E is incorrect.

2. **C** Because two files (`outline.pdf` and `Outline.PDF`) have names that differ only in case, and because FAT is a case-insensitive filesystem, one of those files will be missing on the copy. (Both files will be copied, but the second one copied will overwrite the first.) Thus, option C is correct. The specified `cp` command does not create links, so option A is incorrect. Because the specified `cp` command included the `-a` option, which performs a recursive copy, all of the files in `MyFiles` will be copied, along with the directory itself, so option B is incorrect. In order to copy all of the files, you will have to manually change one file's name; however, `cp` won't do this automatically, so option D is incorrect. Because option C is correct, option E is not correct.

3. **A, B** If you try to create a directory inside a directory that doesn't exist, `mkdir` responds with a `No such file or directory` error. The `--parents` parameter tells `mkdir` to automatically create all necessary parent directories in such situations, so option A is correct. You can also manually do this by creating each necessary directory separately, so option B is also correct. (It's possible that `mkdir` one wouldn't be necessary in this example if the directory one already existed. No harm will come from trying to create a directory that already exists, although `mkdir` will return a `File exists` error.) Option C will have no useful effect; at most, it will change the time stamps on the `mkdir` program file, but if you type it as a normal user, it probably won't even do that. Options D and E are both based on the premise that you must remove directories that already exist with the names that you want to use, but this isn't true, so these options are both incorrect.

4. **True** Symbolic links work by storing the name of the linked-to file in the symbolic link file. Linux reads this filename and transparently substitutes the linked-to file. This process works both on a single filesystem and across filesystems, so the statement is true. Hard links, by contrast, work by providing multiple directory entries that point to a single file. This method of creating a link does *not* work across low-level filesystems.

5. **False** Linux's security features prevent accidental damage when you work as an ordinary user. You must be more careful when you acquire root privileges to perform system maintenance, though.

6. **True** The touch command updates a file's time stamps, and for this purpose, a directory counts as a file, so this statement is true.

7. -u or --update

8. rm -R junk, rm -r junk, or rm --recursive junk

9. ?

Chapter 8

1. **D** The less program, like more, displays a text file a page at a time. The less utility also includes the ability to page backward in the text file, search its contents, and do other things that more can't do. Thus, option D is correct. The grep command searches a file for a specified string, so it doesn't do a task that's similar to more, and option A is incorrect. The Hypertext Markup Language (HTML) is a file format, often indicated with the filename extension .html, that's commonly used on the Web. As such, it's not a better version of more, so option B is incorrect. The cat command can concatenate two or more files, or display a single file on the screen. In the former capacity, cat doesn't do the task of more, and in the latter capacity, cat is less capable than more. Thus, option C is incorrect. The man command displays Linux manual pages. Although man uses less by default, man is not itself an improved version of more, so option E is incorrect.

2. **D** man pages are intended to give you quick information on commands, configuration files, or the like. HOWTOs are intended as introductions to packages or broad topics. Thus, option D is correct. Both man pages and HOWTOs are available on the Internet, and both can be installed on your computer, so option A is incorrect. Both man pages and HOWTOs are available electronically, and it's easy to print either type of document, so option B is incorrect. Some man pages are intended for ordinary users and others are intended for programmers. The same is true of HOWTOs, so option C is incorrect. man pages are "flat" (non-hyperlinked) documents, whereas many HOWTOs are hyperlinked, so option E is incorrect.

3. **C** The whatis command searches a database that contains man page Name sections for matches on the specified keyword and returns the names of the commands whose man pages include that keyword. Thus, option C is correct. Options A, D, and E are essentially fictitious descriptions. Option B describes the output of the which command.

4. **True** When you want to override man's search order, you specify the desired manual section between man and the command name, filename, or other name on which you're searching.

5. **False** Although info pages, like Web pages, use hyperlinks to tie related documents together, the two systems use different formats and protocols. info pages also reside on the computer's hard disk; they require no Internet access to read. For these reasons, info pages are *not* Web-based.

6. **False** Individual program authors decide on documentation file format based on their own idiosyncratic needs and preferences. Although some documents are in OpenDocument Text format, many documents are not.

7. **5**

8. **node**

9. `locate`

Chapter 9

1. **E** The apt-get utility is a network-enabled tool that can resolve dependencies and retrieve all the required packages to install a package that you specify. Debian and its derivatives all use it, so option E is correct. The yum and zypper programs are conceptually similar to apt-get, but they work on Red Hat (and its derivatives) and SUSE distributions, respectively, so options A and B are both incorrect. The dmesg program displays the kernel ring buffer; it has nothing to do with package management, so option C is incorrect. The rpm program is a non-network-enabled program for managing packages on an RPM-based system, not on a Debian system, so option D is incorrect.

2. **A** Typically, Linux starts init as the first process, so option A is correct. bash is a Linux text-mode shell program. Although it's important for user interaction, it's far from the first process Linux starts. The cron daemon manages timed execution of programs to handle routine maintenance tasks. It's started automatically in the boot process, but it's not the first process the kernel starts, so option C is incorrect. Although the login process is critical to logging in users in text mode, it's started by init or by another process, so option D is incorrect. The GRand Unified Bootloader (GRUB) boots the computer, so parts of GRUB run *before* the kernel. Several Linux programs help manage a GRUB installation, but the kernel doesn't start any of them automatically. Thus, option E is incorrect.

3. **A** Option A, /var/log, is the standard home for log files in Linux. Options B through E all present fictitious locations and so are all incorrect.

4. **True** Network-enabled package managers, such as APT, yum, zypper, and urpmi, can automatically download and install packages on which a package you want to install depends.

5. **True** The top program sorts a process list by CPU use, so the topmost item in the list is currently consuming the most CPU time. You can change the sort order in various ways, though.

6. **True** Like on-disk log files, the kernel ring buffer (which dmesg displays) changes as the computer runs. Thus, its contents immediately after booting are not likely to be the same as its contents after the computer has been running for weeks.

7. **package database**

8. **child**

9. **syslog**

Chapter 10

1. **A** The grep utility finds matching text within a file and prints those lines. It accepts regular expressions, which means you can place in brackets the two characters that differ in the words for which you're looking. Option A shows the correct syntax for doing this. The tar utility creates or manipulates archive files, and option B's syntax is incorrect for any use of tar, so that option is incorrect. The find utility locates files based on filenames, file sizes, and other surface features. Furthermore, options C and E both present incorrect syntax for find, and so are incorrect. Option D's cat utility displays or concatenates files, so it won't have the desired effect and this option is wrong.

2. **E** The >> operator appends standard output to a file, so option E is correct. The vertical bar (|) is the pipe character; it ties one program's standard output to another's standard input, so option A is incorrect. The 2> operator redirects standard error, not standard output, and it overwrites the target file. Thus, option B is incorrect. The &> operator redirects *both* standard output *and* standard error, and it overwrites the target file, so option C is incorrect. The > operator redirects standard output, but it overwrites the target file, so option D is incorrect.

3. **D** With the tar utility, the --list (t) command is used to read the archive and display its contents. The --verbose (v) option creates a verbose file listing, and --file (f) specifies the filename—data79.tar in this case. Option D uses all of these features, and therefore does as the question specifies. Options A, B, C, and E all substitute other commands for --list, which is required by the question, so all of these options are incorrect.

4. **True** The special characters [^x] match any single character *except* x, and .* matches any sequence of any characters. The string Linus Torvalds is just one of many strings to match the specified regular expression.

5. **True** You can use the -size *n* option to find to locate files based on their sizes.

6. **False** The zip utility creates or manipulates zip archive files. This file type supports compression directly, as does the zip program. Thus, there's no need to involve another compression program to compress files archived with zip.

7. ^

8. &>

9. **lossless**

Chapter 11

1. **D** LibreOffice, like most word processors, uses a binary format that can't be properly parsed using an ASCII or Unicode text editor. Thus, nano won't be useful in examining such a document, making option D correct. The other document types described in options A, B, C, and E are all likely or certain to be stored in ASCII or Unicode format, which nano can handle, making them all incorrect choices.

2. **B, E** The F6 and Ctrl+W keystrokes both invoke the search function, so options B and E are correct. The F3 key writes the current buffer to disk, so option A is incorrect. The Esc-S keystroke is an obscure one; it enables or disables smooth scrolling, so option C is incorrect. Ctrl+F moves forward one character, so option D is incorrect.

3. **A** In Vi, dd is the command-mode command that deletes lines. Preceding this command by a number deletes that number of lines. Thus, option A is correct. Although yy works similarly, it copies (yanks) text rather than deleting it, so option B is incorrect. Option C works in many more modern text editors, but not in Vi. Option D works in emacs and similar text editors (including pico and nano), but not in Vi. Option E, or something similar, works in many GUI text editors, but not in Vi.

4. **False** Unicode provides support for most alphabets, including the huge logographic systems used in common East Asian languages.

5. **False** Support for underlining, italics, multiple fonts, and similar advanced formatting features is present in word processors, not plain text editors—even GUI text editors lack such support.

6. **True** The convention of using a hash mark to identify comments is common, but not universal, in configuration files.

7. **128**

8. **Ctrl+\ and Esc-R**

9. **u**

Chapter 12

1. **A** Scripts, like binary programs, normally have at least one executable bit set, although they can be run in certain ways without this feature, so option A is correct. There is no standard /usr/bin/scripts directory, and scripts can reside in any directory, so option B is incorrect. Scripts are interpreted programs, which means they don't need to be compiled. Typing **bash *scriptname*** will run the script; option C is incorrect. Viruses are extremely rare in Linux, and because you just created the script, the only ways it could possibly contain a virus would be if your system was already infected or if you wrote it as a virus. Thus, option D is incorrect. Most spell-checkers are intended for English or other human languages, so they lack valid Bash commands such as esac. Furthermore, even if every keyword is spelled correctly, the script could contain bugs. Thus, option E is incorrect.

2. **C** The cp command is the only one called in the script, and that command copies files. Because the script passes the arguments ($1 and $2) to cp in reverse order, their effect is reversed—where cp copies its first argument to the second name, the cp1 script copies the second argument to the first name. Option C correctly describes this effect. Option A ignores the reversed order of the arguments, so this option is incorrect. The cp command has nothing to do with compiling C or C++ programs, so neither does the script, making option B incorrect. Since cp is a simple file-copying command, it can't convert a C program into a C++ program, making option D incorrect. The script's first line is a valid shebang line, contrary to option E, so that option is incorrect.

3. **C** Conditional expressions return a true or false response, enabling the script to execute one set of instructions or another or to terminate or continue a loop. Option C is another way of saying this, and so is correct. Conditional expressions need have nothing to do with license conditions (option A), displaying information on the environment (option B), Pavlovian conditioning (option D), or executing the script at certain times of day (option E). That said, conditional expressions *could* be used in service of any of these goals, but that's not their purpose.

4. **False** The $0 variable holds the name of the script—myscript in this example. To access the first parameter passed to the script (laser.txt), the script must use the $1 variable.

5. **True** You can use for to execute a loop a fixed number of times, whereas while and until execute until a test condition is no longer met or is met, respectively.

6. **False** The effect of the specified script is to launch three instances of terminal *sequentially*; the second launches only after the first terminates, and the third launches only after the second terminates. To do as the question specifies, you should include a trailing ampersand (&) in at least the first two calls to terminal (as in terminal &); this causes them to run in the background, so that the script can continue to execute to launch the remaining instances of terminal.

7.   `#!/bin/sh`

8.   echo

9.   case

Chapter 13

1.   **A** UID 0 is reserved for the system administrator's account, also known as `root`, so option A is correct. The first ordinary user account is not a system account, and its UID is normally 500 or 1000, depending on the distribution, so option B is incorrect. Because A is correct, C cannot be correct. The association of UID 0 for administrative tasks is very basic in Linux, so you won't find variation on this score, making option D incorrect. Option E describes the nobody account, which does not have a UID of 0.

2.   **A, C, E** The `/etc/passwd` file's fields specify the username, an encrypted password (or x to denote use of shadow passwords, which is more common), a UID number (option A), a *single* default GID number, a comment field that normally holds the user's full name, the path to the account's home directory (option C), and the path to the account's default text-mode shell (option E). Option B is incorrect because, although `/etc/passwd` includes the user's *default* group, the user *may* belong to additional groups that are defined elsewhere. Option D is incorrect because the user's default desktop environment is defined in the user's home directory, not in `/etc/password`.

3.   **A** The sudo command is the usual way to execute a single command as `root`, and option A gives the correct syntax to use it as the question specifies. There is no standard `root` command, so option B is incorrect. The passwd command changes passwords, so option C is incorrect. Although you can use su to execute a single command as `root`, you must use it with the `-c` option to do this, as in **su -c** "**iptables -L**", so option D is incorrect. Option E's admin is a fictitious command, so this option is incorrect.

4.   **False** The whoami command displays your username only. The id command displays your username, your UID number, your primary group name, your primary GID number, and the group names and GID numbers of all your groups.

5.   **False** The name for the group data file in Linux is `/etc/group`, not `/etc/groups`.

6.   **True** It's possible to do more damage to a computer as root than as an ordinary user. Thus, you should be extra cautious when using root—run only trusted programs, double-check your commands for errors, and so on.

7.   `/etc/passwd`

8.   w

9.   **system**

Chapter 14

1. **C** The userdel command deletes an account, and the -r option to userdel causes it to delete the user's home directory and mail spool, thus satisfying the terms of the question. Option A deletes the account but leaves the user's home directory intact. Option B does the same; the -f option forces account deletion and file removal under some circumstances, but it's only meaningful when -r is also used. Option D's command will probably have no effect, since rm works on directories only in conjunction with -r, and /home/nemo is probably the user's home directory. Option E's rm command deletes the user's home directory (assuming it's located in the conventional place, given the username) but doesn't delete the user's account.

2. **B** The password in option B uses a combination of upper- and lowercase letters, numbers, and symbols, and it doesn't contain any obvious word. Furthermore, it's a long password. All of these characteristics make it unlikely to appear in an intruder's password dictionary and make it hard to guess. Thus, option B represents a good password, and the best of those shown. Option A is the name of a well-known celebrity (at least in the Linux world!); such a name is likely to appear in password-cracking dictionaries, and so makes a poor password choice. Option C is an extremely common password, which makes it a bad choice. Furthermore, it's short and it consists of just one symbol type (digits). Option D is another popular (and therefore very poor) password. It's a single common word in all-lowercase and it contains no numbers or other non-alphabetic symbols. Although option E is fairly long, it consists entirely of lowercase letters, and it's three related words, making it a poor password.

3. **A** The groupadd command creates a new group, as described in option A, so that option is correct. To add a user to a group, as suggested by option B, you would use the usermod utility. No standard command imports group information from a file, as option C suggests, so this option is incorrect. (Some network user management tools do provide such functionality, though.) To change a user's default group or list of supplemental groups, you would use usermod, so options D and E are both incorrect.

4. **True** System accounts have UID values between 0 and some number (normally 499 or 999), whereas user accounts have UID values above that number (starting at 500 or 1,000, typically).

5. **False** The usual command-line command for changing passwords is passwd.

6. **True** Although the userdel command's -r option deletes the user's home directory and mail files, this command doesn't track down the user's files stored in more exotic locations. You can use find to locate such files if you want to delete them or transfer ownership to another user.

7. `-u 1926 theo`

8. `usermod -l emilyn el211`

9. `-r` or `--system`

Chapter 15

1. **D** Option D is the correct command. Typing **chown ralph:tony somefile.txt**, as in option A, sets the owner of the file to `ralph` and the group to `tony`. The chmod command used in options B and E is used to change file permissions, not ownership. Option C reverses the order of the filename and the owner.

2. **C, D** The d character that leads the mode indicates that the file is actually a directory, while the r symbol in the r–x triplet at the end of the symbolic mode indicates that all users of the system have read access to the directory, so options C and D are both correct. Symbolic links are denoted by leading l characters, which this mode lacks, so option A is incorrect. Although the x symbols usually denote executable program files, as specified in option B, in the case of directories this permission bit indicates that the directory's contents may be searched; executing a directory is meaningless. The only permission field set for write access is in the first triplet, which refers to the file's owner, so only that user, and not other members of the file's group, may write to the file, contrary to option E.

3. **E** Although the chgrp command is the usual one for changing a file's group, you can also use chown to do the job, so option E is correct. Option A's groupadd command adds a new group to the system, so this option is incorrect. The groupmod command can modify details of a group definition, but it doesn't change the group associated with a file, so option B is incorrect. The chmod command changes a file's mode (that is, its permissions), but not its group association, so option C is incorrect. You can use ls to learn a file's current group (among other things), but not to change it, so option D is incorrect.

4. **True** The octal permission of 755 corresponds to a symbolic representation of –rwxr-xr-x, which includes world read permissions (in the final three bits of r–x). Thus, anybody can read the file.

5. **False** Any user may use chmod; however, only a file's owner or root may change the permissions on a file.

6. **True** Although an ordinary user can use chown to change a file's group, ordinary users cannot change a file's ownership.

7. -R or --recursive

8. r-x

9. a+x

Chapter 16

1. **D** The /usr/lib directory holds library files, as stated in option D. These files contain code that can be used by multiple programs. Using libraries reduces the sizes of the other programs and can simplify upgrades and bug fixes. Options A, B, C, and E are all fictitious file types.

2. **A** The -l parameter produces a long listing, including file sizes. The -a parameter produces a listing of all files in a directory, including the dot files. Combining the two produces the desired information (along with information about other files), so option A is correct. The -p, -R, and -d options don't have the specified effects, so options B, C, D, and E are all incorrect.

3. **C** The set user ID (SUID) bit enables programs to run as the program's owner rather than as the user who ran them. This makes SUID root programs risky, so setting the SUID bit on root-owned programs should be done only when it's required for the program's normal functioning, as stated in option C. This should certainly *not* be done for all programs because the SUID bit is *not* required of all executable programs as option A asserts. Although the SUID root configuration does enable programs to access device files, the device files' permissions can be modified to give programs access to those files, if this is required, so option B is incorrect. Despite the similarity in acronyms, the SUID bit has nothing to do with accessing user ID (UID) data for accounts, so option D is incorrect. Although SUID root programs are a security risk, as stated in option E, they're a necessary risk for a few programs, so option E goes too far.

4. **True** The /var directory holds variable data files, which are quite diverse in their purpose. One of the many types of files that resides in /var is print spool files, as noted in the question.

5. **False** Normally, the sticky bit is set on /tmp, which prevents anybody but the directory's owner (normally root) or the file's owner from deleting files within it, even though the directory's world write permission bit is set.

6. **True** Dot files are created by placing a dot (.) as the first character in a filename. As such, converting an existing file into a dot file means that its filename has changed, and any existing references to the file must change if they're to continue working.

7. /media

8. /var/tmp

9. a+t

Chapter 17

1. **C** The gateway computer is a router that transfers data between two or more network segments. As such, if a computer isn't configured to use a gateway, it won't be able to communicate beyond its local network segment, as option C suggests. (If your DNS server is on a different network segment, name resolution via DNS won't work, although other types of name resolution, such as /etc/hosts file entries, will still work.) Lack of a gateway address will not cause the symptoms described by options A, B, D, or E.

2. **B, C** When used to display information on an interface, ifconfig shows the hardware (option C) and IP (option B) addresses of the interface, the protocols (such as TCP/IP) bound to the interface, and statistics on transmitted and received packets. This command does *not* return information about programs using the interface (option A), the hostname associated with the interface (option D), or the gateway with which it communicates (option E).

3. **A, E** DNS problems can manifest as an ability to connect to computers using IP addresses but not using hostnames. Thus, options A and E (and various other DNS-related problems) could create the symptoms described. If the target system were configured to ignore ping packets, as described in option B, it wouldn't respond when you identified it by IP address. The target system's DNS configuration (option C) doesn't enter into the equation, because it responds to the ping request via IP address alone. Your computer's local hostname configuration won't affect its ability to send or receive packets, even by hostname, so option D is incorrect.

4. **True** IPv4 addresses are four bytes long, and are typically expressed as four decimal numbers separated by dots, as in 192.168.0.1.

5. **False** The /etc/resolv.conf file holds DNS server information—the IP addresses of up to three DNS servers and domain names that should be searched when the user omits them.

6. **True** When used without any other options, the route command displays the current routing table.

7. netstat

8. eth0

9. **firewall**

LPI's Certification Program

The purpose of the Linux Essentials Program is to define the basic knowledge required to competently use a desktop or mobile device using a Linux operating system. The program guides and encourages those who are new to Linux, and to open source in general, to understand the place of these tools in the context of the broader IT industry.

The program is made up of several main components:

- ▶ Linux Essentials Exam and Certification

- ▶ Support for worldwide participation in the World Skills Information and Communications Technology Category, IT Network Systems Administration

- ▶ Regional links to employability and apprenticeship programs available to youth

- ▶ Research and resources supporting youth entry into Linux and open source careers

- ▶ Linux Professional Institute (LPI) support for regional government and educational qualification authorities where appropriate

- ▶ LPI support for teacher collaboration and sharing of projects and exercises for the Linux Essentials knowledge base

- ▶ Resources for youth describing jobs and industries requiring Linux skills

The Linux Essentials Certification

The successful Linux Essentials candidate should have an understanding of the Linux and open source industry and knowledge of the most popular open source applications. The candidate should understand the major components of the Linux operating system and have the technical proficiency to work on the Linux command line. The candidate has at least a basic understanding of security- and administration-related topics such as managing users and groups, working on the command line, and using permissions. An LPI Linux Essentials Technician (LPI LET) is most likely the end user of a mostly managed system.

The LPI LET, at a minimum, typically:

▶ Has a basic understanding of free and open source software, the various communities and licenses

▶ Understands the basic concepts of processes, programs, and components of an operating system

▶ Has a basic knowledge of computer hardware

▶ Has a basic appreciation of system security, users/groups, and file permissions for public and private directories

▶ Has a basic understanding of how to make the system accessible and is able to connect to other computers on a local area network (LAN)

▶ Demonstrates a knowledge of open source applications in the workplace as they relate to closed source equivalents

▶ Understands navigation systems on a Linux desktop and where to go for help

▶ Has a rudimentary ability to work on the command line and with files

▶ Is able to make and restore simple backups and archives

▶ Can use a basic command-line editor

▶ Understands file compression

▶ Is able to create and run simple scripts

Certification Objectives Map

Table B.1 provides approximate objective mappings for the LPI Linux Essentials Program. It identifies the chapters and sections where the exam objectives are covered. Be aware, however, that some specific programs and technologies are mentioned in multiple objectives, so you may find more complete coverage of some topics in chapters other than those noted in Table B.1. Consult this book's index if you need help finding a specific subject.

TABLE B.1 LPI Linux Essentials objectives map

Objectives	Chapter(s)
Topic 1: A Career in Open Source and Joining the Linux Community	
1.1 Linux Evolution and Popular Operating Systems	Chapters 1, 2
1.2 Major Open Source Applications	Chapter 4
1.3 Understanding Open Source Software and Licensing	Chapter 3
1.4 ICT Skills and Working in Linux	Chapter 4
Topic 2: Finding Your Way on a Linux System	
2.1 Command-Line Basics	Chapters 6, 12
2.2 Using the Command Line to Get Help	Chapter 8
2.3 Using Directories and Listing Files	Chapter 6
2.4 Creating, Moving, and Deleting Files	Chapter 7
Topic 3: The Power of the Command Line	
3.1 Archiving Files on the Command Line	Chapter 10
3.2 Searching and Extracting Data from Files	Chapter 10
3.3 Turning Commands into a Script	Chapters 11, 12
Topic 4: The Linux Operating System	
4.1 Choosing an Operating System	Chapter 1
4.2 Understanding Computer Hardware	Chapter 5
4.3 Where Data Is Stored	Chapter 9
4.4 Your Computer on the Network	Chapter 17
Topic 5: Security and File Permissions	
5.1 Basic Security and Identifying User Types	Chapter 13
5.2 Creating Users and Groups	Chapter 14
5.3 Managing File Permissions and Ownership	Chapter 15
5.4 Special Directories and Files	Chapter 16

INDEX

Note to the Reader: Throughout this index **boldfaced** page numbers indicate primary discussions of a topic. *Italicized* page numbers indicate illustrations.

A

AbiWord program, 60
absolute file references, 108–110, *109*
accounts, **217**
    creating, 235
        GUI tools, 239–241, *240*
        shell, 241–243
    deleting, 250–252
    features, 218–220
    group strategy, 235–236
    groups, 222–223
    identifying, 220–221, *221*
    modifying, 244–245
        GUI tools, 245–246, *246–247*
        shell, 247–249
    network databases, **222**
    passwords, 236–239
    root user, **226–231**, *229*
    tools, **223–226**
administrative tasks, 227
administrator skill requirements for distributions, **16**
administrators. *See* root users
Advanced Package Tool (APT), 153
algorithms, 35
alpha software, 17
American Standard Code for Information Interchange (ASCII), **185–186**
ampersands (&)
    background programs, 105
    conditional expressions, 211
    redirection operator, 173
    scripts, 205
    symbolic links, 107
AND operators in conditional expressions, 211
Android operating system, **16**, 27, 62–63
angle brackets (<>) in HTML files, 200
Apache licenses, 43
aplay command, 212–213
appliances, 28, **60–63**
apps, 62

apropos command, 133
APT (Advanced Package Tool), 153
Aqua interface, 10
Arch distribution, 17
archiving data, **176**
    compression, **179–180**
    copying files, 120
    tape archiver, **176–179**
    zip command, 180–183
arguments in scripts, 207–208
Artistic licenses, 43
Artwork program, 60
ASCII (American Standard Code for Information Interchange), **185–186**
aspect ratio, 91
assembly language, **70**
assignment operator (=) for variables, 209
asterisks (*)
    account passwords, 219
    case statements, 212
    file listings, 108
    file manipulation, 123
    grep, 169
    info pages, 139
    passwords, 221
    regular expressions, 166
    traceroute, 301
ATA Packet interface (ATAPI), 81
Audacity program, 61
Author section in man pages, 135
authors, program, 145
automatic license distribution, 41
availability of distributions, **15**

B

background, running programs in, **105–106**
backslashes (\)
    directory separators, 108
    regular expressions, 166–167

backtick characters (`) for commands, 176, 208

base 8 numbers, 264

Base program, 60

bash (Bourne Again Shell), 3

    default shell, 100

    editing and command history features, 113

    scripts, 72

Basic Input/Output System (BIOS), 83

basic regular expressions, 166

batch files, 203

Berne Convention, 34

beta software, 17

bg command, 105

/bin directory, 275–276

binary code, 2, 9

binary packages, 150

BIOS (Basic Input/Output System), 83

BIOS partitioning, 82

bit depth of CPUs, 77

BitchX IRC client program, 146

Blender program, 61

Bookmarks feature, 55, *56*

/boot directory, 274

boot.log file, 160

Bootstrap Protocol (BOOTP), 64

bounties, 45

Bourne Again Shell (bash), 3

    default shell, 100

    editing and command history features, 113

    scripts, 72

brackets (<>, [])

    HTML files, 200

    regular expressions, **166**

    wildcards, 123

breaks in connectivity, 300–301

broadband routers, 287

BSD licenses, 42

Btrfs filesystem, 9, 86

buffers, ring, **162–163**

bug fixes for drivers, 95

Bugs section in man pages, 134

business models, open source, 44–45

bzip2 program, 179–180

C

C language, **71**

C++ language, **71**

Calc program, 60

cameras, 93

car computers, 28

carats (^)

    regular expressions, 166

    text editors, 190

case of characters in passwords, 237

case sensitivity of filenames, **123–124**

case statement, 212

cat command, 104, 110

cat/proc/cpuinfo command, 78

cd command, **108**

cdrecord tool, 88

cell phones, 27, 93

cfdisk tool, 84

cgdisk tool, 84

changing directories, 108

channels in IRC, 146

characters in regular expressions, 166

Chatzilla IRC client program, 146

chgrp command, 110, 261

children processes, 154

chipsets, 79

chmod command, 110

    permissions, 266–267

    scripts, 204

    special execute permissions, 280

    symbolic code, 278

chown command, 110, 260–261

Chrome browser, 58

click-through licenses, 36

click-wrap licenses, 36

clock rate, 76

cloud computing, **62**

Cocoa interface, 10

code pages, **186**

code types, 9–10

colon commands, 194

command line, **99**. *See also* shells

    file manipulation, **106–111**, *109*

    generating, **175–176**

    launching terminals, 100–102, *101*

    overview, 2–3

    remote logins, 103

    running programs, 103–106

    shell features, 111–114

    starting, 99–100

    text-mode console logins, 102–103

commands
   completion, 111–112
   history, 112–114
   scripts, 204–206
comments
   accounts, 218
   configuration files, 198–199
   scripts, 204
commercial software, 25
common port numbers, 63–66
compiled languages, 9, 69–70
completion of commands, 111–112
compression of files, 179–180
Computer category, 55
concatenation, 104
conditional expressions, 210–212
configurability of Linux vs. Windows, 12
configuration directory, 276
configuration files, 197–199
connections, network. *See* network connections
connectors, motherboards, 79
consoles, text-mode, 102–103
context menus, 52
control characters, 186
cooperative multitasking, 22
copying
   directories, 127
   files, 118–120
copyleft licenses, 37
copyright law, 33–36
core Unix tools, 13
costs
   Linux vs. Windows, 11
   open source software, 26
cp command, 110, 118–120
cpio program, 176
CPUs (central processing units), 75–76
   bit depth, 77
   distributions, 16
   families, 76–78
   identifying, 78
Creative Commons, 41–42
cron log file, 161
cups directory, 161
curly braces ({}) for functions, 213
cut command, 206

D

daemons, 67
dashes (-) in regular expressions, 166
databases
   network account, 222
   package, 150
Debian package system, 15, 150–151, **153–154**, *154*
default permissions, **267**
default shells, **219**
deleting
   accounts, 250–252
   directories, 125–126
   files, 122–123
   groups, 255
denial-of-service (DoS) attacks, 68
dependencies in packages, 150–151
deprecated programs, 302
derived works in Open Source Initiative, 41
Description section in man pages, 134
desktop computers, 28–29
desktop environments, 6–7, *7*, 49
   choosing, 50–51, *51*
   file managers, 54–55, *55–56*
   launching programs, 52–54, *53–54*
   productivity software. *See* productivity software
   program suites, 3
   server programs, 63–67
   Unix, 9
desktop icons, 52
desktop menus, 52, 57
/dev directory, 275
device names
   network, 296–297
   partitioning, 85
Devices category, 54
dhclient program, 295–296
DHCP (Dynamic Host Configuration Protocol)
   client programs, 295
   description, **286**
   overview, 288
dhcpcd program, 295–296
Digital Video Interface (DVI) cables, 91, *91*
digital video recorders (DVRs), 28
directories, 124
   changing, 108
   creating, **125**
   deleting, 125–126

important, 274–277
listing files in, 5, 106–108
managing, **127**
permissions, 171
viewing, 281–282
discrimination in Open Source Initiative, 41
Disk Operating System (DOS), 22
diskless configurations, 81
disks, **81**
    filesystems, 85–88
    interfaces, 81
    partitioning, 81–85, *82*, *85*
    removable and optical, 88, *89*
    USB devices, 93
displays, **89–92**, *91–92*
distribution-specific network scripts, 295–296
distributions
    common, 14–17
    components, 13–14
    new, 24
    release cycles, 15–17
dmesg command, 162–163, 175
DNS (Domain Name System)
    description, 285–286
    port numbers, 64
    testing, **302**
do command, 213
document properties, 55
document viewer programs, 60
documentation
    online, 144–145
    programs, **141–143**
dollar signs ($)
    arguments, 207
    exit status variable, 210
    prompts, 5
    regular expressions, 166
    usernames, 218
    variables, 208
Domain Name System (DNS)
    description, 285–286
    port numbers, 64
    testing, **302**
donations in open source business models, **45**
DoS (denial-of-service) attacks, 68
DOS (Disk Operating System), 22
dot files, 280
dots (.) in regular expressions, 166
down command, 296
Draw program, 60

drivers
    locating and installing, 94–95
    open source business models, 44
    types, 93–94
    Wi-Fi, **292**
Dropbox cloud provider, 62
dual licensing, 44
DVI (Digital Video Interface) cables, 91, *91*
DVRs (digital video recorders), 28
Dynamic Host Configuration Protocol (DHCP)
    client programs, 295
    description, **286**
    overview, 288
dynamic Web-based content, 59

E

e-book readers, 28, 93
Ease program, 60
echo command, 111, **206**
editing files, **185**
    configuration files, 197–199
    editors
        choosing, 187–188, *188*
        conventions, 190
        launching, **189**
        pico and nano, 189–193
        vi, 193–197, *194*
    text files, 185–187, 199–200
EIDE (Enhanced IDE) interface, 81
else keyword, 211–212
emacs editor, 140, 187–188
email clients, 59–60
embedded systems, 17, 22, 27–28
emergency discs, 219
encryption
    hashes, 219
    passwords, 238
    SSH, 103
    WiFi, 291
end of line in regular expressions, 166
end-user license agreements (EULAs), 36
Enhanced IDE (EIDE) interface, 81
environments
    desktop. *See* desktop environments
    script, 207
    variables, 210
equation editor programs, 60
esac statement, 212

escaping regular expressions, 166–167
/etc directory
    init.d directory, 67
    man.conf file, 132
    purpose, 274, 276
    rc.d directory, 67
/etc/fstab file, 88, 276
/etc/group file, 222–223, 254
/etc/passwd file, 218–222, 276
/etc/resolv.conf file, 295, 297, 302
/etc/rsyslog.conf file, 162
/etc/samba file, 276
/etc/services directory, 63
/etc/shadow file, 218–220, 222, 272
/etc/X11 file, 276
/etc/X11/xorg.conf file, 90, 92
Ethernet network hardware, 286
EULAs (end-user license agreements), 36
Evince program, 60
Evolution program, 59–60
exclamation marks (!)
    account passwords, 219
    scripts, 204
executable directories, 276
execute permissions
    directory, 265
    special, 279–280
exit command, 214
exit values, 210, 214–215
experts, consulting, 57, 145–146
expiration of passwords, 219–220
expressions
    conditional, 210–212
    regular, 165–167
ext2fs (Second Extended Filesystem), 85
ext3fs (Third Extended Filesystem), 86
ext4fs (Fourth Extended Filesystem), 86
extended partitions, 83
extended regular expressions, 166
Extents File System (XFS), 86
extracting data
    find, 170–171
    grep, 167–170
    wc, 171–172

F

fair use principle, 34
FAQs (Frequently Asked Questions), 144

FAT (File Allocation Table) filesystem, 87, 124
fbdev driver, 91
fdisk tool, 84
FDL (Free Documentation License), 38
fg command, 105
fglrx driver, 91
FHS (Filesystem Hierarchy Standard), 273–274, *274*
fi keyword, 211
File Allocation Table (FAT) filesystem, 87, 124
file managers, 7
    for ownership, 259–260, *260*
    for permissions, 266
    working with, 54–55, *55–56*
File Transfer Protocol (FTP), 64
files, 117
    absolute and relative references, 108–110, *109*
    case sensitivity, 123–124
    compression, 179–180
    copying, 118–120
    creating, 118
    in deleted accounts, 250
    deleting, 122–123
    directories. *See* directories
    editing. *See* editing files
    hiding, 280–281
    links, 121–122
    listing, 106–108
    log, 160–163
    manipulation commands, 110–111
    moving and renaming, 120
    script commands, 205–206
    security features, 126
    system, 271–273
    wildcards, 123
Files section in man pages, 134
Filesystem Hierarchy Standard (FHS), 273–274, *274*
Filesystem Standard (FSSTND), 273
filesystems, 271
    directories, 274–277
    FHS, 273–274
    files vs. system files, 271–273
    hiding files, 280–281
    special execute permissions, 279–280
    sticky bits, 277–279
    viewing directories, 281–282
find utility, 170–171, 206
Firefox program, 53–54, *54*, 58
firewalls, 304
flexibility of open source software, 26
FLOSS (free/libre open source software), 40

flowcharting programs, 60
for loops, 213
force overwrite option, 119
foreground programs, 105
forks, program, 8, 60
formats, file, 143
formatted text files, editing, **199–200**
FOSS (free and open source software), 40
FOSSFactory site, 45
Fourth Extended Filesystem (ext4fs), 86
free and open source software (FOSS), 40
free command, 104, 155, **159–160**
Free Documentation License (FDL), 38
free/libre open source software (FLOSS), 40
free redistribution, 40
free software, 37–39
Free Software Foundation (FSF), 8, 36–39
freeware, 25, 37
Frequently Asked Questions (FAQs), 144
FSF (Free Software Foundation), 8, 36–39
FSSTND (Filesystem Standard), 273
FTP (File Transfer Protocol), 64
functions in scripts, 213–214

G

Galeon program, 58
gateways, 287
gdisk tool, 84
gdm directory, 161
gedit editor, 188
General Public License (GPL), 36, 38
Gentoo distribution, 15, 17
getent passwd command, 221
gibibytes (GiB), 84
GID (group ID) numbers, 223
    accounts, **218**
    cross-installations, **258**
    deleted accounts, 250–251
    displaying, 224
GIMP (GNU Image Manipulation Program), 61
Globally Unique Identifier (GUID) Partition Table
    (GPT), 83
globbing, 123
GNOME (GNU Network Object Model Environment), 3
    description, 50–51, *51*
    Office applications, **60**
GNU GPL, 38, 42

GNU Image Manipulation Program (GIMP), 61
Gnumeric program, 60
GNU's Not Unix (GNU) project, 8, 23, 36
Google Apps cloud provider, 62
GParted tool, 84, *85*
GPL (General Public License), 36, 38
GPT (Globally Unique Identifier (GUID) Partition
    Table), 83
GPUs (graphics processing units), 76
graphical user interface (GUI) tools and programs
    accounts
        creating, 239–241, *240*
        deleting, 251, *251*
        modifying, 245–246, *246–247*
    groups, 252–253, *252–253*
    network connections, 293–295, *293–294*
    overview, 3, 6–8, *6–7*
    running, **105**
graphics processing units (GPUs), 76
graphics programs, 61
greater than signs (>) for redirection operator, 173
grep utility
    with redirection, **174**
    scripts, 206
    working with, **167–170**
group ID (GID) numbers, 223
    accounts, 218
    cross-installations, 258
    deleted accounts, 250–251
    displaying, 224
groupadd command, 253–255
groupdel command, 255
groupmod command, 254
groups, 217
    deleting, 255
    fields, 222–223
    managing
        GUI tools, 252–253, *252–253*
        shell, 253–255
    permissions, 263
    strategy, 235–236
groupware programs, 60
growisofs tool, 88
GTK+ widget sets, 50
guides, 144
GUIs. *See* graphical user interface (GUI) tools and
    programs
gzip program, 179–180

H

HandBrake program, 61
hard links, **121–122**
hardware, **75**
    CPUs, **75–78**
    disks. *See* disks
    displays, **89–92**, *91–92*
    drivers, **93–95**
    Linux vs. Windows compatibility, **11**
    motherboards, **78–80**
    power supplies, 80
    USB devices, **92–93**
hash marks (#)
    comments, 142, 198–199
    prompts, 5, 101, 228
    scripts, 204
hashbangs, 204
hashes for passwords, 219
hashplings, 204
HDMI (High Definition Multimedia Interface), 91
head command, 111
header files, 71
headers, email, 187
help, **131**
    experts, **145–146**
    info pages, **138–140**
    man pages. *See* man pages
    online documentation, **144–145**
    productivity software, 57
    program documentation, **141–143**
HFS (Hierarchical File System), 87
HFS+ (Mac OS Extended) filesystem, 87–88, 124
hidden bit, 280
hiding files, **280–281**
Hierarchical File System (HFS), 87
hierarchy of processes, **154–155**, *155*
High Definition Multimedia Interface (HDMI), 91
history command, 114
history of commands, **112–114**
History section in man pages, **134–135**
home directories, 273
    description, **218**
    in File Managers, 55
    purpose, 275
    references, **108–109**
hostnames in DNS, **285–286**
HOWTO documents, 144
HTML (Hypertext Markup Language), **199–200**

HTTP (Hypertext Transfer Protocol), 65
HTTPS, 66
human interface devices, 93
HURD kernel, 8
Hypertext Markup Language (HTML), **199–200**
Hypertext Transfer Protocol (HTTP), 65

I

id command, **224**
IDE (Integrated Device Electronics) interface, 81
identifying
    accounts, **220–221**, *221*
    CPU, 78
    processes, *157*
    protocols and programs, **63–66**
identity, discovering, **224**
IEEE-1541 prefixes, **83–84**
if keyword, **210–212**
ifconfig program, 295
ifdown command, **298–299**
ifup command, **298–299**
ImageMagick graphics programs, 61
IMAP (Internet Message Access Protocol), 65
inetd daemon, 67
info pages, **138**
    purpose, **138–139**
    reading, **139–140**
init process, 154
Inkscape program, 60
input, redirecting, **172–176**
installers for distributions, **13–14**
installing
    drivers, **94–95**
    server programs, **67**
Integrated Device Electronics (IDE) interface, 81
interfaces
    disks, **81**
    network, 302
    user
        GUIs, **6–8**, *6–7*
        Linux vs. Windows, **12**
        text mode, **4–6**, *5*
Internet, defined, 286
Internet Message Access Protocol (IMAP), 65
Internet Relay Chat (IRC) tool, **146**
internets, defined, 286
interpreted languages, 9, **69–70**

inventions, 35
IP addresses, 285–286
IP masquerading, 303
IPv4 addresses, 286
IPv6 addresses, 286
IRC (Internet Relay Chat) tool, 146
Irssi IRC client program, 146
ISO-9660 filesystem, 87–88
Itanium CPU, 77
iwconfig utility, **292**
iwlist command, **291**

J

Java language, **71**
Joliet filesystem, 87
Journaled File System (JFS), 86
journals, 85

K

Kate editor, 188
KCells program, 60
KDE (K Desktop Environment), 7, *7*
    description, 50–51
    Kicker, 57
    launching programs, 53–54, *54*
kernels
    development, 8
    distributions, 13
    improvements, 24
    overview, 1–2
    patches, 13, 95
    process hierarchy, 154
    ring buffers, 162–163
kibibytes (KiB), 83
Kivio program, 60
klog daemon, 162
klogd daemon, 162
KMail program, 59
KOffice office suite, **60**
Konqueror file manager, 54, 58
ksh shell, 100
KWrite editor, 60, 188

L

laptop computers, 28–29
last program, 245
LaTeX format, 61
launching
    editors, **189**
    programs, 52–54, *53–54*
    server programs, **67**
    terminals, 100–102, *101*
LDAP (Lightweight Directory Access Protocol), 65
LDP (Linux Documentation Project), 144–145
less program, 111, **135–137**
less than signs (<) for redirection operator, 173
Lesser GPL (LGPL), 38, 42
levels of info pages, 138
/lib directory, 275
libparted library, 84
libraries
    LGPL, 38, 42
    overview, 3
    packages, 150
library directories, 276
LibreOffice office suite, **60**
licensing
    Linux vs. Windows, 11
    software. *See* software licensing
Lightweight Directory Access Protocol (LDAP), 65
Lightweight X11 Desktop Environment (LXDE), 50–51
links, 117
    file, 121–122
    symbolic, 107, **265**
Linus's Law, 26
Linux Documentation Project (LDP), 144–145
Linux overview, 21
    changes over time, 23
    open source software, 24–27
    origins, 22–23
    roles, 27–30
    as software integrator, 27
listing files, 5
ln utility, 111, 122
load averages, 158
local experts, 145
locate command, 142–143
locating drivers, 94–95
locations, 54
locked account state, 243

log files, **160**
    creating, **162**
    kernel ring buffers, **162–163**
    locating, **160–161**
    verbose entries, **162**
logged-in users, checking for, 245
logical operators in conditional expressions, 211
logical partitions, 83
login prompts, 4–5
logins
    date and time display, 225
    remote, 103
    as root, 227
    text-mode consoles, 102–103
logout options, 7
loopback devices, 297
loops in scripts, **212–213**
lossless compression, 180
lossy compression, 180
ls command, 5, **106–108**, 111, 281–282
lscpu command, 78
lspci tool, 79, 292
LXDE (Lightweight X11 Desktop Environment), 50–51
Lynx program, 58
LyX program, 60

M

Mac OS Extended (HFS+) filesystem, 87–88, 124
Mac OS X operating system, **10**
mail command, **206**
mail spool files, 243
mailing lists, **145**
mainboards, 79
make tool, 118
malware
    Android apps, 63
    dynamic Web content, 59
    network connections, 304
man pages, 104, **131**
    less program, 135–137
    purpose, 131–132
    reading, 134–135, *135*
    searching, 133
    section numbers, 132–133
Market app, 62

masks
    network, 286
    user, **267**
masquerade information, 303
Massachusetts Institute of Technology (MIT)
    licenses, 43
master boot record (MBR), 82–83
Math program, 60
maximum display resolution, 92
MBR (master boot record), 82–83
mebibytes (MiB), 84
/media directory, 275
memory leaks, 159
memory use by processes, **159–160**
messages log file, 161
metacharacters, 190
Metro interface, 12
microkernels, 23
Microsoft Office Web Apps cloud provider, 62
Minix OS, 23
MIT (Massachusetts Institute of Technology)
    licenses, 43
mkdir command, 111, 125, 127
mkfs command, 230
mkisofs tool, 88
/mnt directory, 275
mobile applications, 62–63
mode command, 125
more pager, 135
motherboards, 78–80
mount command, 88
mount points, 85
mounted partitions, 85
moving
    directories, 127
    files, **120**
Mozilla Public License (MPL), 43
MS-DOS partitioning, 82
multi-core CPUs, 78
multimedia applications, **61**
multiple desktops, 7
multitasking, 22
music players, 93
mutt email reader, 59
mv command, 111, **120**
MythTV package, 28, 61

N

Name section in man pages, 134
names
    DNS resolution, 285–286
    files, 120
    groups, 223
    usernames, 218–219
nano editor, 5, *5*, 187–193, *188*
Nautilus file manager, 54, *55–56*
ndiswrapper package, 292
NEdit editor, 188
Netscape Public License (NPL), 43
network account databases, 222
network appliances, **16**
Network category, 55
network connections, 285
    configuring, 287–288
    DHCP, 288
    GUI tools, 293–295, *293–294*
    security, 303–304
    testing, 299–303
    text-based tools, 295–299
    Wi-Fi, 289–292, *289–290*
Network File System (NFS), 66
Network Information System (NIS), 222
network masks, 286
Network Time Protocol (NTP) daemon, 198
networks
    device names, 296–297
    features, 285–287
    status checking, 302–303
new hardware, drivers for, 94
New Technology File System (NTFS), 87, 124
newgrp command, 223
news reader programs, 146
newsgroups, 145–146
NFS (Network File System), 66
NIS (Network Information System), 222
nodes for info pages, 138
nouveau driver, 91
NPL (Netscape Public License), 43
nslookup program, 302
NTFS (New Technology File System), 87, 124
NTP (Network Time Protocol) daemon, 198
numbers in passwords, 237
nvidia drivers, 91

O

object-oriented features, 71
octal code for permissions, 264–265
    chmod, 266–267
    modes, 125
    special execute, 280
    sticky bits, 278
ODF (OpenDocument Format), 60
office tools, 60–61
online documentation, 144–145
online users, 225–226
open ports, 303
Open Source Initiative (OSI), 39–41, *40*
open source software, 24
    business models, 44–45
    defined, 10
    licenses, 42–44
    principles, 24–26
OpenDocument Format (ODF), 60
OpenOffice.org office suite, **60**
OpenWrt distribution, 16
Opera browser, 58
operating systems
    characteristics, 2–4
    distributions, 13–17
    kernel, 1–2
    Linux vs. Mac OS X, 10
    Linux vs. Unix, 8–10
    Linux vs. Windows, 11–12
    user interfaces, 4–8, *5–7*
optical disks, 88, *89*
optimum display resolution, 92
Options section in man pages, 134
OR operators in conditional expressions, 211
OSI (Open Source Initiative), 39–41, *40*
output, redirecting, 172–176
owner permissions, 263
ownership, **257**
    copied files, 120
    file managers for, 259–260, *260*
    overview, 258
    shell for, 260–261
    UIDs and GIDs, 258

P

package databases, 150

package management, 149
   distributions, 15
   package systems, 150–152, *151*
      Debian, 153–154, *154*
      RPM, 152–153
   principles, 149–150
pagers, 135
paid consultants, 145
panels, 52, *53*
Parallel ATA (PATA) interface, 81
parameters in scripts, 207–208
parent directories, 125
parent process ID (PPID) numbers, 155
parent processes, 154
parentheses () in regular expressions, **167**
Parted Magic tool, 16–17, 230
partitioning disks, 81–85, *82, 85*
passwd utility, 132, 247
passwords
   accounts, 218–219
   groups, 223
   login, 4, 6
   network connections, 304
   remote logins, 103
   root users, 229–230
   selecting, 236–238
   servers, 68
   text-mode consoles, 102
   web sites, 59
   Wi-Fi, 290, *290*
   worst, 238–239
PATA (Parallel ATA) interface, 81
patches, kernel, 13, 95
patents, 35
path command, 104
paths for files, 276–277
pattern matches in case statements, 212
Perens, Bruce, 39
Perl language, **71**
permissions, 257
   copied files, 120
   default, 267
   directories, 171
   file managers for, 266
   file type codes, 262–265
   listing, **261–262**
   shell for, 266–267
   special execute, 279–280
phishing, 59, 304

PHP: Hypertext Preprocessor (PHP) language, **71**
pico editor, 187–190
PID (process ID) numbers, 155–157
ping utility, 208–209, 299–300
pipes, **175–176**
plus signs (+) in regular expressions, 167
ports for server programs, 63–66
Post Office Protocol (POP), 65
pound bang lines, 204
power supplies, 80
PowerPC CPU, 77
PPID (parent process ID) numbers, 155
preemptive multitasking, 22
prefixes in IEEE-1541, 83–84
presentation programs, 60
primary partitions, 82–83
principles
   fair use, 34
   open source software, 24–26
printers, 93
privileges of root users, 227–229, *229*
process ID (PID) numbers, 155–157
process tables, 155
processes, 149
   hierarchy, 154–155, *155*
   identifying, 155–160
   memory use, 159–160
processors. *See* CPUs (central processing units)
productivity software, 56–57
   choosing, **57**
   cloud computing, 62
   email clients, 59–60
   mobile applications, 62–63
   multimedia applications, **61**
   office tools, 60–61
   overview, 3
   Unix, 9
   Web browsers, 58–59
program authors, 145
program launchers, 7
programming languages, 69
   common, 70–72
   compiled vs. interpreted, 69–70
programs
   documentation, 141–143
   launching, 52–54, *53–54*
   log files, 160–163
   productivity. *See* productivity software
   running, 103–106
   server, 63–68

project groups, **236**
prompts
    login, **4–5**
    terminal programs, **100–101**
properties of documents, 55
proprietary drivers, **95**
protocols for server programs, **63–66**
ps tool, **155–157**
punctuation in passwords, 237
pwd command, **110–111**
Python language, **71–72**

Q

Qt widget sets, 50
question marks (?)
    case statements, 212
    exit status variable, 210
    filenames, 123
    regular expressions, 167

R

ranges in regular expressions, 166
Raymond, Eric S., 26, 39
reading
    info pages, **139–140**
    man pages, **134–135**, *135*
README files, **141–142**
recursive acronyms, 9
recursive copies, 120
Red Hat distribution, 24
Red Hat Enterprise Linux (RHEL) distribution, 15
redirecting input and output, **172–176**
redistribution of open source software, 40
refresh rate, 92
regular expressions, **165–167**
ReiserFS filesystem, 86
relative file references, **108–110**, *109*
release cycles for distributions, **15–17**
remote host field for who command, 225
remote logins, **103**
removable disks, 88, *89*
renaming files, 120
repetition in regular expressions, **166–167**
repositories for packages, 151
Request for Comments (RFC) documents, 63
resolution, display, 91–92, *92*

return values, 210
RFC (Request for Comments) documents, 63
RHEL (Red Hat Enterprise Linux) distribution, 15
ring buffers, **162–163**
rlogin program, 103
rm command, 111, **122–123**
rmdir command, 111, **125–126**
Rock Ridge filesystem, 87
rolling release cycles, 17
root directory, 108, *109*
    file references, 109
    purpose, **274–275**
root filesystems, 85, 271
root users, **226**
    passwords, **229–230**
    permissions, 265
    privileges, **227–229**, *229*
    safe use, **230–231**
    and system files, 273
    working as, 227
/root/xorg.conf.new file, 90
rotated log files, 161
route command, 295, 299
routers, 287
routing information, 303
routing tables, **299**
RPM Package Manager (RPM) system, 15, **150–153**
runlevels, 122
running processes, identifying, **155–160**, *157*
running programs, **103–106**

S

SANE (Scanner Access Now Easy) software, 93
SAS (Serial Attached SCSI) interface, 81
SATA (Serial ATA) interface, 81
saving
    nano changes, **193**
    vi changes, **197**
/sbin directory purpose, **275–276**
/sbin/init program, 154
Scanner Access Now Easy (SANE) software, 93
scanners, 93
scripts, **203**
    arguments, **207–208**
    beginning, **204**
    commands, **204–206**
    conditional expressions, **210–212**
    distributions, 13

exit value, 214–215
functions, 213–214
loops, 212–213
network, 295–296
shell, 72, 203
variables, 207–210
SCSI (Small Computer System Interface) interface, 81
search features, 52, 57
searching
for data
find, 170–171
grep, 167–170
wc, 171–172
man pages, 133
for programs, 52
Second Extended Filesystem (ext2fs), 85
section numbers in man pages, 132–133
sectors, 81
secure log file, 161
Secure Shell (SSH) protocol
port numbers, 64
remote logins, 103
security
files, 126
Linux vs. Windows, 12
network connections, 303–304
servers, 68
web sites, 59
Wi-Fi, 290–291
sed command, 206
See Also section in man pages, 134
semicolons (;) in case statements, 212
seq command, 213
Serial ATA (SATA) interface, 81
Serial Attached SCSI (SAS) interface, 81
Server Message Block (SMB)/Common Internet File
    System (CIFS) protocols, 65
servers, 63
computers, 29–30, 66–67
installing and launching, 67
protocols, 63–66
securing, 68
shutting down, 303
Unix, 9
service set identifiers (SSIDs), 289
services in open source business models, 44
set group ID (SGID) permissions, 257, 280
set user ID (SUID) permissions, 257, 279–280
sfdisk tool, 84

sgdisk tool, 84
SGID (set group ID) permissions, 257, 280
shareable files, 273–274, *274*
shareware software, 25
shebangs, 204
shells, 2–3. *See also* command line
accounts
creating, 241–243
deleting, 251–252
modifying, 247–249
command completion, 111–112
command history, 112–114
groups, 253–255
for ownership, 260–261
for permissions, 266–267
scripting. *See* scripts
shortcut lists for text editors, 190
shortcuts to files, 121
Showcase program, 60
shrink-wrap licenses, 36
shutting down unused servers, 303
Simple Mail Transfer Protocol (SMTP), 64
site licenses, 36
size of passwords, 237
Slackware distribution, 15, 24
slashes (/)
absolute references, 109
directories, 107–108, 119
HTML files, 200
root filesystems, 85, 108
Small Computer System Interface (SCSI) interface, 81
SMTP (Simple Mail Transfer Protocol), 64
soft links, 121–122
software availability in Linux vs. Windows, 11
software integration, 27
software licensing
and copyrights, 33–36
Creative Commons, 41–42
Free Software Foundation, 36–39
Open Source Initiative, 39–41, *40*
open source licenses, 42–45
source code, 71
availability, 41
description, 9–10
integrity, 41
source packages, 150
special execute permissions, 279–280
spreadsheet programs, 60
SQL (Structured Query Language), 65

square brackets ([])
  regular expressions, 166
  wildcards, 123
SSH (Secure Shell) protocol
  port numbers, 64
  remote logins, 103
SSIDs (service set identifiers), 289
Stallman, Richard, 36
standard error, 173
standard output, 173
start of line in regular expressions, 166
startup scripts for distributions, 13
static files, 273–274, *274*
status bars in text editors, 190
sticky bits, 265, **277–279**
Structured Query Language (SQL), 65
su command, **227–228**
subexpressions, 167
substituted commands, 176, 208
sudo command, **228**
SUID (set user ID) permissions, 257, **279–280**
summary searches for man pages, 133
super servers, 67
superusers. *See* root users
supplemental software in distributions, 13
support
  improved and new tools, 24
  open source business models, 44
SUSE distribution, 15
suspending programs, 105
swap space, 34, **159–160**
symbolic code
  special execute permissions, 280
  sticky bits, 278
symbolic links, 107, **121–122**, 265
Synopsis section in man pages, 134
syslog daemon, 162
syslog log file, 161
syslogd daemon, 162
system accounts, 217
system-config-users command, 239, 245, 251
system files, **271–273**
system log daemons, 162
system messaging, 162

T

tables of equivalents, **57**
tablet computers, 28

tabs for terminal programs, 102
tags for HTML files, 200
tail command, 111, 161
Tanenbaum, Andrew, 23
tape archiver, **176–179**
tar utility, 15, **176–179**
tarballs, 15, **179–180**
TCP/IP (Transmission Control Protocol/Internet
  Protocol) standards, 287
tcsh shell, 100
tebibytes (TiB), 84
technology neutrality in Open Source Initiative, 41
telnet protocol
  limitations, 103
  port numbers, 64
terminal identifiers for who command, 225
terminal programs, 6, 52, **99–102**, *101*
test keyword, 211
testing network connections, 299–303
text-based tools for network connections, 295–299
text files, **185–187**
text mode
  logins, 102–103
  running programs, 104
  user interfaces, 4–6, *5*
then keyword, 211–212
Third Extended Filesystem (ext3fs), 86
thorough searches of man pages, 133
Thunar file manager, 54
Thunderbird email program, 59
tilde (~) character for home directory references, 100,
  109, 218
title bars for text editors, 190
TiVo, 16–17
tkinfo program, 140, *141*
/tmp directory, 273, **275–276**
Tomato distribution, 16
top command, **157–158**, *157*
Torvalds, Linus, 2, 8, **22–23**
touch program, 118
traceroute command, **300–301**
trademarks, 35
Transmission Control Protocol/Internet Protocol
  (TCP/IP) standards, 287
tunnels in SSH, 103

U

Ubuntu distribution, 16

UDF (Universal Disk Format) filesystem, 87
UEFI (Unified Extensible Firmware Interface), 83
UID (user identification) numbers
    accounts, 218
    cross-installations, 258
    deleted accounts, 250–251
    displaying, 224
umasks, 267
umount command, 88
uname command, 78
uncompressing files, 182
uncompression programs, 179
UNetbootin tool, 14
Unicode formats, 185–186
Unicode Transformation Format (UTF) schemes, 186
Unified Extensible Firmware Interface (UEFI), 83
Unity desktop environment, 50
Universal Disk Format (UDF) filesystem, 87
Universal Serial Bus (USB) interface
    devices, 92–93
    disks, 81
Unix operating system
    development of, 22–23
    vs. Linux, 8–10
unprivileged accounts, 227
unshareable files, 273–274, *274*
until loops, 213
unused servers, shutting down, 303
unusual hardware, drivers for, 95
unzip command, 182
update copies, 120
upgrading package systems, 153
USB (Universal Serial Bus) interface
    devices, 92–93
    disks, 81
Usenet newsgroups, 145–146
User Accounts tool, 220–221, *221*
user identification (UID) numbers
    accounts, 218
    cross-installations, 258
    deleted accounts, 250–251
    displaying, 224
user interfaces
    GUIs, 6–8, *6–7*
    Linux vs. Windows, 12
    text mode, 4–6, *5*
User Manager utility, 239–240, *240*
user masks, 267
user productivity programs. *See* productivity software
user tasks, 227

useradd command, 241–243
userdel command, 251–252
usermod program
    groups, 254
    users, 247–249
usernames
    accounts, 218–219
    login, 4
    text-mode consoles, 102
    who command, 225
users
    accounts. *See* accounts
    groups. *See* groups
    root. *See* root users
/usr directory, 275–276
/usr/bin directory, 276
/usr/lib directory, 276
/usr/sbin directory, 276
UTF (Unicode Transformation Format) schemes, 186
utility programs, 3

V

values in configuration files, 198
/var directory, 275–276
/var/log directory, 160
variable files, 273–274, *274*
variables
    configuration files, 198
    scripts, 207–210
vector graphics programs, 60
vendor lock-in, **26**
vertical bars (|)
    conditional expressions, 211
    pipes, 175
    regular expressions, 167
vesa driver, 91
VGA (Video Graphics Array) cables, 91, *91*
vi editor, 187, **193**
    modes, 193–194
    saving changes, 197
    text-editing procedures, 194–197, *194*
video cards, 91
Video Graphics Array (VGA) cables, 91, *91*
virtual desktops, 7
Virtual Memory System (VMS), 22
Virtual Network Computing (VNC), 103
virtual terminals (VTs), 102, 225

W

w utility, **226**, 245
WAPs (wireless access points), 291
wc utility, 111, 167, **171–172**
Web browsers, **58–59**
web forums, **145**
Web searches for help, 146
WEP (Wired Equivalent Privacy) protocol, 291
whatis command, 133
whereis program, 143
which command, 205
while loops, 213
whitespace in configuration files, 198
who utility, **225–226**, 245
whoami command, 224
Wi-Fi, 287
    connections, **289–292**, *289–290*
    drivers, **292**
    security, **290–291**
Wi-Fi Protected Access (WPA) security, 291
widget sets, 50, 90
wildcards
    case statements, 212
    directories, 281
    files, 108, 117, **123**
window controls, 7
window managers, 90
Windows operating system, **11–12**
Wired Equivalent Privacy (WEP) protocol, 291
wireless access points (WAPs), 291
word count utility, **171–172**
word processor programs, 60
workstations, 28
world permissions, 263
worst passwords, **238–239**

WPA (Wi-Fi Protected Access) security, 291
WPA2 security, 291
write permissions, 265
Writer program, 60

X

X Window System, 3, 9, **89–90**
x86 CPU type, 16, **76**
x86-64 CPU type, 16, **76**
xargs command, 173, **175–176**
Xfce desktop environment, **50–51**
XFS (Extents File System), 86
Xft library, 90
XHTML, 200
xinetd daemon, 67
xman program, 135
Xorg.0.log file, 161
Xorg-X11 system, 9
xz program, **179–180**

Y

Yumex tool, 153
yumremove command, 153

Z

Zettabyte File System (ZFS), 9
zgrep utility, 179
zip command, **180–183**
zsh shell, 100